HENNING MELBER

The Long Shadow of German Colonialism

Amnesia, Denialism and Revisionism

HURST & COMPANY, LONDON

First published in the United Kingdom in 2024 by
C. Hurst & Co. (Publishers) Ltd.,
New Wing, Somerset House, Strand, London, WC2R 1LA
© Henning Melber, 2024
All rights reserved.

The right of Henning Melber to be identified as the author of this publication is asserted by him in accordance with the Copyright, Designs and Patents Act, 1988.

A Cataloguing-in-Publication data record for this book is available from the British Library.

ISBN: 9781805260455

This book is printed using paper from registered sustainable and managed sources.

www.hurstpublishers.com

THE LONG SHADOW OF GERMAN COLONIALISM

To Sue and for Tuli

*In memory of
Salomea, Gretel, Rainer and Mary*

CONTENTS

Preface   xi

1. Introduction: Which Past, Whose Past?   1
   Blind-Spot Colonialism   3
   New Agenda—Old Blinkers   5
   One's Own and Others' Past   7
   Beyond Tokenism?   10

2. Enlightenment, Racism, Colonialism and Genocide   15
   The Dark Side of Enlightenment   16
   Colonial Mass Violence and the Notion of Genocide   20
   Towards Decolonisation   24

3. The German Colonial Brand   29
   Germany Goes Overseas   30
   The German Colonies   34
   Some Colonial Leftovers   77
   Colonial Discourses at Home   81
   Colonialism without Colonies   87
   Africans in Colonial Germany   91

4. (Post-)Colonial (West) Germany   97
   West German Africa   100
   Colonial Remnants in United Germany   107
   Black Germany   115

CONTENTS

	Reactionary Revisionism: The Case of the AfD	121
	Light at the End of the Tunnel?	127
5.	Germany and Namibia	135
	An Initial Caveat	136
	The Historical Record	138
	A German Sonderweg?	142
	The Long Denial	144
	The Return of Human Remains and Looted Artefacts	148
	Negotiating Genocide	154
	The Joint Declaration and Its Aftermath	161
	Reparations and Intertemporality	166
	Namibian Disagreements	170
	Ploughing Through	172
	No End in Sight	179
6.	Challenging Colonial Asymmetries and Blind Spots	185
	Selective Memory	186
	Learning from the Past	190
	The Coloniality of Power	196
Acknowledgements		199
Notes		201
Bibliography		249
Index		321

AUTHOR'S BIOGRAPHY

Henning Melber moved to Namibia in 1967, as the son of German immigrants, and joined the anti-colonial movement SWAPO in 1974. He was Director of the Namibian Economic Policy Research Unit in Windhoek, Research Director of the Nordic Africa Institute and Director of the Dag Hammarskjöld Foundation, both in Uppsala, Sweden. He is Extraordinary Professor at the Department of Political Sciences at the University of Pretoria and at the Centre for Gender and Africa Studies at the University of the Free State. He is Senior Research Fellow at the Institute of Commonwealth Studies of the University of London.

His previous books include *Understanding Namibia: The Trials of Independence* and *Dag Hammarskjöld, the United Nations and the Decolonisation of Africa*, both published by Hurst.

PREFACE

This book explores a subject which at the time of writing displays shifting (or at least adjusting) perspectives. The journey into the heart of colonial Germany and its remnants today is also a personal one. After all, we all live in the shadows of a colonial past, though this is acknowledged (or ignored, if not denied) in different ways. What follows therefore also has to do with positionality.

Postcolonial theories have since the late 1990s strongly advocated a change in narratives to critically deconstruct colonial forms of knowledge. But colonial mindsets have not been entirely superseded or abandoned in Western anti-colonial counter-narratives. Historical writing remains largely confined to standardised modes rooted in Western traditions, often without being aware of or without reflecting self-critically on these limitations. Whether we like it or not, we are moulded by our socialisation and our experiences.

Looking at the world through the eyes of others borders on a mission impossible and may even turn into another form of appropriation. In our eagerness to conform to such a shift of perspectives, we risk becoming patronising or paternalistically arrogant by claiming to speak on behalf of those who continue to remain silent, silenced or unheard. Scholars and activists alike should accept that their engagement is limited to their own voices and perspectives when they confront other narratives seeking to downplay the trauma of colonialism. We address matters in which we have a shared history with others, through our own perspectives and views. But we cannot replace our own upbringing with the

PREFACE

upbringing of someone else. We can only engage in our own way. This also means fighting for a due recognition of humanity by claiming and practising our own humanity and human values.

While the answer to the question of what and how to acknowledge, commemorate and seek redress changes all the time as new dynamics unfold, this book remains focused on the task of how best to come to terms with our colonial past. I am grateful to Michael Dwyer for the opportunity to share the results with a wider audience. When we met last before the Covid-related travel restrictions, he asked what I would like to tackle next. When I shared this idea with him, his response was simply: "Go for it." I hope what follows justifies his trust and patience.

Uppsala, January 2024

1

INTRODUCTION

WHICH PAST, WHOSE PAST?

"We cannot change the past, but we can change our blindness to the past."[1]

At the beginning of the 21st century a voluminous collection of essays was published in German with the title "Remembering Crimes". Its subtitle described its focus as an engagement with the Holocaust and genocide. It suggested that it consisted of self-critical explorations seeking to come to terms in the present with a violent past. The book was subsequently widely distributed at a subsidised price by the Federal Agency for Civic Education. The first part included cases from a variety of countries stretching over a century—starting with the Armenian genocide, followed by case studies on South Africa, Algeria, the Netherlands, the Soviet Union, Japan and the former Yugoslavia. In this volume of 30 essays, German colonialism does not once appear as a subject.[2] A similar absence marked the three volumes published around the same time on German memory sites, which claimed to be a wide-ranging attempt to take stock of the cultural memory of Germans. Nowhere in it was there a separate entry on colonialism.[3]

While these examples are indicative of the relative blindness that existed at the time of publication, there is some reason to believe that twenty years later similar projects are less prone to such disturbing oversight and omission and that some of the violent excesses of German colonial rule—not least the genocide committed in South West Africa—can no longer remain ignored. However, as late as 2013, a work compiled by the academic services of the German parliament conceded, quite disarmingly, that German citizens are only to a very limited degree aware of the colonial empire of the *Kaiserreich* in Africa and other parts of the world.[4] As the paper concluded, it was Germany's colonial past in Namibia that was most likely to have *Erregungspotential* (to be potentially exciting in the sense of upsetting).[5]

This study is another modest effort to contribute to and possibly enrich this potential. By doing so, it seeks to undertake a precarious balancing act. As Carsten Stahn observes:

> A critical interrogation of colonial practices by Western voices is a double-edged sword. It may contribute to a rethinking of past and contemporary approaches by the Global North and Europe. But it also carries inherent limits and ambiguities. ... Any Western perspective may easily become entangled in its own contradictions or perpetuate inequalities. It may render other voices less visible or present dilemmas of inequality, structural injustice, or oppression through the voice of "a dominant group", rather than those who have been marginalized ("whitesplaining").[6]

While aware of such pitfalls, I join Stahn in tackling the challenge. To some extent I find comfort in the relative safety of the particular focus of what follows, which is mainly a view of "us" (as German-born offspring of the generations directly involved in colonial expansion and oppression) and not "them" at the receiving end. "Taking African agency seriously", as Olùfémi Táiwò demands,[7] does not mean remaining silent as one of the descendants (and thereby beneficiaries) of the perpetrators in colonial history. We cannot step out of this history. But we can distance or rather dissociate ourselves from the dominant narratives. We can, and should, claim agency too—not for others, but for ourselves in our quest to dismantle the legacies of a specific violent past with consequences for today. These reflections are also

INTRODUCTION

grounded in the desire to find out how best to deal with, if not overcome, the inherited injustices reproduced and operative in the mindsets and policies of today. Both history and memory need permanent interrogation.

Blind-Spot Colonialism

The coalition agreement of 12 March 2018 between the Christian Democratic Union (CDU), the Christian Social Union (CSU) and the Social Democratic Party (SPD)—dubbed the "grand coalition"—opened a new chapter in German governance. For the first time the parties acknowledged the need to address the colonial past. Under the subtitle "Commemoration and Memory", the agreement declared that without remembrance there can be no future and that dealing with Germany's colonial history is part of the basic democratic consensus.[8] But this remarkable statement was followed by an exclusive focus on the Nazi era and the East German (GDR) state. The words "colonial" and "colonialism" appear five times throughout the 173 pages. They feature only in reference to the declared intention of increasing cultural collaboration with Africa especially through a reappraisal of colonialism, the construction of museums and cultural institutions in Africa and a commitment to thorough archival research.[9] While being welcomed as new declarations of intent, these promised commitments were also met at the same time with some sceptical reservations about the seriousness of the engagement.[10]

Indeed, it did not take long before the sobering reality became apparent. In October 2018 the government replied to a minor interpellation by the Green Party on the cultural-political treatment of the German colonial era.[11] The question about what concrete government measures would be taken to recognise German colonial crimes was answered by referring to the declared intention of the coalition agreement (as mentioned above). This was followed by a list of several institutions involved in a number of funded activities (such as securing archival material, exhibitions in museums, archival research and cultural events). It was finally pointed out that the German government had already acknowledged the crimes committed during colonial times by returning to Namibia in August 2018 the human remains of subject people which had originally been brought as trophies or specimens to Germany.[12] When asked if it was planned to include the remembrance of colonial crimes in the official memorial scheme (which embraced the Nazi and GDR eras), the government replied in the negative: because of the different historical contexts and commemoration sites, the colonial era was not part of the memorial scheme.[13] Asked what role colonial times should have in the federal programme Youth Remembers, as announced in the coalition agreement of March 2018, the government explained that this was focused on the crimes of the Nazi era so as to deal especially with current antisemitism and hostility to the Roma, but that it included as well the East German dictatorship (*SED-Diktatur*). Other aspects of German history would not be included in the programme.[14] Perhaps most revealingly, the question whether the government agreed with the demand for the establishment of a central commemoration and documentation site in memory of the German colonial era received an evasive answer: it would be best for such an initiative to be based on a decision taken by parliament.[15]

Such an initiative had not been undertaken by the end of 2023, either by the parties of the earlier coalition or by those in government since December 2021. Instead, parliament decided in 2020 to establish a new documentation centre in Berlin to commemorate German atrocities committed during the World War II occupation of foreign countries; this was conceptualised and contextualised as a European project. The new coalition government has since then proceeded with the implementation of its plans, with a parliamentary hearing taking place in late November 2022.[16] While the centre will host a permanent exhibition on the subject, the declared intention is to complement this with temporary exhibitions on various historical aspects before and after the war. During the hearing, documented in 30 pages, not a single reference was made to colonialism.

This continued blind spot is in step with a position paper on transitional justice published in mid-2019 by the Foreign Ministry. It "advocates a *comprehensive understanding of confronting past injus-*

tices".[17] The approach includes "violations of economic, social and cultural rights" and "various dimensions of justice (such as retributive, distributive and restorative justice)", with transitional justice forming part of the process of social transformation.[18] It advocates "*participative processes with a broad scope* ... to ensure that transitional justice is not perceived as a project of the elites, and that the expertise and political ideas from civil-society organisations and groups (particularly those that represent victims and survivors, or have direct access to them) can be put to use".[19] The paper presents examples of transitional justice in Germany in "*acknowledging and providing reparations for past injustices*". Reference is made to "reparations and compensation for National Socialist injustices". It maintains: "Given its decades-long and multifaceted experiences in this policy area, Germany can provide information about basic requirements, problems and mechanisms for the development of state and civil-society reparation efforts."[20] Strikingly, the term "colonialism" does not feature once in the 32-page document.

New Agenda—Old Blinkers

Since then, at least in official government discourse, some shifts have been visible. In December 2021, the SPD, the Green Party (Bündnis 90/Die Grünen) and the Liberal Party (FDP) formed a new coalition government. Under the heading "Colonial Legacy", its negotiated agreement expressed an intention to reappraise German colonial history with special reference to the restitution of objects from colonial contexts. It also undertook to develop a plan for a place for learning about and remembering colonialism. The coalition wanted to put an end to existing continuities with the colonial past and initiate independent academic studies reappraising colonialism.[21] Under the section on foreign cultural and educational policy, it added that reconciliation with Namibia remained an indispensable task arising from Germany's historical and moral responsibility. As it declared further, the Joint Declaration—the so-called reconciliation agreement—could mark the beginning of a joint process of reappraisal.[22]

In June 2022, the monthly newspaper of the German Cultural Council, the publicly funded umbrella organisation of German cultural associations, published a series of short statements by spokespeople of the six political parties in the Bundestag. They had been invited to summarise their priorities for foreign policy on culture and education.[23] The representatives of the governing "traffic light coalition" (*Ampelkoalition*, referring to green, yellow and red, the colours associated with the three parties) had remarkably little to say on colonial history. There was nothing at all in the statement by the SPD MP Michael Müller. The Green MP Erhard Grundl mentioned in passing a culture of remembrance with regard to ethnological collections from former colonies, and exchange and collaboration with their countries of origin. There were also no words from the liberal-democratic FDP MP Thomas Hacker. He instead stressed that his party would not promote cultural imperialism while advancing their European values. On behalf of the CDU and CSU the former Minister of State for Culture and Media Monika Grütters only referred in passing to discussions about the return of the Benin Bronzes (in the negotiations for which she had been involved as Federal Commissioner for Culture and the Media in the previous government).

Interestingly, only the party representatives on the right and left of the political spectrum paid more attention to the issues. As the AfD (Alternative für Deutschland) MP Matthias Moosdorf emphasised, "our" history, values and achievements are unique, often exemplary for other cultures and societies worldwide. He asked who, if not "we", was best placed in the world to talk about the mutual relationship between freedom and responsibility. A sensible appraisal of the colonial legacy, as he stressed, should not ignore the fact that European civilisation still had much to offer. Collaboration would be much more sustainable than singular symbolic acts of reparation. The counter-position was presented by MP Sevim Dağdelen of the Left (Die Linke). With half of her statement devoted to the colonial legacy, she was the only one who gave the topic priority. Referring to the German–Namibian agreement addressing the genocide committed in South West Africa, she stressed the need for critical reflection on public commemoration culture in Germany and for the decolonisation of a foreign policy imbued with a colonial mindset. She concluded that reconciliation

INTRODUCTION

with Namibia was just the starting point of a process of coming to terms with German colonial and war crimes, which required German foreign policy to be decolonised on all levels.

As these statements suggest, there remains a certain disconnect between the coalition agreement and the priorities of its representatives in the sphere of foreign cultural policy.

One's Own and Others' Past

Despite all the evidence of a continued lack of serious engagement with Germany's colonial past, the year 2022 ended with a spectacular gesture in accord with the declared commitment to returning objects taken from colonial contexts. On 20 December 2022, the German Foreign Minister, Annalena Baerbock, and the Minister of State for Culture and the Media, Claudia Roth, together with the directors of several prestigious German art and history museums, returned 20 sculptures known as Benin Bronzes to Nigeria's Culture Minister, Lai Mohamed, in a ceremony held in Abuja at the country's Foreign Ministry. The artefacts were originally looted in their thousands by British soldiers at the end of the 19th century, mostly from the royal palace of the Benin kingdom (today the Edo federal state in southern Nigeria). Many of them subsequently ended up in other countries' museums and art collections. Some 1,130 of these are known to be in Germany. In a pioneering move, their ownership was legally transferred to Nigeria on 1 July 2022 after years of foot dragging.[24] This caused raised eyebrows especially in the UK, since the British government has stubbornly refused to do likewise.

During the handover ceremony, Foreign Minister Baerbock declared: "It was wrong to steal these bronzes. It was wrong to keep these bronzes and their return to their home is long overdue." And she added: "This step is also important for us because we are dealing with our dark colonial past."[25] And Claudia Roth promised: "This is not the end of a process but the beginning. It marks a turning point in international cultural policy."[26] Baerbock had already tweeted before her departure for Abuja that the return of the Benin Bronzes would mark a long-overdue step. It would not heal all wounds of the past but would show Germany's seriousness in its reappraisal of its "dark" colonial history.[27] "We are here to make amends for injustice", declared Baerbock in Abuja. "This is a history of European colonialism, a history in which our country played a grim role."[28]

This act, which was widely reported in the German and international media,[29] received much praise.[30] But, indicative of the colonial revisionist counterculture still very much alive in Germany, it also provoked scathing attacks from those objecting to such initiatives. One misleading impression created as a result was that the Foreign Minister was uninformed and ignorant of the fact that Nigeria had not been a German colony.[31] It therefore is only fair to quote from her official speech:

> Today, we are here to return the Benin Bronzes to where they belong, to the people of Nigeria. We are here to right a wrong.
>
> Officials from my country once bought the bronzes, knowing that they had been robbed and stolen. After that, we ignored Nigeria's plea to return them for a very long time. It was wrong to take them. But it was also wrong to keep them.
>
> This is a story of European colonialism. It is a story in which our country played a dark role, causing tremendous suffering in different parts of Africa. The return of the bronzes today is therefore a crucial step towards addressing this chapter in the way that it should be addressed: openly, frankly, with a willingness to critically assess one's own actions. And, crucially, by listening closely to the concerns of those who were the victims of colonial cruelties.[32]

Without ridiculing or belittling what can be recognised as a significant symbolic gesture, one feels that a bit more modesty would have been in order, given the largely uncritical and celebratory tone of the German speeches. Despite all the limitations of the gesture in the overall picture, Germany was lauded as a model country (*Musterland*).[33] This generous praise bestowed by Nigerian state officials is certainly understandable. After all, the exchange made it possible to name and shame the British reluctance to return their share of the looted objects. To that extent London had every reason to respond indignantly to the German declaration made in mid-

INTRODUCTION

2022 that all Benin Bronzes in German public institutions would be transferred to Nigerian ownership—albeit most of them would remain for the time being as displays on loan in German museums, which practically made little difference beyond the legal change of ownership.[34] This recalls a comment made earlier by Klaus Lederer of the Left, from December 2016 to April 2023 Deputy Mayor and Senator for Culture and Europe in the federal state of Berlin and a driving force behind the support given to local postcolonial initiatives. As he warned, we cannot apply the same discriminatory views from the past and hold that while looted cultural artefacts from Africa now belong to all, European cultural goods must continue to remain only European possessions. Instead, there must be a true and fair common collective ownership of cultural goods—similar to the reconstruction of a common history, which often includes deeply violent, exploitative and inhuman practices.[35]

This needs to be kept in mind when considering Claudia Roth's declaration in Abuja that Nigeria offered Germany the chance to engage with its colonial history, which was "important for our memory culture".[36] Would Germany's colonial atrocities dating back to the *Kaiserreich* not be a more suitable reference point and priority for dealing properly with its colonial past? Returning the loot taken by other European countries, which ended up in German possession, is an easy gesture of remorse—even more so when the objects are handed over to the government of a country whose people were never subjected to German imperial power. It is another story altogether to return (where possible), for example, looted land to the descendants of those who were robbed of their territories by German soldiers, administrators and settlers. When resisting German colonial invasion, indigenous communities were ruthlessly punished by military expeditions (*Strafexpeditionen*), which escalated into genocidal warfare. This looting of land was an integral part of European imperialism, based on the claim of racial superiority. As a result, in Namibia the (often German-speaking White) beneficiaries of the previous settler-colonial minority regime, built on the ruins of local societies, still occupy large parts of the land taken by brute force.

In a unique symbolic act, the first of its kind, German President Frank-Walter Steinmeier visited the Maji Maji Memorial Museum and met descendants of Chief Songea Mbano in Songea, Tanzania, on 1 November 2023.[37] For his resistance to German colonial rule, Chief Songea Mbano and 66 other Ngoni warriors were executed in 1906. He was decapitated and his head, like thousands of other human remains (mainly from the East African and South West Africa colonies), now lies unidentified in a German depository.[38] A review presented at the end of 2023 recorded more than 17,000 human remains in the 33 German institutions examined. Almost half of these could not be geographically assigned.[39] In his speech, Steinmeier declared:

> I ask for forgiveness, and I want to assure you that we Germans will together with you look for answers to the unresolved questions that haunt you. ...
>
> I have come to Songea today as President of a different Germany. Of a country different from the one that your ancestors had to encounter. Germany stands ready to address the past together. No one must forget what happened back then.[40]

Beyond Tokenism?

While President Steinmeier's declared remorse received much media attention back home in Germany, not all reactions were uncritically positive. Welcoming the "right words", Dominic Johnson warned that the statement of a Federal State President does not automatically have any practical political relevance. This was "a signal, but not yet policy".[41] One dismissive commentator observed that the President did not have historians in his company but members of a business delegation. He suggested that the "crocodile tears" showing remorse for the past should not take attention away from the ongoing neo-colonial extraction of natural resources.[42] In contrast, Steinmeier's "honest words" were appreciated by Andrea Böhm as more far-reaching than any other statement by a European leader—not least when compared with the vague words of the United Kingdom's King Charles III, who at the same time had visited Kenya. She wondered if the explicit apology and appeal for forgiveness could be understood as an admission of

INTRODUCTION

guilt in the legal sense, which might consequently trigger justified demands for reparations.[43] In an interview, Michael McEachrane—Rapporteur of the UN Permanent Forum of People of African Descent—considered Steinmeier's apology a good beginning, with moral and legal consequences. But, as he added, real efforts need to follow.[44]

Being serious about the appraisal of "our dark colonial past", as Baerbock tweeted on 18 December 2022 ahead of her visit to Abuja,[45] which was in a way re-emphasised by Steinmeier at Songea, means that one needs to walk the walk. This includes paying more adequate domestic attention to the crimes committed in the name of German "civilisation" abroad by dealing with these skeletons in the closet in as strict a way as with the later Nazi mass extermination at home. As Klaus Lederer, then Berlin's Senator for Culture and Europe, observed, a truly decolonial transformation involves extensive measures at all institutional levels and in many social spheres. One needs to be aware of this when, in the narrower sense of the cultural sphere, decolonisation and restitution are tackled. Otherwise, culture risks being reduced to a fig leaf of progressive discourses conducted inside a relatively protected terrain.[46] The coalition agreement mentioned above stressed the need to commission independent academic studies to review colonialism. One cannot but wonder what the purpose for this may be beyond foot dragging. The bibliography and references in this book suggest that German colonialism is no longer an under-researched topic. Knowledge exists in a variety of perspectives. What additional knowledge is required before it can be actively implemented and applied? What the British historian David Andress observes about other former colonial powers seems applicable to Germany too:

> the layering of mythology around history is not something that can be simply and uncontroversially pulled back by the application of expertise. The West's current relationship to the past is not the passive victimhood of an individual dementia sufferer, but rather an actively constructed, jealously guarded toxic refusal to engage with facts that are well-known but emotionally and politically inconvenient, and with other experiences that are devastating to

the collective self-regard of huge segments of societies that have no visible desire to come to terms with reality.⁴⁷

This is where Critical Whiteness Studies come into the picture. They challenge the assumed ignorance of a colonial past, which is not so much the result of an absence of knowledge but rather a "product of deliberate practices"—an "ignorance contract" involving White collusion, which sustains racial (understood as racist) hierarchies not by accident, but on purpose, as a choice.⁴⁸ They expose "moral non-knowings", in which "whites [are] aprioristically intent on denying what is before them", as "the mystification of the past [that] underwrites a mystification of the present".⁴⁹ "The aim is an identity that is not blameworthy": "White unknowing derives from unremembering which emphasises the active engagement in knowing and not knowing, a turning away so as not to know the injustice on which white privilege is founded. Memory is about forming identities in the present."⁵⁰

Such lack of memory concerning European involvement in a centuries-long trajectory of violence and oppression outside Europe is by no means limited to Germany. As Hans Kundnani suggests with his use of the term "Eurowhiteness", the Europe formed since the mid-20th century has used its focus on inter-European reconciliation and unification to claim it has learned from history. By doing so, it has prevented a similar engagement with its bloody "civilising mission" abroad. By concentrating on the Holocaust, memory culture has promoted imperial amnesia.⁵¹ Post-World War II Europe became almost self-contained in its understanding of itself by bringing Europeans together "to think about their histories almost exclusively in relation to each other".⁵²

Current efforts to address the history of White oppression and exploitation are therefore not applauded by everyone. In a scathing critique, the new trends in Europe for restitution have been dismissed as a dishonest strategy of appeasement in the service of the status quo:

> The violence of the past is far from over. But it is disguised in many ways, made invisible and normalised. ... The language of restitution fails to take into account historical responsibilities. ... The language of restitution and provenance is a "new" spectacle, a way

INTRODUCTION

of remembering colonialism and writing colonial history. Restitution is declared and controlled in the metropoles and governed by museums, provenance researchers, archives and curators there. ... The rhetoric of restitution celebrates colonialism and imperial relations of power ... demonstrating that the imperial will to know is the will to dominate.[53]

For there to be long-term credibility beyond one-off gestures, more soul-searching and practical consequences are thus required. German official policy and initiatives to address colonial wrongs should not be confined to symbolic acts, significant and even laudable though they might be. They risk being somewhat misleading: creating comfort and peace of mind. If German policy is serious about tackling "our dark colonial past", it should go beyond words and gestures. There should be, in the first place, a domestic agenda, fostering public awareness and enlightened education based on the knowledge and insights already available. Returning some of the Benin Bronzes "could mark the beginning of a new, more self-critical era in Germany's postcolonial politics of memory. Yet, the widely praised decision might also remain a mere political symbol enabling it to portray itself as a role model at the international level."[54]

On this question the jury is still out.

2

ENLIGHTENMENT, RACISM, COLONIALISM AND GENOCIDE

Colonial mass violence and genocide need to be contextualised in a historical perspective. This chapter therefore offers some points of reference to place German colonialism, its genocidal acts and consequences within a wider picture. Offering a background to German expansionism as an integral part of European imperialism does not, however, seek to downplay the ruthless execution of self-proclaimed supremacy but rather to describe the process more generally. Part of the standard repertoire and fall-back position of apologists of German colonialism is the exculpatory reference to other colonial powers and the crimes committed by them—as if this could justify the atrocities committed. What follows, therefore, contextualises in order to explain, not excuse, what happened during the period of European conquest of other parts of the world and the lasting consequences of this interaction.

It was in the era of Enlightenment that Western modernity and its notion of civilisation took root at home and abroad. The idea of progress and development, which was equated with civilisation, was declared a universal notion, and was imposed during the colonial period on foreign peoples and territories. This process was accompanied by organised violence as an integral part of European expansion into the rest of the world. Since then, violence has remained an element of the project of globalisation. It has also infected those in charge in the former so-called periphery when exerting control over their people. Forms of domination rooted in the colonial mindset of White supremacy are no longer limited to Eurocentric or European regimes but are alive elsewhere too. This should not come as an excuse for Europeans not to deal with their own legacy of brute force and oppression.

There is a long history involving the West and the rest. This chapter critically engages with aspects of the seemingly neutral notion of modernity, which is often associated with development and progress. The way these paradigms were imposed on people at home in Europe as much as on the rest of the world had devastating effects and permanent, irreversible consequences. The export of so-called civilisation was a very uncivilised mission. But it created new and lasting realities, often reproducing the old in the new. The resulting mimicry, which has been brought to attention not least by postcolonial and subaltern studies, should be a reminder that the universal claim inherent in many Western models and lifestyles had indeed been infectious. Genocidal practices, for instance, are no longer the exclusive domain of Western imperialism but lead an independent life.

This unholy state of affairs, which contributes to the perpetuation of organised forms of mass violence with the intent to destroy people on account of specific features attributed to them, has been reproduced since the age of imperialism in all parts of the world by unsavoury regimes. In this chapter, we look at the historical roots of European modernity and violence so as to trace their consequences for the emergence of colonial mindsets and practices.

The Dark Side of Enlightenment

In 1550 the philosopher Ginés de Sepúlveda (1490–1573) and the Dominican friar and bishop Bartholomé de Las Casas (1484–1566) conducted a lengthy debate at the Spanish court in Valladolid. Their subject was the annihilating effect of the *Conquista* on the South American indigenous population and their decimation as a result of forced labour in the local mines. The two men's deliberations were a kind of marker of the entry into what might be termed European modernity in the wake of Europe's first stages of colonial-imperial expansion since the "Conquest of Paradise" in 1492.[1] This legal-philosophical exchange also signals the advent of the era of Enlightenment. "Enlightened" rationality paved the way for the development of secular concepts of humanity, guided by philosophical reason and rationality. In this view, Man (indeed in the exclusively male form) was thought to have stepped out of nature and religious faith to tame the natural, challenge tradition and authority, and thereby create new ideas and forms of culture. These involved the domestication of women and children as well as the introduction of notions of "normality" as opposed to "unnormality".[2]

Ironically, if not tragically, this emergence from a preconceived natural determinism also introduced a naturalist conception of humanity rooted in the principles of biological classification systems. This was combined with the introduction of a pseudo-scientific racial (and racist) hierarchy, presented in its infant stage by Las Casas. The world's people were perceived as forming a pyramid, with the most civilised European nations and their members ranked at the top. The South American Indians, according to Las Casas, were to be spared from destruction, for they had the potential to become civilised. As a suitable replacement, Las Casas suggested importing slaves from Africa, as they were in his view inferior to the Indians and not yet human beings.[3] For Sepúlveda the perceived inequality between Europeans and South Americans simply testified to the natural condition of the human species—a hierarchical society of peoples subdivided into superiors and inferiors. In his argument the dualism of thinking created oppositional equations: the relation of Indians to Spaniards was like that of children (sons) to parents (fathers), women (wives) to men (husbands), animals (apes) to humans.[4] These dichotomies underlay the asymmetric power structures and justified the control of inferiors by superiors, if necessary by elimination, just as the natural man required the control and direction of reason and rationality (which White men embodied).

Columbus's explorations (which had been a two-way event, though much to the disadvantage of the indigenous people) shifted

European perspectives by revealing the variety of social formations and communities elsewhere in the world. This promoted the advancement of Eurocentric criteria based on Europe's own cultural norms and values as the highest and only acceptable universal ones, synonymous with progress and development. This equation was also translated into a hierarchical, evolutionary natural order. The Swedish medical and biological scientist Carl von Linné (Linnaeus, 1707–1778) turned such a world view into a classification system for flora and fauna, which is still in use today. Linné included the human species in his system as part of the order of primates. While he stopped short of ranking human "subspecies", he articulated clear, generalised preferences. Europeans were characterised as "acute" and "inventive", being "governed by laws", while Black people were in his view "crafty, indolent, negligent" and "governed by caprice".[5]

Such a ranking of humans guided even those who subsequently advocated human rights for all. The French mathematician, aristocrat and *citoyen* Marquis de Condorcet (1743–1794)—who himself became a victim of the French Revolution, in which he actively participated—developed a more liberal mystification of the idea of progress already advocated by Las Casas, appealing to bourgeois humanism. His linear evolutionism represented an absolute belief in progress and development rooted in the conviction that all human beings are entitled to rights.[6] But his perspective was also limited by a hierarchical world view, which placed the Western and Central European nations and their educated elite at the top of the pyramid. Education was for him the key to humanity. All other people, while recognised as human beings, had to be uplifted to the level of European modernity through the civilising mission—or else had to disappear. An advocate of the abolition of slavery, he nevertheless was caught in a mindset which considered emancipation of one's fellow human beings as the domestication of the "savage" to the lifeways of the French and Anglo-Americans, the most civilised species. Such evolutionary progress eliminates any respect for "otherness" as an independent subject and potentially turns the emerging Western nation-state into a colonial and colonising power.

ENLIGHTENMENT AND GENOCIDE

The German philosophers Immanuel Kant (1724–1804) and Georg Wilhelm Friedrich Hegel (1770–1831), representatives of the era of the so-called Late Enlightenment (*Spätaufklärung*), were prominent proponents of such a Eurocentric civilising mission.[7] They provided philosophical points of reference for an understanding of how to compare different societies at different stages of development, though this fed into negative attitudes towards the "less developed".[8] John Stuart Mill (1806–1873), writing in the tradition of the Philosophical Radicals, personified these ambiguities in the emerging industrial-capitalist society of Britain. Modernisation was about "development" and what this supposedly entailed for people affected by economic growth and imperial expansion. The "developmental" goals defined by European colonialism were moulded in these Eurocentric notions of progress formed over generations.[9] Progress, in such a perspective, was tantamount to civilising the "savages" and, if they objected to this destiny, one might be required to "exterminate all the brutes".[10]

European colonialism was based on the ideological premises of this self-declared civilising mission—a mission whose original targets were subjects at home. These were people who had not yet internalised the values and behaviours appropriate to the industrial-capitalist mode of production then in the making. In parallel processes, "savages" both at home and abroad were trained to become either citizens or subjects, and domesticated as units of labour within a new system of social reproduction. The analogy between "savages" abroad and those at home was commonly used. William Booth, founder of the Salvation Army, published in 1890 a manifesto called *In Darkest England and the Way Out*, in clear reference to the explorer H.M. Stanley's travelogue *Through Darkest Africa*. Processes of forming peasants and "vagabonds" into workers, with corresponding norms and values, drew on ideas of discipline that originated in the development of the "disciplinary society" of the modern bureaucratic state.[11]

This process of domestication concerned the subjection of inner nature, which went hand in hand with the taming of outer nature, the wider world and its inhabitants. European conquest and expansion into other territories involved both an interior, mental landscape (the socialisation of the "savage" psyche) and the exterior, physical world (the subjugation of "savages" in the colonies). Colonisation was a parallel process, occurring both at home and abroad. A closer look at these parallel forms of indiscriminate violence reveals that the real "brutes" were not so much the victims as the perpetrators. What Zygmunt Bauman calls the "gardening state", one prepared to resort to destruction and extinction in order to "weed out" lesser forms,[12] was consolidated in the era of colonial expansion. The fatal consequences in mainstream perceptions have never been rigorously dealt with since then, as can be seen from the rise of new racist forms of exclusivist nationalism in European states in the present era of right-wing populism. Such forms of "patriotism" revive the old Eurocentric world view, in which "otherness" is defined in terms of a value system that denies that we share a common humanity despite our diversity.[13]

Ever since the debate between Ginés de Sepúlveda and Bartholomé de Las Casas, pseudo-scientific theories of "White supremacy" have provided an ideological justification for colonial expansion. The foundations were laid by the evolutionary theories of the French biologist Jean-Baptiste Lamarck (1744–1829) and were further developed in the *Essay on the Inequality of Human Races* (1853–1855) by Joseph Arthur Comte de Gobineau (1816–1882) and by the evolutionary theories of Charles Darwin (1809–1882), not least in his magnum opus *On the Origin of Species* (1859). These contributed to a geo-racist determinism, which, especially in Germany, fell on fertile ground.[14] They also fuelled antisemitism, culminating in the two volumes by Houston Stuart Chamberlain (1855–1927), originally published in German in 1899 as *Die Grundlagen des 19. Jahrhunderts*, and in English in 1913 as *Foundations of the Nineteenth Century*.[15]

Colonial Mass Violence and the Notion of Genocide

Colonial strategies of oppression, subjugation, warfare and the imposition of foreign minority rule introduced new forms of mass violence and extinction. These led in their extreme versions to the elimination of indigenous people in the settler colonies.[16] In the

ENLIGHTENMENT AND GENOCIDE

territories of empire, the industrial mass production of the metropole translated into a willingness to resort to corresponding forms of organised mass killing.[17] Frontiers of empire were turned into battlegrounds, with Europeans defensively "waiting for the barbarians".[18] This underlines Raphael Lemkin's insight that genocides have their roots in colonial minds.[19] By "uncovering the colonial roots of the genocide concept itself", we can "operationalize Raphael Lemkin's original but ignored insight that genocides are intrinsically colonial and that they long precede the twentieth century. The history of genocide is the history of human society since antiquity."[20]

Such an exploration of ideological (as well as individual biographical) continuities and links,[21] which considers colonial genocide and its mindset as a kind of prelude to—though not predetermining—the Nazi expansion into Eastern Europe and the Holocaust, remains contested.[22] The ongoing controversy over the status of genocides (in the plural) and the singularity of the Holocaust—not least genocides committed by colonial regimes—at the same time brings the relevance of postcolonial perspectives to the fore.[23] One appropriate approach may be to view the linkages between colonialism and the Holocaust in Germany's early 20th-century history as a kind of nexus (*Verknüpfungen*).[24]

The lawyer Raphael Lemkin (1900–1959), a Jewish-Polish refugee, coined the term "genocide" in 1944[25] for what Winston Churchill had called in a broadcast speech of 1941 "a crime without a name".[26] Lemkin worked relentlessly to find an international, legally defined and informed response to the Holocaust. Significantly, his concept reached far beyond the singularity of the Shoah. It also explicitly referred to earlier colonial wars of extermination. Not least, it acknowledged the colonial war of extermination conducted by the German imperial state in its colony of German South West Africa.[27]

Owing to Lemkin's initiative, the concept of genocide as a violation of international law was accepted by the United Nations as a normative framework.[28] On 11 December 1946 the UN General Assembly unanimously adopted Resolution 96(1). It stated categorically that "genocide is a crime under international law which the civilised world condemns—and for the commission of which principals and accomplices, whether private individuals, public officials or statesmen, and whether the crime is committed on religious, racial, political or any other grounds, are punishable".[29] It took more lobbying and several compromises—in fact, watering down the original definition, and reducing it to a much narrower concept—before the essentials of this resolution were finally adopted by the General Assembly on 9 December 1948 as the Convention for the Prevention and Punishment of the Crime of Genocide. It went into force three years later.[30] The Convention defined genocide as "acts committed with intent to destroy, in whole or in part, a national, ethnical, racial or religious group", and it made genocide a crime punishable under international law.

While the Convention came about as a response of the international community specifically to the Holocaust, the study of the origins, historical and social contexts, and specific forms of genocide requires further analyses in a comparative perspective. This includes mass violence perpetrated during the process of colonisation and other forms of expansion by war or similar violent means. It includes too the use of degrading names and terms for subject people to dehumanise them and lower the threshold for their killing.[31] Such hate speech allows for the elimination of others. The "civilising mission" of colonial expansion, justified by the claim of racial superiority, was one of the cradles for the development of "modern" forms of mass violence, culminating in the extinction of local communities who resisted foreign occupation. Despite there being a variety of colonising powers, all resorted to practices that had similar if not the same roots, and transcended national identities, with the result that during the phase of colonial expansion "European civilisers" acted on common values in what has been called an "imperial cloud":

> European expansion during the nineteenth and twentieth century appears more and more as a shared colonial project characterised by common basic assumptions, as well as patterns of thought and techniques. Examples of these collective conceptions included the imagination to "civilise" the colonised, efforts to settle a terra nullius and the widespread attempt to place colonisers and colonised

in segregated living spaces in colonial cities. Considering such similarities, it is fitting that, for instance, British, Belgian or German men on the spot—but also at home—often first started to perceive themselves as "European" when they were confronted with the colonial "others" in the imperial periphery.[32]

Despite the differences between the imperial powers, extreme violence as an integral part of colonial rule was a "trans-imperial" phenomenon.[33] This did not exclude specific trajectories among the colonising states. Translated into forms of German colonial practice, the "social Darwinian racism of the settlers was, by its nature, clearly comparable to, and a component of, the völkisch territorial propaganda that is required for the creation of an apartheid society".[34] Such an obsession with racial superiority created fertile ground for colonial practices and treatment of the "natives". If challenged and met by their resistance, such treatment could culminate in forms of genocide, which, as Henry Huttenbach argues,

> in essence ... is a variant of totalist thought, a particular form of mentality. Totalism sees the world in polarizing absolutes: friend/ enemy, good/evil, right/wrong. ... A satisfactory definition of genocide must take into account the totalist dimension in the definition of genocide. ... There must be some form of a direct endangerment of a group's existence, a fact already acknowledged by Lemkin.[35]

A pioneer in the promotion of Genocide Studies, Huttenbach challenges the fixation on Holocaust Studies as "a hierarchy of massacres over which the Holocaust reigns supreme" with "its own definition that applies only to itself".[36] He dismisses the notion of a "supergenocide that cannot be compared with other genocidal incidents",[37] and challenges "the determined practice of dichotomously separating the Holocaust from other genocides" while advocating a comparative approach and the need for contextualisation.[38] This approach is guided by the insight "that the phenomenon of genocide has no single cultural or even chronological origins. Genocidal behavior has been shown to respect no boundaries, neither temporal nor spatial or cultural. Like war, it has manifested itself in the past and present *globally*, regardless of local variations."[39]

THE LONG SHADOW OF GERMAN COLONIALISM

According to this summary:

> Lemkin and the Genocide Convention ... must be understood in the context of the Holocaust—but by no means exclusively so. Just as Lemkin resisted the temptation to elevate the Holocaust to the status of the singular archetype of genocide, so too is the convention designed to capture a range of different events, the common core being a pattern of acts and omissions oriented around the goal of destroying groups as such, social collectives *qua* social collectives—or, as Lemkin himself put it, "a coordinated plan of different actions aiming at the destruction of essential foundations of the life of national groups".[40]

Towards Decolonisation

The link between colonialism and genocide remains an integral part of European modernity and its legacy. Yet up till now this link has hardly been acknowledged in the dominant cultures of the former colonial powers. To do so requires questioning fundamental values and norms which guide the exercise of power and the ways of dealing with deviations from what are considered acceptable norms. This would involve a thorough redefinition of concepts currently applied in terms of social engineering and so-called good governance. It would replace the present hegemonic discourse with reflections on new concepts of power and equality, of the same and the other. If otherness could be regarded as possibly (though not necessarily) different but always as equal, the implicit justifications of discriminatory practices would lose their pseudo-legitimacy.

The systems and conditions created during Western European processes of industrialisation and imperial expansion had long-term effects. They formed an integral part of modernisation theory, whatever its political or ideological orientation (including orthodox Marxism). Not surprisingly, decolonisation from about the mid-20th century never emancipated people—whether colonisers or colonised—from the dominant paradigms of development and similar notions of modernity. The virus survived, even in the ambivalences of Hannah Arendt's Eurocentric critique of the origins of totalitarian rule.[41] A clear indication of the success story of bringing Europe to most other parts of the world is that the institutions of the European state and its agencies reproduced in substantial ways the colonial system. They have remained largely unquestioned and intact in the reproduction of given systems of power and control. While the individuals controlling and executing social and political power might have changed, the concept of power and its applications have not.

Similarly, the colonial legacy in most former colonising nations has hardly been fundamentally questioned and critically examined, especially in terms of the dominant ideology applied within these countries to "civilise the natives", both at home and abroad. The hegemonic discourse has in principle changed little since then. The "inability to mourn", first diagnosed by the Mitscherlichs with reference to post-World War II Germany's inability to come to terms with both the victims and, even more so, the perpetrators of the Nazi regime,[42] applies also to the colonial era. This coincides with a refusal to rethink power and dominance within such notions as development, progress and modernity—all defined in a hegemonic mode of thought as normative and absolute paradigms. None of the former colonial powers has hitherto truly accepted the fundamental challenge of deconstructing in its collective memories and commemoration practices the basis upon which the colonial mindset abused the "civilising mission" to exploit and prey upon others.

Revisiting European modernity and its notions of progress and development may be a particular challenge to those who, because of origin and tradition, were socialised within a culture of domination and imperialism on the part of former generations of perpetrators. They are confronted with the painful task of decolonising their minds by means of critical reflection on the nature of their socialisation. Having said this, a similar challenge exists also for those on the other side of the same historical processes. For if one continues to maintain an us–them divide, separating the "goodies" and the "baddies" according to pigmentation or cultural roots, one is simply reversing the two sides of the dichotomy instead of changing the nature of people's perceptions. It just remains a form of polarisation with mutually exclusive domains and entitlements. After all, being the descendant of an erstwhile victim does not stop one from turning into a perpetrator. Having been discriminated against does not exclude one from engaging in discriminatory practices oneself. Nor does one's origin in a group of perpetrators (in a historical and collective sense) prevent individuals from being able to emancipate themselves from this legacy in terms of their own perceptions, concepts, convictions, commitments and deeds—with all the ambiguities such socio-political, cultural and indeed psychological processes of mental decolonisation may involve.

The basic question is to what extent current practices and mindsets, as reproduced in the still-dominant concepts of progress and development, represent a continuity with colonial thinking. The Age of Enlightenment was also the Age of Reason. In its uncritical belief in man-made progress (indeed, in the male reductionist version), the era saw—as Max Horkheimer and Theodor Adorno argued—the emergence of the first rays of a mythical sun of calculating rationality, under whose icy light the seeds of a new barbarism began to ripen.[43] This rationality took shape as the European project of hegemonic expansion, claiming a universal omnipotence and omniscience to solve the problems of our world (at the cost of the extermination of millions of species—ultimately including us too). Its consequences have been the subject of critical reflections which remain an integral part of the legacy of the Age of Enlightenment. It also produced those who questioned the dominant paradigm to which that age gave birth.

Already during this transformative period, when world views and philosophies changed in line with the transformation of modes of production (and reproduction), representatives of a Radical Enlightenment began to challenge some of the dominant justifications for inequality and injustice.[44] They resisted the prevailing notion of progress. Instead, they embarked upon a critique of the kind of progress that implied the advancement of power in forms which turned such progress into regression. As the co-founders of Critical Theory warned, the curse of unstoppable progress is unstoppable regression.[45] As this chapter indicates, my approach identifies with the critical tradition which engages with a history that is still alive in the present. This is particularly so in the case of Germany, with its reluctant and limited treatment of its colonial legacy.

3

THE GERMAN COLONIAL BRAND

As the introduction to the 2014 edited volume *German Colonialism in a Global Age* put it, "Writing the history of German colonialism has never been simple."[1] Lasting as it did only three decades, from 1884 to World War I, the relatively short-lived German colonial era is often considered rather negligible. This has for long been a dominant perception in post-World War II (West) Germany. The neglect of this history is illustrated by the sparse coverage the subject once received in school textbooks and curricula.[2] The blind spot was only gradually and partly corrected.[3] From the late 1950s to the late 1980s the engagement with the German colonial era was markedly different in the German Democratic Republic (GDR). In contrast to the Federal Republic of Germany (FRG), historians in the GDR engaged in greater depth with the subject. The result in terms of scholarship was considerable and pioneering, as the references in this book show. On the other hand, a nearly 500-page volume on "modern colonial history" published in 1970 in West Germany made do without any chapter on German colonialism.[4] Today, however, the evasive non-treatment of German colonial and imperial history in the public sphere is out of step with more recent scholarly endeavours, which have engaged much more seriously with German colonialism in a variety of aspects. They have provided new insights and knowledge, which have fostered a grow-

THE LONG SHADOW OF GERMAN COLONIALISM

ing awareness that what was once often belittled as a mere "episode" forms an integral part of German history. Its effects include a lasting impact on German identities, too, and challenge established self-perceptions. As a series of discussions on teaching history in German schools concluded, the emergence of postcolonial theories, which have inspired many of the more recent works of historical scholarship, has placed the revision of Germany's collective identities and internalised perceptions firmly on the agenda.[5]

Germany Goes Overseas

The German nation-state and its agencies did not have any influence on the early stages of formal colonial rule by European powers. During the initial period of European expansion, Germany conducted no meaningful sea-based operations beyond Europe, and Germany only achieved official statehood as a unified country in 1871. While Germany can therefore be considered a latecomer in the competition for colonial territories, German merchants and explorers nonetheless played an active role from early on.[6] Germans participated in colonial enterprises right from the initial stages of European colonial expansion.[7] From 1528 the merchant Bartholomäus Welser (1484–1561) from Augsburg collaborated with the Spanish Crown in lucrative colonial projects in Venezuela.[8] His Augsburg rival Jakob Fugger (1459–1525) engaged in similar dealings with the Portuguese empire.[9] In 1682 the Brandenburg African Company established the small trading post of Great Friedrichsburg on the coast of what is today Ghana.[10] Apart from these instances of early German involvement in the exploitation of overseas resources, German traders benefited in many ways from participation as individuals in the colonial expansion of other countries, not least in the slave trade and the plantation economies.[11] While these short-lived overseas enterprises were of a limited nature, they inspired colonial imaginaries in Germans back home, fuelling notions of superiority and imperialist greatness within German literature.[12]

After the traders, missionary societies were next in line in preparing the way for Germany to enter the era of colonial rule.[13] As "civilising agents", missionaries promoted and imposed their Christian–European value systems as a universal norm, thereby displaying the ethnocentric arrogance of a "paternalistic developmental dictatorship" involved in a project of cultural imperialism. This went hand in hand with the promotion of an early-capitalist work ethic.[14] Beginning in the 1820s, the Protestant Berlin Mission and the Rhenish Missionary Society established stations in South Africa. From there, the Rhenish Mission entered in the 1840s the northern territory of what later became German South West Africa. Through their economic activities, including trade in European goods, those in charge of the mission stations soon gained considerable influence in local dynamics.[15] About the same time the North German Mission began to work among the Ewe on the Slave Coast of West Africa in 1847. Given the usefulness of missionary activities for colonial interests, it is no wonder that missions became associated with ambitions to establish formal foreign rule.[16]

A growing number of so-called explorers helped identify worthwhile investments overseas for merchants and traders. Beyond a purely scientific interest in nature and culture, they roamed overseas territories in search of potential resources that could be identified and exploited for profitable businesses. It is worth noting that the focus of these explorers and their expeditions shifted as a hierarchical, Eurocentric view began to entrench itself after the Age of Enlightenment. While earlier travelogues often showed an open attitude to "otherness", free of value-based judgements, this was mostly replaced during the 19th century by a "White supremacist" world view, exploring opportunities for economic gain.[17] Travelogues increasingly described "discoveries" from the perspective of investigating potential investments that offered returns. Starting in the mid-19th century, the number of self-styled German "Africa travellers", who considered themselves representatives of a proper profession, began to increase.[18] Their reports contributed to a growing enthusiasm about the potential for Germany to secure its share in the colonial enterprise. They often achieved celebrity status among the public at home.[19]

The first claims to ownership of overseas territories were made by merchants in charge of big companies, mainly operating from the Hanse towns of Hamburg and Bremen, who staked their claims to land through their individual enterprises and in this way opened the way for the later proclamation of official colonial rule by the imperial German state. Prussian-brewed *Kartoffelschnaps* (potato schnapps) was one of the means for realising the "civilising mission" and an integral part of German encroachment overseas, with a long-term impact on almost every sphere of German influence. It was not only of strategic importance in creating dependency, but also of economic interest. During the early period of German colonialism in Togo, the export of potato schnapps was the biggest trade item.[20] For the Hamburg merchant Adolph Woermann, the lucrative trade in schnapps was, besides the profit it generated, a *Reizmittel* (stimulant) for promoting the civilising mission.[21]

German ethnologists, reflecting the colonial attitudes of the time, were divided over whether it was better to acquire colonial territory than maintain free trade. But they willingly accepted funding by colonial interest groups.[22] So did the explorers and geographers roaming overseas territories.[23] A total of 15 professors specialised in colonial geography and conducted field research in the colonies between 1884 and 1919, displaying a close ideological and institutional affinity with the colonial state.[24] The colonial lobby, composed of representatives of economic interests, academics, adventurers and politicians, started to campaign through pressure groups such as the African Society of Germany (founded in 1878), and associations and societies seeking the acquisition of colonies such as the German Colonial Union (founded in 1882), renamed the German Colonial Society (in 1887), and the Society for German Colonisation (established in 1884).[25] They argued that Germany needed to catch up in the competition for colonial acquisitions with other industrialised countries by securing access to resources and markets. Another argument was to stop German emigration—mainly to North America—by redirecting it to Germany's own colonies.[26]

As an ideological project and projection of the notions of cultural greatness, superiority and the social Darwinist struggle for survival, colonial propaganda soon added to its arsenal of pseudo-scientific racial theories,[27] by resorting to popular culture in fiction

THE GERMAN COLONIAL BRAND

(novels, poetry and, later, narratives written by settlers and soldiers) and film. Both media were in extensive use for decades until the end of the Nazi regime.[28] *Völkerschauen*—rather euphemistically translated as "ethnological shows"—achieved similar prominence well before the establishment of the first German colonies, displaying humans from overseas in zoo-like settings. This form of dehumanising exoticism became a popular attraction and, like novels and films, created entertainment for a considerable number of people in daily German life for decades to come.[29] Hand in hand with anthropology, they propagated "a new antihumanist worldview", which "had some of its most important and far-reaching effects" in Germany.[30]

While historians have discussed at length Chancellor Otto von Bismarck's initial reluctance to enter the colonial race, there seems to be wide agreement that ultimately, for mainly domestic reasons, he was willing to jump on the bandwagon. The motives and move were described as "social imperialism".[31] This suggested that the orientation outwards towards the colonies was an attempt to distract from and compensate for social tensions at home, fuelled by socio-economic changes during an age of further industrialisation, resulting in the pauperisation and proletarianisation of a growing number of German people. The vision and promise of a "place in the sun" (*Platz an der Sonne*), coined in 1897 in a speech in parliament by the State Secretary in the Foreign Ministry, Bernhard von Bülow, captured the spirit of the move in a prominent slogan and metaphor. This became an effective catchword, similar to earlier efforts to channel potential social-revolutionary ambitions into promises of a better life abroad.

In 1884 the first colonial annexations were officially declared by hoisting the German flag and thereby placing (or rather forcing) territories and their inhabitants under the official "protection" of the *Kaiserreich*. This in fact offered protection only to those individuals and their property acquired at best under dubious circumstances as "rogue empires".[32] The hosting of the Berlin Africa Conference of 1884–1885 (also dubbed the *Kongokonferenz*) marked Germany's entry into the club of colonial powers, who took it upon themselves to negotiate the division and distribution of the African continent as a form of property among the European imperial states.[33]

The German Colonies

By the turn of the 20th century, imperial Germany had become one of the biggest colonial empires in terms of foreign territory, euphemistically dubbed "acquisitions".[34] In the following sections, the process of colonisation and some features and consequences of colonial rule for the people in these territories are summarised briefly. There is nowadays considerable information available not only in historical but also interdisciplinary studies on German colonialism, in the form of general overviews, edited volumes, scholarly monographs, journal articles and chapters in books.[35] In increasingly nuanced and critical analyses, the devastating impact of German colonialism has been well researched and presented, though the insights remain largely marginalised or ignored in the public and political spheres.[36]

Instead of adding another general summary account here, the focus in the following sections is on some of the specific features of each case.[37] They show that the inter-colonial German network linked some of the colonies in a variety of ways. First, those seeking profits overseas, not least trading houses such as Woermann,[38] were present in more than one of the colonies and benefited from a variety of increasingly diversified activities. This is true also of individual colonial administrators—such as Theodor Seitz (1863–1949),[39] who was governor of both Cameroon and South West Africa. And it applies even more so to officers in the army: most prominently, Lothar von Trotha (1848–1920), who waged war in three of the colonies; as well as Franz Ritter von Epp (1868–1947),[40] who in addition to two colonial wars had a career in the Nazi regime; and Paul von Lettow-Vorbeck (1870–1964),[41] who was dubbed the "lion of Africa", roaming its battlefields. After his triumphant return to Germany, he wrote a book which was translated into several other languages and which remained in publication until the 1950s.[42] Back in the *Kaiserreich*, the nationalist media contributed to the general mobilisation of support for the unleashing of violence against everything resisting German colonialism.[43] Many drawn from the ranks of those serving colonialism abroad continued with their colonial propaganda when holding leading positions in Germany during the Weimar Republic. Some subsequently entered high-profile careers in Nazi Germany. Interestingly, "German Africans" even sought a return to their "lost *Heimat*" from within the Permanent Mandates Commission of the League of Nations,[44] while others established and maintained their *Heimat* abroad.[45]

"Colonial subjects" were also engaged in or forced into intercolonial mobility. They could be migrant labourers such as the Kru from West Africa who were employed as a kind of African "labour elite" in South West Africa;[46] or recruits for local policing units; or soldiers fighting in different colonial armies and territories;[47] or deportees from their home countries to other German colonies: Nama were deported to Cameroon and Togo,[48] while deportations also took place from Cameroon to South West Africa. One special case was a Nigerian serving in three African colonies, first under British and later under German command, during which time he was deported from Cameroon to South West Africa.[49] Far bigger plans to ship prisoners from one colony to another—including the idea of establishing penal colonies for Africans on the Pacific islands—were thwarted by internal disagreements, legal disputes and financial implications.[50] While the colonial entities are usually presented as separate from each other, they were in varying degrees an integral and interlinked part of the overall colonial system. This does not mean that colonial policies were monolithic or uniform. They were always shaped by local contexts and by the role of individuals in the colonial administration, who at times had very different views and approaches.[51]

As the cases below also show, German occupation of territories by no means involved *terra nullius* ("the land of no one") or happened in a political or socio-economic vacuum. The areas occupied were characterised by their own hierarchical power structures and forms of interaction among the inhabitants, involving local dynamics and interests at play. Some local communities or sections of those communities made the strategic decision to collaborate with the intruders for their own gains, while others adopted resistance to the external threat of disempowerment. In all cases the local communities were actors in their own right and pursued their own processes of strategic decision-making. They were subjects, not helpless victims. Once co-optation based on mutual interests failed during interactions, the claimed superiority of the coloniser turned out to be mere hubris. For the colonisers, the loss of imagined authority created a feeling of weakness, if not threat, resulting in attempts at physical subjugation of the colonised, using more sophisticated military equipment to enforce the colonisers' system through brutal violence.[52]

As a general point of departure, it must be taken for granted that the local communities and their leaders acted as subjects, basing their decisions on their assessment of the unfolding situation. One needs to avoid the trap of assigning them the exclusive status of victims. This overlooks not only the existence of elites as a feature of local hierarchies, but also their proactive, conscious role in the colonial world. Indigenous people were at times collaborators and accomplices for their own gain, though more often they were opponents resorting to non-violent sabotage or armed resistance to foreign rule. Some of them—most prominently the Bell family in Douala—engaged in fairly sophisticated ways in direct interaction and legal disputes with the authorities in Germany, bypassing the colonial authorities.[53] All these responses underline the fact that there were interest-based agencies among the colonised and that they carried influence. They were by no means passive objects. As Matthew Fitzpatrick points out:

> Understanding the role of these extra-European monarchs in responding to and partially shaping the German Empire helps put paid to the assumption that Africa, Asia and the Pacific have only a colonial past, while Europe alone has a political, military, and diplomatic history. The role played by monarchs and their domestic advisors, supporters, and detractors clearly dispels this myth, showing how those outside of Europe prosecuted their own form of international politics and diplomacy with—and indeed from within—the German Empire.[54]

That, in the end, the rules of interaction were imposed and coerced by foreign powers through sheer violence is part of the nature of colonialism. But this cannot rob the colonised of their history of engagement, nor deny them the recognition that they acted and responded to foreign encroachment, whether by means of passive or active resistance, including a variety of forms of sabotage,[55] or collaboration.

South West Africa

From the mid-19th century, local communities of the Ovaherero and Nama (also at times acting in inter-ethnic alliances) were increasingly absorbed in efforts to gain hegemonic control over the eastern, central and southern parts of the territory between the Orange River in the south (separating it from the northern Cape Colony) and the Kunene in the north (the natural border with southern Angola).[56] Although nomadic herders, they were also engaged in mining activities and trade (there was a long-distance trade route supplying the island of St Helena with cattle). The northern parts of the territory (as well as southern Angola) were settled by Oshivambo-speaking communities. They cultivated the land and engaged in crafts and trade activities. So-called Ovamboland and other regions in the north-east remained under German and South African indirect rule (and hence feature less prominently here). In contrast, the central, southern and eastern parts of the country, climatically suitable for European settlement, were increasingly penetrated by missionaries and traders, who in interaction with the local communities fuelled rivalries for the sake of their own interests.[57]

As individual German merchants began searching for direct access to and control over territories abroad, Adolph Lüderitz from Bremen took the initiative to establish what was later called Lüderitzland. This coastal area was a barren strip of desert along the Atlantic Ocean and so the territory had been for a long time of little interest to Portuguese and other seafarers.[58] Lüderitz eyed the bay of Angra Pequena (later Lüderitz Bay) as providing an opportunity to benefit from the longstanding exploitation of rich guano deposits on the small islands in the vicinity and as an entry point for access to mining sites for copper that already existed in the interior. Other incentives were the potential profits from trade in ostrich feathers and cattle as well as guns. Another strong motive was the hope of discovering diamonds and other mineral wealth.[59] A detailed plan and official appeal was submitted to the German Foreign Ministry in November 1882, requesting the protection of the German flag for his enterprises, but it received no answer. Lüderitz nevertheless dispatched Heinrich Vogelsang as his emissary to the bay in April 1883.

On 1 May 1883 Vogelsang concluded an initial treaty with a leader of one of the local communities, followed in August 1883 by a second treaty. The size of the land exchanged for 60 guns and £500 was set at a radius of 20 "geographical miles". This left the deliberate impression that the English mile (1.6 km) was meant, being the only locally known measurement. But the demarcated land area followed a radius based on the German mile (7.4 km). Lüderitz in a letter to Vogelsang explicitly approved of the fraud and told him to continue with such deals. On the basis of these land claims, the German flag was hoisted in the bay for the first time on 7 August 1884 to declare the protectorate (*Schutzgebiet*) of German South West Africa (Deutsch-Südwestafrika). This marked the official entry of the *Kaiserreich* into the club of colonial powers. When the fraudulent land deals continued, Bismarck's official representative, Gustav Nachtigal, expressed his concerns in a letter to Lüderitz in November 1884. As he explained, this was not for the sake of any "factual relevance", but because it could create a "certain impression" to outsiders.[60]

In the end, greed took its toll and Lüderitz could not swallow and digest the prey. Facing bankruptcy, he transferred the usufruct over the vast land he had accumulated to the German Society for South West Africa, which was founded for this very purpose. Not that this made any significant difference in the years to come, since the only meaningful activities that took place were land speculation, the exploitation of natural resources by private "concessionary companies" and trade (not least in alcohol). The absence of any significant investment in infrastructure and of hardly any influx of Germans indicated that the vast territory was initially anything but a settler colony.

THE GERMAN COLONIAL BRAND

In 1893 an official German administration was established. Despite its infancy, the colonial apparatus changed the local dynamics and was soon headed for violent clashes with the local communities standing in the way of further encroachment. Their leaders who resisted cooperation were coerced into "protection treaties" by force of arms or else were executed. After a military attack on his retreat at Hornkranz, in which women and children of the community were killed, Hendrik Witbooi, who was the most important leader among the southern Nama communities, was forced to surrender and end his resistance.[61] Among the Ovaherero communities, the German administration promoted Samuel Maharero to the hitherto unknown position of paramount chief in return for his loyal support.[62]

By the mid-1890s the colonial administration was for the first time in some control over the southern and central parts of the territory. This prompted an increase in settlers seeking their fortune as farmers by means of extensive cattle ranching. As land and livestock were both still mainly in the possession of the local communities, the settlers sought to appropriate these by violent and fraudulent practices with the "legal" backing of the colonial administration. Despite the growing onslaught, the economy remained to a large extent under the control and influence of local Ovaherero communities, who still held possession of both land and cattle. Their dominance was only ended as a result of the devastating consequences of the cattle plague, or rinderpest, in 1896–1897. After the outbreak of rinderpest, the northern regions (mainly so-called Ovamboland as well as the north-eastern parts) were separated from the rest of the territory by a "Red Line", which was established as a veterinary cordon. It turned into an internal border between the northern parts, which were placed under indirect rule, and the southern parts, which were declared a "Police Zone".[63]

The immense loss of cattle made the Ovaherero more vulnerable and reliant upon goods offered by traders, and land as well as labour became the basis of exchange relations. By the turn of the century, Whites had encroached on land previously in indigenous ownership, and the local economy fell more and more under settler-colonial dominance. Deutsch-Südwest became an extension of *Heimat* or the "Imperial Homeland".[64] German capital investments in infrastructure (including a railway line from the coastal town of Swakopmund to the interior) contributed to long-term plans for the more systematic exploitation of resources. New forms of local resistance ended in military defeat and the imposition of new restrictions, including the creation of "native reserves" to limit mobility and expand settler control. Rebellious leaders unwilling to comply with the enforced "protection treaties" were executed, land was confiscated and forced labour was introduced, mainly for railway construction. At the same time, the abusive treatment of workers, and of women, as well as outright crimes committed by Whites against Africans, was ignored by the colonial authorities. In contrast, even minor violations of the laws by Africans were punished excessively.

The injustices and existential threats ultimately reached a point at which, under pressure from his own people, Samuel Maharero abandoned his loyalty to the colonial administration. In January 1904 he issued an order to attack and kill German men. Caught by surprise, the Germans responded with unlimited force of arms once troop reinforcements and weapons arrived from Germany. Having observed the German warfare escalating into forms of indiscriminate mass killing of the Ovaherero, Hendrik Witbooi decided to join the resistance in late 1904, at a time when the Ovaherero were already decisively defeated (see chapter 5 for further details). While Maharero escaped to the neighbouring British protectorate of Bechuanaland, Witbooi died in October 1905 of wounds suffered in battle. Today both are celebrated as leaders of the primary stage of anti-colonial resistance,[65] together with Jakob Marengo (of Ovaherero–Nama descent), who engaged in guerrilla warfare before being killed in September 1907.[66]

With the defeat of the local communities there, final control over the territory was established and consolidated. This paved the way for the establishment of a settler-colonial economy. Nama and Ovaherero who had survived the war against German occupation were incarcerated in concentration camps and used for forced labour (on the construction of railway lines, for instance), resulting in horrific death rates.[67] New regulations introduced from 1905 effected strict physical and social separation between the colonisers and the colonised (including the prohibition of mixed marriages in 1905).[68] A tight, closely controlled and regulated system, motivated not least by fear,[69] emerged by way of legal ordinances. The strict segregation that was introduced was a precursor of apartheid. While the term is usually associated with the White minority regime of South Africa, it was initially a German form of social engineering in its colony. In 1906 all non-Ovambo were prohibited from entering the northern part. In the same year almost all communal land and cattle in the Police Zone were expropriated, and communities were separated and confined to reserves. In 1907 pass laws further limited mobility and could be enforced by the direct authority of any White person.

With the unfolding colonial-capitalist settler economy in dire need of Black workers and servants, the northern area of the Ovambo became a reservoir for cheap and rightless contract labour.[70] By then an inter-colonial network had already drawn on migrant workers from Cameroon for the supply of labour.[71] In 1911 the first labour management agency for contract workers was founded at the border with Ovamboland. From 1912 agents began to recruit migrant workers from the northern regions.[72] By 1913 the colonial economy had absorbed almost all adult male Africans in the Police Zone, mainly on farms, in mining, within colonial state structures and as domestic servants. By then more than 10,000 contract labourers had been added to the workforce. The policing of African labour for the settler-colonial economy, involving openly violent practices, as well as the continued extermination of San (Bushmen), became an important function in the years following the genocide.[73] The process of proletarianisation[74] had been accelerated by the discovery of diamonds in the vicinity of Lüderitz Bay in 1908,[75] with deposits stretching along the coast to the banks of the Orange River. The area was subsequently declared a restricted area (*Sperrgebiet*) to protect the monopoly in exploration.[76] The diamond rush dramatically increased total exports in the period between 1907 and 1913 from 1.6 million to 70.3 million Deutsche Marks, while the number of local Germans more than tripled from 4,700 in 1903 to 14,800 in 1913.[77]

THE LONG SHADOW OF GERMAN COLONIALISM

If there are any keywords to characterise the main effects of German colonial rule for the indigenous people, these would include land fraud, genocide, contract labour and apartheid. Apartheid was proudly supported and propagated by Heinrich Vedder (1876–1972). He came to the colony in 1905 as a missionary and later taught at a missionary college, the only lower-secondary school at the time for Africans. He published extensively on local history. Exerting much influence on colonial-apologetic narratives, he became a widely celebrated authority and icon, not only among German-speaking Whites. In 1951 he was appointed to the South African Senate as representative for "the Natives of South West Africa". His most notable contribution there was a speech in 1956, during which he praised apartheid as an invention by the Germans:

> in South West Africa we have the only country in the world where *apartheid* has been exercised in an increasing degree since 50 years. ... The mixing between Europeans and non-Europeans has since 1908 been prohibited by law. Europeans and non-Europeans are pleased about those apartheid laws. ... There is no sensible person among the Europeans and the Natives who seeks to break down those walls and change that foundation.[78]

At the beginning of World War I, South Africa as a member of the British Empire dispatched its army to occupy the adjacent German-controlled territory, and the German troops and authorities there capitulated by mid-1915.[79] The German possession was handed to the successor colonial power on a silver platter: the pioneering work of colonial subjugation had been completed, and a lasting structural legacy had been created. In 1917 the first South African administrator recognised the German achievement in having "laid the foundations of a progressive administration" in a country "exceptionally well equipped" to benefit from "its vast unexploited and, to a great extent, unexplored resources".[80] This was clearly the view of those who had no other intention than incorporating the country as a fifth province of South Africa. Building on the foundations established by German rule, South Africa consolidated the settler-colonial structures.[81]

Cameroon

Already before imperial Germany settled on an official colonial policy, West Africa had been an important market for the export of spirits from Prussian factories. In July 1883 the Hamburg Chamber of Commerce endorsed a memorandum drafted by Adolph Woermann, which advocated the annexation of the Cameroon coast.[82] This would enable German merchants to avoid taxation on trade routes imposed by the British and French colonial powers. It also served the ambition to gain access to the hinterland. One obstacle to this was the close control of the coast and any inward penetration exerted by the local ruling royal houses of the Duala families of Bell, Akwa, Dido and Hickory, who, despite internal differences and competition, had been institutionally linked since the early 1800s in the Traditional Assembly of the Douala People.[83] They were in contact with English and German traders and benefited from charging a duty on trade within their home turf.[84] To gain a foot in the colonial door, there were initiatives in Cameroon similar to the private transactions undertaken on behalf of the Bremen merchant Lüderitz that led to the official proclamation of German South West Africa.

> From 1883 to 1907 individual Germans or representatives of the German state signed ninety-five treaties and contracts with various chieftains in Cameroon. ... The most famous of these was signed on July 12, 1884, by King Bell and King Akwa. ... The treaty was not signed directly by German officials but merely by private German business representatives. Nevertheless, the German government recognized it as binding on the state and used it to proclaim sovereignty over the territory ... based on the will of the Cameroonian people.[85]

On 14 July 1884 Gustav Nachtigal, acting as the official representative of the German state (*Reichskommissar*) for West Africa—he subsequently also served as Germany's initial emissary to South West Africa—hoisted the German flag. This happened with the consent of some of the local Duala kings—most importantly, with King Ndumbé Lobé Bell and King Akwa (Dika Mpondo Akwa)—after the agreement of 12 July 1884[86] had fully endorsed their conditions as laid down in a document entitled "Our Wishes" and as elaborated in a complementary memorandum.[87] It included their continued ownership of the land and recognition of the local chiefs as rulers of the "Cameroons". This was a clear attempt at limiting direct foreign influence, with the aim of keeping any infringement of their own authority at bay.[88] Given the later history of colonial encroachment, this turned out to be wishful thinking.

Despite their co-signature of the "wishes" statement, the Germans made it clear in their public and confidential statements immediately following annexation that they had every intention of destroying the Duala trade monopoly in order to exploit Cameroon more effectively. The problems were, first, settling colonial claims with Britain, which might take diplomatic advantage of the Duala protest, and second, creating the means for penetrating the interior.[89]

Soon, disagreements and conflicts erupted over the degree to which local control had to be surrendered to the German authorities in the light of different interpretations of the notion of "sovereignty". The continued local ownership of land as well as control over trade relations by local middlemen was never really respected.[90]

Adolph Woermann, who was the mastermind behind the contractual arrangements, had a primary interest in land speculation, in addition to trade, in creating a plantation economy—with rather mixed results.[91] But many of the local communities that exerted control over land were never part of the initial agreement with the Germans. Thus, they did not feel obliged to comply with the agreement or any interpretation of it. Among them was Lock Priso (Kum'a Mbappé) of Hickorytown (Bonabéri), who had favoured an arrangement with the British and refused to accept the German "protection treaty", which he had never signed. From 20 to 22 December 1884, two ships of the German navy attacked and stormed villages and bombed Bonabéri[92] to "restore order".[93] Such forms of "pacification" became almost routine.[94]

By means of an imperial charter, the *Kaiserreich* transferred the administration of the territory initially to the chartered trading companies, as had happened in South West Africa. These companies, however, had no interest in such a financial burden. As a

THE GERMAN COLONIAL BRAND

result of their neglect of this obligation, they were finally superseded by a direct form of German colonial administration in 1889.[95] The subsequent extension of German control, now financed by the German state, was to a large extent conducted by means of military attacks, imposing as retribution a variety of reparations on the defeated (such as monetary payments, forced labour, appropriation of land and extraction of ivory). This militarisation included the recruitment of a mercenary unit from Dahomey slaves in 1891, euphemistically called a "police force" (*Polizeitruppe*). Its members were ordered to use particularly brutal acts of violence and atrocities in their operations against the locals en route to the interior.[96]

Futile demands for better remuneration and food caused growing frustration among the legionnaires. Their women were forced to perform unpaid work for the colonial government in the capital and were, notoriously, sexually abused. When on 15 December 1893 more than twenty of them were publicly stripped naked and flogged with the notorious *Nilpferdpeitsche* (hippopotamus-hide whip)[97] in front of their men, the latter started a mutiny. They managed to occupy the government building for a week before a company of German naval infantry could restore control. All those captured were immediately executed. But news of their treatment, which had triggered the rebellion, became a matter of German domestic controversy over the nature of colonial practices and resulted in disciplinary measures against the two leading colonial officials involved.[98]

As a consequence of the insurrection, military units were formed from Africans recruited elsewhere (Dahomey, Lagos and Egyptian Sudan), and tasked with meting out exceptional brutality against the local population in the further seizure of territory.[99] Until the mid-1890s direct control over the colony was mainly limited to the coastal area. Only during the time of Governor Jesko von Puttkamer (1895–1907) was territorial expansion pursued in earnest and broughted to completion. The German advance to some extent benefited from the support of local leaders who, in competition with rivals, sought advantages through collaboration. A prominent example was Sultan Ibrahim Njoya of the Bamum.[100] But the colony was never truly "pacified". Military administration (in contrast to a civil one) lasted until the end of German colonial rule in half of the proclaimed territory, with several districts under a civil administration headed by former officers of the *Schutztruppe*. For a long time, the colonisation of Cameroon was in German official historiography misleadingly labelled a "peaceful pacification", but the degree and intensity of German warfare laid the basis for the transformation of the local economy and society.[101]

As the plantation economy gradually developed, the search for labour led to forced recruitment and human trafficking, which also involved local leaders as suppliers of young men.[102] The imposition of an arbitrary tax system forced locals into a monetary economy by selling their labour. In return they secured a small amount of cash that was offered under appalling conditions of employment with no rights and a high mortality rate among the workers on the plantations. Forced labour for the colonial economy also weakened and undermined the subsistence production of local communities and further entrenched impoverishment and dependency. This went hand in hand with legal rules and regulations which codified a racially divided society based on systematic discrimination against Africans,[103] with the rule of law being—as in all other colonies—blatantly the law of the rulers. Forced labour was also used to provide transport services during expeditions into the interior and for the construction of infrastructure, such as railways and administrative buildings. Corporal punishment by flogging with the notorious *Nilpferdpeitsche* was a standard practice applied not only to workers and other men, but also to women and children. In reference to the average number of strokes inflicted, Cameroon (and Togo) soon became known as "the twenty-five country".[104]

While these practices provoked further resistance to foreign occupation and rule, the colonial power benefited from the fact that local communities were diverse and dispersed. They were often engaged in competition with one another for influence and control over resources, which meant there was an absence of an overriding alliance guided by common interests. This resulted in mainly discrete forms of war-like interaction, which in turn was a disadvantage for the entrenchment of colonial control. This was especially the case during the expansion into the interior, where isolated and remote settlements were found scattered in the bush: when a local community was defeated and the soldiers moved on to the next military encounter, those left behind often managed to withdraw from direct control. One exception was an insurrection starting in 1904 in the north-west, where several communities of different backgrounds united to fight off the German advance. Despite superior weaponry, the colonial mercenaries took half a year to defeat the attackers and end the war by executing the leaders, with some of their fellow combatants being hanged as late as 1910.[105]

Some influential and resilient local communities involved in direct exchange relations with the colonial authorities in pursuit of their own interests, such as the Duala and Akwa families in the coastal region, resorted to petitions as a form of engagement.[106] Their stance should be understood against the background of local competition with other kings seeking hegemonic control through alliances with the colonial powers, triggered mainly by rivalries between the Bell and Akwa clans. One of the first protest letters was addressed by Manga Ndumbe Bell in 1888 to Chancellor Bismarck, launching an official complaint against Governor Julius von Soden. In 1892 the Duala kings addressed Soden in protest against the abuse of power and the disrespect shown to the local rulers. They bemoaned the undermining of their role as trading middlemen, the inhuman forms of corporal punishment, dehumanising insults and interference in matters regarding women.[107] In 1902 King Duala Bell, King Dika Akwa and King Deido (Jim Ekwalla/Epee Ekwalla Deido) travelled to Berlin to protest against the restrictions on hunting elephants.[108] King Deido used the opportunity to visit the grave of his first-born son, who "like dozens of other male youngsters from elite Cameroonian and Togolese families ... was sent to school in Germany" but died within months of his arrival in 1891.[109]

In 1905 the Akwa Duala petitioned the German parliament (Reichstag) and government to end the torments inflicted by the local colonial administration, by sacking all the responsible officials. Governor Puttkamer retaliated by means of a court verdict punishing the Akwa king and four other signatories with imprisonment with forced labour of between eighteen months and nine years, while eighteen more signatories received three months' imprisonment with forced labour. When Social Democrats in the German parliament attacked this judgment as a breach of the law, the steeper sentences were reduced, and the lesser ones increased. Some of the chiefs were removed from their positions. The judge argued that the punishment was justified because the Africans had disregarded their subordinate status.[110] Despite such setbacks, these forms of civil resistance through "petitionism" were an effective way of claiming agency and voice vis-à-vis German parliamentarians so as to influence policy debates and, at times, even party policy.[111] Petitionism was cultivated as a particular Duala trademark:

> In doing so, the Duala assumed the role of equal political subjects, of subjects of the German Reich. They undermined the racist image of a [sic] "savage" and "primitive" Africans. These petitions to the German Government and parliament in Germany also questioned the authorities in the colony by taking their political demands to the metropole. This questioned the competence of the institutions in the colony and drew attention to their practices.[112]

In the context of such non-violent protest, Prince Mpondo (also Mpundu or Mpundo) Akwa, son of King Dika Akwa, deserves recognition as "one of the most important figures of the German colonial period in Cameroon who remain unknown to the public".[113] Like other sons of the nobility, he attended schools in Germany (from 1888 to 1893). Soon he was considered difficult and his insufficiently subservient behaviour was duly noted and recorded.[114] Back in Cameroon, he had a short stint as official translator/interpreter for Governor Puttkamer. Mutual dislike caused his resignation after six months. This added to his unpopularity in the colonial administration, which accused him of incitement to rebellion.[115] In 1902 he was a member of the delegation to Germany already mentioned. An article in the *Hamburger Nachrichten* quoted him as categorically stating that they would refuse to be deprived of their Black culture, law and habits, which had existed long before the encounter with Whites.[116]

THE GERMAN COLONIAL BRAND

While the rest of the delegation returned to Cameroon, Mpondo Akwa stayed in Germany, where he continued to be a nuisance: "The presence of Mpundo Akwa as a representative from a German colony in the metropole, dressing, and acting according to the cultural repertoires of the white bourgeois subjects, troubled many of the prevalent and specifically German assumptions and conceptions of blackness."[117] In 1905 he faced two accusations in court. Thanks to the lawyer Moses Levi, he was not convicted.[118] Lisa Skwirblies presents the Akwa petition and the trial of Mpondo Akwa as "significant examples of resistance against the colonial system as the Duala and Mpundo Akwa successfully acquainted themselves with a German understanding of the law and legal procedures as well as with a particular German understanding of 'honour' and used this to undermine the legitimacy of the colonial project".[119]

After a few more years as a "troublemaker", Mpondo Akwa finally returned in June 1911 to Cameroon. Celebrated locally for his rebelliousness, he was considered a risk to the colonial administration. Together with his father, he was arrested in September 1911 and, "accused of making Germanophobic remarks",[120] sentenced to imprisonment in 1912. At the outbreak of World War I, he was extrajudicially executed by a firing squad. His story has only more recently (re-)entered the public domain and is a significant reminder that the widely shared perception of determined resistance as associated mainly, if not only, with the Bell family is at best misleading.

Despite this remarkable tradition of resistance, especially by members of the coastal communities, new dynamics in colonial penetration gained momentum with advances in territorial control of the interior (including efforts to integrate local small-scale agriculture into the colonial market economy), further investment in infrastructure (such as railway construction), the expansion of the plantation economy—based on the recruitment of forced labour[121]—and the intensification of trade.[122] For the first time, an infant industry was created with the establishment of factories for the processing of palm oil from 1908 onwards. The value of exports tripled between 1906 and 1914, mainly of tropical raw material, in particular rubber, but also cacao. The colonial economic upswing, also based on the recruitment of local labour especially in the coastal region and the south, did not benefit those forced to work under often appalling conditions. Mortality rates on plantations could reach as much as 20 to 30 per cent annually, and for workers constructing the railway line over 10 per cent. Forced recruitment had devastating impacts on the local African economies and on demography in view of the de-population of younger men.[123] Rigorous sanctions based on the legal rules of the colonial masters tried to curb the growing forms of resistance and withdrawal. Verdicts with harsh punishments more than doubled between 1907–1908 and 1910 and had almost doubled again by 1912–1913.[124]

Throughout the German colonial era, the relative weakness of the state was obscured behind pompous symbolism and displays of violence—complementary forms of terror and intimidation—both in the judicial system and on the battlefield.[125] The so-called Morocco–Congo Treaty signed on 4 November 1911 between Germany and France saw a considerable portion of the French Congo passing into formal German possession in return for the transfer of rights claimed by Germany over Morocco to France. This increased the territory of Cameroon from some 465,000 to 760,000 square kilometres. Although this expansion created some dispute in Germany (the German colonial secretary resigned over the issue), it had little impact in the colony even though historians consider it a contributory factor during the build-up of tensions in Europe before World War I.

Land expropriation in the heartland of the Duala reached new dimensions in 1910, when it was decided to remove the Duala from the town bearing the same name. It was the centre of trade and transport and was now designed to serve exclusively as an economic hub for European settlement. While the Duala had previously cooperated with the German administration for their own gains—albeit with growing suspicions over the constant violation of what they considered the essential elements of a mutual recognition of interests when entering the protection treaty in 1884—they now faced an existential threat. They felt betrayed by the disregard shown for the initial contractual agreements signed with the

Germans. Their enforced resettlement to areas outside the town was imposed with an offer of ridiculously inadequate financial compensation. This further undermined their already weakened economic basis. Rudolf Duala Manga Bell, head of the Bell family since 1908, was elected by all Duala groups to protect their interests. He had been to school in the southern German towns of Aalen and Ulm from 1891 to 1897.[126] Identifying with German culture, speaking and thinking German (and therefore nicknamed by his people "the German"), he had a strong belief in German justice, the rule of law and the legal enforcement of contracts. In his engagement with the Germans, he acted like one of them.[127] In the footsteps of Mpondo Akwa, he raised "petitionism" to a new level after 1911 and managed to engage German authorities and individuals seriously and sympathetically when he brought the Duala case to their attention.

The 1884 treaty became a contentious issue and a matter of conflicting interpretations. The controversy involved the Reichstag and the Imperial Colonial Office, which were in partial disagreement with the local colonial government. German parliamentarians were willing to consider the Duala claims sympathetically. When Manga Bell was denied access to Germany, he dispatched his close confidant, Ngoso Din, in 1913 as his emissary to champion his case. Din's efforts were supported by some journalists and members of parliament. The efficient awareness campaign placed added pressure on the Cameroon authorities. They built a case against Manga Bell by claiming he did not represent the Duala majority and that his actions would be a betrayal of their interests. In a further development, flimsy evidence was finally constructed (or rather invented) claiming that Manga Bell had plotted to overthrow the German colonial government with support from the British. These accusations discredited Manga Bell to the extent that the number of those willing to support his case in Germany was considerably reduced, not least within officialdom.

Manga Bell and Ngoso Din were arrested in May 1914. The two-day trial in early August, which took place in the context of the first few days of World War I (starting on 28 July 1914), lasted for only some hours and bordered on a kangaroo court. The prominent defence lawyers of the accused[128] were denied a presence. Duala Manga Bell and Ngoso Din were sentenced to death for high treason. Their public hanging the next day (8 August 1914) was a deliberate and calculated judicial murder, executed in cold blood despite all protest.[129] Occurring just a few days into World War I, their trial and execution was emblematic of the mindset and practices of colonialism. It "occurred against a background of petitions, public discussion, protests to the Reichstag, ministerial briefings and appeals to expert metropolitan and colonial opinion. ... It offered not so much an illustration of the limits of the German *Rechtsstaat* in colonial matters as a demonstration of the cruel functioning of those norms in favour of the colonising power."[130]

As the case of Mebenga m'Ebono, another exceptional figure in the fight against German colonial rule, shows,[131] resistance took very different forms. While in the service of a colonial officer, he came for schooling to Germany in 1891. Baptised as Martin Paul Zampa (or Samba) in the same year, he returned to Cameroon as a soldier in the colonial army. Decorated with several military medals, he ended his service in 1899 and became a wealthy merchant cultivating a European lifestyle. He is mentioned again in the colonial records of 1914, being accused of instigating a revolt and of secretly training young men to fight German rule. He was also executed on 8 August 1914.

The Germans were unable to reap the fruits of the seeds of terror they had sown. A joint British and French military invasion of the colony, launched both from the sea and from the interior, lasted—with the interruption of heavy rains—from September 1914 until January 1916 and brought to an end the German presence. Cameroon was shared and divided as prey between the British and French under League of Nations mandates, which sowed new seeds of chronic internal conflict and violence, infused by a colonial legacy of hostilities and divisions.[132]

Togo

As Dennis Laumann observes in his overview, literature on this German colony, "as compared with that of most of the other for-

THE GERMAN COLONIAL BRAND

mer European colonies on the African continent, is far from extensive".[133] This paucity of information is to some extent reflected in the following section.

During a short stopover on his way to Cameroon, Gustav Nachtigal signed an agreement on 5 July 1884 with a local headman from one of the Ewe communities. This served as the formal justification to proclaim a German protectorate over a small stretch along the West African coast between the British-occupied Gold Coast and the French-controlled territory of Benin. After negotiations over the territorial borders with Great Britain and France, the colony of Togo came on the map. It stretched from the coastal strip further inland. The more densely populated hinterland remained in large parts under the control of local communities, with only a few German outposts situated there. The region gained prominence as a result of the "Togo hinterland expedition" of 1894–1895. This served the dual purpose of underlining the German claim to the territory vis-à-vis British and French rivals by means of partly imposed treaties with local rulers, while at the same time collecting (when necessary, also through looting) local cultural artefacts.[134] The presence of a contingent of 25 soldiers showed just how much the expedition's motives were anything but purely scientific in nature or "civilian".

> The expedition finally reached the river Niger in February 1896. It had penetrated far into areas beyond formal German colonial rule and had attempted to tie rulers to the German Reich through alliance treaties. Even though it was emphasized in public that this would be a scientific expedition, the actions of those involved clearly demonstrate that this was primarily a matter of expanding and consolidating German colonial rule.[135]

After a base had been established in the region, further expeditions into northern Togoland between 1896 and 1901 met armed resistance from the local Konkomba communities, which made the area hardly "governable".[136] Rather, it became another hunting ground for colonial loot. Lieutenant Gaston Thierry, second-in-command since August 1896 of a colonial outpost at the town of Sansanné-Mango in the region, who was responsible for the physical elimination of the local Biema dynasty in 1897, became the most notorious of all the thieves.[137] On his return to Germany in August 1899, some 1,700 items appropriated mainly from the former ruling families formed part of his luggage and, as his private collection, were offered for sale. After some haggling, the items were acquired by the Berlin Ethnological Museum, the Linden Museum in Stuttgart and the Ethnological Museum in Leipzig. It is not only these goods that still await return to their places of origin: "More than sixty ancestral remains from northern Togo dug up by Thierry are indeed in the custody of the Foundation Prussian Cultural Heritage."[138]

Thierry's self-enrichment was too much even for the German colonial administration. A year later he was dismissed. Governor Köhler motivated this step in a letter addressed to the Colonial Department of the Foreign Office. As he stated, Thierry's "main activity consisted in leading the life of a *Landsknecht* [mercenary soldier], repeatedly absconding from the station for many months without reporting to the government, and undertaking one punitive expedition after another, always resulting in abundant spoils of war which provided the basis for his business".[139] So much for the "civilian" (not to mention "civilising") nature of the colonial enterprise.

As the smallest of the African territories, the German presence never included German soldiers as a permanent military component, and it relied on a very lean administration. Germans in the country numbered less than 400 at any given time. This kind of modest approach created "a romantic legend of the model colony".[140] The image was fed by the perception that Togo was the only colony which was not in its operations a loss-making liability for the German state. With its trade and a limited number of plantations (mainly for palm oil and kernels), it never became a major economic enterprise and therefore was a limited drain on the German exchequer. But a closer look at the seemingly rosy picture and at the colonial practices reveals that the belittling image of a *Musterkolonie* (model colony) was a fantasy of colonial apologetics.[141]

The claim that it was self-financing was a distortion overlooking the true state of affairs, as it received indirect subsidies through an *Afrikafonds* (African fund) and other allocations compensating for the discrepancy between income and expenditure.[142] By recruiting

THE GERMAN COLONIAL BRAND

an African mercenary force of 600 men instead of deploying any German soldiers as *Schutztruppe* for operations against the local population and limiting the number of police officers to ten for overseeing African recruits,[143] advocates of colonisation could argue that there was no German blood sacrificed and that lives were spared. This was trumpeted back home in Germany as a glorious story of peaceful occupation. Such mystification benefited from the fact that local resistance took place in fairly isolated and limited incidents, which did not translate into massive military clashes that might arouse public attention in Germany. But, overall, more than fifty officially recorded military campaigns took place, conducted with ruthless brutality.[144]

Direct occupation of Togo was limited and was often only marked by outposts that had symbolic rather than material value, as the northern parts of the territory were hardly accessible or ventured upon. Togo was the weak colonial state par excellence, often influenced by and responding to African dynamics in its operations. As in Cameroon and East Africa, the physical presence of colonial rule could be characterised as a series of islands in an African sea.[145] As the example of the capital Lomé shows, development—like the establishment of colonial rule—was the result of a complex series of interactions with agencies and interests within the local population, at times involving a pragmatic give and take.[146] In the early years the relatively marginal status of Togo, compared with the other German colonies in Africa, fostered among the rather small number of German officials in the local administration a unique identity and understanding of how best to handle the situation on the ground. This resulted in a certain aversion to orders from home, which were considered ignorant of local realities. This created differences with, if not opposition to, the perspectives of Berlin and bordered on occasional resistance to directives.[147] Such disagreements and competing views were also the order of the day elsewhere. Depending on the complexity of the issues, the dividing line fell not only between the colonial administration and Berlin,[148] but within German society as well, for colonial policy and practices became a matter of controversy in Germany too.

The African police force served a wide range of repressive purposes and complemented the military force. It was increased from an initial 35 members in 1889 to 250 in 1900 and peaked at 600 in 1913.[149] Policing included the recruitment and oversight of forced labour and capital punishment of villagers resisting subjugation. Just like Cameroon, Togo became known in West Africa and beyond for practices of physical mistreatment as the "land of the twenty-fiver" because of public floggings of naked "delinquents", consisting of 25 blows with the end of a piece of rope, which left deep wounds on the body. This corporal punishment was turned into a terrorist ritual, during which the colonial official would add another stroke, exclaiming "And one for the Kaiser". Despite massive criticism in Germany, the number of these official punishments increased from 162 as recorded in 1901–1902 to 832 in 1912–1913, with the actual number most likely being much higher.[150] This was tantamount to a "regime of corporal punishment".[151]

The positive image of a *Musterkolonie* was also bruised by scandals which became known and debated in Germany. These were a kind of normality in the colonies, often connected to acts of rape or other forms of excessive physical brutality.[152] For Togo it was the "Atakpame scandal" that stood out, like the tip of an iceberg.[153] A missionary disclosed that the German administrator in charge of the Atakpame district had sexually abused a minor. The affair became a matter of political debate in the German parliament. It finally ended in a classic case of colonial injustice when the perpetrator was found not guilty in the local Atakpame court despite overwhelming evidence of his misdeeds. This staged trial testified to the double standards of the so-called rule of law and was just one of the more prominent cases among numerous similar occurrences in all the colonies.[154]

As a typical example of colonial spaces of traumatic violence (*Gewalträume*),[155] the "Atakpame scandal" is also linked to the violence of utopian colonial ambitions to reconfigure and transform agrarian structures in Togo through the *Volkskulturprojekt* (folk culture project). This term was associated with the introduction of cotton cultivation, imposed on the local peasantry by means of forced labour, which involved the same German official who had been acquitted in the Atakpame case. It was based on assumptions which clearly indicated the ignorance of the colonisers regarding indigenous cultures. They misleadingly labelled local lifeways as "folk culture", thereby displaying a Eurocentric blindness towards the local communities' core values, norms and practices.[156]

There was a transnational dimension to this failed project, linking the history of German colonialism and the American Southern states through what was called the Tuskegee Expedition.[157] In collaboration with the German administration, the influential African American educator Booker T. Washington initiated an experiment to translate the experiences and practices of cotton farms in Alabama to plantations in Togo. This has been described as the export of "the racial political economy of the New South".[158] Staff of Washington's college at Tuskegee, Alabama, were responsible for establishing experimental cotton farms and agricultural schools in Togo between 1902 and 1908. Despite increasing the annual cotton exports from Togo almost sixtyfold over the years, the output remained rather meagre. Forced peasantisation through small-scale cotton production for a European market on individual plots failed to integrate (or rather coerce) young Togolese men into the colonial economy. The scheme came to an end in 1911, signalling the failure of colonial utopian visions of agricultural transformation.[159] It nevertheless illustrated that colonial economies were not only confined to direct links with the "motherland" but at times also sought comparative advantages globally: "the Tuskegee expedition appears as a quilting point, stitching together and thus permanently transforming three powerful networks: German social science, New South race politics, and African cash cropping. At their points of intersection, these three networks produced objects whose apparent stability both conceals and results from a dynamic and transnational history: blackness, peasants and cotton."[160]

The real lesson was that local producers based their decisions on their own interests and not on those of an imposed foreign regime, whether administratively, politically or in economic terms. Neither the plantation economy nor the *Volkskultur* was attractive enough for African peasants to participate voluntarily under colonial supervision. Rather, where production for external markets was successful, it was the result of independent local initiatives, such as the cultivation of cacao in parts of the hinterland where the German presence was thin.[161]

The beneficiaries of the local peasantry's market-related production (of palm oil and rubber) were not only the trading companies, but also some highly influential local traders operating mainly in the coastal towns. They became the core of the first forms of anticolonial resistance, by petitioning initially the local governor, then the German colonial secretary of state during an inspection visit in 1913, and finally the Reichstag in two parallel submissions in 1914. Togolese also voiced their frustrations by publishing petitions and letters in African newspapers in the neighbouring Gold Coast, which secured international attention. These documented the injustices and atrocities that had been committed and demanded an end to German colonial rule, thereby presenting a striking contrast to the cultivated image of a *Musterkolonie*.[162]

At the beginning of World War I, local communities showed no interest in keeping the Germans in their country, nor did the hired mercenaries in the army and police show any desire to defend the territory. Within weeks of being invaded by the British and French Allies from neighbouring colonies, the German administration capitulated in August 1914. But its special brand of ruling by violence through recruited Africans created a legacy which would shape the foundations of the later independent state and its hierarchies of power and control. Those recruited by the Germans for the African army and police force had been mainly Hausa and Kru mercenaries from the Gold Coast and Liberia. Local Africans joining these units (mainly from the northern hinterland) were never deployed in their home region or villages but operated in places where they were strangers. The rule of terror by these mercenary forces instilled a lasting popular rejection of the army and police as state agencies, way beyond the German colonial era. The rift between the coastal Ewe and the hinterland created deep-seated, lasting ethnic aversions between the local communities in these regions, and this remains a factor in domestic politics to this day.[163]

East Africa

The role played by Adolph Lüderitz in the proclamation of South West Africa, and by Adolph Woermann for that of Cameroon, was

THE GERMAN COLONIAL BRAND

filled by Carl Peters in the lead-up to German colonial rule in East Africa. Yet historical processes are more than just the work of individuals. As already shown, German policy under Chancellor Bismarck was initially reluctant to join the race for colonial territories. Part of Bismarck's change of mind was the growing influence of lobbying agencies and entrepreneurs hoping to generate individual fortunes. These circles included well-connected, influential trading houses with access to policymakers. Their agitation contributed to creating a public opinion that welcomed such expansion and paved the way for private acquisitions (obtained in dubious circumstances) to secure German protection and thereby subsume indigenous communities under foreign rule.

Carl Peters and his partners represented another motivation for colonialism. In contrast to Lüderitz, Woermann and other traders with African business interests (such as Vietor in Togo), Peters—who left behind an academic career[164]—was mainly motivated by an imperialist nationalism, combined with social Darwinism, to join the scramble for Africa. What lay behind his ambitions and campaigns was a nationalist ideology, not an economic agenda for private gain. Instead of promoting the approach that private endeavours would pave the way for hoisting the German flag, he was of the opinion that colonial wealth would follow the proclamation of colonial territories.[165] When he founded the Society for German Colonisation in March 1884, there were no firm interests in economic overseas enterprises connected to the move. Instead, the movement was "mainly supported by emigration enthusiasts and ardent nationalists".[166] Peters organised an expedition in November 1884 to Zanzibar and the coastal mainland, where some local leaders were persuaded to enter into obscure contracts. These provided the justification for demanding official German protection of the acquisitions he claimed to have made. Initially reluctant, Bismarck finally issued a *Schutzbrief* (Royal Patent of Patronage) on behalf of and in the name of Emperor Wilhelm II at the end of February 1885:

> Under the conditions that the aforesaid society remains a German society and that the directorate or other leaders of the organization, as well as their successors, remain citizens of the German Reich, we

grant authorization to it for the exercise of all rights stemming from the treaties, including legal justice for the natives and citizens of the Reich and other nations who may settle in the territories for business or other purposes, and we place it under the control of our government through this our Letter of Safe Conduct.[167]

This opened the way for what was now called the German East Africa Company (DOAG) to pursue further pseudo-legal territorial claims. As a follow-up to the Berlin Conference, the hinterland beyond the East African coast (controlled mainly by Arab traders and local communities under the suzerainty of the Sultan of Zanzibar) was divided into a British and a German zone of influence. The ultimate size of the area officially demarcated on the basis of treaties with Great Britain and Portugal in late 1886 amounted to almost a million square kilometres (including present-day Tanzania and parts of Rwanda and Burundi) and it became the largest German colony. But it mainly existed on paper, "on European maps, in the minds of German colonial enthusiasts and agitators", and "had to be made".[168]

Between 1884 and 1893, when his career ended abruptly, Carl Peters shuttled frequently between Germany and the new colony. He was the brutal conqueror par excellence, a megalomaniac convinced that ruthless violence was the only language the locals understood.[169] This violence was more an indication of weakness than strength and was similar to the violence unfolding in South West Africa that led to strategies of extermination. The "weak state" compensated for its limitations by pompous symbolism, displaying pseudo-power in "theatrics of rule". This was combined with warfare, based on superior weaponry, that was prepared to physically eliminate any resistance.[170] As has been observed: "Violent resistance and repression were endemic to the colonial subjugation project."[171] Further encroachment by the colonial power gradually turned East Africa into what has been characterised as a permanent state of war.[172] Priority was given to internal control, limited as it was, based on "bloody proofs of superiority".[173]

The invaders with their expansionist ambitions soon clashed with the local population and those who were in control of the region.[174] The *Schutzbrief* triggered further territorial expansion by

THE GERMAN COLONIAL BRAND

the DOAG. This was followed by the establishment of company stations (there were 18 of these by April 1888), staffed with inexperienced, young agents and resembling Potemkin villages in some respects. Plantations established for the cultivation of tropical products failed to make a profit, not least because they lacked direct access to the coastal centres. Based on a "lease agreement" of April 1888 with the Sultan of Zanzibar, the DOAG claimed ownership over the entire mainland coastline, which had been under the control of the local communities. The first forms of protest and resistance that were recorded took place in early 1887. Once it was realised that they had been subjected to a formal "takeover", open violence erupted in September 1888, and all stations except Bagamoyo and Dar es Salaam had to be abandoned. The resistance consisted of a combined Swahili and Arab response of the coastal and hinterland communities, led in the north by Al Bashir bin Salim (known as Abushiri or Bushiri) and in the south by Hassan bin Omari "Makunganya".

Under pressure, Chancellor Bismarck justified preparations for a large-scale military retaliation. The fictitious claim that it was a fight for the abolition of the slave trade secured the necessary domestic support for funding in the German parliament.[175] Rallying behind this pretext,[176] a joint German–British–Portuguese–Italian blockade of the East African coast was put in place in late November 1888: this revealed the shared agenda of the colonial powers to protect their common interests in maintaining control over their colonies. With the German state taking over the administration of the colony from the DOAG, Hermann Wissmann was appointed as commissioner (*Reichskommissar*) for East Africa. He arrived at the end of March 1889 in Zanzibar to oversee and conduct the war. Wissmann thought nothing of resorting to massacres on a routine basis, thereby indicating the omnipresence of violence in his campaigns for conquest, during which he displayed his abilities as a master in the staging of power.[177] His recruits (dubbed the "Wissmann Truppe") were foreign mercenaries mainly of Sudanese, Somali and Zulu background under the command of German officers. In contrast to the *Schutztruppe* in Cameroon and South West Africa, they engaged as Askaris[178]—similar to the units operating in Togo—in fighting and looting throughout the German period of occupation.[179] Wissmann showed no mercy and was quick in sentencing suspected leaders to death in military tribunals, often displaying thereafter their corpses publicly. The Consul General in Zanzibar called Wissmann's rule a military dictatorship.[180] While Wissmann posed as an abolitionist, he had no scruples in collaborating with slave owners and traders. If it happened at all, slavery was reduced as a result of the initiatives of those kept in slavery. German colonial authorities never abandoned the system. They were instead keen to maintain a close collaboration with the local slave-owning elites to secure their support for colonial rule.[181]

Despite all the evidence, Wissmann, like Gustav Nachtigal,[182] entered the colonial pantheon. Wissmann (1835–1905) was killed by his own gun in a hunting accident near his Austrian residence in Styria. In 1908 he was honoured with a statue in Bad Lauterberg in the Harz, where he regularly used to visit his mother and sister. Unlike his monument in Hamburg, the statue was still standing at the end of 2023.[183]

The militarily superior mercenary units soon gained the upper hand and increasingly isolated Abushiri. After his capture in December 1889, it was not enough to sentence him to death. Systematic humiliation was a method used to dehumanise those who dared to resist, before eliminating them. The delinquent "was dressed in full Arab costume complete with sword and dagger and photographed. Then he was stripped naked and again photographed with chains on his arms and legs, and a halter around his neck. Finally he was hanged."[184] In May 1890, Makunganya was also captured, sentenced by a military tribunal, and hanged. This brought an end to the resistance. Some objects looted then made their way into the collections of the Ethnological Museum in Berlin.[185]

After the situation was stabilised to some degree, Germany and Great Britain decided to share the regional colonial cake in line with their geostrategic interests by entering the Heligoland–Zanzibar Treaty of 1 July 1890.[186] The exchange ratified by the treaty added a narrow, lengthy corridor to the north-east of South West Africa, stretching between Northern Rhodesia and Bechuanaland to the vicinity of the Victoria Falls. The so-called Caprivi Strip (named after the German Chancellor of the time, Leo von Caprivi) formed part of the deal on the (incorrect) assumption that it would provide a land bridge that would ultimately connect South West Africa with East Africa. Instead, the geographical monstrosity has remained a territorial anomaly and would lead much later to local demands for secession of this strip from the independent Namibian state.[187]

Following the temporary "pacification", the Askari soldiers were, in a way similar to what happened in South West Africa and Cameroon, turned nominally into a *Schutztruppe*.[188] Under German command, they remained a peculiar conglomerate of African mercenaries recruited from other regions, often dispatched to conduct punitive expeditions with brute force to further extend and entrench colonial rule.[189] It did not take long for new large-scale resistance to erupt. The Wahehe kingdom in the south-western parts of central Tanganyika was at the time ruled by Mtwa Mkwavinyika, more commonly known as Mkwawa. He himself was not opposed to violence and raiding, and the expansion of his sphere of influence was not confined to local fights with neighbouring communities. It included the raiding of caravans on the route from Bagamoyo to the coast and, in this way, he challenged German interests and influence. His warriors clashed for the first time with the advancing colonial army in 1890. In the process of securing the area for German control, Mkwawa was considered a nuisance, and though diplomatic efforts were made that resulted in occasional accords, they did not bring the confrontation to an end.[190] A punitive expedition led by the *Schutztruppe* commander Emil von Zelewski ended in disaster when it was ambushed in August 1891. In what has been dubbed the "Battle of Rugaro", Zelewski was killed together with several other German officers and several hundred African soldiers and porters.[191]

The defeat was followed by a mixture of negotiations and military confrontations between the Wahehe under Mkwawa and the Germans under Governor Eduard von Liebert and the newly appointed military commander Lothar von Trotha. In October 1894 the *Schutztruppe* destroyed the fortress that served as Mkwawa's headquarters and forced the Wahehe to capitulate.

Mkwawa escaped and tried to organise further resistance by means of guerrilla warfare. But his support was waning. In line with the idea of a war of extermination advocated by Liebert, a scorched-earth policy was adopted which killed an estimated hundred thousand Wahehe.[192] In July 1898 a patrol cornered Mkwawa, who, instead of surrendering, killed himself.[193] A head believed to be his was brought to Germany as a trophy and symbol of victory. What is said to be Mkwawa's skull (though this is disputed) was finally returned in 1954.[194] A tooth of Mkwawa was returned in 2015 from the private possession of descendants of the soldier in charge of the patrol.[195] These violent interactions towards the end of the 19th century had wider consequences beyond the Iringa region, which lasted until the end of German colonial rule.[196]

Re-enter Carl Peters, who had been left with no role to play since 1889. In 1891 he was appointed as *Reichskommissar* for the Kilimanjaro region. His brutal conduct here, in which he displayed the character of a pathological megalomaniac, led to local resistance. But events that began unfolding from mid-1892 brought an end to his colonial career. Feeling cheated by his African concubine Jagodja, who had a love affair with his servant Mabruk, he personally sentenced Mabruk to death by hanging. Jagodja fled to a Wachaga village. When the local leader refused to hand her over to Peters, he ordered the destruction of the village. Jagodja was sentenced to death for conspiracy and executed three months after Mabruk. While this abuse of power was initially covered up, Peters was eventually recalled in 1893 and sent on leave. In 1896, after he moved to London, his actions turned into a public scandal in Germany, when the Social Democratic leader August Bebel revealed to the Reichstag Peters's promiscuity with local women and his punishment of "infidelity". Nicknamed "Hanging Peters" (*Hänge* Peters), he was officially dismissed from the public service for breach of duty in 1897. In 1905 Emperor Wilhelm II rehabilitated Peters by awarding him the title *Reichskommissar* without any accompanying duties. He also granted him a pension in 1914 in recognition of his abilities.[197]

Clashes with the Chaga had already started in February 1891,[198] triggered by German efforts to gain control over the southern

Kilimanjaro region. Trying to take advantage of internal tensions between different communities seeking hegemony in the region, the *Schutztruppe* attacked Mangi Sina of the Chaga at Kibosho. This marked the beginning of the end of Chaga dominance in the region and led to continued fighting between various local communities and the colonial army. Moshi under Manga Meli was conquered in August 1893. On 2 March 1900, Meli and 18 other leaders, accused of conspiracy, were hanged. Although it is suspected that the heads of some of those executed were also brought to Germany, they have not been found and the search for them continues.[199]

The state of emergency that prevailed in the colony, with its simmering tensions and hostile antagonisms, finally escalated into the Maji Maji war.[200] Between 1905 and 1907 over twenty communities of different backgrounds, languages and cultures formed an alliance to rise up against the Germans in the southern parts of the territory.[201] Their eventual defeat came at enormous human cost. The estimated numbers of those killed differ but are thought to amount to several hundred thousand as the result of a systematic scorched-earth strategy. Depending on the definition applied, this was another extermination strategy tantamount to genocide.[202] By mid-1906 most of the resistance was broken, though fighting continued locally. In July 1907 the war was officially ended. Along with the warfare against the Ovaherero and Nama in South West Africa, the Maji Maji war features prominently in the literature on German colonial wars as an example of a deliberate war of extermination. While there exists no "explicit order to prove genocidal intent, ... that intent can be inferred from the perpetrators' actions".[203]

There were numerous ambiguities and contradictions in both the forms of resistance in the colonies and in the nature and operations of the colonial state. This was especially apparent in East Africa, where, as elsewhere, control over territory was a driving motive.[204] But the degree of interplay with local elites in the process of economic penetration was at times decisive in either securing collaboration or causing the outbreak of organised resistance: "distinct strategies of extraction produced distinct outcomes in terms of violent antistate rebellion in the early phases of state building".²⁰⁵ In addition, the working conditions imposed on Africans often resulted in a refusal to submit to the colonial order of labour.²⁰⁶

Economic extraction was mainly confined to cash crops (rubber, sisal, cotton and coffee), cultivated in plantations or by smallholders, if necessary by forced labour. The colonial economy became more important only towards the end of the German period.²⁰⁷ It included the effort to promote African small-scale agriculture as *Volkskulturen* (folk cultures) alongside the European plantation economy. Exports almost tripled from 1907 to 1913, and the German East Africa Company remained the dominant economic player both in trade and in its involvement in the plantation economy. But the scar of the wars, which resulted in a long-lasting decimation of the potential labour force, imposed a constant limitation, similar to the aftermath of the genocidal war in South West Africa. Taxing the locals was the main instrument used to generate an income for the colonial state, by forcing people to engage in market-related production so as to earn the money required for taxation. The taxes also forced people to work on the plantations or in the construction of railway lines, which served the export of raw materials as transport routes. The investments in colonial infrastructure (roads and railways) are often used by colonial revisionists as a positive example of the benefits that colonisation created for the colonised. But this myth has been exposed by Andreas Greiner in respect of the building of roads in East Africa:

> Vernacular structures and patterns of mobility proved resilient against German rule while the agency of those Africans subjected to colonial space simultaneously subverted its transformation. ... Colonial infrastructure development (and, through it, spatial appropriation) in the German colony was not a streamlined process, but a contested field in which infrastructure schemes planned from office desks were constrained by and collided with established structures and practices on the ground.²⁰⁸

More than most other German colonies (with the exception of settler-colonial South West Africa), East Africa was a place where experiments with "modernisation" took place in the course of eco-

THE GERMAN COLONIAL BRAND

nomic development and in the role played by science.[209] The introduction of wildlife conservation left a lasting legacy of imperial intervention in the environment and on human–animal relations. It was influential in shaping a colonial-oriented view of natural habitat management that has obtained until today, informing current hunting and conservation practices.[210] The territory's people also served as an important laboratory for tropical medicine,[211] in particular for Robert Koch's trypanosomiasis (sleeping sickness) research, which was subsequently continued with increasing experiments on people in Togo.[212] What has often been praised as evidence of the achievements of the "civilising mission" and used to highlight the blessings and benefits of colonialism came at an unethically high cost to human life among the subjects of the research and has triggered the current debate about the renaming of the Robert Koch Institute.[213]

Related to this is the debate in present-day Germany about renaming (or correcting, if not removing) the public memorials that still exist of General Paul von Lettow-Vorbeck, who before his deployment to East Africa had been involved in wars in Qingdao and South West Africa.[214] At the end of German colonial rule in East Africa he once again personified the brutal violence meted out to the local population. While the colonial administration and army in all other colonies capitulated rather quickly when World War I broke out,[215] Lettow-Vorbeck embarked with his *Schutztruppe* on a drawn-out guerrilla campaign, roaming over the territory. His use of Africa as a mere battleground (or rather landscape for his escapades to avoid capitulation) cost the lives of several hundred thousand people. Because of his stubborn determination to escape the British-led Allied forces, World War I ended for East Africa not on the official date of 11 November 1918 but a week later, when Lettow-Vorbeck finally capitulated.[216] Dubbed "the Lion of Africa", he received upon his return to Berlin in March 1919 an enthusiastic hero's welcome with a public parade at the Brandenburg Gate.[217]

The iconography linked to Lettow-Vorbeck also promoted the myth of the loyal Askaris, praised for their selfless services rendered to Emperor and Fatherland. This was entirely invented and constructed, to counter accusations that Germany was an unpopular colonial master. In reality, most of the Askaris were mere soldiers of fortune. When they realised that they had ended up on the "wrong side", they deserted in their thousands. Interestingly, but not surprisingly, while some of the novels of the 2021 Nobel laureate in literature, Abdulrazak Gurnah, make much reference to the not so romantic lives of the Askaris and the *Schutztruppe* in German East Africa before and after the outbreak of World War I,[218] by far the most widely read works of fiction on the subject in German have been in much lighter vein.[219] They mostly consist of an entertaining collection of incidents between the German and British opponents. In contrast, some of Gurnah's novels—which until late 2021 were largely unknown in Germany—present the perspectives of the Askaris and their interaction with the Germans.[220]

As a result of the Treaty of Versailles, German East Africa was divided: the British were given charge of the administration of Tanganyika (which after independence in 1961 merged with Zanzibar to form Tanzania), while Belgium received Rwanda and Burundi. As in all other cases, the local population was not consulted. Colonised people were treated—just like all other natural resources—as an imperial commodity in the possession of others.

South Sea/Pacific Islands

Given the plethora of islands in the South Seas and the Pacific, which during the last 15 years of the 19th century, were added bit by bit to the collection of German colonial property, it is impossible within the confines of this general overview to record their indigenous people's interaction with German foreign rule (where visible and experienced) in sufficient depth. What follows is therefore limited to some select aspects presented in the literature available. The patchwork nature of the discussion testifies to the fact that these colonial escapades were geographically remote and diverse, while at the same time being a prominent screen for projecting male sexual desires linked to the myth of the "noble savage".[221]

Colonial rule in the western Pacific was preceded by a long history of interactions.[222] These were largely connected to trading bases initially established by the Hamburg-based company of

THE GERMAN COLONIAL BRAND

J.C. Godeffroy & Sohn, which was succeeded after its bankruptcy in 1879 by the German Trading and Plantation Society of Hamburg for the South Sea Islands (DHPG). It campaigned for the colonial annexation of Samoa to secure its interests (such as copra plantations) there. Beginning in 1884, a chequered series of islands (or even only parts of them) were formally turned into protectorates. Unbeknown to them, people in north-eastern New Guinea (Kaiser Wilhelmsland) and the Bismarck Archipelago were brought by proclamation under German "protection". In 1885 the same happened with the Marshall Islands and the northern Solomon Islands. While Samoa had been a centre of German activity since the mid-19th century, parts of it only joined the German constellation in 1899, when the Treaty of Berlin divided the islands between Germany (western islands), the United States, and Britain (which secured rights over Tonga). After being defeated in the Spanish–American War, Spain sold its remaining possessions, known as the "Spanish East Indies" (the islands of the Carolines, Palau and the Marianas), to Germany in 1899.[223] There was great diversity among the individual islands, whose indigenous peoples had different histories, languages and cultures. The label "Micronesia", for example, suggests a homogeneous conglomerate, which did not actually exist. The division into island groups such as the Marianas, the Carolines and others was a purely European construct, which wrongly suggests the presence of collective identities.[224]

The widely cultivated "crush" or love affair with the South Seas[225] helped colonial propagandists in the empire to rally support. But from as early as 1872, before the official German appropriation, Germany had a free hand in conducting a total of 196 recorded punitive expeditions against indigenous communities there.[226] Instead of opening the gates to paradise, the initial stages of the German administrative presence were a fiasco. From 1885 to 1889 New Guinea descended into chaos under the governance of the recently established New Guinea Company. The total ignorance of local conditions shown by company staff resulted in political and economic inefficiency, erratic behaviour, an absence of any meaningful administration, and a racist colonial legal system. Discredited by its failures, the company transferred the administration of the territory in April 1889 to the German state.[227]

Constraints remained: the islands were immensely far from Germany (it took between 42 and 49 days to travel by sea from Hamburg to the local capital of Rabaul), and there were problems to do with local transport and communication logistics as well as climate-related health problems. German farmers and plantations battled with labour shortages and the administrations exercised patchy control. Overall, Pacific Islanders seemed to be luckier than many other colonised subjects elsewhere: "The home government's failure to provide sufficient support for rapid commercial growth, and the unwillingness of *Grosskapital* interests in Germany to invest where returns were still small and uncertain, saved the Pacific colonies from large-scale economic penetration and helped to preserve local social structures."[228]

While German Samoa, acquired as a result of the Tripartite Agreement of 1899 with Britain and the United States, was the latecomer in the history of German acquisitions, it soon competed with Togo for the title of "*Musterkolonie*", despite its inauspicious beginnings: "By the 1880s, Germany was the power least trusted by the Samoans, as German merchants were ruthless in seeking conditions favourable to the development of their lands and business."[229] Despite these onslaughts, the local elites were "still very much in control of social and political activities, and they were extremely jealous of their prerogatives".[230] This fed into the "noble savage" myth and created a favourable ground for interaction. It appealed to a sense of White superiority, as involving "a duty towards the Samoans", and to a fundamentally benevolent paternalism,[231] most likely encouraged by the lack of power and authority on the part of the local authorities.

With too many conflicts in the other colonies already on their hands, the lack of any meaningful size and the absence of any reason to make use of physical force, especially as there were no soldiers stationed on the islands, the German state never showed any interest in strengthening the power of the local administration beyond facilitating interaction with the local people as much as possible. This "lean system" also provided opportunities for the colonised: dubbed "coconut colonialism",[232] it created space for local responses and strategies of adaptation. These were able to find ways of secur-

THE GERMAN COLONIAL BRAND

ing advantages for themselves by (re)defining their role locally as well as in their relations with the foreign power and the wider outside world. As Peter Hempenstall suggests:

> German rule in the Pacific was a process of constant compromise between relatively weak and highly personalised administrations on the one hand and the leaders of Island communities on the other. Whether in New Guinea, Ponape or Samoa, the Germans never gained absolute control over the politics of their Island populations. ... Pacific Islanders, through their leaders and institutions, often took the initiative in colonial politics, while the Europeans struggled to make responses which accorded with their colonial objectives and their own image of themselves.[233]

Such "colonialism lite" did not eliminate all physical encounters and conflicts. The biggest clash took place in 1910–1911 when the Sokeh on Ponape (nowadays Pohnpei) of the Caroline Islands group of Micronesia took up arms and thereby disrupted the imaginary South Sea idyll.[234] It was the imposition of a head tax—payable if not in cash, then by an equivalent in labour—that caused their resistance. After a worker was physically mistreated during road construction, his fellows laid down their tools. When a German official appeared the next day for negotiations, he and three other officials and Melanesian policemen in his company were killed. Several ships of the South Sea naval squadron manned by 700 marines and auxiliary troops were dispatched to fight some 270 Sokehs, who resorted to guerrilla warfare. Only by means of a scorched-earth strategy, which cut the locals off from supplies, were the German troops finally able to break the resistance. Fifteen of the leaders were executed. The Sokeh were deported to the far-away island of Yap to undergo forced labour in a phosphate mine. Under Japanese colonial rule, the survivors were able to return in 1917 to Ponape, where, in 1942, only 242 Sokeh were counted.

The German Pacific empire ended with World War I in 1914, when the administrations capitulated in August to New Zealand troops in Samoa, and to Australian troops in New Guinea and Nauru in September, while Japanese troops occupied the Marshalls, Carolines and remaining islands north of the equator in October.[235]

In fairness, we need to acknowledge that, in contrast to other colonies and colonisers, Germans continued to enjoy a good reputation in the memory of Pacific Islanders. In particular the administration of Samoa under Governor Wilhelm Solf was recognised as having made efforts to win the respect and recognition of local communities. While his governance style did not exclude patronising undertones, it was certainly preferable to that of others in similar positions elsewhere. He has even been considered a hero, "set apart from the normal run of European adventurers",[236] and has been praised for "his ideas and policies", which "represent an achievement in the realm of colonial history".[237] In his engagement with locals he went as far as to comply with requests by villages to support local brass bands.[238] In 1923, while acting as the German ambassador to Japan, Solf received a telegram from Samoan leaders, asking him to return as their Governor.[239]

However, while this may well document a local elitist perspective and is eagerly used as evidence of colonial benevolence, it should be taken with a pinch of salt. Those who collaborated with the colonial administration of "culturally adept governors"[240] should not be considered the sole representatives of the colonised. As the counter-narrative aptly summarised by Matthew Fitzpatrick suggests, Samoa (like most other islands in the region under German rule) "remained a colonial site in which dissent was expressed in both word and deed".[241] That wholesale bloodshed was avoided, in contrast to the massacres bordering on genocide in other German colonies, "seems an artificially low benchmark for a comparative assessment that positions Samoa as an exemplar of benign imperial rule".[242] What took shape as a "culturally eclectic" colonial administration, recognising and accommodating local features, was "a pragmatic response to the precarious security position of a colony in which Germans were outnumbered roughly 100–1 by those they ruled".[243] That Samoans were disempowered by predominantly peaceful methods without military destruction "should not be seen as simply a form of benign colonial rule informed by the cultural acumen of its governors",[244] but rather as giving preference to domination by other means—not least because of the actual power relations that existed.

THE GERMAN COLONIAL BRAND

Qingdao/Tsingtao or Jiaozhou (Kiautschou) Bay[245]

Strictly speaking, the lease territory (*Pachtgebiet*) of the Bay of Kiautschou was not—as the name indicates—a colonial property, though in contemporary perceptions there was no major difference from other territories claimed by Germany. Legally, it had the same status as Hong Kong, which from 1842, under the British Crown, was the blueprint for subsequent ambitions and treaties of other Western powers to secure a formalised presence in China. With the proclamation of German protectorates in the South Sea, a geostrategic interest in China and the desire to obtain a stopover along the East Chinese coast of the Yellow Sea became ever more pronounced after 1885. German gunboats had been roaming East Asian waters since 1869–1870.

To realise its territorial cravings, the German empire ruthlessly exploited a "window of opportunity" to force China into a 99-year lease agreement for the small enclave on the Bay of Kiautschou, including special economic privileges in the hinterland of Shandong Province. Since China's defeat in the war with Japan of 1894–1895, its regional hegemony had been damaged. Western imperialism was eagerly seeking to secure more entry points. Germany pursued similar ambitions as its influence had till then been limited to a less formal presence by way of local economic (in the main, trading) activities. In 1896 Admiral Alfred von Tirpitz, in charge of the East Asia Squadron, while searching for a naval base under German control, identified the Bay of Kiautschou as a suitable port and started to plan its occupation.[246] A window of opportunity opened shortly afterwards when in November 1897 two missionaries of the Steyeler Shandong Mission, operating since 1882 in the area, were killed.[247] This was the pretext for direct intervention by the navy. Foreign Minister Bernhard von Bülow used the incident in parliament in December 1897 to justify Germany's claim for a "place in the sun" as legitimate. According to the official record, he stated:

> The massacre of our missionaries was the obvious, compelling reason for our intervention, since we did not believe that these devout people, who were pursuing their sacred offices in peace, could be regarded as outside the law. ...

THE LONG SHADOW OF GERMAN COLONIALISM

> We must demand that German missionaries, merchants, goods, as well as the German flag and German vessels be treated with the same respect in China that other powers enjoy. (Loud applause)
>
> We are happy to respect the interests of other powers in China, secure in the knowledge that our own interests will also receive the recognition they deserve. ("Bravo!")
>
> In short, we do not want to put anyone in our shadow, but we also demand our place in the sun. ("Bravo!")[248]

On 6 March 1898 China signed an agreement, leasing the Bay of Jiaozhou for 99 years to the German empire. Hereby China surrendered her sovereign rights within a radius of 50 kilometres around the bay, granted Germany mining concessions and the right to construct railways in Shandong Province, and awarded preferential treatment to all German businesses.[249] In contrast to the other colonies, the lease was placed, on account of its military-strategic importance, not under the Colonial Office but the Imperial Navy Office. Since June 1897 Tirpitz had been its state secretary, with ambitions to enlarge the fleet so as to enable the navy to play a proactive role in further colonial expansion.[250]

With Qingdao as its centre, Shandong was turned into a "proto-colonial" territory.[251] Its resource-poor north-western parts became the breeding ground for anti-colonial riots among a peasantry with a distinctive martial culture. Originally known as Yihequan (the Righteous and Harmonious Fists), they soon were branded the Boxers. They gave rise to a blend of self-organised protest of an anti-imperialist kind with superstitious and secretive features, which sought to defend their indigenous rights against foreigners, missionaries and local Christian converts.[252] This turned into the Boxer War, involving the mobilisation of several hundred thousand peasants. Starting in late 1899, they burned, killed and looted in a war against the allied powers in response to what they perceived as an invasion threatening fundamental change to their lifeways.[253] The Boxer War demonstrated that there did not have to be direct colonisation for colonialism and anti-colonial resistance to come about. When the Boxers besieged the diplomatic quarter in Beijing in mid-1900, the conflict escalated into the biggest operation of all

THE GERMAN COLONIAL BRAND

colonial wars by a united military intervention of eight countries (Austria-Hungary, France, Germany, Great Britain, Italy, Japan, Russia and the United States). This "punitive expedition" marked the first official German colonial war beyond the military suppression of local resistance elsewhere and signalled Germany's ambition to play a leading role among the imperial powers.[254] It was conducted with uninhibited brutality, which found its expression in the infamous *Hunnenrede* (Hun speech) by Emperor Wilhelm II when addressing soldiers about to leave for China on 27 July 1900 at Bremerhaven:

> Should you encounter the enemy, he will be defeated! No quarter will be given! Prisoners will not be taken! Whoever falls into your hands is forfeited. Just as a thousand years ago the Huns under their King Attila made a name for themselves, one that even today makes them seem mighty in history and legend, may the name German be affirmed by you in such a way in China that no Chinese will ever again dare to look cross-eyed at a German.[255]

Such an annihilation strategy was already by then a violation of international law, codified and also signed by the German empire. Article 23 of the regulations of the 1899 Hague Convention—"a statement of international customary law"[256]—expressly prohibited the following actions:

(b) To kill or wound treacherously individuals belonging to the hostile nation or army;
(c) To kill or wound an enemy who, having laid down arms, or having no longer means of defence, has surrendered at discretion;
(d) To declare that no quarter will be given.[257]

In violation of these principles, the German intervention helped mould a specific brand of military commander for subsequent extermination warfare in the African colonies, for it saw the first missions of Lothar von Trotha and Paul von Lettow-Vorbeck. German conduct in the Boxer War can be seen as an immediate precursor of the extermination strategies subsequently applied in East and South West Africa. By the time of the arrival of German troops in China, the Boxers had already been defeated. While the other countries' contingents were reduced or even withdrawn, the Germans entered on a killing spree.[258]

In contrast, further developments in Qingdao were fairly peaceful and turned into a form of give and take with the Chinese residents, who were able to strongly influence the agenda for their own benefit, thereby limiting colonial dominance.[259] The German claim of a *"Musterkolonie"* was, on a closer look, based on considerable Chinese contributions and an adjustment by the Germans to Chinese initiatives and undertakings. But daily life remained much characterised by a racist divide. Until 1914, Chinese residents in Qingdao were not allowed to live in the "European" parts of town.[260] At the same time, the way the German establishment embedded itself in its Chinese surroundings, and the Chinese ownership of local assets, helped create intercultural interactions and exchanges, with Chinese agencies as active counterparts of German actors and interests, in contrast to the colonial hierarchies and asymmetric power relations elsewhere.[261]

Given the relatively pleasant surroundings, Germans felt at home here: "many acknowledged Qingdao as a new or second Heimat and within the context of colonialism it was seen as a 'deutsche Heimat' that was in tight interconnection with the first".[262] Here, too, innovations were considered a "laboratory of modernity".[263] Although Qingdao was from a Chinese perspective certainly no *"Musterkolonie"*, at least it was a place where one could live.[264] But, as was so often the case, this also depended on one's social status.

At the beginning of World War I, the German South Sea squadron happened to be on an inspection tour of some of the Pacific islands. When war broke out, the only cruiser left behind quickly vacated the harbour of Qingdao to escape the British fleet. Despite this less than heroic end, the Chinese enclave soon turned into a lasting object of mystification back home in Germany.[265] Among such reminders are the names of the German naval vessel *Iltis*, its commander Lans and the fort Taku, which was attacked during the Boxer War in 1900. These three became prominent street names in German cities such as Cologne and Berlin.

THE GERMAN COLONIAL BRAND

Some Colonial Leftovers

While the colonial lobby in the German empire argued that colonies would create wealth and provide opportunities for emigration, on balance this remained wishful thinking. Few companies and individuals made a fortune from colonial enterprises, while emigration continued to other destinations. The colonies were a loss-making enterprise for the German state since the costly wars fought there far exceeded the revenue from resource extraction. Another kind of reckoning shows that while many tend to downplay the thirty years of overseas empire as a negligible historical episode bordering on the harmless, it had devastating results for those at the receiving end. As figures suggest, during the whole period the number of Germans in the colonies at any given time remained—even at the peak periods when soldiers were deployed—less than 50,000. But far more than a million locals paid with their lives in the direct warfare conducted in the territories, while even more lives were damaged or destroyed as a result.

In recent years, the historical and cultural legacies of German colonial rule have become a matter of growing interest.[266] As could be expected, these play out in rather different ways and forms. While the colonial period is still often dismissed or downplayed in Germany as an insignificant footnote of imperial history, it has left a much more direct and lasting imprint in the consciousness and awareness of the colonised, as literary works engaging with the period have documented since then as well.[267] It also had a lasting political impact on the way local communities position themselves:

> the afterlives of the shortest-lived colonial empire in Africa reveal the protracted nature of decolonization on the continent. ... Invoking German rule became a language through which Namibians and Tanzanians negotiated with subsequent rulers, explored the meaning of the colonial encounter, and formulated claims for recompense. It thus highlights that remembering colonialism became integral to the assertion of African sovereignty and the emergence of modern restorative justice politics.[268]

In some parts of the former overseas empire, the limited period of German colonial rule served as a comparative advantage. As has been noted for Papua New Guinea: "Germany seems to have won the colonial popularity contest by losing its colony long before decolonialization could ever be even conceived of."[269] Pro-German sympathies also existed in Samoa at the time of the 1916 takeover by New Zealand.[270] Some justification for the positive reference to German colonial rule in the Pacific islands lies in the far greater neglect and devastating effect of the takeover by the successor colonial powers, New Zealand and Australia. Given the traumatic changes and cost of lives that the neglect of these two countries wrought, local inhabitants have been left with more positive traces of German rule in their cultural memory, and they still feel more closely related to the German South Seas today.[271] Similar perceptions and sentiments have also been recorded for the West African and East African territories, where fairly muted memories and legacies could be interpreted more as a criticism of the successor French and British colonial rulers than as a nostalgic desire for continued German rule.[272] This nostalgic desire also existed on the German side in the fields of arts and culture, where the South Seas occupied a special place in the idea of the "noble savage" as a place of remembrance and desire.[273] Indigenous art labelled as *art primitif* had a great following among the cultured avant-garde of the Weimar Republic. Their use of this art as an inspiration for their own creative work was another form of appropriation.

Not surprisingly, South West Africa has been an exception to such romanticising, apart from the heroic narratives about pioneering German settlers in the colonial literature (more on this later). The South African successors were not much welcomed by either the German settlers or the colonised. But with the détente soon established between the remaining Germans and the arriving South African Whites and the further expansion of settler-colonial rule, the colonial subjects were firmly handed over from one apartheid system to another. The special role of Namibian Germans as a distinct group not only with a history but also of present relevance remains a contentious issue.[274] The German language has not only survived as a means of communication in Namibia,[275] but it has continued with a life of its own after the period of German rule elsewhere too, when the German language was used as a tool of cultural policy.²⁷⁶ Testifying in its own way to colonial amnesia, "research into linguistic aspects of German colonialism and especially into colonial varieties of German is still fairly underrepresented in both Germanic linguistics as well as in pidgin and creole studies".²⁷⁷ Though largely overlooked, "*Unserdeutsch*" was a German legacy in Papua New Guinea.²⁷⁸ German colonialism even brought about a "Germanophone" elite in Douala after 1914²⁷⁹ and aroused sympathies in Cameroon and Togo for Hitlerian Germany.²⁸⁰ The German language has in both countries remained a well-established subject at universities.²⁸¹ Togolese descendants of German fathers claimed their specific identity through fluency in German and the cultivation of features and attributes considered as German values and culture. In 1934 a Club of German Mixed-Bloods (Club der deutschen Mischlinge) was formed as a private association with 153 members. By the mid-1980s their numbers had declined to a mere 15.²⁸²

Instead of digging deeper into the structural and socio-cultural legacies, which would go beyond the limited scope of this volume (with its focus mainly on the German colonial side), a few lighter aspects are presented here to illustrate the long-term effects of the comparatively short-term colonial rule, at least in some of the societies exposed to the dubious blessings of *Herrenmenschen* ("master race") culture. In China, German lager beer is the most popular brand and Tsingtao Beer is by far the most prominent label (it is in demand also internationally).²⁸³ There is a museum and an annual beer festival in its name. In Namibia, Namibian Breweries (until the takeover by Heineken in 2023, owned and managed to a large extent by local German-speaking Whites) proudly cultivates a history loyal to the German (Bavarian) *Reinheitsgebot* (Purity Law) dating back to 1516.²⁸⁴ Apart from this quality assurance, the history of German beer in the country is seemingly protected by ideological purification and gatekeeping.²⁸⁵ Needless to say, there is an annual Oktoberfest. At this increasingly popular local attraction, traditional Bavarian costumes are worn by all varieties of Namibians (though predominantly still by White German-speakers), who enjoy the drinking spree to the accompaniment of an imported *Wiesn* band.²⁸⁶ The post-Covid Oktoberfest in 2022 was officially opened by the Windhoek mayor with entertainment provided by the German groups Die Kirchdorfer and Schuhplattler, and with beer brewed exclusively for the occasion.[287] Togolese have developed their own version of the Oktoberfest with an annual beer festival.[288] The legacy of strong alcohol imported from Germany is also visible in Cameroon.[289] No such alcohol-related traces can be discovered in today's Tanzania, where at least an Askari monument remains prominently placed in central Dar es Salaam.[290] However, this monument was only unveiled in 1927 to give recognition to the Askaris who fought on the British side against the Germans and hence should not be mistaken as a nostalgic memorial of German colonial rule. It is a reminder that the term Askari can be associated with different colonial contexts. On the other hand, monuments and buildings as well as other remnants in the public mnemoscape and memory landscape remain an integral—though declining—part of Namibian daily life and a continued attraction for parts of the German-Namibian tourism industry.[291] While such public monuments are rare in other former German colonies, those interested (and willing to pay a minimum of 3,000 euros) can spend 16 days in Cameroon, Ghana and Togo discovering the traces of the German colonial past.[292]

A particularly obscure remnant of Germany's colonial past in Togo was the regular visits of the President of the Bavarian Federal State and Cabinet Minister, Franz Josef Strauss (1915–1988), and his friendship with the dictatorial President Gnassingbé Eyadéma (1935–2005)—both were passionate hunters and co-presidents of the Bavarian–Togolese Society.[293] When visiting in May 1983, Strauss was welcomed in Lomé like a head of state.[294] One of the favourite slogans of Strauss, for decades leader of the CSU, was (with regard to his predilection for Togo and to the colour associated with the Union parties in Germany) "We blacks have to stand together". He is not on record as having used this slogan in his frequent visits to South West Africa, where he once declared, "Ich bin ein Südwester."[295]

The Strauss escapades inspired a Togolese–German theatre production (*Wir Schwarzen müssen zusammen halten*), supported by the Goethe Institute and video-streamed for the first time in March

2021 when it was performed at the Munich Studio Theatre.[296] It was one of three projects initiated by the Goethe Institute to develop transnational understanding with the people of the six African countries (Namibia, Burundi, Rwanda, Tanzania, Cameroon and Togo) once under German colonial rule.[297] Other efforts to address some of the injustices of colonialism and their consequences include the restitution of looted cultural artefacts and the return of human remains,[298] and demands for the full rehabilitation of Manga Bell and Ngoso Din. These and other matters will be discussed in the following chapter.

Colonial Discourses at Home

The German nation-state in the making was accompanied by the notion of *Pangermanismus* (Pan-Germanism). It aggressively channelled and projected existential fears during Germany's transformation towards an industrialised society not only into growing antisemitism but also into dreams of a greater German empire, promising a solution to the economic crisis through colonial expansion. The myth of the colonial promise became the mantra for an ideology of integration, which cultivated the belief that stability could be attained by channelling class conflicts outwards through an expanding empire.[299] The desire to become a colonial power was an effective vehicle for achieving a collectively shared domestic aspiration, transcending in part class boundaries and identities in the hope of securing a better life for all. It was a useful instrument in helping construct a nationalist cultural identity. The initiatives towards colonising remaining territory in Africa could initially count on the Social Democrats in parliament: when there was a debate in 1885 on a 50 per cent increase of the *Afrikafonds* budget of the African Society, they voted in support of this motion, which was tabled by Bismarck. As they argued, this scientific society would be able to determine whether tropical Africa was suitable for settler colonialism.[300]

The controversies over the colonial wars that soon erupted also helped to integrate the organised labour movement into Wilhelmine imperialism. From the turn of the century Social

THE LONG SHADOW OF GERMAN COLONIALISM

Democratic members of parliament increasingly criticised Prussian militarism and brought into the open colonial scandals involving atrocities committed in putting down anti-colonial resistance. But criticism remained for most of the time implicit. It focused on the practices and methods of colonial rule, and only on rare occasions questioned colonialism as such.[301]

August Bebel (1840–1913) was not only a prominent but also an exceptionally principled voice in expressing disagreement with colonial policy. An early example was his lengthy intervention of January 1889, when the official takeover of administration in East Africa by the German state was discussed in parliament, using the pretext of the abolition of slavery as a motive. His speech provides evidence that the spirit of the times was not as all-pervasive and predominant as some apologists for colonialism would maintain.

> What is this East African Company? It is a small circle of big capitalists, bankers, merchants, and industrialists, i.e., a small circle of very rich people whose interests have nothing at all to do with the interests of the German people; who as far as this whole colonial policy is concerned have nothing but their own personal interests in mind. ... Basically, the essence of all colonial policy is the exploitation of a foreign population to the highest degree. Whenever we look at the history of colonial policy over the last three centuries, we encounter violent acts and the oppression of native peoples, and not infrequently this ends in their complete extermination. ... In order to go on exploiting the African population to the fullest possible extent, preferably undisturbed, millions are to be spent from the pockets of the Reich, from the pockets of the taxpayers; the East Africa Company is to be supported with funds from the Reich in order to secure its business of exploitation. ... We, as opponents of any form of oppression, will not lend any support to this.
>
> ... If a European or German colonial society were to cultivate the East African territories placed under the German protectorate, no advantage whatsoever would arise for the inhabitants of the respective countries. ...
>
> It is maintained that the goals are to spread European civilization, European culture, to spread Christianity, and above all to end the

horrible slave trade and the slave hunts. But, Gentlemen, you do not wish to abolish the central cause of the slave trade and the slave hunts in the first place—slavery in and of itself. So far, not one of you has even thought of emphasizing or even hinting at that. ...

Gentlemen, to involve us in this type of adventure, without the faintest prospect of it being advantageous to the overwhelming majority of the population—whereas, on the contrary, all the benefits from such an undertaking will go to a small minority of the rich, who if they wish to increase their wealth may do so at their own cost—that is something we cannot get enthusiastic about. ...

... We declare that we will vote against this bill, regardless of whether this stance is described as some kind of treason or high treason. I also declare that I do not have enough confidence in the current leadership of German Reich policy to believe that it will, insofar as it has its officials in Africa, make any particular efforts to conduct the colonization of the territory in a truly humane and so-called Christian manner.[302]

Germany's Social Democrats at the time were not all as clear and uncompromising as August Bebel (who himself was not without flaws) but were fairly divided over colonialism. They included a revisionist camp supporting what was called "social imperialism". Party members even advocated an imperialist policy, justifying colonial expansion as an economic necessity; this led to huge internal differences and debates, within the international labour movement too.[303] Despite all its criticism of details of colonial policy, the German—and, more generally, European—labour movement tended to side with the colonial project if it benefited the workers at home.[304] As Bebel himself made clear in another speech in 1906 in the flowery language of the time: colonial policy in itself was no crime, it could even be a cultural act. If representatives of cultivated and civilised people came to foreign people as liberators, as friends and mentors, as helpers in need, to bring them the achievements of culture and civilisation and educate them to become people of culture, colonisation could be an act noble in intention and correct in its approach. Then the Social Democrats would be the first, so he assured his speakers, willing to support such colonisation as a great cultural mission.[305]

Such statements were not unusual. Referring to the German example, Reinhart Kössler suggests: "The trajectory of socialism, in particular party politics, with relation to colonial issues ... has shown basic contradictions."[306] The Eurocentric model of human evolution was as internalised among the Left as among the Right, the only difference being that Social Democrats in the main proposed other methods to carry out the "civilising mission". The Social Democratic MP Eichhorn, for example, criticised the extermination strategy in South West Africa because it destroyed the labour force. He demanded protection of the "natives" so they would be able to work. What's their use, he asked, if they are almost starved to death with a mortality rate of up to 60 per cent? They are only a burden. One needs to take appropriate measures, less from a sense of humanity and feeling of empathy, and more with the intention of securing the assets of the colony and making the "natives" useful for the Germans.[307]

On one point, however, the Social Democrats differed in their approach from most of the members of other parties: on the whole they conceded that the colonised had the potential to be elevated to the higher level of European culture and civilisation if they received suitable care and support. This view was expressed by the MP Henke, among others. Refuting the view expressed by fellow members of parliament that n-----s were not humans—referring to the use of the term *Arbeitstiere* (workhorses)—he maintained that those in employment performed well in their work. This was for him proof that they were suitable human beings who could ascend to a higher cultural level. He therefore demanded that as a matter of duty the culture of the n----- should be uplifted.[308] Despite attacking the racist dehumanisation of the local people, his arguments are another manifestation of the dominant, internalised notion of White supremacy. Views like these show that the European working class and their representatives had been, like other members of Western European societies, domesticated in the course of the early industrial revolution. They shared with other social classes the outward perspectives of dominance and subordination in colonial power relations, defined as a civilising mission. This (mis)understood colonialism as a form of development aid. Despite all their moral and ethical objections to crude forms of subjugation, the Social Democrats' view in its cultural-imperialist variations was not far from the reasoning of the *Kolonialreformer* (colonial reformers).[309] The latter's most influential representative was the banker and liberal politician Bernhard Dernburg (1865–1937), who was Secretary for Colonial Affairs and head of the Imperial Colonial Office from May 1907 to June 1910.[310] Colonial reformists were aware that an extermination policy destroyed the local labour force as one of the most important natural resources of the colonies, and that such destruction also put paid to any attempt to integrate the colonised into colonial capitalist market structures.[311]

Another prominent and articulate critic of colonial scandals, besides August Bebel, was Matthias Erzberger (1875–1921) of the Centre Party (Zentrum), who was assassinated by an ultra-right terror squad.[312] Morally and ethically guided by his strong Christian beliefs (the Catholic Centre Party was the predecessor of today's Christian Democratic Union), he vigorously attacked the blatant abuse of power and injustices in the colonies. In particular, he was among the strongest critics of the prohibition of mixed marriages.[313] He showed through his stance that fundamental values were not necessarily confined to a party-political affiliation. At the same time, his views resembled the "benevolent paternalism"[314] shared by many others critical of the methods and brute force of German colonialism.

The parties with critical views on the brutality of colonial warfare brought about a domestic policy crisis.[315] In December 1906 a supplementary budget was tabled in parliament. This was required because of the high costs caused by the war in South West Africa, which was still dragging on, as the military focus shifted to the Nama (denigrated in racist German terminology as *Hottentotten*).[316] Social Democrats and the Centre Party, holding almost half the seats in parliament (45 per cent), refused to endorse the budget. They were joined by several small parties representing national minorities, amounting to over 10 per cent of votes. This added up to a majority who objected to the increase in military allocations. Chancellor Bernhard von Bülow immediately drew the consequences, dissolved parliament and announced a snap election. This took place within a matter of weeks on 25 January 1907 with run-off elections on 5 February. The short and intensive election campaign focused on colonial policy and was commonly known as the *Hottentottenwahlen* (Hottentot vote)—so much for the supposedly marginal role of colonialism in Germany during those days. The electorate was made to believe that this was a matter of life or death in the fight to fend off the onslaught by savages and barbarians in the colonies and protect and defend civilisation.

In view of the strategic alliances formed by the conservative parties, the election result was devastating for the Social Democrats. Despite a considerable increase of votes (a quarter of a million), the loss of 38 seats (from 81 to 43) was dramatic. This decimated the faction in parliament critical of colonialism and paved the way for a dominant conservative alliance (known as the Bülow or Hohenzollern blocc). With the new majority, parliament approved the increase of funds for financing colonial warfare while at the same time expanding investments in a naval policy that sought an increased global influence. The defeat (despite an increase in voters' support) also encouraged the revisionists within the Left to formulate a reformist colonial policy.[317] Carl Ballod (1864–1931), an economist and later a follower of Karl Liebknecht and Rosa Luxemburg in the Independent Social Democratic Party (USPD), warned that it would be suicidal for a race and nation to leave the vast, fertile and sparsely populated parts of the globe only to the lower, coloured races. This would lead to the downfall of culture and civilisation.[318]

That these attitudes were nevertheless a matter of personal choice was perhaps best personified by Hans Paasche (1881–1920), who is recognised for his resistance to German militarism and colonialism, as well as for pioneering ideas about ecologically aware sustainability.[319] As a naval officer he participated in 1905–1906 in the East African war. In 1912 he started publishing in a magazine a series of critical observations on the European way of life through the letters of an entirely fictitious African on a visit to Germany. These were also published posthumously as a book, which achieved a certain cult status after being rediscovered in the 1970s.[320]

THE GERMAN COLONIAL BRAND

Paasche became a pacifist during World War I and was dismissed from the army in 1916. During 1920 he was murdered by a right-wing commando on his estate in what is today Poland. The burial site became a memorial in 2005.[321]

Colonialism without Colonies

As should now be obvious, the colonial expansion of the German empire not only left traces in the colonised territories and among those surviving there, but it also made a considerable contribution to the formation of the German nation-state. Not surprisingly, the historical analyses of this period remain contested terrain. They include the debate over the role colonialism played,[322] though it is now widely accepted that the pervasiveness and presence of colonial discourse left lasting marks on German daily life.[323] But oversights still happen. A recent history of Germany—much praised by parts of the "establishment" and widely recognised—emphasised democratisation and female emancipation during this time as a progressive "departure into modernity",[324] yet it did not consider colonialism of sufficient relevance to engage with. While this could be seen as further (albeit fading) evidence of colonial amnesia, the massive criticism it received for neglecting the military nature of this era testifies to a growing awareness of the legacies of colonialism, which could give rise to a conservative backlash in the public discourse.[325]

Whatever the importance we may attach to the colonial era, it can be safely maintained that with the formal end of German colonial rule as a result of the Treaty of Versailles, the German colonial mentality and mindset did not end. It survived in "the complexity in specific cases of connections among colonialism, organized domestic politics, ideology, and constructed social identity".[326] Nor did the "dream of empire" come to an end, for it lay just below the surface during the Weimar Republic and it gave birth to new desires (and even plans) under the Nazi regime.[327] "Colonialism, in a multiplicity of forms and functions, was a continuous and central concern during the entirety of this period. ... If not the ultimate expression of German empire, colonialism was certainly one enduring expression."[328] Colonial rule infected the dominant popular culture and subsequent political developments in a way not limited to the *Kaiserreich*.[329] The Weimar Republic emerged as an amputated state whose colonies had been redistributed to other powers. This was seen as a national humiliation and denial of the claims of White superiority, which at the time were dressed up as a civilising mission: "colonial ideology was instrumental in the Weimar years, lighting a world stage where many Germans believed themselves to have been cast in the role of victim".[330]

In the view of most Germans, the "diktat of Versailles" robbed them of their legitimate overseas possessions. Demands for the return of these territories were not limited to the agitation of colonial and economic interest groups but included parts of the Social Democrats.[331] An everyday public culture embracing the "colonial thought" was actively shaped and promoted by institutionalised state agencies. Cultural norms and values showed the importance of the German colonial afterlife to interwar politics.[332] Romantic memories of the glory days abroad mushroomed and fed the desire for Germany to reoccupy its place in the sun: "memorials to those who had fallen overseas became manifest symbols demanding the return of the 'stolen German colonial empire'".[333] Expansionist geopolitical thought, fostered throughout the Weimar Republic, gave birth to the *Lebensraum* propaganda of the Nazi regime.[334] Remnants of the colonial past survived in many spheres and forms. They were deliberately cultivated in a diverse range of physical, cultural and mental memory politics.[335] "Weimar colonialism" flourished.[336] As Florian Krobb and Elaine Martin have said: "Loss of face internationally coupled with a postwar identity grounded in the conviction of victimhood gave rise to a distinctly frenzied colonial dialogue that posited the immediate resumption of the colonial project as the 'cure' for the 'illness' that had beset the German body politic."[337]

New reference points were created in the (re-)naming of streets. As a study of around a hundred cities documents, this served to reinstate the notion of colonial superiority, which assumed a new momentum during the Nazi regime, involving colonial renaming in the territories Nazi Germany annexed from the late 1930s.³³⁸ These practices awarded a heroic status to individual colonial actors, above all to Carl Peters. He was portrayed as a patriotic martyr in a 1941 propaganda cinema movie in which the prominent actor Hans Albers played his role.³³⁹ One particularly proactive lobby group was the *Kolonialdeutsche* (colonial Germans). They campaigned both for rehabilitation from the stigma of being "bad colonisers" and for a return to their *Heimat* (which as a notion is poorly captured by the English term "home").³⁴⁰ For them, home was neither the Weimar Republic nor Nazi Germany, despite the latter's slogan of *Heim ins Reich*, demanding the return of the colonies. Many of these Germans, coming from a background in the colonial service, decided to engage in the international arena, in particular the League of Nations, to promote Germany's rehabilitation: "Given the huge level of not only financial, but also cultural and moral investment that many Europeans had placed in colonialism, it is hardly surprising that Colonial Germans were indignant at being excluded from the civilizing mission with the stigma of atrocity. Empire and the 'othered' colonized subject had both played roles in European self-identification, including German identity construction."³⁴¹

Over and above the area of policy, the relatively short period of direct physical German colonial rule—still often downplayed as a mere episode—had disproportionally lasting effects: "Germany's postcolonial experience—what might be called 'colonialism without colonies'—became the fundamental factor in the interwar radicalization of pre-World War I ideas and practices of expansionist biopolitics."³⁴² These were manifested not least in the further development of the pseudo-science of *Rassenkunde* (racial–in the sense of racist–science),³⁴³ triggered earlier by discourses on "racial mixture",³⁴⁴ which had fatal consequences for millions of people in Germany and abroad.³⁴⁵

The themes of the far-reaching and lasting impact of colonial *Herrenmenschentum*, its claim of a civilising mission as a legitimate strategy for the survival of the fittest, and the demand for a "place in the sun" can all be illustrated by reference to popular literature with an enduring impact. This genre acquired new dynamics in the Weimar Republic and boomed in Nazi Germany.³⁴⁶ It nourished the convictions of racial superiority and the need for war in defence of one's own race as the ultimate form of human development. There are two spectacular examples to illustrate this trajectory. One is the prominent North German *Heimatschriftsteller* (native writer) Gustav Frenssen (1863–1945), who left his home soil of Holstein and the Lüneburg heath and moved to the colonial territory of South West Africa. In 1906 he published a fictitious *Feldzugsbericht* (field campaign report) as *Peter Moors Fahrt nach Südwest* (Peter Moor's Journey to South West), claiming to be based in part on narratives of returning *Schutztruppe* soldiers who had fought in the war against the Ovaherero.[347] The book elevated the Germans' ruthless extermination strategy into a moral obligation of the civilising mission, as a kind of service to humanity. It thereby gave shape to the idea of a *Rassenkrieg* (war of the races): "A fundamental racial otherness encoded in the terms 'black' and 'white' determines an irreconcilable antagonism of 'culture' and 'wilderness' and—closely associated with it—the contrast of 'order' and 'amorphous mass'."[348] While first published in the immediate aftermath of the genocidal warfare in South West Africa and subsequently also issued in other languages,[349] it later became an ideological narrative serving the military expansion to the East by the Nazi regime. This accounts for its subsequent distribution until the end of World War II.[350] It has retained its ideological currency by remaining in circulation and distribution, both in print and as an e-book.[351]

Frenssen's social Darwinist glorification of the colonial extermination policy was complemented by a similarly widely distributed and even more ideologically enduring novel by Hans Grimm (1875–1959). It appeared twenty years later, and its author became even more prominent than Frenssen. Grimm, who returned in 1910 from South Africa, published several colonial-patriotic narratives set in southern or South Africa.[352] In 1926 he achieved lasting fame with the publication of a long-winded novel with the title *Volk ohne Raum* (People without Space), which in its unabridged original version is 1,299 pages long.[353] Considered "poorly written and full of digressions",[354] it was the literary work most effective in supporting the notion of *Lebensraum*. At the German stand at the World's Fair in Chicago in 1933, it was exhibited next to the six most important achievements in German technology and economy as the only book worth displaying and the greatest product of the German mind.[355] Grimm's colonial narrative became an integral and substantial part of Nazi propaganda for its expansionist policy, directed at creating *Lebensraum* in Eastern Europe.[356] Like Frenssen's fictitious *Feldzugsbericht*, Grimm's main opus, which has sold close to a million copies so far, remains a fundamental part of colonial-apologetic propaganda in all its various editions and reprints.[357]

As we can see from these and other studies of how colonialism permeated daily life in Germany,[358] a colonial mentality remained an intrinsic part of the Weimar Republic and the Nazi era.[359] While it would be a simplification to assume a linear continuity from the era of colonial expansion overseas to the Nazi regime's invasion and occupation of Eastern Europe, the perpetuation of the colonial mindset was a substantial factor.[360] As Bradley Naranch notes, it was the foundation of a continuing imperial project:

> That project took multiple forms and functions in the decades that followed but never entirely went away or erased all connecting links to the earlier colonial past. These connections are not always obvious nor are they all-embracing. German territorial ambitions in parts of the European East, for example, easily outlasted the end of colonial experiments in East Africa and East Asia. These respective arenas were never entirely equivalent at any specific moment in time, but they did have connections, and these connections matter.[361]

While German colonial history was, over and above romanticising nostalgia, a matter of pride and praise, the flipside of the colonial project was the price paid by those on the receiving end of the daily execution of claims of racial superiority. White supremacy was exercised at the expense of those who, as a result of colonial interactions, came to be present among the colonisers at home.

Africans in Colonial Germany

For reasons obvious from the preceding sections, "colonial Germany" began with the early European expansion and only ended with the defeat of the Nazi regime in World War II. By then Africans had been present in Germany for centuries.[362] With the emergence of a postcolonial movement, there have been increasing efforts to make them more visible.[363] Restoring "fleeting memories" counteracts colonial amnesia and brings "forgotten figures" alive.[364] There is evidence that Africans were part of German royal courts from the 13th century, if only to serve in the main as status symbols and retainers to promote the "cosmopolitan" image of the regional rulers.[365] One of the first recorded visits by Africans with an impact beyond tokenism took place in the mid-17th century, when the Rome-based Ethiopian Jesuit abbot Gregorius (1600–1658) arrived to foster Ethiopian studies in the duchy of Gotha between 1649 and 1652.[366] The most prominent example of an African who left his mark in Germany before the days of the empire was the philosopher Anton Wilhelm Amo (c.1703–1759?) from Ghana. He taught at the universities of Halle and Jena before returning disillusioned to Ghana. Amo has become a prominent figure in more recent efforts to give recognition to the history and contributions of Africans in Germany.[367]

Subsequent to the failed attempt to establish a Brandenburg colony in the late 17th century, it became fashionable in Prussia to add African musicians to military bands. The son of a Nubian, who as a young boy was brought from Egypt to Prussia in the mid-19th century, Berlin-born Gustav Sabac el Cher (1867–1934) became the most prominent. After studies at the music college in Berlin-Charlottenburg, he advanced to the position of bandmaster of the First East Prussian Grenadier Regiment and in this role turned many women's heads. He married the daughter of a wealthy estate agent (in other sources, of a teacher) and later became owner of a garden restaurant.[368] The couple received late recognition when portrayed in an oil painting of 1890 with the title *Preußisches Liebesglück* (Prussian fortune of love), which has been on display since 1992 in the German Historical Museum.[369] Subsequent curiosity about the history of the family, whose members survived the Nazi era and continue to live in Germany, resulted in a book and a documentary film.[370]

The presence of Africans markedly increased with the empire's expansion in the late 19th century.[371] This came about because of exchanges initiated by missionary societies such as the Ewe school, which trained evangelists from Togo.[372] The era of direct German colonial rule paved the way for more Africans to enter Germany. As servants, sailors or exhibits on display in human zoos, as Robbie Aitken points out,[373] they mostly stayed only temporarily and remain largely unaccounted for in the archival records. As a kind of personal property, treated with paternalistic and patronising care, at one end of the scale, and with racist abuse and dehumanisation at the other, personal servants formed a significant proportion of Africans in Germany at the time. In contrast to these servants and to the "natives" displayed as "exhibits" at the notorious *Völkerschauen*, the offspring of influential local African families who interacted with the colonial regime on an equal footing were sent for study and training to Germany.[374] While they were initially considered a worthwhile investment by the German authorities, antipathies and hostilities soon took over and limited if not the educational, then at least the social and professional, advancement of Africans with a privileged background. Many of them sooner or later returned disillusioned to their home countries before the end of Germany's colonial rule, confronted by the limits of the "civilising mission" when it came to opportunities for them in the belly of the beast.

Members of the Bell family from Cameroon had particularly sobering, even deadly experiences. In 1912 Richard Manga Bell, who had obtained a formal education at a gymnasium in Berlin, was employed in a supervisory position over German workers by a company. This caused an uproar in colonial circles. An article in the organ of the German Colonial Society warned that the reputation and position of Whites needed to be better protected. The author insisted that it should be made impossible for a person of colour to boast upon return to his home country that he had been senior to and carried authority over White Germans.[375] Richard Manga Bell was the brother of Rudolf Duala Manga Bell. As we have seen, his belief in the German justice system and the rule of law ended in his execution, and that of Ngoso Din, on fabricated charges of high treason.[376] Their determined resistance was— albeit much more costly—similar to that of other Africans who took the authorities in Germany to task and campaigned for their rights instead of remaining passive victims.[377] Throughout the period of German colonial rule, migration from the colonies to the "motherland" faced legal restrictions. "Colonial wards" were not supposed to stay on in Germany forever and were therefore not entitled to equality before the law through German citizenship.[378] As Elisa von Joeden-Forgey argues, the long-term impact of the three decades of formal German colonialism resulted in the idea of race becoming an operative principle in Germany's political culture.[379]

With the end of formal colonial rule, the situation of Africans in Germany did not ease. While the Weimar Republic offered some windows of opportunity for a few in the cultural sphere and in the entertainment industry, the "racialisation" of humans and the subordination of people of colour to White supremacy advanced further, ending in the Aryan obsession of the Nazi era. Black people in particular were exposed in ordinary daily life to conflicting views about how they should be treated[380] and faced growing discrimination. Some, like Joseph Ekwe Bilé (1892–1959), responded with political activism.[381] In 2022 he was honoured with a plaque for his determined fight for rights during the 1920s in Berlin.[382] Martin Dibobe (1876–?1922 or later) took a stand in petitioning for civil equality in the Weimar Republic together with 17 co-signatories from former German colonies. He has been recognised by inclusion in the list of "*100 Köpfe der Demokratie*" (100 heads of democracy).[383] Like many others, he finally turned his back on Germany. In 1921–1922 he tried to return to Cameroon. As he was refused entry by the French, he ended up in Liberia, but what happened to him thereafter remains unknown.[384]

With the gradual takeover by the Nazi regime, Africans and Afro-Germans became, even more than before, victims of the effects of applied *Rassenkunde*.[385] The presence of African soldiers stationed after World War I by the French army in the occupied parts of the Rhineland fuelled these sentiments further. Their deployment was widely seen as another act of humiliation by the Allies. They became the target of racist public campaigns.[386] Women involved in relationships with them were ostracised, considered shameful and treated as a disgrace, if not scum. Even more so than their mothers, children born of these relationships had to endure life-long ordeals. They were often forcibly taken from their homes, sterilised and ended up as young adults in wartime camps.[387]

Some of the life histories of those with an African parent or parents living in Germany between the two world wars have now been recorded and allow more intimate insights into their sufferings.[388] Their memories are a painful reminder of a still largely ignored chapter, which remains in the shadow of other crimes.[389] Africans living in Germany and entering bonds with German women were punished for such "transgressions". The prominent case of Mahjub bin Adam Mohamed (1904–1944) serves as the end of the novel *Afterlives* by Abdulrazak Gurnah (although he is unacknowledged in the book).[390] As a young boy he joined his father as an Askari child soldier, and after several years in the employment of German companies, he moved in 1929 to Berlin, where he became known as Bayume Mohamed Husen. He had minor roles as an actor in 23 movies, for the last time as a servant in the film *Carl Peters*. His affairs with local women were considered a form of *Rassenschande* (racial defilement). In late 1941 he was incarcerated in the concentration camp Sachsenhausen, where he died three years later. In 2007 his memory was honoured by the first *Stolperstein* ("stumbling block") placed for an African.[391] Established on the initiative of the artist Gunter Demnig,[392] these memorial cobblestones have become an integral part of German memory culture. As a reminder of the victims of the Nazi regime, they mark a specific place connected to the person or persons in question. Another *Stolperstein* (put in place in 2009) commemorates Hagar Martin Brown (1889–1940), killed by Nazis in Frankfurt/Main. In 2021 two more were installed in Berlin to commemorate Martha Ndumbe (1902–1945) and Ferdinand James Allen (1920–1941).[393]

As these known cases document, Nazi Germany became a lethal place for people of African descent during a time when there was a further radicalisation of ideas of racist dehumanisation, including the will to kill.[394] But at the same time Nazi Germany continued to benefit from the presence of Africans, and not only as exotic actors in movies or other displays nurturing a superiority complex by degrading them to stereotypes of serving subordinates.[395] During and after direct colonial rule, Africans played crucial—though usually unacknowledged—roles until the late 1930s in academic scholarship related to African languages and culture, thereby often helping promote the scholarly careers of their German "mentors"[396]—they were Africans who "developed" Germans.

While gaps in knowledge are being increasingly filled, not least through a growing number of local studies based on archival material by members of postcolonial initiatives who seek to trace the individual histories of Africans in Germany,[397] the efforts to document the overall impact of Black communities in Germany until the 1950s remain a challenge. This is, as Kira Thurman notes,

> because Germany's black residents were always policed, stymied, and scattered about in ways that hindered collectivization. The fact that communities formed at all should be understood as an Olympic feat in overcoming what were nearly insurmountable odds. Placed in isolation and prevented from forming meaningful bonds with other people of colour and with white Germans, black Germans' fragmentation explains why it has been so difficult to trace a distinct Afro-German culture.[398]

The changes that have taken place since then will be the subject of the next chapter. It includes a look at the formation of an Afro-German community acting in their common interest and claiming a respected place in their German home.

4

(POST-)COLONIAL (WEST) GERMANY

Memories of the colonial era and engagements with it did not end with the defeat of the Nazi regime. As part of the new West German political establishment, "Old Africans" (*Alte Afrikaner*), who had personal or familial connections with the colonies, helped influence "development policy" as it emerged after the war.[1] Their role also made clear that the African part of the German empire was a decisive and permanent point of reference in the shaping of continued affinities with the colonial past. In the field of literature, several authors, writing less for the mainstream, also explored the colonial legacy though it was not so much focused on Africa;[2] but in terms of popularity, colonial romantic fiction continued to predominate and influenced a wider public and popular culture.[3] South West Africa/Namibia remained a major focus culturally, politically, diplomatically and academically, partly due to the continued presence of a German-speaking minority there. Chapter 5 will be devoted to this special relationship. It provides the most obvious case of the intergenerational transmission and conservation of colonial historical memory, often (though not always) in the form of a romanticising nostalgia as part of family history.[4] Beyond these personal intergenerational memories,

> the years after 1945 were characterized by a general amnesia about the German history of colonialism or a selective reinterpretation

of that history. Images of Germans as benevolent colonizers had become prevalent already during the interwar years. Perhaps because Germany lost its colonies at the hands of other European powers and the United States and never faced a successful colonial revolt, Germans developed a particular sentimental attitude toward former colonial subjects.[5]

This chapter focuses on the Federal Republic of Germany (FRG). The different way in which the German Democratic Republic (GDR) engaged with the colonial past is evident from the many references in chapter 3 to scholarly works published there from the late 1950s.[6] Remarkably, this trajectory of knowledge production had hardly any impact on or overlap with the specific way that West Germany's memory culture developed. The Iron Curtain was more than just a physical partition. The markedly different ideologies and policies of the two states reflected differences in the way they positioned themselves in the post-World War II era of confrontation and competition between two power blocs, in an effort to gain wider influence in the international arena on the basis of geopolitical affiliations.[7] These differences could be seen in the engagement with the colonial era. For many in the West, "Germany's own colonies and the German colonial period survived in memories and histories produced in the shadow of the Holocaust either to rehabilitate German identity or discredit the precursors and successors to Nazi rule".[8] While such (mis)appropriation was taboo for GDR citizens, at least in public, this did not prevent East Germans from reproducing colonial racist patterns in their treatment of Africans who came to the country as students or migrant workers or in state-sponsored forms of interaction and collaboration.[9]

In the first two decades after 1945, the Cold War left German colonialism as a matter of critical engagement to East Germany. In West Germany, the focus on 20th-century history was almost exclusively limited to the Nazi regime in a rather ahistorical (and selectively narrow) manner. Similarly, support for anti-colonial struggles especially in Africa became part of official GDR state policy, finding institutional expression in the GDR Committee for Solidarity with African Peoples from 1960 to 1964, the Afro-Asiatic Solidarity Committee from 1964 to 1973, and the Solidarity

(POST-)COLONIAL (WEST) GERMANY

Committee of the GDR from 1973 to 1990.[10] In the Federal Republic it was a matter for sections of civil society, evolving within the wider student movement from the 1960s.[11] With rare exceptions—such as protests against the Wissmann monument in Hamburg commemorating the German governor of East Africa[12]—such support was almost entirely disconnected from the colonial heritage, though the first serious critical scholarly analyses in these years began to challenge the hitherto largely superficial engagement with colonialism. While for both German states the period from the 1960s to the end of 1970s offered (for different reasons) occasional room for debate about the colonial past, the subject was reduced to "peripheral appearances" during the 1980s.[13]

Critical analyses of German colonial history entered the wider scholarly discourse in West Germany to a significant extent only from the late 1990s, partly as a result of the rise of African, Development, Cultural and Postcolonial Studies. The numerous publications of the last two and a half decades cited in the bibliography of this book testify to this turn. It took even longer for a critical engagement with German colonialism to appear in the wider public discourse. This remains an uphill battle, not least because of the separation maintained between the Holocaust and colonialism, even more so in public life than in the field of scholarship: "We must assume that the German state's memory politics, which after 1989–90 elevated remembrance of the Shoah to *Staatsraison* (national interest) ... did not encourage the two fields to move closer together."[14] Instead, Germany's politics of memory can be more appropriately understood by the term *Deckerinnerung*, which Michael Rothberg uses in Freud's meaning of "screen memory":[15] as a "covering memory" that occludes or ignores the past. This points to the fact that attempts to create a hierarchy or scale of atrocities tend to promote blind spots.[16] Until the end of the 20th century, therefore, Lora Wildenthal could still recognise that

> the absence of colonialism from the German past became a quiet, but stubborn, part of German identity. (The German Democratic Republic was, at least at the official level, an exception.) German identity after 1919, that is, German postcolonial identity, has been insular, even self-consciously provincial. ... General works on

modern Germany reflect a certain provincialism and a quiet, but stubborn, white identity for Germans.[17]

West German Africa

In the first decades after the war West Germans were preoccupied with more pressing needs and traumas than dealing with the colonial past prior to the Nazi regime. Instead, the period when Germans had been engaged in a "civilising mission"—while not openly celebrated—offered some comfort and refuge, drawing on family histories and related narratives. Generally, colonial remnants survived untouched and were—if at all consciously acknowledged—seen more as belonging to a bygone era associated with "better times". Colonial history and its relics remained an integral part of ordinary daily life, surviving in place names, monuments and language with racist connotations.

The year 1956 marked the foundation of two associations that signalled a continued affinity with the German past, especially in Africa. The German African Society (DAG)[18] was to a large extent the initiative of *Alte Afrikaner*—diplomats and politicians with a family connection to the continent. The association was closely linked with economic interests and official West German foreign policy, and was partly funded by the state. It published a glossy magazine, *Afrika heute* (Africa Today), which carried not the faintest criticism of colonial times, but instead promoted West German relations with independent African states willing to seek partnerships with the West. In parallel, 1956 also saw the foundation of the Traditional Association of Former Schutztruppen and Overseas Forces (Traditionsverband ehemaliger Schutz- und Überseetruppen).[19] From 1969 its annual general meetings were held in Bad Lauterberg, and included a wreath-laying ceremony at the Wissmann statue, which was still standing at the end of 2023.[20] The association's constitutional mandate (in the version of 2019) includes support for historical research; undertaking and supporting the writing and publication of truthful accounts and correcting untruthful ones; and preserving the memory of the victims of war.[21] As a cursory inspection of its activities reveals, these are euphemisms for a blatant form of colonial apologetics. Not surprisingly, members of the Traditionsverband show ideological overlaps with and linkages to the political party Alternative für Deutschland (AfD), about which more will be said below.

While the ideological basis of the Traditionsverband never aroused any temptations for a takeover, the DAG became a site for political-ideological battles over influence during the early 1970s. By then the Union of Africanists in Germany, established in 1969 and subsequently renamed the Union for African Studies in Germany (VAD), had consolidated itself after an intense internal debate between the various disciplines over the association's political positioning in the face of demands for it to adopt a critical stand against the colonial history of earlier German African Studies.[22] Due in large part to the new spirit of international solidarity emerging since the mid-1960s in the student movement, the scholarly and political profile of the younger generation of scholars in the VAD's ranks signalled strong support for anti-colonial movements and fostered critical assessments of neo-colonialism. This is apparent from the list of its publications between 1970 and 1999—in the main, edited volumes of contributions to general conferences.[23]

In the approach to colonial history, this period also saw the start of new research. The ambiguities which such new approaches created were illustrated in a review essay by Winfried Baumgart.[24] As its author concluded, the latest research had examined in detail the effects of policy of various interest groups and made plain the "seemingly unexpected collision of interests". He conceded that the numerous dark or obscure spots had not become clearer. But with the growing distance in time one could also see the positive sides of colonialism. In a subsequent monograph the same author ended his chapter on colonial policy by approvingly quoting the opinion of a British author that the German colonial administration had been very strict, sometimes harsh, but always just.[25]

The new academic discourse was accompanied by the first fundamental dismantling of the claims of the colonial "civilising mission" in a more popular non-fictional format.[26] In this spirit, VAD members played a decisive role in the takeover of the DAG in 1971–1972. Replacing the conservative "Old Africans" through a coup at an annual general meeting, members of the new internationalist movement used the opportunity for a substantial repositioning of the journal *Afrika heute*. But the glorious victory was short-lived. As a result of the radical change in stance, financial support from the Foreign Office was stopped in 1974,[27] and the DAG closed shop in 1975. With the DAG becoming obsolete after its successful hijacking, the German Africa Foundation (DAS) was established in 1978. It has operated since then in close association with official policy, adjusting over time to new developments.[28] The institutional contexts and trajectories of the Traditionsverband, the DAG and the VAD were all indicative of the dynamics unfolding in the 1960s and 1970s, influencing the discourses and illustrating the debates in search of a viable position on the colonial past in democratic West Germany.

This peculiar atmosphere, spanning a wide spectrum from reactionary and racist colonial-apologetic mindsets to critical analyses of the colonial legacy, can also be illustrated by reference to two films of the mid-1960s. Just as with the popular 1959 documentary movie *Serengeti darf nicht sterben* (Serengeti Shall Not Die),[29] the reactions to these two films showed how the topic of Africa continued to resonate with the German population, though in rather different ways. Released in August 1966, *Africa Addio* (also released as *Africa: Blood and Guts*) by Italian filmmakers Jacopetti and Prosperi provoked a storm of protest about their manipulated footage filmed in East Africa. Presented as a documentary, it was viewed with the strongest repugnance by the renowned film critic John Berger, who observed: "'Africa Addio' is a brutal, dishonest, racist film. It slanders a continent and at the same time diminishes the human spirit. And it does so to entertain us. ... If 'Africa Addio' is to be believed, Africans have engaged in an orgy of bloodletting and pillage since the Europeans left."[30] At its premiere in West Berlin, it drew massive criticism from the mainstream media, including conservative publications.[31] Violent student protests led to the trashing of the cinema, which added another dimension to the furore. Ultimately, this student intervention distracted from the movie and from any engagement with colonial-apologetic propaganda and shifted attention to the forms of protest. It also contributed to a refocusing by the protesting students on German fascist history, which acted as a smokescreen that obscured the track record of German colonialism.[32]

Only two months after the first screening of *Africa Addio*, the documentary *Heia Safari* by Ralph Giordano (1923–2014) created another minor uproar, this time from the opposite political direction.[33] Broadcast in two parts of 45 minutes each on two evenings in October 1966 by the state TV channel ARD with the revealing subtitle "The Legend of the German Colonial Idyll",[34] it offended a mainly older generation of viewers. In response to strong protests, including phone calls by the leading CDU politician Eugen Gerstenmaier, President of the Bundestag, and Franz Josef Strauss after the showing of the first part, demanding that the broadcast of the second part the next evening be stopped,[35] a two-hour discussion was recorded in December ("Heia Safari: Für und wider"—for and against) and broadcast in February 1967. While the discussion could not bridge the divide, it partly illustrated the generational nature of the conflicting perspectives.[36] The arguments also revealed a pattern which since then has been repeatedly reproduced: while some complained that one should not open old wounds but treat past history as a closed chapter, advocates of colonial revisionism (who prefer to indulge in nostalgic reminiscences) claimed to find inaccuracies in the historical details. While *Heia Safari* is widely considered a milestone in the history of TV documentaries, it took another twenty years until German television broadcast further documentaries with a similar critical perspective on the subject.[37]

That Giordano's documentary was received overwhelmingly positively by a younger generation was an indication of shifting perspectives, which also found expression in the student movement's demands for a coming to terms with the Nazi crimes and for taking to task those former Nazis who continued to occupy senior positions in the democratic state's institutions. The 1960s was also the decade when an anti-imperialist and anti-colonial solidarity movement first emerged in the West, which led to new dynamics in the 1970s. In Freiburg, Action Third World was established in 1968. It acted as the midwife for the founding of the

THE LONG SHADOW OF GERMAN COLONIALISM

Information Centre Third World (Informationszentrum Dritte Welt/Iz3w), which from 1970 published the journal *iz3w* (originally as *Blätter des iz3w*).[38] The Information Centre Southern Africa (Informationsstelle Südliches Afrika/ISSA)[39] was founded in 1971 with an office in Bonn and started publishing *Informationsdienst Südliches Afrika* (from 1994 as *afrika süd*) in 1972. With its focus on southern Africa, ISSA gave special attention through its journal and many publications (in several series of books) to the subject of early German colonial rule, especially in South West Africa.[40] Unlike other organisations such as the Anti-Apartheid Movement (1974–1994) and several Christian or church-related initiatives that were motivated by an agenda of international solidarity with the "Third World" movement of the 1970s and 1980s, both Iz3w and ISSA remain in existence despite difficult conditions. The same resilience has been shown by the quarterly journal *Peripherie: Zeitschrift für Politik und Ökonomie in der Dritten Welt* (Periphery: Journal of Politics and Economy in the Third World)—more recently titled *Peripherie: Politik-Ökonomie-Kultur*. It was founded in 1980 by a handful of young scholars in the early stages of their careers, who, while working entirely independently, shared similar values of international solidarity and a commitment to value-based academic analysis.[41]

The growing awareness of a violent German colonial past was illustrated in 1978 by the screening of the documentary *Die Liebe zum Imperium* (Love of empire)[42] by Peter Heller,[43] and by the publication in the same year of Uwe Timm's novel *Morenga*. In the following year Gert von Paczensky's first popular non-fiction assault on colonialism appeared in a revised edition. As the renowned journalist warned his readers: in Germany, people like to believe that there is not much to tell because of the relatively short duration of German colonial history. His book shows just how wrong this belief is.[44] With its particular focus on demystifying Carl Peters, Heller's one-hour film, *Die Liebe zum Imperium*, became prominent as a popular source of counter-information. In the absence of other visual sources with similar information, it gained almost cult status within those segments of civil society critical of colonialism. As with *Heia Safari*, opponents criticised the film because of several inaccuracies and mistakes in the detail. These included the unacknowledged use of material from other colonies besides East Africa, though this did not by any means alter the substance of the message. But the inaccuracies came in handy as ammunition for those wishing to discredit the authenticity and credibility of the film. This has remained a common tool used by the Traditionsverband and similar organisations. Colonial enthusiasts continue to use the knowledge they have acquired from their meticulous collection of items of the colonial past as their hobbies (coins, flags, uniforms, stamps and so on) as testimony and proof of authority.[45] They point out that the tropical helmet was different in East Africa from that in Cameroon, but this only serves to distract from the real issues at hand. It is as if someone who does not know how the specific uniforms of the *Schutztruppe* looked in each of the colonies is disqualified from making any reliable judgement on the devastating consequences of their warfare.

To dismiss colonial-critical *Nestbeschmutzung* (nest soiling), apologists also tend to make use of what could be cynically called *Autobahnargumente* (autobahn arguments).[46] They misleadingly create a kind of "balance sheet" listing individual cultural and scientific achievements as evidence of the "civilising mission" to set against the devastating structural consequences of colonialism. Such flawed record-keeping has been put straight by the historian Gesine Krüger. As she maintains, even if all colonial officials and soldiers had been benign, which they weren't, it would not have made any difference to the partitioning of Africa among European powers, which was carried out with a willingness to meet resistance by brutal means.[47]

That this kind of "balancing act" was still stubbornly alive came to the fore at the time of the centenary of the Berlin Conference in 1984, marking the hundredth anniversary of the *Kaiserreich*'s emergence as a colonial power. For the first time, critical assessments of the colonial era contributed to a growing number of activities—including the VAD conference on a hundred years of interference in Africa[48]—and produced a range of publications.[49] Notably, these also included the first demands made for the restitution of looted artwork in German possession.[50] At the same time, the subject remained to a large extent dominated by attitudes that ranged from blatant glorification[51] to rather mild justifications of Germany's colonial record. To illustrate the point, a former ambassador with a long diplomatic career in African affairs repeatedly referred to the *Aufbauleistungen* (achievements) of the colonial past and saw no reason to look at its downsides through a magnifying glass.[52] *Aufbauarbeit* was also part of the rhetorical repertoire of a colonial historian who concluded that ultimately Robert Koch balanced out Carl Peters.[53] He also argued that thirty years of German colonialism was far too short a time to achieve much more. After all, these colonies—like those of other colonial powers—had to be conquered before something could be constructed on the remains of what had been destroyed.[54] In any case, he argued, if the Germans hadn't arrived, others would have come in their place.[55] Such blinkered perceptions were interpreted as a refusal to be reminded of the violent episodes in German society, which cannot all be reduced to the work of the "demon" Hitler. Rather, they go back to "normal" times and actually happened in the "good old days".[56]

As if the balancing acts in 1984 were not enough, one of the doyens of colonial history a year later concluded his academic overview written for university students in a similar downplaying fashion. He compared German colonialism to development policy as an *Entwicklungsdiktatur* (development dictatorship) and *Modernisierungsmodell* (modernisation model), which created the preconditions and means for the later struggle for freedom and for cultural and political reintegration (*sic*) into a larger community.[57] Such perspectives continued to prevail, albeit there was a growing discomfort whose effects were clearly visible by the late 1990s. But alongside a willingness to acknowledge the horrific chapter of the Third Reich in the 20th-century history of Germany, there stood in contrast the widely internalised attitude that colonialism was a matter for "others" to deal with.[58] Efforts to downplay German colonialism as a "short-lived adventure" or "episode"[59] have survived as part of popular German perceptions. Such euphemisms used by the editors of a widely praised volume did not prevent the book's dissemination by the Federal Agency for Civic Education in 2018.

(POST-)COLONIAL (WEST) GERMANY

Colonial Remnants in United Germany

The increasing number of scholarly texts on colonialism since the mid-1990s[60] has given rise to the observation that as a result of a postcolonial turn "German colonial history ... has developed into a fashionable topic".[61] In what is seen as a paradigm shift, new studies have increasingly included "a cultural history vein: discourse and representation, colonial knowledge, and memory".[62] These advances in scholarship testify to the considerable disconnect between scholarly insights and public awareness, as well as to the long-lasting failure of politicians (which has only gradually ceased) to recognise the challenges of dealing with the colonial past. Their ignorance was apparent at a seminar arranged in 2001 by the parliamentary wing of the Green Party. In his closing remarks as chairperson of the meeting, MP Hans-Christian Ströbele (who at the same time was a member of the parliamentary committee for development policy) observed that Germany was lucky to have been forced to give up its colonial empire. This gave it an opportunity to play an unencumbered, and therefore pioneering, role in international relations.[63] That this view is by no means restricted to Germans was revealed at the same event. Ströbele's remarks followed a speech by the Nigerian ambassador to Germany, who reminded the audience of a proposal by President Obasanjo of Nigeria on a visit to Berlin in December 1999. He had then suggested that a "New Berlin Conference" be called to redefine European–African relations, since Germany was morally and historically well positioned to take the initiative for such dialogue.[64] In all fairness, it should be stressed that Ströbele (1939–2022) thereafter became, during his later years in parliament (until 2017), one of the most active MPs promoting awareness of Germany's colonial past. He thus convincingly showed that neither initial ignorance nor age prevents one from constantly learning.

The pitfalls of a colonial past still alive in the present are also evident in everyday discriminatory language, which often continues to bear racist stereotypes or connotations.[65] These have been internalised to such an extent that they are at times used without any conscious intention to discriminate. Such gaffes—without being excused—can thus be considered as a kind of aphasia (a disorder that affects how you communicate). At the same time, the ignorance about the context which shaped such language borders on amnesia (memory loss).

Popular Literature

The problem is also manifest in a popular genre of fiction which has discovered the "postcolonial" narrative.[66] It shows that even the best of intentions (assuming they exist) cannot always protect people from a lack of sensibility. Thus, an artist well known for his anarchistic cartoons in the 1970s–1990s drew inspiration from a visit to Namibia. In a novel he subsequently wrote, he engaged with the genocide of 1904–1908.[67] It turned into "nostalgic obfuscation",[68] "a form of cultural engagement with German colonialism that takes postcolonial criticism for granted and invites readers to indulge yet again in African exoticism, colonial fantasies, and historical nostalgia", thus raising "the prospect of a literary memory of colonialism beyond postcolonialism".[69] It reminds one strongly of romantic conceptions of European life in African colonies popularised by the Hollywood movie *Out of Africa*: "Fictionalizing colonial history from a seemingly historiographical or rather an antiquarian point of view paradoxically achieves very similar effects to re-enactments of colonial life in prime-time German television features, where since the millennium docudramas have been just as popular as in literature."[70]

This kind of colonial gaze is reproduced in a whole range of narratives in which women describe their interactions with locals, even if they do not quite "go native". Among the most prominent and successful examples is *Die weiße Massai* (The white Massai).[71] The book was such a bestseller that two more novels followed.[72] It was also turned into a movie, and the author summarised her passion for Africa in another monograph.[73] As Dirk Göttsche has observed:

> One of the modern twists in the reenactment of colonial myths ... is the shift from the male heroes of colonial novels to the female protagonists of recent works. These sometimes combine the fascination of colonial adventure in exotic terrain with the stance of a

courageous anticolonialism in colonial space which gives rise to yet another myth, which is postcolonial only in the historical sense of the term, namely the myth of a "better colonialism" (Sartre's term) which history failed to give a chance to develop.[74]

Many of these narratives reinforce in the reader a sense of paternalistic faux open-mindedness that views the "other" through the lens of a dominant monocultural Germany:

> Novels angled at the bestseller market of literary entertainment clearly continue to draw on the allure of an imaginary landscape from the pressures of modernity into the perceived "paradise" of tropical exoticism, the promise of unfettered colonial adventure, the excitement of an alleged closeness to "original" nature, both in the wildlife and countryside and in the culture of the "native" Africans encountered by the German protagonists. . . .
>
> In a universe of global communication, exchange and migration, which nevertheless continues to be marked by serious imbalances in power, prosperity, participation and opportunities, the imagination of adventures in exotic terrain and the exoticist othering of Africans lose their innocence. Replicating patterns of perception and discursive practices that are ultimately colonial in origin, they raise ethical issues along with political concerns.[75]

This contrasts with the case of the renowned South African novelist André Brink (1935–2015): counteracting romanticising clichés, he described the brutality of colonial frontier society in *The Other Side of Silence*, a novel that evoked the particular horrors of war in German South West Africa, including the gendered violence of that conflict. Many of André Brink's novels, located in mainly historical colonial settings of South Africa, were published in Germany by the large publishing house Kiepenheuer & Witsch. *The Other Side of Silence*, however, was considered unsuitable for a German audience—which indeed might have been true for a public caught up in colonial amnesia or at least an unwillingness to face the brutal side of history. It required a rather small publisher to produce a German version. While of late the combination of postcolonial and memory studies has provided a productive context for narrative literature as well,[76] this should not lead us to hastily conclude that they have already decisively shifted public mainstream discourses. Nor has the genre avoided the danger of regressing into appropriations, re-mystifications and stereotyping.[77]

An overview of recent African literature published in German could create the misleading impression that this genre is widely established and recognised.[78] But African literature remains, with very few exceptions, a niche genre and is mainly published by committed smaller publishing houses.[79] While a few novels of the Tanzanian-British writer Abdulrazak Abdulrazak Gurnah were translated and distributed by mainly smaller publishers in limited print runs between 1986 and 2006, these were all unavailable at the time he was awarded the Nobel Prize in Literature in October 2021.[80] That Gurnah, despite his literary engagement with German colonial East Africa, was considered by the German media to be widely unknown can be dismissed as a bid to justify their own ignorance. His novel *Afterlives* had received prominent reviews as a masterpiece in the established international media.[81] But the Nobel Prize was disparagingly declared a reward for "identity politics".[82] Fittingly, the author in the initial version misplaced Zanzibar as an island off the Kenyan coast (this was later corrected). A leading journalist in the supplement of *Die Welt* (part of the Springer press consortium) quoted in a tweet the citation of the Nobel Prize Committee, which stated that Gurnah was selected "for his uncompromising and compassionate penetration of the effects of colonialism and the fate of the refugee in the gulf between cultures and continents".[83] The journalist then commented: "well-behaved".[84] The contrast between such an arrogant and limited view and the inclusive empathy of Gurnah could hardly be stronger. It illustrates the divide between the tunnel vision of White supremacy, a form of mental imprisonment, and universal humanism. Years before, Gurnah had disclosed in an interview with the German newspaper *Stuttgarter Zeitung* that as a 15-year-old he cried when reading *Anna Karenina*, despite knowing nothing about 19th-century Russia. Tolstoy, he explained, writes about human emotions which can be understood by all.[85] As this shows, while all humans are able to share a certain understanding of feelings, if not the feelings themselves, this does require a certain willingness and openness.

(POST-)COLONIAL (WEST) GERMANY

Humboldt Forum

In June 2013 the foundation stone was laid for the reconstruction of Berlin's imperial palace, known as the *Stadtschloss*. It was for centuries the seat of the royal Prussian Hohenzollern dynasty. Located on the Museum Island in the East Berlin part of the divided city, it was seriously damaged during World War II. In 1950, the ruins—considered by the new government in East Germany as remnants of an imperialist past—were demolished. In its place the Palace of the Republic—also known as the People's Palace—was built in the early to mid-1970s. From 1976 it hosted the East German People's Chamber. With German unification in 1990, the building's main function became obsolete. In 2003, the German parliament—now again located in Berlin—adopted a resolution to replace the asbestos-contaminated building (closed and vacant for health reasons) with a replica of the old castle. As a showcase of Berlin's links to the world, it was designed to accommodate the Humboldt Forum—named after the explorer Alexander von Humboldt (1769–1859) and his brother Wilhem (1767–1835), founder of the Humboldt University—to exhibit the collections of the city's previously separate Asian Art Museum and Ethnological Museum.

If anything has been achieved by the newly established Humboldt Forum, which the Minister for Culture,[86] Monika Grütters, declared in 2016 was "currently the most ambitious cultural project in Germany"[87]—it is that it has given rise to a vibrant debate over many years. Not only did it spark a discussion on the role of ethnology.[88] More importantly even, it remains a contested subject between those who see it as a museum of world cultures (as its protagonists confidently claim) or (as the critics anticipated) a treasury of colonial artefacts.[89] As a result of prominent media coverage the debate has given greater visibility to and created greater awareness of the German colonial past, looted colonial objects and their restitution. The numerous articles published between 2016 and 2019 in the monthly paper *Politik & Kultur* of the German Cultural Council, which have since been compiled in a volume, are in themselves testimony to the wide range of opinions on the subject.[90] The ongoing debate is also well illustrated in numerous articles addressing a non-German audience.[91]

THE LONG SHADOW OF GERMAN COLONIALISM

There was no lack of grandiose promises made at the start of the project. Hermann Parzinger, president of the Prussian Cultural Heritage Foundation, a federal institution, and one of the three founding directors of the Humboldt Forum, declared in mid-2016 that the museum would, in the best tradition of Humboldt, "please and educate" visitors, who would be left "wondering about fascinating linkages"; in the end, they might gain a better understanding of the world. As a result, the Humboldt Forum could become a place of self-affirmation in a more interconnected world.[92] Such whitewashing covered over the brute force of colonial oppression and the looting of resources in many parts of the world, with numerous objects ending up on display, thereby documenting the "interconnected world" of imperial times.

It was to some extent thanks to the uncompromising attitude of the French art historian Bénédicte Savoy (as well as the principled demand for the restitution of looted objects) that the Humboldt Forum gained more attention in the German media. Savoy, a professor at the Technical University of Berlin, resigned in July 2017 from the expert advisory board of the Forum, after asking how much blood was dripping from each artwork. As she said in a newspaper interview,[93] the collections represented "300 years of collecting activity with all of the nastiness and hopes that are bound up with it. That is us, that is Europe. One could imagine so much if it wasn't all buried under this lead, covered like nuclear waste just so that no radiation leaks out. The Humboldt Forum is like Chernobyl."[94]

Parzinger denounced her criticism as "cheap self-profiling" and claimed to detect in it a "postcolonial hate of institutions" which likes to attack ethnographic museums.[95] This evasiveness and denial was topped by Horst Bredekamp, another of the founding directors of the Humboldt Forum, who declared in a radio interview that Savoy was "playing a game to put colonial history in the spotlight".[96] Such dismissals were echoed in the conservative media, which demanded "glamour and magic instead of joyless and hyper-correct colonialism debates".[97] In an ironic twist, the much-scolded Savoy, together with the Senegalese scholar and artist Felwine Sarr, was commissioned in 2018 by President Emmanuel Macron of France to investigate the return of cultural objects from public French institutions to African ones. Their report[98] was a major step forward in the campaign for restitution. Its publication in a German translation[99] also added to the debate on the Humboldt Forum. The two have been much recognised since then: in 2020 they ranked third in the list of "most influential people in the art world" by the magazine *ArtWorld* and were included by *Time* among the "100 most influential people of 2021". Savoy countered earlier criticisms of her stand with the simple statement that "a society is better if it knows its past".[100]

But knowing the past should also find expression in a willingness to give up stolen possessions. That, despite growing demands, this should remain a much-contested matter has been apparent in the debate triggered by a 15-metre-long outrigger boat from Luf island in the German colonial Bismarck Archipelago of what is today Papua New Guinea.[101] Brought to Berlin in 1904, it is now one of the attractions on display in the Humboldt Forum. Because of its size, it was installed in the shell of the building while still under construction in 2018. Its removal would require some massive engineering work and might add to the reluctance to engage in the necessary research on its provenance or findspot. Defending its appearance on display, Parzinger declared in an interview that there was no demand for its return.[102] At the opening of the museum, he explained that it represented a "memorial of the horrors of the German colonial era".[103]

A similar evasiveness was displayed by the Minister of Culture, Monika Grütters, in July 2021, a few days before the first of several official opening events at the Humboldt Forum. Her views reveal how colonial amnesia survives not only in the architecture and conception of the museum,[104] but also in the form of euphemisms. She said that the Forum was a "base camp for a trip around the world". Commenting on the prominent display of the well-known Benin Bronzes,[105] she stressed how important it was "to show the world how one deals with humanity's cultural heritage, which at some time was devolved upon or entrusted" to others.[106] The Humboldt Forum, as she explained further, had therefore, already before its opening, initiated important debates about how to handle, for example, cultural goods from colonial contexts. It thus, she went on, not only deals with the big themes of human existence but also contributes to reconciliation in colonial contexts. Just a few days later, at the first official opening on 20 July 2021, Grütters praised the reconstruction of the castle as "a gift for Berlin and the entire Germany, which can here present herself as a driving force for inter-cultural understanding".[107] This was more evidence of a discourse which some critics saw as a turn to the right as far as cultural memory relating to imperial Germany was concerned.[108]

The decision taken in 2002 to replace the former GDR Palace of the Republic with a replica of the Prussian castle initially sparked debates about public memory of German history. The subsequent decision to accommodate the Humboldt Forum within its walls shifted the focus towards imperial and colonial memory: "While Forum enthusiasts saw the move as a brilliant stroke of genius that would cement Berlin's status as a world-class cultural capital, its critics saw a thinly disguised form of neo-exoticism and imperial nostalgia."[109] This set off a new debate about Germany's colonial past, marked by the announcement of an alliance of postcolonial initiatives as *No Humboldt 21* in June 2013.[110] Unintentionally, however, this risked turning colonialism into an exceptional and exotic episode in German history, rather than a process with a long-lasting legacy that has been insufficiently dealt with.[111] In hindsight, "the symbolism of rebuilding an imperial palace, crowned with a golden crucifix, as a showcase for colonial booty now seems almost comically misjudged".[112] This misjudgement may make room for counter-narratives to gain ground:

> Myths are made in the telling, and it matters who eventually gets to tell—and to contest—the story. The Humboldt Forum started out in the grips of an exculpatory discourse, but it does not have to end that way. It would be ironic indeed if the champions of the myth of innocence end up creating a museum that shows its very impossibility.[113]

Pointing in this direction was the speech given at the second official opening ceremony in September 2021 (following the first in July 2021) by no less than Germany's head of state, Frank-Walter Steinmeier. He said in his speech:

as Federal President, I must say quite clearly that, even if the Second Reich began its quest for a "place in the sun" relatively late, there is no reason to have a clear conscience. And so this reborn palace must also serve us as a reminder and a warning: of militarism, of nationalism in the Second Reich, and of German colonialism, too.[114]

After visiting the exhibitions in mid-2023, George Steinmetz ended his observations with two recommendations about how the Forum could come closer to its self-declared aim of making visible the complexity of colonial histories and their entanglement in the present. Firstly, it should lay a stronger focus on the overlapping of culture and colonialism/postcolonialism, imperialism and anti-imperialism, by treating German colonialism not only in the context of imperial Germany, but also of later eras of German society. Secondly, while attention has been paid to the imperial context in which the artefacts on display were appropriated, the Forum has neglected to show how colonialism, imperialism and globalisation resulted in a continuous mix of forms of cultural expression. As Steinmetz observes, most provenience research ignores the fact that colonising and colonised cultures are interwoven in multiple ways and does not ask how these interactions changed them (and the context and meaning of the artefacts).[115] At the same time, the Humboldt Forum offers new food for thought about the role and function of memory culture in the wider German historical context, as it is represented (or ignored) in the variety of museums and collections on the Museum Island in Berlin.[116]

Black Germany

Of late, the history and present existence of a Black diaspora in Germany have been increasingly well documented.[117] While White Germans can afford to feign ignorance or unawareness of their country's colonial past, this is not the case for Black Germans (henceforth referred to as Afro-Germans), who are confronted daily with the vestiges and consequences of colonialism and its inherent racism. The equation of Germans with Whiteness remains an exclusivist and thus excluding perspective on who Germans are.

THE LONG SHADOW OF GERMAN COLONIALISM

In this regard Afro-Germans have a tale to tell—and it's not a pleasant one.[118] While most of their personal accounts now available remain largely confined to the West German decades up to 1990, more studies are gradually emerging that look more closely at the situation of Africans in the former GDR.[119] Not that this is of any comfort: evidence suggests that, despite a markedly different official narrative, the experiences of Afro-Germans in East Germany were often not fundamentally different from those in West Germany and they were hardly protected at all from racist experiences. The partial racism in the GDR, manifest in the treatment of Black students, migrant workers and Afro-Germans in daily life, was in striking contradiction to the official policy of international solidarity with African struggles for liberation, which included support for the US Black Power movement.[120]

The first encounters of Afro-Germans with the discriminatory racist (and cultural) exclusivity of post-World War II Germany were mainly those of children of Black American soldiers of the Allied forces. These *Besatzungskinder* (war children, or less euphemistic children of occupation),[121] as they were called, are estimated to have numbered around 400,000 in total (of whom a much smaller number had Black fathers). They—and their mothers too—were ostracised and shamed. In the main they were a fatherless generation, at times also abandoned by their mothers, and, if not targeted for racist abuse, forced into invisibility.[122] Only when West Germany gradually became a welcome member of the Western alliance as the Cold War intensified in the 1960s did the search for the fathers become possible and, in some cases, bear fruit. Bärbel Kampmann (1946–1999) met her Afro-American father when she was 40 years of age.[123] Ika (Erika) Hügel-Marshall (1947–2022) met hers at the age of 46.[124] By then she had become a pioneer in the Afro-German movement.[125] Many of this generation, in so far as we know, have been denied the opportunity for self-discovery and a confident and strong identity necessary to survive.[126] The failure was not theirs, but that of the majority or mainstream society, which unfeelingly denied them a deserved, respected and equal position within a plural society. Instead, many different historical and social as well as cultural identities and forms of expression were ruthlessly excluded and silenced for generations.[127] The colonial divide between coloniser and colonised under the control of a "master race" lived on, sacrificing diversity to a cleansed and pseudo-sanitised uniformity.

Black German football players were among the first to enter more prominently the West German public sphere. Erwin Kostedde was, in 1974, the first Afro-German to wear the shirt of the national team on the soccer field. After that, several Afro-German women and men represented Germany in international competitions, but they remained targets of racist abuse and continued to be confronted with racial discrimination,[128] as were Black players in the various German leagues.[129] Besides a few men and women in the sporting world and in the entertainment industry, Black visibility gained some ground in politics, arts and culture only from the mid-1980s, while racist treatment also gradually—if only in peripheral areas—became more recognised as an issue.[130]

In 1985 the first meeting of Afro-Germans to organise themselves took place, and resulted in the formation of the Black German Initiative (Initiative Schwarzer Deutscher/ISD).[131] The mid-1980s also saw the beginnings of a powerful Black German women's movement, which gained institutional form in ADEFRA (ADEFRA e. V.—Schwarze Frauen in Deutschland, or Black Women in Germany),[132] inspired by exchanges with the African American writer and feminist Audre Lorde (1934–1992) in Berlin. She also contributed a message of greetings to the first, path-breaking book on Afro-German feminism, published with the title *Farbe bekennen* (which can best be rendered as "confessing" or "claiming colour"). Its publication was tantamount to liberation from the bonds of silence. As a scathingly honest engagement with Black history and experiences, it revealed, as Lorde put it, "an invisible bloody childhood … as stained or imperfect Germans".[133] This pioneering intervention was based on the understanding that the common denominator in their lives was not a biological but a social factor: living in a White German society.[134] The volume signalled not only the dismissal of White supremacy. In it the women also laid stubborn claim to being part of German society and belonging. While Afro-Germans are excluded from the consciousness of most

Germans, who regard them as non-existent, they are, after all, at home in Germany: home understood as an inner point of reference and a feeling that one is part of it.[135] Not by coincidence or accident, this book has become a classic of self-assertion.[136] Since the time of its publication, Afro-Germans have been on the move.[137]

Several biographical accounts have given voice to the experiences of Afro-Germans and added to their claims for acknowledgement and recognition.[138] This has marked a shift in their search for identity through literature,[139] bordering on a "poetry of survival".[140] But it was not survival for all, as the tragic story of May Opitz (1960–1996) illustrates. Changing her name to May Ayim in acknowledgement of her African roots, she was at the forefront of writing essays and poetry.[141] "Her writing was not merely a component of her politics, but it was her politics."[142] She took her own life on 9 August 1996 in Kreuzberg (part of former West Berlin), where she had lived since 1984. In this district a riverside road along the Spree was renamed May-Ayim-Ufer in 2010.[143] As a "champion of People of Colour", she is included in a list that recognises a hundred outstanding people of democracy.[144] Her legacy remains alive through numerous publications in her honour.[145]

During recent years, Afro-Germans have made further advances in public life. As has been noted: "Due in part to a shift in scholarly focus but also to the publication of new memoirs written by Afro-Germans, historians are increasingly successful at recovering the voices of black Germans."[146] They gained visibility in the political sphere as members of the German parliament, the European parliament and parliaments in the German federal states, as well as at community levels, and have formed the Association of Elected Officials of African Descent. At the end of June 2022, Aminata Touré became the first Afro-German member of cabinet in a federal state government, when she was appointed in the new CDU–Green Party coalition in Schleswig-Holstein as Minister for Social Affairs, Youth, Family, Senior Citizens, Integration and Equality. In April 2023 Joe Chialo of the CDU became the Berlin Senator for Culture and Social Cohesion. Afro-Germans have also become recognised in their own right as media journalists and as actors in television productions. They take part in decolonial activities and

(POST-)COLONIAL (WEST) GERMANY

other public awareness campaigns through their work in academia, museums, arts and culture.[147]

A particularly noteworthy initiative is the pioneering joint project Decolonial Memory Culture in the City, started in Berlin in 2020. Funded by the Berlin Senate and the German Federal Cultural Foundation, it is an alliance of Afro-German and Afro-diasporic agencies and postcolonial initiatives and the Berlin City Museum Foundation.[148] They are jointly engaged in the task of promoting critical colonial memory to create greater public awareness by dismantling colonial-racist structures and legacies in the public sphere.[149] Among the significant outcomes has been the collaborative project *zurückGESCHAUT | looking back*.[150] This exhibition opened in October 2017 in the local Museum Treptow. It gave a face to most of the 106 individuals brought from overseas as human exhibits for display at the first German Colonial Exhibition in Berlin's Treptower Park from May to mid-October 1896. Many of them had not been aware of the plan to display them as colonial objects in a human zoo.[151] The initial exhibition of 2017 had several shortcomings, and consequently the photographic portraits of the 106 children, women and men from Africa and Oceania were revised and further research was undertaken into their biographies to highlight their resistance.[152] Additional information was also obtained on the background and context of the colonial exhibition. In late 2021 *ZurückGESCHAUT* re-opened with a new design and concept as a permanent exhibition at the Museum Treptow and has since then received wide recognition and praise.[153]

Despite greater public visibility, Black Germans (not to mention People of Colour more generally as well as the victims of other racist forms of discrimination)[154] still face an uphill battle to overcome daily discrimination, racial profiling and physical attacks because they may look different from other Germans. But Germans they are, and they contribute to a Germany that is more than just a White society with roots in a colonial past. In 2017, a report by a Working Group of the United Nations Human Rights Council presented this sobering reality:

> While people of African descent are a diverse group, their daily lives are marked by racism, negative stereotypes and structural

racism. They are targeted and are victims of racist violence and hate crimes. They fear for their safety and avoid certain places as they believe they will be attacked. They are subjected to racial discrimination by their classmates, teachers and workmates and to structural racism by the Government and criminal justice system. In Germany, negative stereotypes of people of African descent remain commonplace. These stereotypes lead to misguided and misinformed perceptions of people of African descent. Despite the gravity of the situation, they are not officially recognized as a group particularly exposed to racism.[155]

The report's recommendations start by contextualising its approach, pointing to the long-term impact of colonial history and the Nazi regime, which has not been properly addressed:

> Germany should recall its role in the history of colonization, enslavement, exploitation and genocide of Africans, and should make reparations to address the continued impact of those acts. … The Working Group emphasizes that the history of racism in Europe should also be understood through an analysis of the events preceding the Second World War, taking into account the correct sequence of historical events.[156]

However, acknowledging the history of Africans and Afro-Germans and giving room to Black voices in Germany should not be confused with active advocacy. As the report of the Working Group pointed out:

> Civil society sources have stated that research in African studies by German academics could, and should, play an eminent role in the analysis of the causal chains that seem to perpetuate racism and racial discrimination towards people of African descent and in highlighting the deficiencies of strategies for containing these social ills that have proved to be ineffective in the past. The situation of people of African descent is currently treated in the context of postcolonial studies, which aim to identify the colonial roots of the persisting discrimination and unbalanced power relations, for example as manifested in language, but not to improve these relations.[157]

(POST-)COLONIAL (WEST) GERMANY

At the end of 2023 the Committee on the Elimination of Racial Discrimination within the Office of the United Nations High Commissioner for Human Rights once again expressed concern "about the structural discrimination and stigmatization against people of African descent".[158] The task remains to embark on vigorous anti-racist political struggles in Germany (and elsewhere) today. This is even more necessary in view of what is almost a crusade by the extreme right. We should not shy away from the fatal attacks they launch on all that they consider a threat to exclusivist White supremacy.

Reactionary Revisionism: The Case of the AfD

Postcolonial civil society and not least the increasing presence of proactive Afro-Germans in public life have made visible inroads into German provincialism and its isolationist views that can only contemplate a "culturally homogeneous" society. Such gains have been met with increasing pushback by White supremacists. They work hand in hand with the populist right, dismissing anything not to their political liking as "woke culture" while themselves resorting to the practices of McCarthyism. This is most pronounced in attacks on postcolonial efforts to bring colonial history into the public realm and to provide adequate forms of memory and commemoration. These efforts are damned as antisemitic for downplaying the singularity of the Holocaust.[159]

At the head of this rearguard action is the AfD (Alternative für Deutschland), which has secured a presence in the German parliament as well as in most of the parliaments of the German federal states. By the end of 2023 it had made increasing inroads in the support for existing parties in terms of both numbers of potential voters and accepted mindsets. With Nazi sympathisers in their ranks, the new right-wing White supremacist reincarnations of megalomaniac ideas and imperial fantasies have emerged on the political scene in full force. Their approach is multidimensional, using various themes and pursuing several agendas in addressing different audiences. As Jonathan Hyslop observes: "Some AfD leaders use rhetoric about contemporary Africa that is shockingly obviously evocative of Nazism, while other opinions appear, superficially, quite 'developmentalist' and sensible. ... The neo-Nazi and libertarian faces of the AfD ultimately justify the same policies: shutting down immigration, ending development aid and opposing multiculturalism."[160]

Having discovered colonial history as a contested battlefield, the AfD recycles the old canard of a guilt complex or *Schuldkult* (cult of guilt), which, as shown in chapter 3, was first successfully tried out as the *koloniale Schuldlüge* (colonial-guilt lie) during the Weimar Republic and the Nazi regime.[161] As Hyslop suggests:

> continuities in the German right's mobilisation of the memory of the Empire, between 1919 and the present, are striking. ... Right-wing populisms build an artificial past, for a representative present, but they do not construct it out of nothing. As the contemporary ultra-right works to create an imagined return to a better age, the Empire that was abolished in 1919 lives on.[162]

On 11 December 2019 the AfD hosted the North American scholar Bruce Gilley for a public lecture in its rooms in the German parliament. His presentation bore the title "The Balance of German Colonialism: Why the Germans Do Not Have to Apologise and Definitely Do Not Have to Pay for the Colonial Era!" Gilley obtained dubious fame in 2017 with an article in which he argued "The Case for Colonialism".[163] Responding to his critics in 2022, he maintained: "If, after due consideration of evidence and logic, a scholar believes that colonialism was an unambiguously 'good thing' in most times and places, then he needs to begin by making that case itself."[164] In his 2019 AfD lecture, he claimed to be competent to discuss the issues in the following way:

> I am not a historian, much less a historian of colonialism. I am a social scientist, and I have come to the conclusion that very little history on German colonialism meets the most basic standards of social scientific research as normally understood. It is ideological, biased, and often self-contradictory. So my main qualification for writing about German colonial history is that I am not a historian of German colonialism.[165]

(POST-)COLONIAL (WEST) GERMANY

Having established his qualifications in this way, he moved straight on to German South West Africa—and demonstrated his deep knowledge by making the factual error that the territory also included "parts of present-day Botswana". He tackled the "genocidal bull" by its horns when stating, "Unless we confront this head-on and get it right, everything we say about the rest of German colonialism will always come with the riposte 'Well, what about the Herero?'"[166] His answer was not meant to be satirical: "let's remind ourselves that Southwest Africa was about 2% of the German colonial population (measured in terms of people-years). Just logically, imagine we conclude that Germany did a really horrible job with this 2% and a superb job with the other 98%. What would our overall conclusion be about German colonialism?"[167]

Without disputing that the Ovaherero were reduced in numbers by 75% and the Nama by 50% because of the German annihilation strategy, he put the blame entirely on General Lothar von Trotha as the military commander and thereby individualised the root cause of the genocide: "Germans and German policy were not genocidal: Trotha was."[168] His unreserved praise song in honour of the German civilising mission ends with the appeal:

> German memory and writing on colonialism continues to suffer from a post-1918 ideological indoctrination campaign redolent of the worse aspects of totalitarianism. Having variously allied itself with totalitarian movements of the left (Soviets) and right (Nazis), this scholarly industry continues to get a free pass and to be accepted as truthful and just. It is neither. Germany's reassertion of its classical liberal and Western identity must begin with a rejection of the dogmatic and totalitarian ideology of anti-colonialism.[169]

His reasoning was in line with an AfD draft resolution, circulated to parliament on the same day, to address the German colonial era in what they call a cultural-politically differentiated way.[170] Referring directly to a controversial statement by the personal representative for Africa of the German Chancellor,[171] the resolution argued that German colonialism contributed to the liberation of the African continent from archaic structures. It then recognised (following Gilley's line) that the war by German colonial troops in

South West Africa led to excessive cruelties, but denied any systematic or intentional genocide by putting the blame only on Trotha. Such personalisation devolves guilt by attributing responsibility to a single individual, not to the system.[172] While the AfD recognises the suffering of the victims of colonial wars, it denies any obligation for compensation. Instead, the amount of development aid given to Namibia since its independence is considered as impressive evidence that Germany has lived up to its historical responsibility towards its former colony. The resolution therefore regarded it as justified to counteract the growing amnesia by spreading awareness through commemoration and cultural-political means of enlightenment. For this it proposed that a federal foundation be established not only to address German colonial history but also to make it known in a differentiated way. It then called on the federal government to develop a commemorative culture that brought to the fore the positive and beneficial aspects of the German colonial era; to work towards a differentiated view of that era; to promote such perspectives in school curricula; to decisively oppose demands for reparations; to refuse demands for the restitution of cultural goods from the colonies on the grounds that colonial times were "criminal"; and to appeal to communities in the federal states to retain those street names which memorialised colonial personages and places.

Importantly, in this draft resolution the AfD sought to claim for its own the term "amnesia", which hitherto had been applied with the opposite meaning by those critical of colonial apologetics.[173] In its justification for the draft resolution, it unashamedly appropriated studies that had a different (arguably ambiguous) intention, for its own purposes.[174] It attacked "cultural Marxist inspired post- and de-colonialism" and bemoaned what it saw as a paradigm shift since German unification, in this way creating the impression that critical colonial-historical studies had since then been indoctrinated by East German ideology and now simply echoed it. It accused the "left spectre" of having imposed its "normative interpretation of the past" as the dominant view and of having turned those sympathetic to the idea of a colonial civilising mission into victims. The demands for the restitution of cultural artefacts were disqualified as "inquisitory logic" aimed at the "removal of inalienable property".[175]

(POST-)COLONIAL (WEST) GERMANY

On 12 June 2020 the AfD tabled another draft resolution seeking to restrict the restitution of cultural artefacts taken from colonial contexts.[176] It argued that these deserve to be conserved in the cultural memory of humankind, which can only be secured under the caring and professional protection of German museums. Restitution, in contrast, would risk their loss to humanity owing to presumed neglect. Such restitution, it claimed, was promoted by a rhetoric of guilt, orchestrated against the colonial era. The resolution asked that Germany should officially counter the demands by categorically stating that no legally valid claims exist for the return of looted objects. It bemoaned the consequent contamination of all colonial history as a crime against humanity, as a result of the hyper-moralistic demands for restitution.

Following the German–Nigerian agreement for the restitution of the Benin Bronzes and ahead of the return of the first twenty of them (see chapter 1), the AfD submitted another draft resolution to parliament at the end of September 2022.[177] It followed seamlessly the earlier initiative in substance and language, replicating parts of its passages. It warned that if the return of artefacts from the Benin kingdom became reality (which it did a few months later), there was the risk of further demands for restitution. These, it claimed, have no legally valid basis and should, with very few exceptions, be dismissed. To judge the merits of such claims, an independent advisory body should be set up to scrutinise each case and artefacts should only be returned if the panel reached such a recommendation. The expert panel to be established should bear the name of Gustav Nachtigal. According to the AfD, his name has been wrongly removed in the recent renaming of streets and places. The naming of the panel in his honour would therefore be an act of historical justice by recognising his qualities.[178] In its reasoning the resolution blamed the media and, increasingly so, politicians for using guiding concepts such as colonial violence, stolen art, and colonial trauma to shape public opinion and frame the story as one in which the cultural heritage of kind, peace-loving peoples fell prey to brutal, looting colonisers.

While the AfD resolutions have not received the necessary parliamentary majority, their influence should not be underestimated.

They receive support in the wider public apart from direct party members and followers. The almost iconic status of Gilley in these circles speaks for itself. His appearance in the parliamentary seminar in December 2019 marked his entry into the club of German patriots who have no problem in discrediting born-and-bred German people of colour as not being truly German, while at the same time embracing like-minded people from very different corners of the world. Encouraged by being welcomed with open arms by "the aptly named Alternative for Germany (AfD), the largest opposition party in the Bundestag",[179] Gilley expanded his presentation into a monograph that was published first in German.[180] He still follows this career path as an advocate of the good German colonialists. Styling himself in a follow-up paper as a martyr and victim of "Woke mobs",[181] he summarised his "profound scholarly dissent from the reigning and strictly policed anti-colonial orthodoxy" in the following way:

> German colonialism was both inherently ethical as well as ethical in practice, in every place where it was found. It arose from natural processes of human endeavor, violated no formal or informal laws in doing so, and found a ready welcome in all places. Its initiation through the Berlin conferences marked it as ethical from the start because of the moral compass established by the Berlin agreements. ... The combination of rule-following, justificatory ethics, and consent-based rule that characterized the German colonial experience marks it as a high-point of the European colonial achievement.[182]

At the same time, one should recognise that debates in Germany about crimes committed in the empire's colonies and about the restitution of cultural artefacts have—thanks to a proactive civil society—made considerable inroads in the public sphere. This may be one of the more positive reasons for explaining the current colonial revisionism of right-wing populists. But it is also a reminder that the uphill battle is far from over. While postcolonial initiatives have made significant advances in creating awareness of historical injustices dating back to the era before the Nazi regime, colonial revisionism and White supremacy in combination with anti-migrant xenophobia have responded with forceful attacks in Germany as well as in other former imperial countries. Significantly, revisionist thinking is not only the preserve of right-wing extremists such as the AfD. Some opinion makers have reversed their positions and backtracked, abandoning earlier anti-colonial positions. Among these is the renowned journalist Bartholomäus Grill. He discovered the writings of Hinrich Schneider-Waterberg (1931–2022), a "Southwester" farmer and amateur historian, who dismissed the genocide in German South West Africa wholesale. Grill gave him prominence by elevating him in the influential *Der Spiegel* to the status of a "crown witness".[183] Hardly by accident, Grill is amply referred to in the AfD resolution submitted in December 2019 to the German parliament.

Light at the End of the Tunnel?[184]

The significant inroads that postcolonial initiatives have succeeded in making into the public discourse since the turn of the century are by no means secure. As we have just seen, there has been a backlash from colonial revisionism and White supremacy, which have reared their ugly heads, in parliament as well. Until recently, colonial-apologetic voices could occasionally still be heard at the highest levels of government: in October 2018 the German Chancellor's personal representative for Africa, Günter Nooke (in office until early 2022), declared in an interview—which the AfD was happy to quote—that colonialism helped Africa to be freed from "archaic structures" and that "the Cold War has done Africa more harm than the colonial era".[185] Opinions of a similar nature remain alive in other spheres of society. Nevertheless, the revisionist forays cannot obliterate the impact of a growing, if still minority, postcolonial mindset in the German public.

An increasing number of mostly localised initiatives have raised awareness about colonial relics in daily life, such as street names and memorials.[186] There are also several websites run by activists, which have diversified the choices of those who are looking for relevant information on the internet. A first sign of progress was the number and range of civil society activities in both Namibia and

THE LONG SHADOW OF GERMAN COLONIALISM

Germany marking the centenary of the genocide in Namibia in 2004.[187] In the fields of scholarship and popular non-fiction, several collected volumes have since then documented efforts to promote critical reflections on how to come to terms with the German colonial past.[188] Similarly, the growing number of local and regional initiatives are indicative of the increased interest in present-day references to colonial history.[189] This important engagement still depends to a large extent on voluntary commitment and remains precarious.[190] But thanks to such local initiatives, the renaming of streets and other public places that once honoured colonial stalwarts provides a sign of visible progress.

German postcolonial initiatives and other civil society agencies demand that colonial atrocities committed by the German empire should enter public memory in forms like the Holocaust memorial[191] in central Berlin, as well as through more local, community forms of remembrance. So far, these efforts have largely been ignored by the German government. But some headway has been made in a few municipalities and federal states. As explained in more detail elsewhere, the initiative Decolonize Berlin got under way in 2020.[192] As a publicly funded civil society network, it represents a broad alliance of Black, diasporic, postcolonial and other initiatives.[193] The federal state of Baden-Württemberg in 2019 organised special activities within a "Namibia Initiative" in the academic, educational and cultural fields.[194] Also noteworthy is an initiative by the South Schleswig Voters' Association, a smaller party in the parliament of the federal state of Schleswig-Holstein, which as early as 2005 recognised colonialism as part of regional history.[195]

Rehabilitation of Manga Bell and Ngoso Din

A special initiative worthy of note as setting an example is the campaign for the rehabilitation of Manga Bell and Ngoso Din, whose roles and subsequent execution were described in chapter 3. On 8 August 2014 an article in *Die Tageszeitung* recalled their hanging a hundred years previously.[196] The Green Party MP Hans-Christian Ströbele asked the government in late October 2014, with reference to the article, why it had not addressed the crimes of the German colonial power in Cameroon and why Germany did not rehabilitate the victims of judicial murder by an Act of parliament.[197] The answer by Michael Roth as Minister of State in the Foreign Ministry on 5 November 2014 was rather evasive and tried to avoid responsibility.[198] He declared that the issue was in the first place a task for historical researchers, seemingly unaware that by then colonial history published in German had already largely accomplished this task. He further explained that the Duala in Cameroon had till then not demanded the rehabilitation of Manga Bell. The Foreign Ministry, he added, had made some financial contributions to a local cultural project, which would remember the fate (*Schicksal*) of Manga Bell. There would also be events held in his honour on the occasion of the centenary of his death (this was said three months after the date had passed).

Ströbele in a follow-up then enquired if the government was willing to initiate a process of rehabilitation or issue a statement of rehabilitation in the German parliament and to the Duala, independent of any formal request by them. Roth then insisted that such a request would be necessary and decisive and repeated that the government was in contact with the descendants of those executed, that it would participate in the festivities and support them financially. Ströbele then referred to the apology extended by Minister Heidemarie Wieczorek-Zeul in 2004 on the occasion of the centenary commemoration of the annihilation of the Ovaherero at the Waterberg (see chapter 5) as an example of how best the matter could be dealt with. In a final response, Roth promised to raise the matter with the Foreign Minister. Despite this promise and the publication of an entire monograph on the subject only a few months later,[199] the matter remained dormant, notwithstanding occasional reports in the German media (often without any mention of Ngoso Din).

Finally, the Rothenbaum Museum—Cultures and Arts of the World (MARKK) in Hamburg drew fresh attention to the execution through its exhibition *Hey Hamburg, kennst Du Duala Manga Bell? / Hey Hamburg, do you know Duala Manga Bell?*[200] Its opening in April 2021 was followed by a privately initiated campaign. After months of internal consultation, a group of eight people released a public petition for the rehabilitation of Manga Bell and Ngoso Din in early 2022. The group included Princess Marilyn Douala Manga Bell and Jean-Pierre Félix-Eyoum, two direct descendants.[201] This led to a minor interpellation by the Left Party at the end of April 2022, which obtained a written answer on 13 May 2022.[202] Asked if it knew whether the legal categorisation of colonial injustices would still be glossed over or legitimised by the application of the principle of intertemporality (see more on this concept in chapter 5), the government responded that it did not share the underlying view of the executions. It then stated that in the course of dealing with German colonial history it would initiate independent academic studies and then take steps in the light of their results. Government then conceded having knowledge of the petition co-signed by Princess Marilyn Douala Manga Bell. It thereafter referred to the significance of matters of identity in postcolonial societies when dealing with the past, which would make it important to obtain a request for rehabilitation. At the same time, it confirmed it was committed to a reappraisal of colonialism and to continued exchanges with Princess Manga Bell, whose activities it supported. Finally, asked if Minister of State Michael Roth had, as he had promised in 2014, raised the matter with then Foreign Minister Frank-Walter Steinmeier (who after 2017 became Germany's President), the government declared it was not obliged to follow up on internal and external communications, but said it seemed from official files that such a conversation had not taken place.

This renewed evasiveness, which shied away from any firm commitments, provoked several critical responses in the media.[203] At the same time, Princess Marilyn, great-granddaughter of Manga Bell, was a guest of the Goethe Institute in Germany at the end of May 2022. This provided her with an opportunity for an informal meeting with the Minister of State in the Foreign Ministry, Katja Keul. According to the Princess, Keul was well informed about the petition and showed a willingness to find a solution.[204] While since then there has been no official rehabilitation until early 2024, the initiatives had several outcomes. On the occasion of a visit to Cameroon for cultural events in early November 2022, Katja Keul

(POST-)COLONIAL (WEST) GERMANY

visited the site of Manga Bell's and Ngoso Din's execution. In a well-prepared speech, she declared among other things:

> Colonialism was nothing but systematic exploitation.
>
> Resources were plundered and borders drawn indiscriminately.
>
> As the German Government, we are determined to face up to this chapter of our history and to put an end to the shortcomings in coming to grips with it. ...
>
> We therefore want to work together to explore ways to commemorate King Rudolf Manga Bell in a dignified way in Germany and in Cameroon.
>
> This is why I have come here to listen to you today.
>
> I want to hear what expectations you have of efforts to come to grips with the past.
>
> You laid the foundations for this when you visited me at the Federal Foreign Office, Princess Marylin [sic]. I would like to thank you for this.
>
> ... We have to admit that we know shockingly little about jurisprudence in the former colonies.
>
> We will therefore set out to research this part of colonial rule, to better identify systematic injustice and to call this out clearly.[205]

In parallel, postcolonial initiatives have achieved significant results in the renaming of public places and streets, some of which now bear the name Bell. On 7 October 2022, the city of Ulm proclaimed the Manga Bell Square next to the old court building and the state attorney's office, close to the school he attended. The occasion was honoured by the presence of a delegation of dignitaries from Cameroon, headed by King Jean-Yves Eboumbou Douala Bell. Also in attendance was the Minister of Justice of the federal state of Baden-Württemberg.[206] On 2 December 2022, the Nachtigalplatz (this was named after the colonial official) in Berlin-Mitte was renamed the Rudolf and Emily[207] Manga Bell Square.[208] In attendance were King Jean-Yves Eboumbou Douala Bell and Princess Marilyn Douala Manga Bell. A long-drawn-out battle that lasted over a decade thus ended with celebrations and a few protests.²⁰⁹ Aalen, the southern German town where Manga Bell attended school before continuing his studies in Ulm, also decided to recognise this history by proclaiming a Manga Bell Square.²¹⁰ Located in front of the school he attended between 1891 and 1896, it was officially inaugurated on 2 July 2023, again in the presence of King Eboumbou Douala Bell, Cameroon's ambassador to Germany and several other dignitaries. Notably, for the occasion the city of Aalen published a teaching manual with documentary material for schools.²¹¹ But the official rehabilitation of Manga Bell and Ngoso Din, who were hanged in a perversion of justice, remained pending. Another petition, initiated on 20 September 2022 and this time directly addressed to parliament, showed that such demands still do not receive much public support. By the time of its closing date of 27 December 2022, the petition had garnered just 1,025 co-signatories within the space of three months.²¹² While there may be some light at the end of the tunnel, the struggle is far from over. The question of when and how the two victims of a perversion of justice would finally be officially rehabilitated²¹³ had not been answered by the end of 2023.

Parliamentary Debates on Colonialism

In line with growing awareness, public exchanges and even policy statements about the restitution of cultural artefacts and human remains have considerably shifted towards a more open engagement with the legacy of the colonial era.²¹⁴ The response by the AfD documented in the previous section confirms this shift. While in 2011, on the occasion of the restitution of the first batch of human remains to Namibia, the German government all but marginalised the event,²¹⁵ more recent debates in parliament have been marked by conservative deputies in particular proudly referring to these and similar achievements. Except for the AfD, there are hardly any longer denialist approaches towards the genocide in Namibia or attempts to counter Namibian demands for reparations with promises of development cooperation, which had made up the arguments particularly of conservatives and liberals only a few years earlier.²¹⁶ On 19 November 2020 parliament debated a whole series of motions on how to deal with the German colonial past. Except for the AfD (as we have seen), a remarkable consensus could be observed among all parties.[217] While speakers of the Left Party criticised the conservatives for a lack of consistency, there was virtually common agreement about the need to seriously address the colonial legacy and to investigate thoroughly the restitution of looted cultural goods in German museums, which had occasioned the debate. One might consider this a major success after years of patient and insistent work by various postcolonial initiatives, mainly based in civil society; but, on the other hand, a very different factor may have contributed towards this surprising unanimity: the onslaught from the right.

Still, even within the "consensus" stressed by conservative deputy Markus Koob,[218] one can recognise clear differences among the parties. Whereas the conservatives and the liberals, much in keeping with their former approach, stressed the achievements of German policy (even though on a clearly different terrain from that before), the Green and the Left parties in particular insisted that there remained unfinished business; they pointed to the need for a proactive policy of remembrance, including bolstering the long-term work of postcolonial initiatives;[219] questioned the adherence to the framework of international law;[220] and called for an immediate apology not only for the genocide in Namibia but for colonial crimes more generally, along with a reconsideration of the broader framework of present-day trade relations with former colonies.[221] Remarkably, a conservative voice stressed the need for "empathy with the victims", which ought to motivate a dialogue with African states in a spirit of true partnership.[222]

"Internal Liberation"?

Speaking at the 75th commemoration of Victory in Europe (VE) Day in May 2020, President Frank-Walter Steinmeier called this a day of liberation imposed by Allied military forces, including the Soviets. But, as he stated, "internal liberation", the coming to terms with the legacy of dictatorship and, above all, the horrific mass crimes of the Nazis, remained "a long and painful process".[223]

Steinmeier's plea to "accept our historic responsibility" met with broad acceptance. "Internal liberation" had come some way—leaving aside comparatively weak statements by the AfD. Even though this attitude and this practice are viewed by many as exemplary, it has some grave shortcomings. German memory politics and practices are not quite as exemplary as much of German mainstream public discourse would like to make us believe. In fact, engagement with the violent past, particularly of the first half of the 20th century, is an ongoing and painful as well as conflictual process. That this process encompasses crimes and victim groups that had previously been silenced only underlines the magnitude of the task. "Internal liberation", as a goal stated in President Steinmeier's VE Day speech, remains hard work on the long road ahead. It means conflict and pain, and it must never end. In the words of Steinmeier: "Remembrance never ends. There can be no deliverance from our past. For without remembrance we lose our future. ... For 'liberation' is never complete, and it is not something that we can just experience passively. It challenges us actively, every day anew."[224]

The battles are far from over. What David Andress has diagnosed in the case of other states applies to Germany too: "there are entire bookshops' worth of good historical work, whole departments of bold young historians (and some grizzled old veterans) who have been telling their students, and anyone else who would listen, how it really was for at least a generation. The problem remains what to do when people don't want to listen, or learn."[225]

Concern has been expressed that in their focus on Germany's overseas colonies, local postcolonial efforts might obliterate Germany's (post-)imperial history within Europe. Such a tendency, it is feared, risks limiting the engagement with racism and coloniality to "Black communities" and dealing with colonialism as a kind of special, separate subject.[226] But, as has been conceded, there is no clear answer as to how commemorative work should look and what forms it should take. The best form of commemoration, therefore, may be a never-ending debate about how such memory work should be pursued and the expansion of such discussion into the arena of the post-imperial.[227]

5

GERMANY AND NAMIBIA

The effects and consequences of colonial warfare waged by the German army, euphemistically called "protection troops" (*Schutztruppe*), and subsequent administrative measures introduced in the territory called German South West Africa between 1904 and 1908 meet the definition of genocide and have been officially recognised as such. This chapter develops the earlier historical overview further, by providing more details on the nature and consequences of the war for the affected communities. It then examines subsequent engagements with the colonial legacy. From the late 1960s, as we shall see, colonial rule in German South West Africa became a subject of scholarly interest in both West and East Germany, albeit there were different government perspectives and public discourses on imperial Germany's colonial past (see chapter 4).

This chapter first recapitulates the events of the war that ended in genocide, and then presents an overview of the debates on the atrocities and their introduction to a wider German public, finally resulting in the official admission of genocide by the German government in 2015. A summary is offered of the processes surrounding the restitution of human remains and cultural artefacts, which started in 2011. The last sections are devoted to the bilateral German–Namibian negotiations since 2015 on how to come to terms with this past, before their preliminary outcome, initialled by the two governments' special representatives in May 2021, is critically assessed. This remained controversial, and the official ratification of a modified version of the agreement was still pending at the end of 2023. But there are signs that both governments seek closure despite continued protest and the rejection of the nature of the negotiations and their result. It is finally argued that what initially seemed to be—more by accident than by deliberate political will—a step in the right direction became entangled in the pitfalls of damage control on the German side. Even if officially adopted, such agreement remains, as a state-to-state affair without the involvement of both countries' peoples, far from true reconciliation. But before turning to these matters, we need to reflect on how to position scholarly advocacy in cases like this where descendants of the perpetrators of the crime deal with the colonial past.

An Initial Caveat

Dealing with any past—and especially a colonial one—is a question of perspectives. As Britta Schilling has pointed out, "incorporating non-European perspectives … remains one of the most important tasks for historians of German colonialism, both in research and in a wider continuing engagement with the colonial past".[1] This is even more of a challenge when, in addition to a general engagement with the past, one has to address such crimes as the genocide in South West Africa and similar extremes of violence elsewhere. In the context of critical engagements with colonialism in Germany, postcolonial theory has since the late 1990s strongly advocated a fundamental change in the perspectives and methods of narratives to deconstruct colonial forms of knowledge and history.[2] As a consequence one needs ask whether colonial discourses have really been transcended or abandoned even in Western anti-colonial counter-narratives. Academic writing remains largely (and often uncritically) confined to standardised forms anchored in Western traditions, without being aware of or self-critically reflecting on these limitations.

Nonetheless, this effort to find a more adequate form of engagement with the colonial past and present is similar to that of other scholars and activists raised in and influenced by specific social contexts and whose mindsets are moulded by their own experiences and perspectives. Transcending these and looking at the world through the eyes of others is not only a huge challenge. It borders on a mission impossible and risks creating new omnipotent claims reminiscent of White supremacy. An eagerness to comply with such a shift of perspectives easily becomes patronising or paternalistic through the claim to speak on behalf of those who continue to remain silent or unheard. It risks ending—despite noble motives of a different kind—in a form of whitewashing. Agency has a different meaning.

This chapter no doubt suffers from these limitations in the absence of accessible, recorded counter-narratives.[3] Scholarship has to humbly accept its limitations in representing "other" views. As Marion Wallace warns: "the genocide debate can also be a hindrance to inquiry, and, above all, to situating the Namibian War as an event in *Namibian*, rather than German history".[4] While this is a necessary caveat, it should not prevent those confronted with the consequences of this history in Germany from addressing them in an effort to come to terms with this past. After all, it was an event that would not have taken place without German colonial intervention, which had long-term implications for Germans back in Europe too. This merits a critical engagement by German or Western scholars so as to create awareness of the consequences and help deal with them. Decolonisation (especially of mindsets) requires engagement by the descendants of those involved on all sides.

Such challenges and responsibilities on the part of the colonisers should not excuse us from creating space for the voices of those whose experiences our Western perspectives and forms of communication cannot articulate. In the case of Namibian–German history and its treatment in the present, it therefore seems appropriate to begin this chapter with a local voice: "We cannot free ourselves from the past until both the victims and villains are atoned with Germany's imperial past in Namibia. The past is like the shade of a thorn tree that covers a pile of thorns for those stepping on it … It is like a weeping grave of an angry ancestor."[5]

THE LONG SHADOW OF GERMAN COLONIALISM

The Historical Record

Much has been researched and published on German colonial rule in what became on 21 March 1990 the sovereign Republic of Namibia. This chapter limits itself to a summary of the consequences of the warfare conducted during the German settler-colonial occupation. The prelude and aftermath of the military encounters starting in 1904 were presented in the overview in chapter 3 and are covered more adequately in several other studies.[6] Here, a short description of the genocidal warfare and its consequences serves as a point of departure.

In January 1904, in a surprise attack Ovaherero forces killed more than a hundred German farmers in an attempt to forestall further encroachment on their land and resist their subjugation under foreign rule. Following an order of Paramount Chief Samuel Maharero, they spared the lives of missionaries, women and children as well as other Whites. Germany responded with a massive mobilisation of troops and military equipment, which were dispatched to the colony. General Lothar von Trotha, who had established a track record of ruthlessness in colonial warfare in East Africa and China, became the military commander of the operations. The entries in his diary, finally published in 2024 after decades of refusal by his family to allow access, reveal a genocidal mindset.[7] In August 1904 the war escalated into a series of military encounters around the Waterberg in the heartland of the Ovaherero. Unable to defeat the Germans, the Ovaherero tried to avoid further clashes. On making their escape, they sought refuge partly in the adjacent Omaheke semi-desert. German soldiers cordoned off the area to prevent those fleeing from clandestinely returning and seeking shelter elsewhere in the country. Trotha issued an order on 2 October 1904, declaring that the Ovaherero were no longer subjects under German rule and were not allowed to surrender. The order was rescinded in December of the same year by the Kaiser under pressure from public protests within the German empire.[8] It declared, among other things:

> I, the Great General of the German Soldiers, address this letter to the Herero people. The Herero are no longer considered German

subjects. They have murdered, stolen, cut off ears, noses and other parts from wounded soldiers, and now refuse to fight on out of cowardice. ... The Herero people will have to leave the country. Otherwise I shall force them to do so by means of guns. Within the German boundaries, every Herero, whether found armed or unarmed, with or without cattle, will be shot. I shall not accept any more women and children. I shall drive them back to their people—otherwise I shall order shots to be fired at them.[9]

This declaration, widely referred to as an "extermination order" (*Vernichtungsbefehl*), has given rise to a variety of conflicting interpretations as regards its intention, purpose and execution. It remains a major reference point in the current debate for agencies of the victims' descendants. But the controversy—whether this order provides irrefutable evidence of a premediated genocidal intention—should not distract us from the overall effect of German colonial warfare and its consequences for local communities in the eastern, central and southern regions of the territory. Estimates suggest that tens of thousands of Ovaherero died of thirst or hunger on their way to neighbouring Bechuanaland (today's Botswana), where descendants of the survivors are still living. Thousands more were captured (often after surrendering to missionaries) and put into concentration camps for use as forced labourers. Imprisoned women were sexually abused in a systematic way. The treatment of those captured even provoked harsh criticism from the chief inspector of the Rhenish Mission Society, Johannes Spiecker, who, like most of the missionaries and the mission society itself, was fully in support of German rule but called Trotha a "butcher".[10]

Several of the Nama communities (insultingly referred to in German as *Hottentotten*) under Captain Hendrik Witbooi and other leaders rose up after witnessing the war against the Ovaherero in late 1904. They resorted to a guerrilla strategy and fought the colonial army for years. On 22 April 1905 Trotha issued another, less widely known order addressing them. He declared that all those who did not surrender should leave the "German territory" or otherwise they would be shot until all were exterminated.[11] Witbooi, then in his mid-seventies, died in October 1905 from a wound inflicted in battle. Jakob Marengo, of Herero and Nama descent, kept the German soldiers busy until 1907. He was finally killed in the border area of the Cape Colony by a German patrol which entered the Cape with the consent of the British. The captured Nama suffered a similar fate to the Ovaherero and were imprisoned in concentration camps under conditions that had fatal consequences for many. More than a hundred of them (including women and children) were deported to Cameroon and Togo, where most did not survive.[12]

In the harbour towns of Lüderitz Bay and Swakopmund along the Atlantic coast the prisoners died of exposure to the harsh climate, malnourishment and the consequences of forced labour. The mortality rate peaked at about 80 per cent on the notorious Shark Island. A rock in the sea off Lüderitz Bay, it "was perhaps the world's first extermination camp".[13] Others have denied that the extreme casualties were intentional, but rather blame neglect, administrative failure and carelessness.[14] But whatever the cause, this did not in any way change the horrific result in terms of the number of those who paid with their lives. As Rachel O'Sullivan has observed: "the question remains: how unintentional can mass deaths over a sustained time period be? Even if the aim of the colonial concentration camps was not annihilation, at what stage does prolonged indifference towards sustaining human life become murder?"[15]

More importantly, such a debate risks reducing the overall assessment mainly to a matter of the concentration camps. This gives rise to the misleading assumption that the camps are central to the categorisation of the war as genocidal. While they were indeed potentially part of what can be described as genocidal practice, they were not a decisive element. Even in the absence of such camps the warfare and subsequent treatment of the survivors amounted to a genocide. In the more recent colonial historical debate, earlier works advocating this assessment have been regarded as teleological in tendency. This is based on the view that the initial military and police force was at best limited and that the use of official source material in these works was at best selective or uncritical.[16] It is argued that the unfolding dynamics were not predetermined and that the escalation of violence was more a sign of German military weakness than of strength, while the subsequent practices of elimination were more an indication of fear.[17] Proponents of such a reassessment of the "intent to destroy" nevertheless reach the same conclusion, that the result "can doubtless be termed a genocide".[18]

In a similar vein, some scholars have questioned the notion of "settler colonialism" as too vague and imprecise a category. "Although this categorisation is not wrong", argues Matthias Leanza, "it might not capture the change and evolution the protectorate underwent." As he reasons: "If one wanted to subsume the entire sequence of trajectories along which the colony evolved under a single category, as 'settler colonialism', this would obscure the profound shifts and transformations shaping its course", culminating in genocidal warfare and subsequent settler-colonial structures in parts of the territory.[19] While these scholarly debates are in many cases fruitful, they are at best of secondary interest (if not insignificant or even irrelevant) for those who demand adequate recognition of the crimes and injustices committed. For the descendants of the affected communities, such scholarly debate on the context and origin of their ancestors' ordeal is of no major interest. This may explain why Trotha's so-called *Vernichtungsbefehl* remains the most prominent example they refer to.

As a result of the war, an estimated two-thirds of the Ovaherero and one third to a half of the Nama died. The Damara (derogatorily called *Klippkaffern* in German), living among and in-between the various Nama and Ovaherero communities, were victims too,[20] while the communities of the San (Bushmen) continued to be targets of decimation throughout the period of German colonial rule.[21] The survivors in these local communities lost their traditional social organisation and lifeways. This was also the consequence of the administrative structures established by the colonial authorities and imposed on the local survivors, which in effect denied them the means to continue their way of life. Apartheid was a German invention and was introduced prior to a similar system in South Africa. While the actual number of those killed remains a matter of dispute, there is clear evidence of the "intent to destroy" as regards the people's way of life. This is a core definition of genocide (see chapter 2). According to this understanding, the Whitaker Report presented to the United Nations Economic and Social Council (ECOSOC) in 1985 listed the German war against the Ovaherero in 1904 as the first genocide of the 20th century.[22] Since then, most scholars who focus on colonial history or international genocide studies have reached the same or a similar conclusion.

A German "Sonderweg"?

The fate of the Ovaherero, Nama and Damara was by no means a unique phenomenon of a particular trajectory in European colonialism, although discussions about a German *Sonderweg* (special trajectory) may be of value if only to suggest that such a *Sonderweg* could have happened elsewhere too and therefore it was not one. Numerous colonial atrocities and crimes against humanity in many parts of the world testify to the fact that colonialism as a system was a form of organised violence, oppression and elimination of other people, amounting to war crimes, crimes against humanity and ethnic cleansing bordering on genocidal practices. Colonial warfare was a trans-imperial phenomenon.[23]

As regards the case of German South West Africa, evidence in the colonial archives in London reveals that the British Foreign Office and the Cape colonial government were not only aware of the German warfare in the neighbouring territory in all its brutal forms, but also a willing supplier of material and thereby an active supporter of the logistics that made possible the extermination of people.[24] Shark Island in Lüderitz Bay, which was a concentration camp for Nama (including women and children), was leased until 1906 by the Cape government to the German administration in South West Africa.[25] The deaths of the majority of Nama imprisoned there under extreme conditions thus took place on British territory, according to existing territorial rights, while officials in the Cape Colony (and those at the Foreign Office in London) closed their eyes.

The Cape administration knowingly conducted business with the perpetrators of genocide in the adjacent German colony through the supply chain fuelling the military machinery that implemented the so-called extermination order and subsequent military operations against the Nama. As the Cape Governor stated in a letter of 16 February 1906 to the Colonial Secretary, Lord Elgin, in London: "the large expenditure by the German government is of great benefit to the Cape of Good Hope, and my ministers are evidently anxious to do nothing to interfere with it". That this was an attitude not based on ignorance of what was going on is shown by the further explanation that they "will shut their eyes to the real destination of the supplies and will not take steps to interfere with the existing arrangements".[26]

The British *Report on the Natives of South West Africa and Their Treatment by Germany* (the "Blue Book"), released in 1918, revealed such atrocities with the aim of discrediting Germany as unfit to be a colonial power.[27] In response, a German "White Book" retaliated in 1919 by accusing the British of similar atrocities.[28] Ultimately, the South African government withdrew the incriminating Blue Book in 1926. This followed a request in a resolution of the Legislative Assembly of South West Africa (then a mandated territory under South African control), denouncing the report as an "instrument of war", and asking for its removal from official files in South Africa and Great Britain, and the destruction of all copies in public libraries and bookstores. This step "relegated the most damning record of the genocide of the Hereros to virtual oblivion, instead of placing it before the world as a possible warning of things to come".[29] The Blue Book had included eyewitness reports from members of the Cape colonial police as well as British army officers accompanying the German troops from 1904 onwards, who had shared in minute detail shocking revelations that were only made public in this document. When in 2014 a research student presented convincing evidence of what amounted to British complicity in the German genocide, and confronted the official in charge of the South Africa desk in the Foreign and Commonwealth Office in London with his findings, he received in reply a letter insisting that these events were not genocide but rather atrocities.[30]

In contrast to such an official view, Marion Wallace puts the German warfare in the colony into an appropriate perspective:

> The atrocities in Namibia can be understood as standing at the extreme end of a continuum of violence and repression in which

all the colonial powers participated. Nevertheless, it is important to name what happened in 1904–8 as genocide, not least because those who deny this continue to foster a debate that is really "a constant exercise in denial of historical evidence" [quoting from an article by Werner Hillebrecht, then head of the Namibian National Archives]. Because of the tenacity with which they make their arguments, it needs to be restated that the way in which they minimise African suffering is contrary to the weight of historical evidence and the conclusion of most recent research.[31]

The Long Denial

As chapter 3 shows, political office-bearers and the wider public in West Germany refused for a long time after World War II to acknowledge the ugly sides of Germany's colonial past. Konrad Adenauer, German Chancellor between 1949 and 1963, and deputy president of the German Colonial Society from 1931 to 1933, was characterised by his biographer as a "late-nineteenth-century colonialist".[32] But with the country claiming it was the legal successor of the German empire, Holocaust commemoration entered the public domain prominently from the late 1960s. This was not entirely voluntary. Dealing with the Nazi era in domestic politics and through remembrance came about not least as a result of the efforts of a generation linked to the student movement of the 1960s. Since then, Germany has been widely applauded for the way in which it has engaged with this chapter in its history. But demands to go back further in time and put the Nazi regime into a wider historical context, including the earlier colonial period, fell on deaf ears. In contrast, East German historians were much more willing to uncover imperial German history in great detail.[33] But their perspective suggested that neither the Nazis nor colonialism had anything to do with the GDR. In a striking parallel, historians from East Germany in 1966[34] and from West Germany in 1968[35] presented similar ground-breaking conclusions in their doctoral theses as regards the German colonial era in South West Africa. Despite different approaches they both tackled the taboo of the "good old days" and provided complementary evidence for the totalitarian mindset, methods, practices and consequences of mass destruction. A more theoretical thesis, drawing on Hannah Arendt's thinking, fairly soon thereafter added another important dimension to these early seminal works.[36]

However, it was fiction which first managed to draw attention to and promote a new perspective on colonial history within the wider West German public. Jacob Morenga (also referred to as Marengo) is the title figure in the still widely read semi-documentary anti-colonial novel by Uwe Timm (already introduced in chapter 4). While bearing his name, the novel has as its main character the German veterinarian Gottschalk, who served in the colonial army.[37] It is a creative blend of facts and fantasy, described as "a pioneering work in the critical memorialization of German colonialism" and "a benchmark for the poetics and politics of postcolonial memory".[38] As a "literary rediscovery of colonialism",[39] it contributed to a growing awareness of this history in West Germany.

Notwithstanding this remarkable exception, efforts by parts of West German civil society and politically engaged scholars to initiate a wider (self-)critical engagement with the colonial past bore little fruit initially. A century after the infamous Berlin Conference of 1884–1885, which marked the formal birth of the German colonial empire, academic inquiry and publication still failed to translate into wider public awareness.[40] Instead, as chapter 3 shows, colonial-apologetic thinking remained widespread and more effective than critical calls for decolonisation of the colonial mindset. Those pointing to the violent trajectory stretching from the mass atrocities in the German colonies to the subsequent world wars remained side-lined. It was evident that colonial-revisionist networks were still more effective publicly and able to drive and shape a selective public discourse about the colonial past.[41]

Until the late 1990s the German–Namibian historical axis was mainly kept alive by a considerable number of German-speaking Whites in the former colony, the so-called South Westers.[42] At the end of the previous decade the geostrategic consequences of glasnost and perestroika had created a new world order, leading not only to German unification but to Namibian independence. While the Berlin Wall fell in November 1989, Namibians were voting for a government of their own, bringing to an end South African foreign rule. Unified Germany and the independent Republic of Namibia entered 1990 in parallel on the international stage. This also led to new relations between the two.

Members of the West German Bundestag were aware of the need to respond to the common history that Germany and Namibia shared. Following a parliamentary debate in mid-March 1989, a resolution passed in anticipation of the forthcoming independence of the colony recognised that Germany held a "special historical responsibility" for Namibia.[43] But the euphemism made no reference to genocide or any other negative connotations. Instead, special mention was made of the interests of the German-speaking minority in the country. German policy seemed more concerned about the descendants of the colonial perpetrators than the descendants of the victims. Tellingly, the resolution's core phrase of a "special responsibility" remained the official point of reference for the next twenty-five years, during which time growing demands for the recognition of the genocide made little headway.[44]

Meanwhile, from the turn of the century, Genocide Studies had emerged internationally as a new scholarly field, transcending the former exclusive focus on Holocaust Studies.[45] Despite accusations that the singularity of the Holocaust has been put in question, genocide scholars have added important perspectives to the field of study. The contextualisation of genocides (in the plural) also helped promote an engagement with the South West African case. Within a short period of time, (mainly younger German) scholars produced a variety of new insights on matters related directly or indirectly to the genocidal warfare in South West Africa.[46] By 2004, a century after the beginning of the war, a growing number of studies were challenging the official denialism through a series of publications,[47] while numerous civil society initiatives were organising a variety of activities related to the war.[48] This was part of a wider move since the turn of the century to lift the veil which had been cast over the German colonial past.[49]

In parallel, a marked (albeit unplanned) shift occurred in official policy pronouncements. The Social Democratic Minister for Economic Cooperation and Development, Heidemarie Wieczorek-

Zeul, attended the main commemorative event held by the Ovaherero communities in August 2004 at Hamakari near the Waterberg, where, a century before, military encounters had triggered the subsequent genocidal practices. In her speech she declared that the atrocities were in our present understanding genocide and that Trotha would today be prosecuted for war crimes. Seemingly moved, she asked for forgiveness in the sense of the petition in the Lord's Prayer. When the audience demanded an apology, she said that her whole speech was an apology. This was mistaken as a change in official German policy. But Germany's Foreign Minister, Joseph (Joschka) Fischer of the Green Party, dismissed her utterance as a purely personal statement, while the German media ridiculed her as a woman who had been carried away emotionally.[50]

Minister Wieczorek-Zeul unilaterally offered a gesture of reconciliation amounting to 20 million euros. This Namibian–German Special Initiative Programme[51] was financed from the German Development Cooperation ministry, but it was considered by the affected communities as mere tokenism. Since the Namibian government felt it had not been properly consulted, it only reluctantly engaged with this initiative. Because of its lacklustre implementation, it by and large became a waste of money.

Already towards the end of 2001, the Paramount Chief of the Ovaherero, Kuaima Riruako (1935–2014), had initiated private claims for reparations from the German government and a few German companies in a United States court.[52] On 19 September 2006, Riruako, as a member of the Namibian parliament for the opposition National Unity Democratic Organisation (NUDO), introduced a motion in the National Assembly demanding adequate commemoration of and reparations for the genocide.[53] In a later session the same year, this motion was adopted by a vote that had the support of most members of SWAPO, the former liberation movement now in political power. But the government did not follow up on this politically within the bilateral relationship it has with Germany. The resolution, however, recognised the legitimate demands for compensation by the affected communities and their direct involvement in matters related to the genocide. Local communities who have felt side-lined by the official bilateral negotiations since the end of 2015 (see below) frequently refer to this motion to argue that the government has not lived up to the decision taken then, which stipulated that representatives of the descendants of the affected communities be included in any engagement with the German state. This disjunction is also visible in the variety of forms of local Namibian remembrance in arts and culture, with state-sponsored commemorations often acting for but not with descendants of the most-affected communities.[54]

The Return of Human Remains and Looted Artefacts

In 2011, 2014 and 2018, a number of skulls and other human remains were repatriated from Germany to Namibia.[55] Most of these were of people killed during the genocide or earlier atrocities under German colonialism, dating back to as early as 1885.[56] It is still not known how many more are stored in German "collections". Their repatriation cannot be separated from the admission of colonial state-sponsored crimes. Looted cultural artefacts in the possession of numerous museums and private collections are further testimony to the challenges facing Germany. The return of two highly symbolic and unique items of historical value in 2019 marked a significant moment. As the occasions show in various ways and contexts, asymmetric power relations and perceptions remain pitfalls, but there are options for handling the contradictions and challenges in different ways.

In 2010 a Charité Human Remains Project funded by the German Research Foundation began a closer inspection of the huge number of objects in its possession (many of them hardly known or properly registered) and also engaged in a wider context with the challenges of provenience (findspot) research. In September 2011 this project had its first outcome when 20 skulls were repatriated.[57] They had initially been used for some of the infamous anthropological studies that preceded the Nazi era.[58] What had been conceived as a solemn handover ended in a minor scandal. The high-calibre Namibian delegation, with over seventy members headed by a minister, felt snubbed and not properly hosted according to protocol (not a single German minister made time for a meeting). The German government kept throughout a deliberately low profile and avoided any official statements that went beyond its earlier position. The state representative attending the handover ceremony maintained the government's evasive line in her short statement by avoiding any reference to genocide, when declaring:

> During the period of German colonial rule in Namibia there was a bloody repression of the uprisings in former German Southwest Africa by the Imperial troops which killed many members of the Namibian peoples. Surviving Herero, Nama and Damara were held prisoner in camps, were subjected to forced labour, the brutality of which many did not survive. On the occasion of today's ceremonial act of return we remember the victims of war and imprisonment.[59]

When activists in the audience expressed dismay and protested when she did not offer an apology, she left the ceremony abruptly before the representatives of the Namibian delegation delivered their speeches. The cold shoulder shown by the German Federal Government prompted the Left Party to submit a minor interpellation on 14 November 2011.[60] The rather evasive answer of 1 December 2011 was revealing.[61] It stressed that the return of human remains and artefacts lay solely within the authority of the individual federal states whose institutions possessed the items and did not form part of the responsibility of the central government. It was pointed out that the Namibian delegation's visit was entirely arranged and funded by the Namibian government and was not at the invitation of the German side. The visit was thus not a matter for the German government to take care of, even though it had offered generous hospitality to the delegation during their stay. The details shared in the response speak for themselves:

> Federal Foreign Office paid a total of €11,195 for the delegation's accompanying cultural programme, and a total of €6,675 for the memorial service and the handover ceremony including the musical programme for both events. Costs of €2,636 were paid for the transport of the skulls including the costs of drawing up the freight documents, delivery of the boxes, labelling and packaging material. The Federal Government also paid for the issue of a Schengen

visa for 70 delegation members who had a Namibian passport or an official Namibian identity card, the costs of which are specified in Article 16 of Regulation (EC) No. 810/2009 of 13 July 2009 (OJ EC L 243/1). Four further delegation members were in the possession of diplomatic passports and did not require a visa to travel to Germany. The German Embassy in Windhoek acted in a service-oriented manner and the staff took a lot of time and effort to ensure that all delegation members received the visa they needed in time despite the fact that some of the applications were made at very short notice.[62]

This business-like handling of the highly symbolic first effort to restore some human dignity and history to members of the Namibian communities whose ancestors had been victims of genocide contrasted with the welcome which accompanied the arrival of the returned human remains in Windhoek.[63] This illustrated the different if not conflicting perspectives of the two parties, which continued to inform the ways each engaged with a shared history.

The handover of a second lot of 14 repatriated human skulls took place at the University of Freiburg in March 2014 in a more low-key, less public fashion. The small Namibian delegation was again headed by a minister, but the ceremony took place in the absence of officials from the German Federal Government.[64] A third handover, this time in a much more prominent and controversial fashion, followed in August 2018 in Berlin. This took place after a significant shift in official German–Namibian relations, for in mid-2015 the German Foreign Ministry had acknowledged in a semi-official way that the acts committed in South West Africa were tantamount to genocide. This led to bilateral negotiations with the Namibian government, starting at the end of 2015 (see the next section). The context of this third repatriation had thus changed considerably, though the contradictions had not.

The Namibian delegation, once again led by a minister, was hosted by the Minister of State for International Cultural Policy in the Federal Foreign Office, Michelle Müntefering.[65] In her welcoming speech on 27 August 2018 she declared: "When I consider the actions of Germans during the colonial period, then I stand humbled and ashamed before you."[66] On 29 August, 27 human remains were

GERMANY AND NAMIBIA

handed over in a Berlin church. Müntefering partly repeated her earlier welcoming remarks. Again, no deep apology was extended. At the end, she "bowed in deep mourning" and asked "from the bottom of my heart for forgiveness".[67] This wording did not go beyond the individual remorse offered in 2004 by the German minister Heidemarie Wieczorek-Zeul at the centenary commemoration of the battle at Ohamakari, when she asked for forgiveness in the style of the Lord's Prayer.[68] In this way Müntefering stuck to the legal niceties favoured by the Foreign Ministry.

This has not been the only sensitive issue. Conflicts have cropped up on account of the approach taken by both governments. In an obvious attempt to keep a low profile on the side of the German state, the responsibility for the ceremony was devolved to the German Protestant Church, acting jointly with the Namibian Council of Churches. Participation in a vigil the evening before the handover was restricted to personal invitations, contrary to the principle that Christian services are open to all. In another twist, the Namibian ambassador to Germany informed the postcolonial civil society group Völkermord Verjährt Nicht (There Is No Statute of Limitations on Genocide) that its members, who had relentlessly campaigned for recognition of the genocide and the renaming of colonial street names, would no longer be invited to the handover ceremony.[69] Representatives of the independent Ovaherero and Nama agencies, as descendants of the victim groups, were only assigned some space at the ceremonies at the last minute. They voiced their frustration accordingly. As Paramount Chief Vekuii Rukoro stated on their behalf: "How do you—the organisers of this event—think of us, Herero and Nama leaders, that our staunch supporters who were responsible for discovering these remains, are kept outside while we are locked up inside and standing next to members of the very church that has committed genocide against our people? Don't you ever have respect for our feelings?"[70]

The human remains were repatriated to Windhoek in the company of Müntefering and the German special envoy Ruprecht Polenz (who had been appointed in late 2015 to conduct the bilateral negotiations). On 31 August 2018 a ceremony with Namibia's Vice President as the keynote speaker took place in the parliamentary garden. While all participants were at pains to maintain decorum, a range of divergent concerns were expressed. Vice President Nangolo Mbumba emphasised the need for reparations.[71] Müntefering mainly repeated her speech given in Berlin, ending with the words:

> We Germans want to stand by your side, now and in the future. Namibia! When we arrived at the airport this morning we all felt that this is a moment in time. Thank you for making it a moment of togetherness. I bow my head in profound sorrow. I cannot undo the terrible injustice committed by our ancestors. But here, in the land of your ancestors, I again ask for your forgiveness from the bottom of my heart. May their souls rest in peace.[72]

In contrast, the representatives of victim communities insisted on a formal apology and reparations. Even the Ovaherero group which cooperated in the bilateral government negotiations, as well as Namibia's special envoy Zed Ngavirue, stressed they would judge any outcome in the light of these essential criteria.[73] Leaders of affected communities who refused to play second fiddle in the government-to-government negotiations insisted that their relegation to a subordinate position as members of a technical committee amounted to a continuation of colonialism.[74] According to all evidence, this third repatriation of human remains was another missed opportunity. Upon the arrival of the delegation in Berlin, Müntefering told reporters that Germany still had "a lot of catching up to do in coming to terms with our colonial heritage".[75] This has not changed since then.

In contrast, a different approach informed the act of restitution undertaken by the federal state of Baden-Württemberg and the Linden Museum in Stuttgart.[76] Its collection included (since 1902) the family Bible and whip of the legendary Nama leader Hendrik Witbooi. They were both looted during an attack on the community's retreat at Hornkranz in 1893, after the Witboois had refused to sign a "protection treaty". After the decision was taken to return the heirlooms by the end of February 2019 to the family descendants and the community at large, both items were displayed at the museum in the preceding months.[77] The objects were then taken to Namibia by a delegation headed by the federal state's Minister for Culture and Art. After a ceremonial welcome upon arrival in the capital Windhoek, the heirlooms were received the next morning by the country's Vice President. Together with the Namibian Minister for Education, Arts and Culture and the leaders of the local communities, the delegation then transported the heirlooms (together with a Nama and a Herero skull) to Gibeon, the main site of the Witbooi community in the country's southern region. Stopovers in three places on the way allowed local communities to witness the return and pay their respects and tributes.[78] The official handover was then made in Gibeon to President Hage Geingob (1941–2024), as the most senior representative of the Namibian state. He then immediately passed the heirlooms to the three great-granddaughters of Hendrik Witbooi and other community elders.[79]

The return was not free from complications, not least as regards the question of ownership and related procedures during the repatriation of the heirlooms. Who are the legitimate recipients or heirs and guardians of objects looted during colonialism from local communities, who since then have become citizens of a sovereign state represented by a central government? What provisions should be made to adequately accommodate and house the returns? Local tensions during the transfer touched on these issues and pointed to a complex and complicated if not contradictory process.[80] Reinhart Kössler, who witnessed the transfer as part of the delegation, has summarised the issues:

> This experience has clearly highlighted the fault lines and potential cleavages that are most likely inevitable features that accompany the restitution of cultural goods. Similar experiences have also been experienced regarding the repatriation of human remains: the claims for ownership and control on the part of the modern independent state countervail the expectations and hopes of the communities whose forbears have been robbed of the objects that are now to be returned. ... The experience surrounding the bible and the whip has shown that doing the right thing is not always without risk.[81]

As one of the most recent of an ongoing series of exchanges, a three-year collaborative project entitled "Confronting Colonial

Pasts, Envisioning Creative Futures" resulted in the return of 23 cultural objects from the Berlin Ethnological Museum to the National Museum of Namibia towards the end of May 2022. While again a most welcome initiative with the best of intentions, it was unable to lift the colonial veil entirely. As was noted with some consternation by postcolonial German initiatives and a wider Namibian public, these objects were initially returned on indefinite loan as part of a "joint reappraisal" of history. In response to the question why these objects were not fully restituted, the explanation given was that the project was part of "a process of rapprochement and that's the way that it was decided the objects would go back".[82] Significantly, public statements both in Germany[83] and Namibia[84] were not free of euphemisms and seemed to avoid language that called a spade a spade. The objects, "acquired" or "collected" during colonial times, were "travelling" on a "journey" to Namibia. This semantic softness contrasted somewhat with the declared aim "to engage with colonial trauma".[85] At the same time it is an indication that the journey undergone in German–Namibian relations from the time of the colonial trauma is far from over. But one can see that lessons have been learned. As announced only a few days later, a decision was taken by the governing Board of Trustees of the Prussian Cultural Heritage Foundation that some or all of the 23 objects might remain permanently in Namibia. Unfortunately (or perhaps revealingly so) the tone of the statement remained rather patronising. Hermann Parzinger, the head of the Foundation, declared: "If we now restitute these objects, then we support our Namibian partners in the reconstruction of their country's history."[86] On the other hand, a German cultural TV programme (*Titel, Thesen, Temperamente, ttt*) broadcast a much more empathetic feature on the transaction; this presented a variety of local Namibian voices under a no-nonsense title that stated that art looted during colonialism was being returned to Namibia.[87]

Negotiating Genocide

While the language of the time, using terms such as *Rassenkampf* (racial struggle) and *Vernichtungskrieg* (extermination war), was clear enough, it took 110 years until a spokesperson of a German government ministry finally admitted that what had happened between 1904 and 1908 in South West Africa was tantamount to genocide. The final admission occurred almost in passing in 2015, after the Bundestag, on the occasion of another centenary, recognised the Armenian genocide.[88] This had not only provoked an outburst by an enraged President Tayyip Erdoğan of Turkey, who pointed to the hypocrisy of this selective perspective given the unacknowledged German colonial genocide. Many of the established German media also noted and questioned the double standards. For the first time, the genocide in Namibia became a wider public issue. Even conservative political party officials realised that only recognition of the historical facts would restore some moral high ground. Last but not least, the Social Democratic Foreign Minister, Frank-Walter Steinmeier, could not escape the fact that his party while in opposition had tabled a parliamentary motion (later dismissed) on Namibia jointly with the Green Party that had introduced the term "genocide". At a press conference in July 2015, a spokesperson of the Foreign Ministry confirmed after repeated enquiries by a journalist that the term "genocide" was now applicable to what had happened in South West Africa.[89]

Bilateral negotiations were resumed between the special envoys Dr Zed Ngavirue[90] and Ruprecht Polenz,[91] appointed by the Namibian and German governments towards the end of 2015. But up to the end of 2023 there has not been an official recognition, by the democratically elected political representatives of the German people, of the genocidal nature of the crimes committed. On 2 June 2016 the German parliament adopted a resolution about the Armenian genocide;[92] a resolution of 30 November 2022 recognised the Holodomor famine committed by the Stalin regime in the Ukraine as genocide;[93] and on 19 January 2023 a draft resolution was adopted[94] that described the Islamic State's crimes against the Yazidi as genocide. As Kössler observes, these resolutions stand in sharp contrast to the continued official silence of the German parliament about the genocide committed in the German colony.[95] As late as August 2017, a government response to the Report of the Working Group of Experts on People of African Descent on Its

Mission to Germany, submitted to the United Nations Human Rights Council, still referred to the genocide as "suppression of revolts in former Southwest-Africa".[96]

The core issues negotiated between the governments were the form of an official apology and adequate compensation—that is, if compensation could ever be remotely adequate given the human costs and the lasting structural consequences of the atrocities of the time, which have shaped parts of Namibian society and the living conditions of several ethnic groups until today.[97] Both an apology and the forms of compensation are closely intertwined since the nature of the apology (as an acknowledgement of the genocide) has legal implications for the extent of compensation. The term "reparations" was deliberately avoided on the German side. It would create a far-reaching precedent[98] and directly affect pending ways of handling German war crimes during World War II. Judgments for compensation to the descendants of victims, as handed down by courts in Greece, Italy and some Eastern European states, have so far not been acknowledged by Germany.[99] The argument is that the state cannot be held liable for crimes committed by individuals.

The Namibian case could open a Pandora's box—not only regarding the unresolved reparation claims from World War II but also as motivation for subsequent claims concerning crimes committed in other German colonies. Moreover, other former colonial powers may fear legal precedents should Germany find a solution in recognising the demands and claims brought by the descendants of mainly Ovaherero and Nama people (but also the Damara and San)—all victims of German colonial warfare and the subsequent annihilation strategies which destroyed their established ways of life and forced them into bondage-like dependency. While chapter 2 offers more on the context of the Genocide Convention adopted by the United Nations, here we can note that its definition of genocide goes beyond the "intent to destroy" in terms of a deliberately planned (though not necessarily executed) physical annihilation of people who have been targeted on the basis of a shared group belonging, and also includes the destruction of cultural identities and forms of social reproduction—all an integral part of settler-colonial rule and frontier societies, as much in Australia and the Americas as in southern Africa.[100] Consequently, one does not have to employ conspiracy theories to assume that the German negotiations have not only been closely followed by other former colonial powers, but most likely have also been a subject of informal exchanges behind closed doors among some foreign ministers in Brussels.

Given this state of affairs, any lasting solution is far from being achieved. After all, even if the two governments have reached a compromise, ratified by both sides, considerable numbers of the descendants of the most-affected communities feel marginalised and not inclined to surrender their claims. They do not acknowledge the Namibian government as the legitimate agency advocating their interests and negotiating on their behalf given their lack of adequate direct representation. In contrast, the Namibian government claims a legitimate monopoly over the centralised state, entitling it to represent the Namibian people, and does not consider the local ethnic agencies, constituted (among others) as the Nama Traditional Leaders Association (NTLA) and the Ovaherero Traditional Authority (OTA), as legitimate negotiators, despite representing considerable parts of their ethnic groups. These groups have, jointly with other communities in the diaspora (mainly in Botswana and the United States), gone to a US domestic court in New York to claim reparations, albeit with no success.[101]

On 5 January 2017 Chief Riruako's successor, Paramount Chief Vekuii Rukoro (1954–2021), and Chief David Fredericks (1932–2018), chairman of the NTLA, as the main plaintiffs, together with the Association of the Ovaherero Genocide in the USA Inc., filed a class action lawsuit in a US federal court in New York, which was finally dismissed in May 2021. The plaintiffs claimed "the legitimate right to participate in any negotiations with Germany relating to the incalculable financial, material, cultural, intellectual, religious and spiritual losses suffered". Their complaint, submitted under the Alien Tort Statute, asked for the award of punitive damages and the establishment of a constructive trust, into which the defendant (Germany) should pay the estimated "value of the lands, cattle and other properties confiscated and taken from the Ovaherero and Nama peoples".[102] Commenting in the German media, the German special envoy Ruprecht Polenz created the impression that the plaintiffs had asked for individual reparation payments. A joint press statement issued on 9 January 2017 by the German initiative "Berlin Postcolonial" and the Ovaherero Paramount Chief dismissed this as "a blatant lie" and a "calculated misrepresentation to deliberately discredit our legitimate and justified campaign for restorative justice".[103] The plaintiffs had also referred to the Declaration on the Rights of Indigenous Peoples, adopted on 13 September 2007 with the votes of Germany and Namibia, by the United Nations General Assembly.[104] Article 18 stipulates that "indigenous peoples have the right to participate in decision-making in matters which would affect their rights, through representatives chosen by themselves". The Namibian government has, however, included a group willing to participate, constituted as the Ovaherero/Ovambanderu and Nama Council for Dialogue on the 1904–1908 Genocide (ONCD 1904–1908), as a consultative body forming part of the Cabinet Technical Committee, which falls under the Namibian Cabinet's Political Committee on Genocide, Apology and Reparations, in advising the special representative.[105]

Germany has conveniently dodged the contested matter of representation by the descendants of the victim groups, by declaring it a purely Namibian affair. This evasive—albeit formally correct—position suits the German side well. After all, Germany would expect the least compromises from the side of those who represent the claims of descendant groups when it comes to the issue of restitution of ancestral land taken under German colonialism. "Retributive justice" is indeed a term missing from the official vocabulary. In an interview with the German radio station Deutsche Welle towards the end of July 2017, the special envoy Ruprecht Polenz[106] stressed once again that Germany would not negotiate over reparations and that this position had been made clear right at the beginning of the bilateral talks. For Germany, the genocide was not an issue to be discussed under international law. While the term "reparation" was a legal category, the matter was a political-moral rather than a judicial one. This, according to Polenz, was not something less but something different. He did not, however, explain why this would exclude adequate forms of compensation as a political-moral consequence (tantamount to, though not necessarily declared as, reparations). Polenz had stated earlier on that efforts to come to terms with the past were about healing wounds. Interviewed too, the Namibian special envoy Zed Ngavirue pointed out that this approach seemed to suggest that the medical prescription was being issued by a doctor in Berlin. But from a Namibian point of view, he added, a medical practitioner in Berlin could not alone decide on an adequate treatment. He insisted that the matter of reparations would remain on the table.[107]

As late as June 2019, the outgoing German ambassador to Namibia, Matthias Schlaga—from November 2023, president of the lobbyist German-Namibian Society[108]—reassured a local German-speaking audience at a public event that the term "genocide" must be understood only in a moral-political context, not in a legal sense, and that reparations would be a "no go". He was quoted as saying:

> Germany is ready to apologise, but first we need to know what we are apologising for. Reparations is a legal term. We do not see a legal obligation to pay reparations but will put in place "measures to heal the wounds" from a historical sense. ... The amount of money to be given is what is stalling negotiations and the difference is quite considerable.[109]

Ambassador Schlaga had a talent for not missing any opportunity to make blunders and gaffes. But insensitivity on the part of representatives of the German state was not confined to Schlaga. In mid-July 2019 Daniel Günther visited Namibia. As Minister President of the German federal state of Schleswig-Holstein and then President of the Federal Council (Bundesrat), he was one of the five most senior representatives of the German state and the first in this league to visit Namibia since President Roman Herzog in 1998. He used his stay to pay his respects at a Swakopmund memorial in commemoration of the victims of the colonial concentration camp there.[110] But he missed the opportunity to fall to his knees as the West German chancellor Willy Brandt had done in 1970 when he turned the page of history in German relations with Poland through his genuflection in Warsaw.

THE LONG SHADOW OF GERMAN COLONIALISM

Günther's statements during his official engagements were indicative of the German approach. In a meeting with President Hage Geingob, he expressed an interest "in finding a quick solution to the genocide issue". The Namibian head of state responded by saying there was no need to rush the negotiation process. Rather, issues should be handled properly.[111] Günther also addressed the unresolved land question. He took the liberty to advise President Geingob to respect property rights, since potential investors—such as the business people in his entourage—would not be forthcoming if property was not protected.[112] This prompted Geingob to assure him that property rights would be respected.[113] In his main speech addressing the National Council (the equivalent of the German institution which he then presided over), Günther drew East German parallels to the Namibian situation inasmuch as thirty years previously developments in the GDR had "forced the government to hold the first and only free elections". He stated further: "I believe that people in the GDR and people in Namibia clearly showed their courage in their struggle for liberation."[114] Comparing the anti-colonial struggle led by the liberation movement SWAPO to the civil rights movement in the GDR testified to the German disconnection from Namibian realities and perceptions. It was at best disrespectful of the human costs of two decades of war against an illegal regime and added insult to injury. And while Günther recognised "historical guilt", he fell short of an apology and avoided meeting representatives of the Ovaherero and Nama, which provoked Paramount Chief Rukoro into describing the visit as a hollow ritual.[115]

From early 2019 (when the eighth bilateral meeting took place in Swakopmund), negotiations had become dormant owing to elections in Germany and Namibia, followed by the pandemic-related lockdown, which put on hold any further meetings. At the beginning of 2020 the Namibian special envoy publicly clarified that the German government had not yet put on the table any definite amount that they were willing to pay as reparations. Referring to plans for the next (ninth) round of negotiations set to take place in February 2020 in Berlin, he indicated that he was "positive that we should make a real advance this time around, but it would certainly not be the conclusion of talks".[116] Given the pandemic-related restrictions, this meeting took place only in mid-May 2021, ending with a preliminary agreement.

The Joint Declaration and Its Aftermath

The document initialled by the special envoys as a "Joint Declaration", dated 21 May 2021, made international headlines.[117] For the first time a former colonial power offered an apology on a state-to-state level for mass crimes that had been committed. The potential legal implications as well as the precedent this might create for other former colonial powers occupied the minds of legal experts and foreign policy pundits.[118] The outcome gave rise to divided responses. Some considered the accord as a potential model for efforts towards postcolonial reconciliation, affecting also other former colonies and colonial powers.[119] This may be so even though the Namibian case went lamentably wrong: reactions among significant parts of the descendants of the main victim communities were overall negative. They dismissed the agreement as an insult[120] and made it clear that, "deal or not, the struggle continues".[121]

What's in It

The Joint Declaration has 22 clauses in five chapters, with the flowery subtitle "United in Remembrance of Our Colonial Past, United in Our Will to Reconcile, United in Our Vision of the Future".[122] With reference to previous resolutions of the German parliament in 1989 and 2004, the Introduction emphasizes "a special historical and moral responsibility towards Namibia". Nine clauses under chapter I then summarise in a remarkably honest way the crimes committed, with the conclusion: "As a consequence, a substantial number of Ovaherero and Nama communities were exterminated through the actions of the German State. A large number of the Damara and San communities were also exterminated." Clause 10 under chapter II continues: "The German Government acknowledges that the abominable atrocities committed during periods of the colonial war culminated in events that, from today's perspective, would be called genocide." Clause 11 under chapter III adds: "Germany accepts a moral, historical and political obligation to tender an apology for this genocide and subsequently provide the necessary means for reconciliation and reconstruction", while clause 13 states: "Germany apologizes and bows before the descendants of the victims." Clause 14 under chapter IV stipulates: "The Namibian Government and people accept Germany's apology and believe that it paves the way to a lasting mutual understanding and the consolidation of a special relationship between the two nations. ... This shall close the painful chapter of the past and mark a new dawn in the relationship between our two countries and peoples."

Both governments undertake to create a "reconstruction and development support programme" (clause 16), which will finance projects in seven of Namibia's 14 regions (in which a majority of descendants of the most-affected communities live). Clause 17 commits the parties to "finding appropriate ways of memory and remembrance, supporting research and education, cultural and linguistic issues, as well as encouraging meetings of and exchange between all generations, in particular the youth". For these commitments the German government promised to put aside a total amount of 1.1 billion euros allocated over thirty years, with 1.05 billion earmarked for the development programme and 50 million "to the projects on reconciliation, remembrance, research and education" (clause 18). Clause 20 then confirms that "these amounts ... settle all financial aspects of the issues relating to the past addressed in this Joint Declaration". The final clause, 22, offers the assurance that Germany will "continue the bilateral development cooperation at an adequate level".

Germany's Foreign Minister, Heiko Maas, officially announced the agreement.[123] He stressed that the admission of genocide did not imply any "legal claims for compensation" and referred to the "substantial programme ... for reconstruction and development" as a "gesture of recognition". (Speaking of recognition, when reading the statement to the press, Minister Maas acknowledged the German special envoy Ruprecht Polenz by name. But, deviating from the written text, he left out the name of the Namibian counterpart, Zed Ngavirue.)[124] During parliamentary question time a few days later, Minister Maas stressed that the agreement was entered on a purely voluntary basis. There were no legal reasons, as he explained, for making or promising payment. It was thus also not comparable to the subject of reparations.[125] Minister Maas also clarified that the signed agreement was not a treaty that would require formal ratification by parliament.[126]

What's Not in It

In a comprehensive critical engagement with the document, members of the European Center for Constitutional and Human Rights (ECCHR) did not mince their words: "That the 'reconciliation agreement' will be published as a mere Joint Declaration speaks volumes. The preceding negotiation process furthermore disregarded international participation rights based both in treaties and customary international law."[127] Their verdict was devastating: "What shows from the choice of title and format of the accord ... the 'semantic struggle' was decided in favor of the German government's take on its responsibility, a responsibility that is normatively very thin, almost void in its recognition of accountability and reckoning with its colonial legacy and guilt."[128]

This corresponded with the lack of inclusivity on the Namibian side in respect of the communities most affected by the genocide. While Minister Maas claimed in his press statement that "the Herero and Nama communities were closely involved in the negotiations on the Namibian side", the ECCHR regretted the inadequate participation of the main agencies of these communities. Referring to several normative frameworks adopted by bodies of the United Nations concerning the rights of minorities and indigenous people, it pointed out: "There can never be justice in a truly restorative sense when affected communities like the Nama, Ovaherero, San and other communities are not included in the negotiations."[129]

As the Declaration clarifies in clause 16, the amount of 1.05 billion euros earmarked over a period of thirty years for development projects is supposed "to assist the development of descendants of the particularly affected communities".[130] This is less than the amount that the German Development Cooperation ministry has spent in the thirty years since Namibia's independence.[131] It turns Germany's willingness to make material compensation into a rather modest and limited, if not embarrassing, "gesture of recognition" (Maas), adding insult to injury. To illustrate the point: after the tsunami disaster at the end of 2004, Germany raised 1.1 billion euros through private donations and official humanitarian aid within six months.[132] For 2021, Germany's capital, Berlin, had budgeted expenditure of 10.5 billion euros for personnel costs only.[133] During the same year, the German Minister for Health wasted a billion euros on face masks, which gave insufficient, substandard protection against Covid-19.[134] Construction costs for the new Berlin airport had by the time of its opening in 2021 exceeded seven billion euros.[135] Estimated costs for the new underground railway station in Stuttgart increased to over nine billion euros in 2022.[136] Similarly, the 50 million euros "dedicated to the projects on reconciliation, remembrance, research and education" in Namibia, which is to be allocated over the same period, can be set against the annual maintenance costs of 60 million euros for the controversial Humboldt Forum, which displays artefacts looted during the colonial era. Even leading members of the governing party SWAPO expressed frustration. For the country's and party's Vice President, Nangolo Mbumba, who was officially in charge of handling the matter, the money was not enough.[137]

Land Matters

"Land Reform, in particular Land Acquisition, within the framework of the Namibian Constitution, and Land Development" are identified in clause 16 of the Joint Declaration as priorities. But it remains unknown how, given the meagre amount allocated, any meaningful changes in terms of land ownership and utilisation can be implemented. This goes to the heart of the question of socioeconomic transformation of property relations and ownership since independence and points to a shared responsibility of both governments. After all, reversing the skewed patterns of land distribution requires the political willingness of both partners in the bilateral negotiations.

The issue of land provides visible evidence of the structurally embedded nature of inequality and injustice in Namibia. As we have already noted, most of the commercially viable territory in the eastern, central and southern regions of the country is still the private property of predominantly White (and often German-speaking) commercial farmers.[138] The general attitude among locals who benefited from colonialism in terms of land ownership does not help in finding a solution: "White Namibians' class privilege seems to have rendered them largely indifferent to the structural violence that land inequality continues to sustain."[139] So far, Namibian government policy has not displayed any determined political will in favour of transferring land back into the ownership of the dispossessed local communities. The beneficiaries of the rather modest redistribution of land since independence have often come from groups and communities in the northern region, who formed the basis of SWAPO and whose land was never expropriated under colonialism. Transfer of land to members of these groups thus arouses immense frustration and anger among the communities who were robbed of their land under colonialism.

Land is, apart from economic considerations, ultimately a matter of identity—for those who currently own it as much as for those who feel it should be theirs.[140] Today's commercial agrarian sector remains associated with land theft. The current system of private land ownership is a constant reminder that colonialism did not end with independence. It continues as long as restorative justice does not become part of the land debate. The second National Land Conference, held during the first week of October 2018, stated in a resolution under issue 38 ("ancestral land rights and claims") that "measures to restore social justice and ensure economic empowerment of the affected communities" should be identified. The next resolution then proposed to "use the reparations from the former colonial powers for such purpose".[141] This might have offered a window of opportunity during the ongoing negotiations between the Namibian and German governments for dealing with their intertwined history—provided both sides were willing to hand over the land to the descendants of those from whom it was stolen.

Germany could have provided the necessary funds for a just (in the sense of fair) expropriation of commercial farms in recognition of the constitutional requirements. Their land was that of the indigenous communities, whose ancestors are buried there. But the transfer of such land can only constitute a first step and needs to avoid turning land once again into another dumping ground (as under the colonial policy of "native reserves"). The German state would therefore have to finance the necessary investments—both in terms of infrastructure and know-how—empowering those local communities willing to return to the land as owners again so that they can fully benefit from resettlement and make a living from land under the conditions of climate change adaptation. The Namibian government, on the other hand, would have to accept that resettlement should involve as its main beneficiaries the descendants of those robbed of their land, and not privilege those whose land was never taken. This would be an investment by both governments in an act of reconciliation contributing to an enhancement of social stability. As such, it would include a constant German policy concern. After all, the situation of the German-speaking community (who are often still German citizens) has been an explicit point of reference for its Namibia policy. The 1989 resolution adopted by the West German parliament on Germany's special responsibility for its former colony made explicit reference to the German-speaking local community, though not to the victims of the genocide.[142]

Reparations and Intertemporality

At dispute is not only the amount offered in the agreement as an ultimate settlement. A related, more profound and serious omission of the Declaration was noted in the ECCHR statement, which identified "a mere shift of an initial refusal to call it genocide to a refusal to apply the legal term 'reparations'".[143] As the ECCHR observed: "Given the joint declaration's wording and lack of the term reparation therein, it avoids comprehensively acknowledging

GERMANY AND NAMIBIA

Germany's legal responsibility for its colonial legacy. ... The gesture of an apology will remain purely symbolic if it is not connected to other means of reparations."[144]

That the term "reparations" was omitted from the Declaration remained indeed a bone of contention between the two governments. While the issue cannot be discussed in detail here, it should be noted that the claim for reparations in respect of colonial crimes is not far-fetched "wishful thinking" but a matter of intense debate.[145] This is also closely related to discussions on intertemporal law, which raises the issue of which laws are applicable at which times. Intertemporality as a principle deals with legal questions based on the laws effective at a specific time. This includes the willingness to endorse the legality of laws considered as a justification for crimes. Germany applies rules of intertemporality ambiguously by refusing to recognise certain Nazi-era laws or those of the GDR. In the latter case, property was restituted after German unification by declaring the laws under which it had been transferred after World War II as illegal and as therefore having lapsed after 1990.[146] Such an interpretation can be applied much more easily and convincingly to the restitution of land misappropriated under German colonialism at the lasting expense of local communities. But, instead, colonial criminal acts are willingly concealed by recognising laws of the time by means of the intertemporal principles. As an earlier principled legal reflection put it: "There are therefore two elements, the first of which is that acts should be judged in the light of the law contemporary with their creation, and the second of which is that rights acquired in a valid manner according to the law contemporaneous with that creation may be lost if not maintained in accordance with the changes brought about by the development of international law."[147]

What is also contested is the definition of legitimate agencies in specific historical (in this case, colonial) contexts. This includes "a conceptual disconnect between the international system and its constitution through imperialism, colonialism and genocidal violence. Consequently, claims for redress of injustices based on substantive colonial relations and their legacies are deflected to a system of rule still infused with imperial law and legislation."[148] As Carsten Stahn has aptly stated:

> Colonial injustice is not a distant wrong that passes away with time. It is an everyday reality that reproduces itself. ... The (after) life of colonialism remains present in our relations to spaces, objects, persons or history. ... Contemporary forms of historical injustice, such as the holocaust, are deemed to be open to legal redress for individuals because some of the perpetrators or (direct and indirect) victims are still alive, while other types of historical injustice are excluded because perpetrators and (direct and indirect) victims have deceased. This agent-related understanding neglects the structural nature of colonial injustice. It restricts redress to inter-personal relations and liability structures. It disregards the fact that colonial injustice results often not so much from the injustice done between particular persons, but rather from the structures of abuse or the institutional systems put in place at the time.[149]

As chapter 3 has already pointed out, the carrying out of annihilation strategies had already been outlawed by the Hague Convention of 1899 as being in violation of "a statement of international customary law".[150] If the Convention embodies principles of international law, then its rules apply not only to its signatories but also to indigenous communities such as the Ovaherero, Nama and others who had "not relinquished their full sovereignty".[151] On this premise one can argue that customs "limiting the use of force in war ... conferred humanitarian rights upon the Hereros".[152]

The Joint Agreement denies such an interpretation. As the ECCHR statement pointed out:

> by relying on the doctrine of intertemporality—the declaration states that the killing of the Ovaherero and Nama 1904–08 is only a genocide "from today's perspective"—the German state reproduces the colonial power structures of hegemonic subordination and the racist exclusion of non-European nations and political entities—the core element of colonialism and colonial injustice. Based on this doctrine and the respective argumentation, it follows that today's international law does not apply to protect the then colonized: they were not part of the so-called civilized nations, that means that legally no genocide was committed, the colonial power did not act unlawfully and thus no reparations are

due. The argument's structure shows how colonial power patterns survive. On the one hand, some acts are outside law, while Germany uses a legal argument based on the doctrine of intertemporality to reject responsibility.[153]

The genocide of 1904–1908 and its consequences for the descendants of the affected communities remain a challenge for efforts to come to terms with the past. They are, rightly so, a matter of intense advocacy and debate, which poses fundamental challenges to any "reconciliation agreement". Despite the admission of genocide (significantly "from today's perspective") and some words of remorse, this agreement avoids the full consequences of bearing responsibility. It is in practice a continuation of the doctrine of an apology without payment for damages, coined by Foreign Minister Fischer some twenty years earlier. As a soft version of denialism, it offers no true reconciliation. Rather, it continues to prioritise major domestic (national) German interests, albeit dressed up in a multidimensional costume.[154] The Joint Declaration simply reconfirms, despite all the rhetoric, Germany's engagement with independent Namibia over the issue of genocide as a refurbished version of asymmetric power relations. It is based on the continued exclusion of those who should be the prime partners in the search for restitutive justice. Instead, the two governments, in complete contempt of their people, decide on their behalf "to accept Germany's apology". German–Namibian bilateral interactions remain a story of the "White Saviour" and aid recipients.[155] The notion of reconciliation is offered as a counter-model and substitute for reparations as material compensation, and a policy that deals with the past turns into development aid for the Namibian state.[156] A general observation that has been made by Tom Bentley on the "sorrow of empire" as a ritual of legitimation applies to the Joint Declaration too:

> On the one hand the politicians do seem to be speaking on behalf of the state (as well as the people) and taking responsibility, but, in the very texts of the apologies, are either using these platforms to employ obfuscating language regarding the transgressions or to evade and plead against aspects of historical responsibility in ways

that overlap with legal expedience. Rather than clarity, it creates a sense of ambiguity, whereby the state both accepts and distances itself from responsibility in the same ritual.[157]

The German–Namibian government-to-government agreement falls into such a category and can be considered symptomatic of a hegemonic state-centred approach.[158] It falls short of the minimum concessions which major parts of the descendants of the most-affected communities can legitimately accept as a true recognition of the historical injustices committed.

Namibian Disagreements

Ratification of the Declaration by the foreign ministers, planned within a matter of weeks during June 2021, remained pending. The intended closure provoked immediate outcry and protest by relevant agencies of the local communities. For the Ovaherero Paramount Chief, Vekuii Rukoro, the agreement added insult to injury.[159] Even the representatives of three Ovaherero royal houses participating in the final round of negotiations declared after their return from Berlin that they would not endorse the agreement.[160] The scheduled debate on the negotiated result in the National Assembly in early June 2021 ended in turmoil. MPs of opposition parties voiced their frustration over the "betrayal".[161] In fact, the parliamentary debate came to a halt before it really began. The growing Covid pandemic (Namibia recorded the highest infection rates worldwide) cost the lives of the Namibian special envoy, Dr Zed Ngavirue, and the Ovaherero Paramount Chief, Vekuii Rukoro. Owing to the strict lockdown, the sitting of parliament was postponed. When it finally re-opened in late September 2021, several hundred demonstrators together with MPs from opposition parties climbed over the fence of the parliamentary garden and stormed the National Assembly building.[162] There was a vibrant debate in the house that lasted until the end of the parliamentary session on 1 December 2021.

Numerous speakers from all parties voiced concern, criticism and rejection. Deputy Minister Esther Muinjangue set the tone. President of NUDO, the only non-SWAPO member of government, she had previously been the chairperson of the Ovaherero Genocide Foundation. Now she declared in parliament: "We have the feeling our government is not supporting us. You hear government-to-government, but where are we?"[163] McHenry Venaani, leader of the official opposition Popular Democratic Movement (PDM), denounced the compensation agreed for the crimes committed as a flagrant display of arrogance and lack of empathy by the German government.[164] Bernadus Swartbooi, leader of the second biggest opposition party, the Landless People's Movement (LPM), commented when referring to the exclusion of the indigenous communities most affected "that this nation-state does not belong to all".[165]

SWAPO MPs voiced their frustration too. Minister Tom Alweendo was concerned about the growing divisions among members of all parties:

> I am troubled by how the conversation has gone thus far. It is now so apparent that the debate has become so divisive. We call each other names. We refer to each other as puppets and sell-outs ...
>
> I am afraid that should we continue with this path, then the legacy left by the divide and rule philosophy will continue to flourish.[166]

As the debate showed, reconciliation not only between the people of Germany and Namibia but also between people within Namibia was further away than before. The so-called reconciliation agreement in fact further divided the Namibian people along lines of ethnic identity. The parliamentary debate closed without any decision being taken. The government announced that in view of the sentiments expressed, it would seek further negotiations with the German side.[167] Once an improved agreement was ratified, the government announced, this would be submitted to parliament for acceptance.

In mid-2022 Namibia's first President, Sam Nujoma, joined the critics. In an interview on the occasion of his 93rd birthday, the widely respected and influential elder statesman, whose words still have considerable weight, declared: "Namibia must return to the negotiating table with Germany, whose offer of N$ 18.4 billion for the Nama and Ovaherero genocide is woefully insignificant." He also acknowledged that the communities of the Damara and San had been "caught up in a cataclysm" tantamount to genocide.[168]

Ploughing Through

In October 2021 the German special envoy Ruprecht Polenz confirmed in an interview that the Joint Declaration would not be renegotiated.[169] Elsewhere he reiterated that the negotiations were closed.[170] But the new government, in office since early December, stressed in its coalition agreement that its commitment to pursuing reconciliation with Namibia was an "indispensable task", for historical and moral reasons. It mentioned the reconciliation agreement as a potential prelude to a further joint reappraisal.[171] This sounded much more open than what a spokesperson of the German government intimated at a press conference in early 2022. According to him, the Joint Declaration was an offer on the table, and it was now up to the Namibian side to decide how to proceed.[172]

In the absence of any visible further progress, German MP Sevim Dağdelen of the Left Party submitted a parliamentary question in July.[173] In a response at the end of August it was categorically stated that the German government considered the Joint Declaration final, though there were ongoing conversations about the implementation of individual aspects.[174] It maintained that the Namibian government, despite the heated debates in the National Assembly, would stick to the draft, while at the same time it conceded that the Namibian side had not yet approved the text.[175] The reply also listed a number of official meetings and conversations between government representatives since the signing of the draft. It stressed once again that the Declaration was not a legal contract in terms of international law and therefore did not require endorsement (ratification) by a vote in the German parliament. It also expressed the view that the Namibian parliament did not have to authorise the signing of the Declaration by the two countries' foreign ministers, while emphasising that both governments agreed that adequate participation by descendants of the Ovaherero and Nama was indispensable for genuine reconciliation.[176]

One wonders about the meaning of "indispensability" in this context. The Landless People's Movement, the Nama Traditional Leaders Association and the Ovaherero Traditional Authority reacted to this statement with a joint legal intervention submitted to Namibia's Foreign Minister and Attorney General.[177] Referring to the concluding statement of Minister Frans Kapofi in Namibia's National Assembly on 1 December 2021 on behalf of the government and to Namibia's constitutional principles, they demanded that there be a final authorisation or ratification of the Joint Declaration by the Namibian lawmakers. They also questioned how the Namibian government could act as negotiator without any parliamentary endorsement and announced that they were willing to take the matter to the Supreme Court to prevent ratification. The Attorney General in an angry response dismissed the "malicious allegations" and "insinuations".[178] But Minister Kapofi expressed his indignation over the German response. For him, reparations remained "an unfinished job that has to be finished. It is something that we need to address as a country."[179]

On 12 October 2022, Katja Keul, Minister of State in the Foreign Ministry, responded to another question in the German parliament in no uncertain terms: the German and Namibian governments would stick to the Joint Declaration. Only matters of implementation remained the subject of confidential talks.[180] Significantly, she also used the opportunity to make a semantic clarification, criticising the use of the term "reconciliation agreement". Though the term had also been used in official German communications before, Keul, referring to the official title of the Joint Declaration, stressed that there was no "so-called reconciliation agreement".[181] She added that it was a pioneering document. This almost aggressive defence of a compromise as a major step forward suggested that German policy under the new coalition government not only held to the negotiated result but seemed to be eager to turn what has been characterised by Franziska Boehme as "reactive remembrance"[182] into a selling strategy. In an address on 17 October 2022, Keul referred to the Declaration as "a milestone in our efforts to remember the painful past and unite behind a common vision for the future. ... Our two governments stand by what we have jointly achieved. And we are currently working on ways to settle the remaining open questions, so that the Declaration can be signed."[183]

In contrast, the Namibian government remained tight-lipped. For the first time, Namibia's Vice President, Nangolo Mbumba, offered a public indication of the official position when on 27 October 2022 he addressed a meeting of the Chiefs' Forum attended by traditional authorities from the most-affected communities who were willing to collaborate in the bilateral negotiations. According to Mbumba, the amount of 1.1 billion euros had to be increased and the thirty-year payment period was too long. The result also failed to recognise victims in the diaspora, especially those living in Botswana.[184] As he elaborated, the technical committees of both countries had "discussed the issue, and proposed that amendments be made to the joint declaration in the form of an addendum, which was submitted to the German government".[185] This clarification made the Joint Declaration in its current form untenable. As Vice President Mbumba stated at a press conference at the conclusion of the Chiefs' Forum, when referring to demands for a much higher sum for compensation: "Hopefully we will reach a figure which Germany is ready to give and which Namibia is ready to accept. The government of the Republic of Namibia is waiting for a response from Germany on the proposed addendum. I am assuring Namibians that no agreement has been reached or signed with Germany yet."[186]

This contrasted markedly with the statements of Katja Keul as a high-ranking political representative of the German government, who pronounced on the Namibian position on several occasions in a misleading manner. According to Bentley, the inherent structure of such dialogue "entails a format that accords the politicians of the transgressor state an elevated speaking position. This results in a ritual predisposed to problematic representations of the colonised and sanitised narratives of the transgressor."[187]

The statement by Vice President Mbumba triggered another parliamentary question by MP Dağdelen to the German government, seeking clarification about the status of the Joint Declaration. The very short answer she received on 9 November

2022 was, in its semantic twists and its vagueness, tantamount to an oracle. It confirmed that both governments would remain committed to the original text of the Joint Declaration but had agreed that questions of implementation would be clarified in additional rather than new negotiations.[188]

While affairs remained pending during 2023, new critical interventions threw spanners in the works: on 19 January 2023 an application by Bernadus Swartbooi of the LPM, the OTA and nine traditional authorities from Nama communities as members of the NTLA was filed at the Namibian High Court.[189] It challenges the constitutional legality of the bilaterally negotiated agreement. The lawsuit seeks a judicial review to set aside the decision by the Speaker of Namibia's National Assembly to note the Joint Declaration and to declare it unlawful in terms of Namibia's Constitution as well as in breach of the motion adopted by the National Assembly in 2006. It argues that the country's international relations remain subject to constitutional control. Until the end of 2023 the case remained frozen in a "status hearing", a suspension to enable the prosecuting party to collect more supporting documents and to prepare a road map for its arguments. For Karina Theurer, who acts as a legal consultant in the lawsuit, it "could be a historical milestone, because it is the first time that an interstate agreement on the reappraisal of colonial crimes is being reviewed in a court of a former colony".[190]

As if this was not enough, seven Special Rapporteurs of the United Nations Human Rights Council submitted a letter to the German[191] and Namibian[192] government on 23 February 2023.[193] With minor variations, these letters

> express grave concern at the alleged failure of the Governments of Germany and Namibia, as parties to the negotiations, to ensure the right of the Ovaherero and Nama peoples, including women, to meaningful participation, through self-elected representatives. ... The legal status of the Ovaherero and Nama peoples and their representatives as indigenous peoples under international and national law is different and separate from that of the Namibian Government itself, and thus requires a place of its own in the negotiations. ... International law requires States to obtain the free,

prior, and informed consent of the Indigenous Peoples concerned through their own representatives before adopting and implementing legislative or administrative measures that may affect them. It also stipulates that mechanisms that aim to redress colonial crimes have to be developed in conjunction with them. The right to meaningful participation in all decisions that have an impact on their cultural life is also guaranteed under international law.[194]

The UN Special Rapporteurs not only bemoaned the "insufficient memorialization" of the genocide in both countries, but also underlined

> that the question at hand is not a demand for assistance but rather, and clearly so, a demand for accountability and reparation for the harm inflicted. This has important ramifications as only full reparation that includes acknowledgement, apology, restitution, compensation, rehabilitation and guarantees of non-recurrence (including the reform of continuous forms of exclusion and discrimination) can effectively remedy past wounds. This fundamental distinction cannot be overlooked or dismissed as in it lies the key to achieving the healing and reconciliation that has evaded both parties for so long.[195]

The Special Rapporteurs requested both governments to clarify certain matters. Namibia responded on 30 May 2023,[196] and Germany on 1 June 2023.[197] Predictably, both responses dismissed the criticism entirely. In particular, they were eager to stress that participation in the bilateral negotiations was at all times open to the representatives of the affected communities but had been declined by OTA and NTLA. This ignores the point made by the Special Rapporteurs "that the refusal to participate in ways which are not in accordance with international law cannot be construed as a refusal to participate in general".[198] The German response insisted that "today's outlawing and prohibition of genocide under international law did not exist in the years 1904 to 1908", and that "the current regime of human rights protection is not a suitable instrument for addressing by legal means events which occurred long before its establishment".[199] It ends with the self-righteous claim that the bilateral negotiations "could serve as a model for addressing colonial injustice".[200] But as Karina Theurer reveals: "In private, German diplomats admit that their legal reasoning is tenuous, but that the floodgates must be prevented from being opened."[201] Such motivation could well have been a contributing factor that explains the eagerness to push through the agreement against all odds. It may also resonate with the Namibian government's desire to bring the pending matter to a close, as the similar responses by both governments suggest.

Namibia's head of state, Hage Geingob, caused much consternation with a statement made when engaging on 15 September 2023 with students at the Paris Institute of Political Studies (Sciences Po) at a stopover on his way to the opening of the United Nations General Assembly in New York. When questioned about the bilateral negotiations, he opined:

> Reconciliation of Germany and Namibia is there. We have diplomatic relations, we have peace. This genocide happened how many years ago? Over a hundred years ago. Then the South Africans took over—they were worse and then Swapo started to fight to free the country. After we freed the country, we now have the right to talk about the genocide. Some people who talk about the time to reconcile were on South Africa's side when we were fighting for freedom. Now all of a sudden, the demand is that they must negotiate themselves. Go and convince Germany.[202]

In a subsequent interview with the news network France24, Geingob indicated that some agreement seemed to have been reached, and his spokesperson revealed a few days later that Geingob had "discussed outstanding matters on genocide reparations with German Chancellor Olaf Scholz".[203] Not surprisingly, this caused considerable public uproar. NUDO demanded an apology, reasoning: "The president is at liberty to play to the international gallery" but should not "do it at the expense of the Ovaherero and Nama people".[204] The NTLA and the OTA lambasted Geingob for "denialist utterances" in an unusually strongly worded joint statement for "behaving repugnantly and self-servingly in particular questions of our existential demands for redress of a colonial past".[205]

THE LONG SHADOW OF GERMAN COLONIALISM

Addressing German-speaking Namibians in late October 2023, Foreign Minister Netumbo Nandi-Ndaitwah revealed that another round of negotiations had taken place in Windhoek from 4 to 6 October. According to her, the focus was on three unresolved issues, namely "the amount offered, the 30-year payment period, and whether the final joint declaration would bring finality to Germany's obligations towards Namibia in the context of genocide".[206] In early November 2023, opposition leader McHenry Venaani claimed that the negotiations had reached agreement to add another one billion euros to the initial amount agreed.[207] In the absence of any official response, this remained unconfirmed. But in another meeting behind closed doors in early December in Berlin, the delegations seem to have reached further common ground. On 9 December 2023 Christoph Retzlaff, director for Sub-Saharan Africa and the Sahel at Germany's Federal Foreign Office, posted on X (formerly Twitter): "Constructive and trustful talks with Technical Committee of Government of Namibia in Berlin. Exchange with MPs of Parliament. Addressing the painful colonial past and jointly shaping our special relationship for the future."[208]

While rumours suggested that a deal had been sealed, by the end of 2023 no official announcement had been made as to how the Joint Declaration had been modified and if the result would be accepted. But even if by the time of this book being published such a ratified agreement became reality, it would not end the controversial debate. What Bentley has dubbed "double ventriloquism" seems an adequate characterisation of any agreement reached. This

> occurs whereby both the (former) colonizing state and the postcolonial government collude to speak for the colonized in respect to offering a narrative of the wrongdoing, determining remedial measures, and agreeing that the issue is "closed". Such collusion frames the state as the sole interlocutor in the transitional justice process and is an exercise in marginalizing the subaltern voices in addressing the past.[209]

As Theurer warns, "if the current German government thinks it will be possible to achieve reconciliation by imposing an agreement that is perceived to reproduce colonial racism and white saviourism and that is rejected by the majority of the affected communities", it might be in for a nasty surprise. Rather, "it amounts to putting more fuel into the fire".[210] The same warning can, of course, be addressed to the Namibian government.

No End in Sight

To take stock: what started as a much-welcomed, long-overdue initiative has turned into a tragically missed opportunity marred by flaws. Even if renegotiations have reached an amicable solution, it remains a major challenge, if not a mission impossible, to obtain approval of the majority among the members of the communities in Namibia and the diaspora most affected by the violent past. At the end of 2023, the leaders of the NTLA and the OTA issued another joint statement, referring to a visit of their delegation to Germany in December and a meeting held with MPs of the Green Party. They blamed the party for having "betrayed our trust", by abandoning its initial position after joining the tripartite government alliance. They accused the MPs of "making it seem as if there is nothing they can do about the more or less concluded negotiations and wanted to camouflage their shame with an addendum". As the statement stressed further:

> Germany must unconditionally acknowledge that it committed genocide, it must unconditionally apologise and it must unconditionally repair the damage it has done. ... Any utterance from German and Namibian officials, whether verbally or in writing, which refers to the genocide as something which "can be considered genocide from today's perspective", is a justification of genocide. It is not an acknowledgement. It is beyond our lay logic how the Namibian government can agree to a document which implies that the victims of the genocide were savages, according to Germany's interpretation of international law.[211]

As a matter of fact, no "official forum, in which perspectives of the Ovaherero and Nama could be expressed and heard, ever existed, was offered or seems to have been envisaged in the Joint

Declaration".²¹² This points to the limitations of government-to-government negotiations if they do not adequately recognise those who mainly bear the consequences of the genocide. The motto of the main agencies representing the descendants of the victims remains "Anything about us, without us, is against us".²¹³ Without their being substantially involved and willing to reconcile, this bilateral exercise in addressing the past remains in their view as patronising and paternalistic as colonialism had been. The asymmetries are a challenge also for those aware of them, since they remain partly intact and are reproduced among critical observers.²¹⁴ Given the structural legacies reproduced in current social realities, there is still a long way to go to accomplish reconciliation.

Any lasting solution is far from being achieved. Considerable parts of the descendants of the most-affected communities are not inclined to surrender their claims. They do not acknowledge the Namibian government as the legitimate agency for promoting their interests and negotiating on their behalf. This confirms the observation that state-to-state negotiations have inherent limitations in the quest for a solution.²¹⁵ Given that local communities in Namibia were exposed to dramatically different forms of colonial oppression and occupation in the course of their regional and ethnic histories, they should be granted agency in their own right to deal with and negotiate on the consequences of the genocide. This by no means disrespects the unitarian state as represented by the Namibian government, but recognises the official slogan once used by SWAPO of "unity in diversity". After all, as Kössler observes, "denial of actual difference amounts to discrimination, which, by implication, might actually jeopardize the goal of unity".²¹⁶ At the end of 2023 the Committee on the Elimination of Racial Discrimination within the Office of the United Nations High Commissioner for Human Rights expressed concern about the lack of "meaningful participation of the representatives of the victims of the Ovaherero and Nama peoples' genocide in the development and adoption of the Joint Declaration".²¹⁷

Given the further entrenchment of intra-Namibian ethnic-regional animosities and identities, not least as the result of adequate representation being denied these groups at the negoti-

GERMANY AND NAMIBIA

ating table, the following argument by Federico Lenzerini is also applicable to Namibia's indigenous communities:

> The recognition and realization of the right to reparation for such peoples—translating in practice to no more than allowing them to "regain control of their lives and their lands"—would not destabilize any state. On the contrary, it would provide great assistance in the realization—in a stable manner—of a fairer society and a more serene social environment, which, in the long run, is favourable to everybody, indigenous or not.[218]

Germany has conveniently dodged the matter of representation of the descendants of the victim groups by declaring it a purely internal Namibian affair. This position avoids any effort to find a solution for the matter. In the face of concerns about creating a precedent in international law, it would be possible to address the Namibian case without being obliged to acknowledge a general commitment to reparations for colonial crimes. After the announcement of the Joint Declaration, Sevim Dağdelen of the Left Party asked the scientific services of the German parliament to explore options for direct payments to Ovaherero and Nama in compensation for their losses.[219] The report indicated that it would be possible to enact a tailor-made Compensation Bill for the specific case.[220] This would require a negotiated agreement with the Namibian government as representative of the state. No such initiative was taken, however, suggesting that there was no willingness to explore this potential solution. After all, Germany would expect the least compromises from the side of those who represent the claims of the descendant groups. This applies especially to the issue of restitution of ancestral land stolen under German colonialism or later expropriated after the defeat of local groups in what they term the Namibian–German War. Instead of recognising the rights of the indigenous groups most affected, Germany "has treated the involvement of the Ovaherero and Nama as if this amounted to establishing bilateral relations with a non-governmental entity", as Judith Hackmack observes. Instead, she argues, "insofar as processes for addressing colonial crimes involve present-day governmental action ... states need to ensure the involvement of the survivors, in accordance with their international human rights obligations".²²¹ The descendants of the most-affected Namibian communities remain caught between a rock and a hard place, fighting "their battles for political recognition and legitimation on the terrain of memory ... as hegemonic state historical narratives are challenged by historically disenfranchised groups who issue legal and political demands for acknowledgement of their own versions of the past".²²²

Retributive justice remains missing from the vocabulary of the Joint Declaration. But already three years into Namibia's independence, a legal scholar suggested—with reference to retroactivity as an essential notion stressed by the International Military Tribunal at Nuremberg—that German liability for the genocide committed in South West Africa would require reparations for the injuries suffered as an appropriate measure for redress.²²³ A similar view has been presented by Esther Muinjangue in an interview:

> Only those whose ancestors went through that horrible experience understand the pain and impact inflicted by the genocide. We can never solve these issues by trying to beat around the bush—we need to call a spade a spade. As long as Germany avoids using words such as genocide and reparation, we can forget about coming closer to closing this chapter.
>
> ... It is critical to have representatives of the two communities at the negotiating table, selected and appointed by themselves. It is simple, we follow the same model that was applied at the Claims Conference with the German Government, State of Israel and 23 groups representing the Jews. If Germany could negotiate with 23 groups, what is difficult to negotiate with 23 groups of Ovaherero and Nama?²²⁴

In a similar vein, Howard Rechavia-Taylor and Dirk Moses wonder why one cannot seek the representation of Namibians beyond the state: "The Herero and Nama genocide and its aftermath are by no means identical to the Holocaust and its aftermath, but that does not rule out comparisons about the seriousness with which the question of reparations has been dealt."²²⁵

While the condition of colonial amnesia is unfortunately still true of many Germans, it is certainly not the case for many

Namibians—especially for the descendants of those communities who resisted and suffered most from German colonisation and subsequent settler-colonial rule. Just imagine for a moment if Germany had offered Jews a similar formula in acknowledgement of the Holocaust, as a genocide seen "from today's perspective". One wonders what the Jewish and wider international response would have been. As Ta-Nehisi Coates points out: "Reparations could not make up for the murder perpetrated by the Nazis. But they did launch Germany's reckoning with itself, and perhaps provided a road map for how a great civilization might make itself worthy of the name."[226]

In his essay "The Burden of Memory",[227] Wole Soyinka insists that distance in time from a crime whose consequences are still alive in the present is no argument for or against a legitimate demand for reparations. For the descendants of those who were destroyed by the genocide at the beginning of the 20th century, this history has had irreparable consequences for their present circumstances in Namibian society. Soyinka refers to the healing trilogy of truth, reparations and reconciliation. As he concludes, the scars of memory weigh heavy in the scales and block the ways to healing. On the way through the portal of healing, which the joint procession of victim and perpetrator must pass to achieve a moral symmetry, reparations are the keystone. Without reparations the portal would collapse and, with it, the two other pillars of truth and reconciliation. The final stone, if only as a symbolic offering, is redress. In his posthumously published notes, James Baldwin categorically underlined this perspective by stating that history is not the past but the present. We carry—and we are—our history. We cannot step out of the shadows of the past. But we can acknowledge them and try to bring light into the darkness.[228]

The Joint Declaration fails to achieve this. Without the descendants of the genocide survivors substantially involved and willing to reconcile, the outcome of the bilateral German–Namibian negotiations remains as patronising and paternalistic as colonialism had been. As the German legal expert Matthias Goldmann critically observed:

> The proposal to use the term "healing the wounds" suggests that it is not. ... It is a posture that inadvertently reproduces colonial

> thinking. For reconciliation to work requires that we stop that kind of thinking and find a genuinely postcolonial, or decolonial, approach. ...
>
> As in the European context, we need to stop using lukewarm legal arguments as an excuse against deeper forms of solidarity. As in the European context, we need to learn to be humble again. Of course, such bonds of solidarity are going to hurt some of our interests and sensitivities. Not just financially. But if it does not hurt, it is not a fix.[229]

There is a long way to travel so as to achieve reconciliation, by embracing justice and fairness.[230] Instead of healing wounds, the so-called reconciliation agreement has opened new ones among those who crave recognition and respect when it comes to the lasting consequences inflicted by colonialism not only on their ancestors but also on them. "It is as if we have never existed," one of them said to a German journalist.[231] This points to the decisive aspect, which goes far beyond material compensation. As the Nama activist Sima Luipert insists:

> No amount of money can ever wholly repair the damage that has been done. It's about recognition. Germany will only recognise us when it sits with us at the table.
>
> It will be like a mirror reflecting back to Germany what it has done. Germany is afraid to look into that mirror because it will see the monstrosity of what it has done. The collective German psyche is not ready.[232]

The question which the late Jewish historian Yosef Hayim Yerushalmi once posed remains valid also for the Namibian case: "is it possible that the antonym of 'forgetting' is not 'remembering' but 'justice'?"[233]

6

CHALLENGING COLONIAL ASYMMETRIES AND BLIND SPOTS

"Instead of self-cleansing we need self-enlightenment."[1]

In taking steps to engage more seriously with its colonial past, notably by negotiating on the subject of genocide with Namibia's government and by acts of restitution, Germany has once more—as in the case of commemorating the Holocaust—won international respect. But even though other former colonial empires may refuse to come to terms with their history of violence and oppression, this should be no reason for celebration. As Claudia Roth, Federal Government Commissioner for Culture and the Media in the Office of the Chancellor since December 2021, clarified in an interview: memory culture has many "white spots". The historical reappraisal of the colonial past has not even started in earnest, and the subject has not yet entered the wider public consciousness.[2]

This final chapter therefore first summarises once again why the current achievements are not sufficient and why public memory is still characterised by deficiencies, contradictions, denialism and an attempt by some gatekeepers to distract from or downplay the need for serious memory work as a domestic policy. It ends with some considerations and proposals for facing the colonial shadows.

THE LONG SHADOW OF GERMAN COLONIALISM

Selective Memory

The historian David Andress describes the phenomenon of "cultural dementia" in approaching the past in the UK, France and the US as "particular kinds of forgetting, misremembering and mistaking the past".[3] This goes beyond amnesia, as he argues: "In most cases, the amnesiac is aware that they do not remember; and knowledge of that lack—and of the potential to fill it from external information—is something to cling to." In contrast, "The dementia sufferer is denied the comfort of knowing they don't remember."[4] With reference to Holocaust commemoration, Andress explicitly excludes Germany from this diagnosis. However, his characterisation of selective (or absent) memory in the three countries he lists applies to Germany too: "They are detached from the actual history of how our societies took on their current social, economic and cultural forms; and they are wrong about where those societies fit into the world around them."[5] Their identity as patriots "embroils people in assumptions that have visible harmful consequences for anyone outside the core of that identity, and where the collective trajectory is towards further exploitation of a historical privilege that is, as much as it is anything else, racial."[6]

What requires clarification, however, is the use of the term "dementia". Cultural dementia, as Andress insists, is irreversible; colonial amnesia is not. As proponents of the notion concede, colonial amnesia is on the retreat.[7] Continued awareness campaigns have left their marks—whether this has to do with the genocide committed in South West Africa, the Humboldt Forum or the restitution of human remains and cultural artefacts. Not least, relentless efforts by local postcolonial initiatives, campaigning for the renaming of public spaces and questioning other forms of colonial memory that have been conserved, have made inroads in everyday life. All of these aspects matter in this book.

Amnesia does not mean that the topic of colonialism is absent from the public sphere. It has hardly ever been. Rather it means—in the sense meant by Andress—that the dominant discourse ignores existing counter-knowledge or applies some degree of immunisation against its revelations. These are available as sources and can be accessed and used for learning by anyone willing to do so. Such knowledge is not expunged from "storage memory" but rather kept away from "functional memory".[8] Its existence does not protect one from amnesia. Nor is the continuous presence of the subject since the days of German colonial rule or the knowledge accumulated over time proof that the term "amnesia" is misleading.[9] Some of those critical of German colonial historiography and the selective, restricted, filtered or biased treatment of such knowledge suggest aphasia as a more appropriate diagnosis—a lack of suitable language rather than a lack of memory. Lack of memory and lack of adequate language can indeed be considered as complementary in disrupting memory, and not as contradictory. Amnesia and aphasia are two sides of the same coin.

Even though sufficient evidence exists for colonial atrocities and the fundamental, systemic injustices that took place with lasting structural consequences, this does not mean that such facts are taken into consideration; nor are they adequately acknowledged in the sense of being integrated in one's (self-)positioning. Denial of empirical facts as well as attempts to shun their moral dimensions and obligations is more than just aphasia. It is the act (at times deliberate) of not wanting to acknowledge what could and should be known. Referring to the archive of the former Imperial Colonial Office, available and accessible after German unification when it was transferred from Potsdam to the German Federal Archives in Koblenz, a staff member wrote how she found it difficult to acknowledge colonial amnesia while as an archivist she was literally sitting among the documents.[10] Such thinking ignores social and political realities. The mere fact that such archives and knowledge exist does not eradicate misperceptions or prevent denialism. All the analyses of German colonial history based on archival material by historians in the GDR (see chapter 3)—as partisan as some might nonetheless have been—were dismissed in the West as purely "ideological", if not fabricated, and thereby denied any factual value or credibility as evidence. As previous chapters have shown, despite the gradual inroads and achievements by postcolonial approaches since the turn of the century, such misconceptions are still rife and even remain dominant.

THE LONG SHADOW OF GERMAN COLONIALISM

Colonial-apologetic efforts—directly or indirectly supported by institutionalised historical studies—set out to counteract and dismiss the new colonial-critical discourses that gained momentum as the international solidarity movement emerged from the late 1960s.[11] As shown in chapter 4, academic debates of the 1980s confirmed the continued existence of colonial-revisionist networks, influencing the public discourse.[12] Such networks have not retreated or become irrelevant. Overcoming the deficiencies caused by amnesia (or aphasia, for that matter) requires a fundamental revision of perspectives, mindsets and behaviour that will translate into everyday practices and shape a common culture based on a shared historical awareness, informing daily life as much as politics. Despite the progress presented in chapter 4, we still have a long way to go, in a world which continues to be governed by asymmetric power relations, both globally and locally.

Loss of memory has been at the heart of national identity formation since the birth of the so-called nation-state, as Ernest Renan observed in a lecture at the Sorbonne on 11 March 1882:

> Forgetting, I would even say historical error, is an essential factor in the creation of a nation and it is for this reason that the progress of historical studies often poses a threat to nationality. Historical inquiry, in effect, throws light on the violent acts that have taken place at the origin of every political formation, even those that have been the most benevolent in their consequences.[13]

As Renan noted, "a heroic past with great men and glory ... is the social capital upon which the national idea rests". It oils the shift of emphasis towards the idea of the nation as a community of "great solidarity"[14]—a solidarity which supports taboos around topics and memory loss, such as characterised the initial years of post-1945 West Germany.[15]

Europe's colonial and imperialist expansion took place at a price—which was paid by others. And remembrance needs to address the memory loss. As a current African perspective articulated by Yvonne Owuor has it:

> Some thinkers-on-trial work is required. Is your culture willing to poke at your Charles Darwins, John Lockes, Carl Linnaeus,

CHALLENGING COLONIAL ASYMMETRIES

Immanuel Kant? Not forgetting that completer of philosophy too, the beloved Georg Hegel who boldly stated that *"man as we find him in Africa has not progressed beyond his immediate existence"*. And we the non-existent, in a Hegelian sense, have had to live out the strong belief of the Occident in this capsule of condensed stupidity.[16]

Hegemonic knowledge and power went (and continue to go) hand in hand in consolidating colonial relations. Even those not blinded by amnesia are not protected from aphasia. For those socialised in a society of colonial perpetrators, knowledge of the true nature of colonial history does not provide reliable protection against infection by patterns of thought from the dominant culture. What is required to reduce (though not eliminate) the risk is reflective self-interrogation, questioning one's own production of knowledge. Is not the fact that we can afford to deal with African history only when it is of direct relevance to our own history and engagement with colonial guilt, nothing but a continued form of colonial dominance?[17]

A past determined by a relationship between perpetrators and victims, such as colonial forms of rule, cannot remain silent on the history of violence or abstain from the necessary engagement with that history.[18] The "long shadow of the Holocaust" resulted in the conceptual and discursive expansion of the diagnosis of trauma. This by no means implies a downplaying of the Holocaust or a questioning of its uniqueness. Rather, it signals a profound moral and cognitive turn in thought as a result, which allows us to view earlier excesses of violence in a new perspective and to describe and judge such occurrences, for which no language or public awareness previously existed.[19]

In the light of such an understanding, there have been increased demands to provide adequate space for the treatment of the colonial history of violence. This has provoked vehement reactions, which in their misrepresentations and claims often make any productive and constructive exchange impossible. Refusal to engage is not confined to the right wing but is well at home in society's middle. For instance, a columnist in the monthly newspaper of the German Cultural Council, a pluralist forum open to colonial-critical deliberations, bemoaned the debates over the Humboldt Forum as a "farewell to our leading memory". He claimed that postcolonial discourse has no place for the singularity of the Holocaust.[20] Resistance to lifting the taboo on the brutal nature of colonial history predating the Nazi regime remains very much alive.

Learning from the Past

Learning from the past for the sake of the future when engaging with colonialism in the present continues to face rejection. This is met with frustration by those who were on the receiving end of colonial history:

> You Germany, with your shrines and reflections on the devastation of the Shoah, that there is to this moment a dispute about what to do with stolen, appropriated, desecrated human remains, the horrific evidence of the Occident's inability to come to terms with its own ghastly conscience, its will to murder, its compromise with intrinsic and moral evil. But for how long, my dears? That this depth and scope of unadulterated evil does not seize the national conscience says all that needs to be said, not only about our fundamental disconnect, but the fact that the site where the most difficult work is to be undertaken is in that space of re-humanisation. So, dear Germany, how often have you asked yourself what it means to be human? And having explored that thoroughly, what is your reply to the sibling question: what does the humanity of the other mean for me?[21]

The German–Namibian Joint Declaration, which received detailed attention in chapter 5, is subtitled "United in Remembrance of Our Colonial Past, United in Our Will to Reconcile, United in Our Vision of the Future". If taken seriously, it could serve as an outline and blueprint for efforts between states and peoples seeking to come to terms with their brutal colonial history in so many parts of the world. Unfortunately, what sounds like a shared commitment fails to live up to its promise. What follows after the embracing formula of the Declaration—the substance of negotiations—is deeply flawed and contrary to any meaningful notion of memory and commemoration. The deal between the two governments has not in any serious way involved the people of both countries, though the governments negotiated on their behalf. They endorse the idea of a *Schlussstrich* (final line), suggesting that history can be put to rest. This is yet more evidence that colonial relations are still being reproduced in the present, not only in the asymmetric power relations of global policy, but also in the domestic policies of countries. The limited compromise negotiated between Germany and Namibia testifies to the existence of a hierarchy when it comes to the treatment of mass violence and genocide in history. That in the shadow of the Holocaust other crimes are reduced to being secondary to the singularity of the mass extinction of the Jews is not only a selective view of the sufferings of other people at other times (or even endured at the same time by members of other groups such as the Sinti and Roma, not to mention those hunted down for political and many other reasons, such as members of the queer and Black German communities). It is also based on a continued colonial amnesia in Germany, which remains an obstacle to the promotion of greater public awareness beyond occasional lip service.[22]

"Was wären Sie bereit aufzugeben?" (What are you willing to give up?) was the reply given by Naita Hishoono, a Namibian raised in the GDR during the 1980s, to the question of how national reconciliation between Germany and Namibia could be achieved. Her answer was made during a panel debate on the second day of the international conference "Beyond: Towards a Future Practice of Remembrance", held at the Frankfurt University of Applied Sciences in collaboration with the Anne Frank Educational Centre on 22–23 September 2022.[23] Her response is entirely justified, not least if we bear in mind the ludicrously modest amount of money allocated for "reconstruction" in the German–Namibian agreement as "a gesture of recognition". But she also could have asked: what are you willing to accept? This touches on the non-material aspect of reconciliation. How much are you willing to engage with, and take in, what we (the offspring of the colonised) have to offer and share as our own feelings, emotions and traumatic memories, having been on the receiving end of mass crimes, genocide and robbery not only of our land but also of our way of life and our culture. What has been observed with reference to the Namibian case is true in a more general context too: "It is well known that truth-telling from the perspective of the survivors, as well as commemoration, can have a reparative and healing effect. They can also contribute toward (re-)establishing the agency of survivors that was lost as a result of the international crimes."[24]

What might a collective world memory consist of, one that includes all human experiences of suffering and the right to share these in narratives, to contribute to a shared inheritance? As several reflections on this insist, if we are to achieve an inclusive attitude guided by solidarity, we need to abandon the notion of a hierarchy of suffering. This requires an understanding of the economy of empathy as a form of mental and emotional self-positioning within a landscape of history, shaped by five hundred years of colonial and postcolonial asymmetries.[25] In our global world of asymmetric power relations, we find a reduced empathy (if any) with the victims of colonialism. Knowledge about the colonial legacy is in most cases unaccompanied by pain or mourning. It is a cold form of knowing. It refuses to consider how our own history has shaped the present; how so-called Western civilisations are structurally embedded in the consequences of the colonial era.[26]

If we are to develop a serious understanding, especially in the context of seeking reconciliation, we need a new, self-critical, reflective orientation and positioning in the shadow of colonial history. We must critically interrogate the cultural and mental foundations of our world views and our framing of knowledge. We need to challenge our perceptions of ourselves and of others. What we take for granted must be questioned. Only then can we begin to make meaningful efforts to understand. This includes the willingness to provide space for the experiences of "the other": not only to be aware of them, but to allow them to penetrate our self-awareness and what we have taken for granted. Reconciliation cannot take place if the process of re-establishing and reconstructing memory as a collective act is impossible because the descendants of those who are commemorated are excluded.[27] As the Ovaherero Paramount Chief Mutjinde Katjiua has stressed, the recognition of injustice matters. As he demanded: "Listen to us."[28]

But even if we are willing and able to walk the painful road, we need to accept our limitations. In NoViolet Bulawayo's novel *We*

Need New Names, a Zimbabwean back home exclaims in an angry exchange with her childhood friend who has relocated to the US: "you are not the one suffering. You think watching on BBC means you know what is going on? No, you don't, my friend, it's the wound that knows the texture of the pain."[29] We cannot experience the pain of others and we cannot speak on their behalf: failure to accept this is another form of appropriation. Salim, the narrator in Abdulrazak Gurnah's novel *Gravel Heart*, when meeting British fellow students eager to involve themselves in making a better world, observed: "If the posters and the campaigns and demonstrations were a guide, any injustice in the world seemed to be theirs to claim, accompanied by frivolities that were like a celebration of disorder. They were fortunate people who desired to own even the suffering of others."[30]

We cannot and should not claim ownership of the suffering and trauma of others that we never have been able nor will be able to experience ourselves. But we can help make such suffering and trauma known so as to gain recognition and respect from others. In this way we act not as their mouthpiece but as people willing to accept their experiences as related to ours in a world of asymmetric power relations. This requires a careful balancing act, which needs to accept the limits of our perspectives as those of members of societies benefiting from global injustices in the past and present. This undertaking does not claim to speak for the victims but seeks to ask how we can come to terms with our past in a better way, as a modest effort to side with those who were far too long on the receiving end, without claiming to join their ranks. Accepting one's own limitations may promote an understanding of solidarity "as ally-ship rather than vanguardism".[31]

This points to the hierarchical selectivity of *Gerechtigkeitsgefühle* (feelings of justice), relating to "affective and emotional dynamics in normative processes of meaning-making".[32] As Charlotte Wiedemann maintains, compassion is not just. It does not follow the principle of human equality. But while it may be impossible to feel the pain of others, we should try to understand and respect them[33]—and, one might add, to endure what this entails.

While many believe in lifelong learning guided by curiosity, this is often merely a matter of pursuing self-affirmative perspectives. But seeking to confirm our own convictions is not learning. Learning is listening. Learning is also more than a cognitive act. Learning—particularly in inter-societal contexts—requires an emotional dimension too. It benefits from empathy, which should translate into creating awareness of and sensitivity towards others. Ideally, learning is more than acquiring knowledge as a cognitive act. It is also a value-based affair with emotional, moral and ethical dimensions. Otherwise, learning remains the acquisition of cold knowledge. Facts do matter, and the transmission of factual knowledge remains an integral part of learning. To that extent, textbook reforms and revised curricula do make a difference as part of organised learning processes in schools and other institutions of learning. They are contributory factors in creating awareness not only of past injustices but also of the need to address them. Access to what is on record remains a precondition for challenging amnesia and denialism and should begin at home and at school.[34] It also requires developing the insight that colonialism was not restricted to lasting consequences for the colonised. It had a lasting impact on the colonisers too, which we need to become aware of and problematise, and accept as a challenge if decolonisation is to be taken seriously. It would require the admission in Germany and also in the wider European continent that the Nazi regime was no atypical exception, but the extreme outcome of racial obsessions anchored in deep mental structures.[35] "Year zero"[36]—1945—marked a new beginning with much baggage carried over from the past, and much of the old—not least in terms of brutality and violence—reproduced in the new. But just as this historical account of 1945 shows, coming to terms with the past needs more than facts and analysis. It needs a human face. The horror of the Holocaust only came to life through visual documentaries and personal accounts, not through the plain statistics and anonymous data of mass extermination: "To recognize genocide is, fundamentally, to confront the validity, legitimacy, and legibility of the thing; to bring it into a fold of *human* experience so that it, too, can become universally acknowledged and henceforth memorialized and mourned."[37] And human experience needs personal interaction:

Understanding injustice, and the crime of genocide specifically, solely in a legal sense does not sufficiently account for the trauma it engenders. ... Finding justice, then, constitutes a multifaceted process of addressing this emotional distress as well as undoing the structural factors perpetuating it. ... An emotions perspective contributes significantly to a more complex understanding of the communities' key demands, in particular their affective content in the sense of being respected, heard and valued in one's personhood. ... Practices such as truth-telling, apologies and reparations may evoke a sense of recognition and help restore victims' dignity. Therefore, they represent a counterproject to the continued sense of degradation and heteronomy lived by descendants throughout their engagement.[38]

Local memory sites can also be translated into transnational memory spaces: "the transnationalisation of memory can evoke empathy and solidarity, as illustrated by the never again discourse".[39] This includes physical locations (using the examples of Robben Island and Srebrenica), and also points to the risk of appropriation "when tourists try to 'relive' the experience of suffering", thereby reducing "deep trauma to a transferable commodity".[40] This is an important warning. Memory and commemoration, like redress, need to be based on the recognition that people have genuine experiences to share, which are not "cast in stone" as sites to be claimed and occupied by others. To that extent, we can make good use of accounts and narratives such as oral records, literature and other forms of creative expression. In the case of Namibia, we can learn from and through shared histories,[41] and other examples of "writing genocide",[42] as well as from greater access to recorded oral history[43] and literary efforts by writers with a different point of departure.[44] Furthermore, recent explorations by German-speakers with family histories in South West Africa and even partly indigenous roots offer new perspectives.[45] This is all educative, and helps us understand that justice matters—not only for the descendants of the communities exposed to genocide and other forms of mass violence, but also for those on the side of perpetrating societies who live—often as beneficiaries—in the shadow of injustices.

THE LONG SHADOW OF GERMAN COLONIALISM

The Coloniality of Power

The growing body of scholarly work on the colonial dimensions of Germany's history from the *Kaiserreich* to the Nazi regime led at one stage to the conclusion that "the basic case for placing the Nazi empire inside a framework of colonialism, whether in the abstract or for purposes of comparison, seems noncontroversial".[46] This has changed recently, if it was generally accepted at all. The inroads made by postcolonial initiatives in civil society, and by scholars often with an affinity for postcolonial theories, demanding adequate recognition of the genocidal mass violence during colonial times, have met with an embittered defence by cohorts of German gatekeepers. The latter maintain that such demands lack respect for and recognition of the singularity of the Holocaust, sometimes even associating these demands for recognition with antisemitic tendencies downplaying the Holocaust. Since the publication of Michael Rothberg's *Multidirectional Memory*[47] in a German translation, this debate has escalated.[48] It centres on the keywords of genocide, reparations and retributive justice, connected to the lasting impact of colonial rule for the descendants of the affected indigenous people.[49] This interrelatedness has also highlighted in the wider public discourse the "emotional relevance of Germany's colonial past", while at the same time "a legal renegotiation of the colonial past is very unlikely because of the ordering effects established by Holocaust memory".[50] Reflecting on the controversial reception of his book in Germany, which "laid bare the gulf between contemporary international research and its translation into public history and debates on memory culture",[51] Rothberg asked:

> what is the meaning of working through the past? Although those hostile to multidirectional and postcolonial approaches to memory return again and again to the question of whether or not colonial violence is the "same" as the Holocaust, the real stakes lie elsewhere. They involve what we do with those histories in the present: how we negotiate lived multidirectionality, relations of difference, and contemporary experiences of subordination and violence, all of which are refracted through the habitus of the dominant German memory culture.[52]

The singularity of the Holocaust provides an excuse in the German debate for the gatekeepers to leave the image of the colonial *Kaiserreich* undisturbed. This compartmentalises and thereby disrupts history for the sake of a selective present. A contrasting African perspective dismisses the exclusivism of the term "holocaust". It is seen as evidence that the "tendency to diminish the pain of Africans is not accidental; it reveals the devious workings of the phenomena of the *coloniality of power* ... in European scholarship that names Africans as less human or Other".[53] As Khatija Khan explains in her conclusion: "to equate the suffering of the Jews under the Third Reich with the experiences of African people under colonial rule in Africa is not meant to minimize the Jewish Holocaust. It is in fact a way of amplifying the historical violence that has been visited on Africans and Jews in history."[54]

For Natan Sznaider, who advocates "vanishing point perspectives" as a third way, one can understand the Holocaust as the ultimate evil in European remembrance, since it was the worst crime that is remembered in Europe. But it is similarly understandable that this is not the case in the world that experienced the mass killing and forced labour of colonialism.[55] In a comment on the debates, it has been suggested that at the core of the controversies is neither comparison nor claimed singularity but commemorative hegemony.[56] These "memory wars" (*Erinnerungskämpfe*)[57] reach far beyond the uphill battles against colonial amnesia or relativism, though they include them as an integral part of coming to terms with the ugly sides of German pasts that have been denied or not fully acknowledged, despite the much-celebrated (albeit selective) memory culture of the Holocaust.

The advances of recent years have been accompanied by setbacks. A painful reminder is the sad example of an initiative to rename Iltis Street in Berlin-Dahlem. Like Taku and Lans streets, it marks a small road in the vicinity of the Free University of Berlin. They are reminders of the naval captain and two gunboats operating in the Pacific during the German colonial "pacification" and the Boxer rebellion (see chapter 3). In mid-2022, alumni of the Otto-Suhr-Institut (which is the home to Political Sciences) started campaigning for renaming Iltis Street as Nora Schimming Promenade, to honour a

THE LONG SHADOW OF GERMAN COLONIALISM

Namibian activist (1940–2018). A former student at the Institute, she served after a long engagement in the anti-colonial struggle as Namibia's second ambassador to Germany (1992–1996).[58] Despite support from a broad local alliance, including a wide range of so-called reputable and respected members of the political, diplomatic and institutional establishment, a local alliance of the AfD, CDU and FDP (!) in the district council of Steglitz-Zehlendorf (tasked to decide on the proposal) used their combined majority to block the name. As of early 2024 the matter remains pending.

But there are also reasons to celebrate. At the official event marking the renaming of two streets in Berlin-Wedding in honour of Rudolf and Emily Duala Manga Bell and Cornelius Fredericks on 2 December 2022, Sharon Dodua Otoo recited her poem "*das erinnern*",[59] which she had composed for this occasion. I take the liberty of ending this book, which deals to a large extent with a German-African past in the present, by quoting its last parts (the translation is my own):

> In heads, in which cheaters are trivialised as explorers in which stolen land is transformed into protectorates, In which true kings are betrayed, In which colonial executions are not followed by official apologies, No appeal to conscience helps.
>
> ...
>
> On those days when I am most optimistic, I know that remembering happens anyway. There are humans, who wear stories on their skin, have innocent blood running in their veins and blossoms along their spinal cord. Some speak softly and keep their eyes lowered, or even the whole head. Here bridges are built, a patient explanation as if it is the first time. There people start marching, because: we finally want to breathe. Tears are shed when laughing and weeping, the earth is intoxicated by it, and some of us do: the remembering. We gift our names to German streets. It happens anyway if the others want to believe or not.

ACKNOWLEDGEMENTS

The writing of this book benefited from the working environment so generously facilitated by the Nordic Africa Institute, to which I remain affiliated as an associate. My thanks go to Therése Sjömander-Magnusson and all her colleagues for creating such an inspiring, supportive atmosphere.

I am grateful to those who at different times and in various ways have accompanied and supported me as seniors since my student days in academia: Franz Ansprenger, Michaela von Freyhold, Dietrich Goldschmidt, Gerhard Grohs, Leonard Harding, Manfred O. Hinz and Werner Ruf. Lennart Wohlgemuth offered me the opportunity to relocate from Namibia to Sweden. I am in debt to them all for playing a role in one way or another during my scholarly and professional development.

I acknowledge the friendships and exchanges with several people who will not see the result of their inspiring interactions with me, most notably Carlos Lächele, Helga and Ludwig Helbig, Gottfried Mergner and Tor Sellström. I miss them dearly. The ongoing collaboration with Reinhart Kössler, spanning more than four decades, has enriched my perspectives. I am also grateful for the exchanges with others, too many to mention, while working in Germany, Namibia, Sweden and South Africa. The recent years of interaction with Uma Kothari and others in the European Association of Development Research and Training Institutes (EADI) have added to my insights. So did the handful of people who made me feel at home in the circle "Fürsorgliche Überzeugungsarbeit". Finally, it is

ACKNOWLEDGEMENTS

thanks to Thomas Fues that I have re-engaged—if only from a distance—in postcolonial German advocacy and activism beyond the German–Namibian case.

My heartfelt thanks go to Michael Dwyer, who fully supported this project. Its result benefited from constructive reviews with suggestions for final improvements and the meticulous language editing by Russell Martin. Adding to my books on Namibia (2014) and Dag Hammarskjöld (2019), it completes the thematic foci closest to my heart and mind. As the saying goes, all good things come in threes.

Finally, without the patience, tolerance and daily support of Sue, this undertaking would have remained work in progress. Owing to the pandemic our shared small home was turned into an office with papers piling up and invading her treasured privacy. She had to pay a high price for loyalty to a pensioner unable to retire. Luckily, we continue to love each other.

pp. [1–5]

NOTES

1. INTRODUCTION: WHICH PAST, WHOSE PAST?

1. Chimamanda Ngozi Adichie in her keynote speech at the opening ceremony of the Ethnological Museum and the Asian Art Museum in the Humboldt Forum, Berlin, 22 September 2022. Accessible as a video at https://www.humboldtforum.org/en/programm/digitales-angebot/digital-en/keynote-spreech-by-chimamanda-adichie-32892/.
2. Knigge and Frei, *Verbrechen erinnern*.
3. Francois and Schulze, *Deutsche Erinnerungsorte*.
4. Wissenschaftliche Dienste, Deutscher Bundestag, *Dokumentation: Zur kolonialen Vergangenheit Deutschlands in Namibia*, 4. Notably, the name of the author and several other references to sources and related information are blacked out.
5. Ibid., 9.
6. Stahn, *Confronting Colonial Objects*, 9.
7. Táiwò, *Against Decolonisation*.
8. Die Bundesregierung, *Koalitionsvertrag vom 12. März 2018*, chapter XIII/2, 165.
9. Ibid., XII/4, 152 and XIII/2, 167.
10. Schwarzer, "Das verdrängte Verbrechen".
11. Deutscher Bundestag, Drucksache 19/5130.
12. Ibid., 4f.
13. Ibid., 4.
14. Ibid., 5.
15. Ibid., 2.
16. Deutscher Bundestag, Ausschuss für Kultur und Medien, Protokoll-Nr. 20/20.
17. Federal Government, *Interministerial Strategy to Support "Dealing with the Past and Reconciliation (Transitional Justice)"* 8. Original emphasis.
18. Ibid., 8f.
19. Ibid., 16. Original emphasis.
20. Ibid., 23. Original emphasis.
21. Koalitionsvertrag, *Mehr Fortschritt wagen*, 125f.
22. Ibid, 126. The draft agreement was initialled in May 2021 after more than five

years of bilateral government negotiations by the special envoys of the two countries but by early 2024 had not yet been ratified. For more details on the process and the controversies, see chapter 5.

23. "Was steht an in der Auswärtigen Kultur- und Bildungspolitik? Die Sprecherinnen und Sprecher der Fraktionen geben Auskunft", *Politik & Kultur*, June 2022, 6–7.
24. The agreement is accessible at Auswärtiges Amt, "Joint Declaration on the Return of Benin Bronzes and Bilateral Museum Cooperation".
25. Both quoted in Al Jazeera, "Germany Returns 20 Benin Bronzes to Nigeria".
26. Quoted in Oltermann, "Germany Returns 21 Benin Bronzes to Nigeria". Notably, the number given in media reports is 20, 21 and 22 respectively. According to a tweet by Baerbock, the number was 20.
27. https://twitter.com/ABaerbock/status/1604492970866229256.
28. Quoted in Schult, "Rückgabe von Benin-Bronzen".
29. For a detailed background article, see Rogers, Lassa and Marshall, "How Germany Changed Its Mind, and Gave the Benin Bronzes Back".
30. The article in *Der Spiegel* has at its main title a quote from the governor of the Nigerian federal state of Edo that Germany is a role model for the world ("Deutschland ist ein Vorbild für die Welt"); Schult, "Rückgabe von Benin-Bronzen".
31. See the factual rejection of such claims by Mallon, "Benin-Bronzen: Baerbock hat absolut recht, ihre Hater blamieren sich".
32. Federal Foreign Office, "Speech by Foreign Minister Annalena Baerbock on the Occasion of the Return of the Benin Bronzes to Nigeria".
33. Koldehoff, "Kommentar zu Benin-Bronzen".
34. As the agreement states in clause 5: "Both sides intend that German public museums and institutions will continue to display Benin Bronzes on loan as set out in the transfer agreements."
35. Lederer, "Wie viel Blut klebt an der Kunst?", 119.
36. Quoted in Schult, "Rückgabe von Benin-Bronzen".
37. For reasons most likely related to the pending negotiations between the German and Namibian governments on the genocide committed in South West Africa (see details in chapter 5), he made no similar appearance in Namibia.
38. For more details, see https://rememberinghumanremains.wordpress.com/songea-mbano/; LeGall and Mboro, "Deutsch-Ostafrika", 109; and Rushohora, "Desperate Mourning and Atrophied Representation".
39. Pérez Ramirez, *Survey on Human Remains from Colonial Contexts Held in Museum and University Collections in Germany*.
40. Bundespräsidialamt, Federal President Frank-Walter Steinmeier on the Occasion of the Visit to the Maji Maji Memorial Museum, 2 and 3.
41. Johnson, "Ein Signal, aber noch keine Politik".
42. Selz, "Krokodilstränen".
43. Böhm, "Europas Angst, sich zu entschuldigen".
44. Hoffmann, "'Wir erleben den Beginn einer großen Dekolonisierungsbewegung'".
45. Note the frequent use of the term "dark".
46. Lederer, "Wie viel Blut klebt an der Kunst?", 115.

47. Andress, *Cultural Dementia*, 144.
48. Van der Westhuizen, "Apology as a Pathway", 146, with reference to Steyn, "The Ignorance Contract", 10 and 12.
49. Mills, "White Ignorance", 27 and 31, as quoted by Van der Westhuizen, "Apology as a Pathway", 146.
50. Ibid.
51. Kundnani, *Eurowhiteness*.
52. Kundnani, *Eurowhiteness*, 4. Interestingly, when making reference to a possible collective Western European (EU) project of reparations, he lists by name France, Belgium, the Netherlands, Spain and Portugal, but not Germany.
53. Moradi, "'Restitution' of Looted African Art Just Continues Colonial Policies".
54. Volk, "Patriotic History in Postcolonial Germany", 286.

2. ENLIGHTENMENT, RACISM, COLONIALISM AND GENOCIDE

1. The title of a movie by Ridley Scott released 500 years later.
2. Especially instructive are the works of Norbert Elias and Michel Foucault, referred to in more detail below.
3. See Hanke, *Aristotle and the American Indians*; Hernandez, *The Las Casas–Sepúlveda Controversy*.
4. For more details, see Todorov, *The Conquest of America*.
5. Fredrickson, *Racism*, 56.
6. Williams, *Condorcet and Modernity*.
7. For a critical engagement with Kant, see Harvey, *Cosmopolitanism and the Geographies of Freedom*; Elden and Mendieta, *Reading Kant's Geography*. Both Kant and (more prominently) Hegel are references for Krell, "The Bodies of Black Folk". See also Hahmann, "Rassismus in der Klassischen Deutschen Philosophie?"; Martinez Mateo and Stubenrauch, "'Rasse' und Naturteleologie bei Kant"; and Zambrana, "Schlechte Angewohnheiten".
8. Koselleck, *Futures Past*. For a deeper engagement with his theory of modernity and theory of historical time, see Weiskott, "Futures Past".
9. See Duffield and Hewitt, *Empire, Development and Colonialism*; Hodge, Hödl and Kopf, *Developing Africa*.
10. A phrase coined by Joseph Conrad in his 1902 novella *Heart of Darkness*. It remains a matter of debate whether this was written with a colonial-critical or colonial-apologetic intention. Conrad's novel inspired the title of a pioneering study on colonial mass violence by the late Sven Lindqvist, *"Exterminate All the Brutes": One Man's Odyssey into the Heart of Darkness and the Origins of European Genocide*.
11. The concept of a disciplinary society has been most prominently introduced by Michel Foucault, see *Madness and Civilization*; *The Order of Things*; *The Birth of the Clinic*; and *Discipline and Punishment*; see also Mills, *Michel Foucault*.
12. Bauman, *Modernity and the Holocaust*. See also his related engagements with the destructive impact of modernity on the devaluation of human lives perceived as different, in *Modernity and Ambivalence* and *Wasted Lives*.

13. For multidisciplinary approaches to genocide, including chapters inspired by critical theory, see Bauman and Foucault, contributions to Kinloch and Mohan, *Genocide*.
14. Zimmerman, *Anthropology and Antihumanism in Imperial Germany*. See also Grosse, *Kolonialismus, Eugenik und bürgerliche Gesellschaft in Deutschland*. For the impact of this on German colonial policy, see also Bauche, "Von der Unmöglichkeit, klare Grenzen zu ziehen".
15. On these foundations laid in the 19th century, see especially Poliakov, *The Aryan Myth*. For the links between colonial racism, antisemitism and the legacies since then, see Kölnische Gesellschaft für Christlich-Jüdische Zusammenarbeit, *100 Jahre deutscher Rassismus*.
16. Madley, "Patterns of Frontier Genocide 1803–1910"; Adhikari, *Destroying to Replace*; *Genocide on Settler Frontiers*; *Civilian-Driven Violence and the Genocide of Indigenous Peoples in Settler Societies*; and "'We Will Utterly Destroy Them'". See also the pioneering study of Bodley, *Victims of Progress*.
17. On various aspects of this interrelation, see the contributions in Dabag, Gründer and Ketelsen, *Kolonialismus*.
18. This is the programmatic title of an early novel by J.M. Coetzee, set in a colonial borderland.
19. See Schaller, "Colonialism and Genocide"; Moses, "Raphael Lemkin, Culture, and the Concept of Genocide"; Schaller and Zimmerer, *The Origins of Genocide*. For a contextualisation of genocides, see Moses, *The Problem of Genocide*.
20. Moses, "Empire, Colony, Genocide", ix.
21. See Melber, "Kontinuität totaler Herrschaft'"; Madley, "From Africa to Auschwitz"; Zimmerer, *Von Windhuk nach Auschwitz?* and *From Windhoek to Auschwitz*; and Baer, *The Genocidal Gaze*.
22. See the debate between Melber, "How to Come to Terms with the Past"; Kössler, "From Genocide to Holocaust?"; Kundrus, "From the Herero to the Holocaust?", and "Colonialism, Imperialism, National Socialism"; Keim, "Colonialism, National-Socialism and the Holocaust"; and Bachmann, *Genocidal Empires*. "A less direct route from South West Africa to Poland" is suggested by Dedering, "Compounds, Camps, Colonialism", 44. For overviews of the controversial debate, see the review article by Zollmann, "From Windhuk to Auschwitz"; Fitzpatrick, "The Pre-history of the Holocaust?"; and Kühne, "Colonialism and the Holocaust". A sober de-escalation of the polemical debate triggered in the early 2020s is presented by Bajohr and O'Sullivan, "Holocaust, Kolonialismus und NS-Imperialismus". An interesting parallel between German colonialism in Africa and the colonisation of Polish people in the Prussian-Polish Provinces is drawn by Urena Valerio, *Colonial Fantasies, Imperial Realities*, chapters 3 and 4. Comparative studies of colonial wars (and more reservations as regards a unilinear continuity in German genocidal practices) are presented in the chapters in Klein and Schumacher, *Kolonialkriege*.
23. See on this Axster, "Licht und Schatten?"
24. Wiedemann, *Der lange Abschied von der weißen Dominanz*, 231ff.
25. Lemkin, *Axis Rule in Occupied Europe*. For popular summary versions explaining

and advocating the use of this term, see Lemkin, "Genocide: A Modern Crime" and "Genocide".

26. Vasel, "'In the Beginning, There Was No Word …'" Churchill's full speech, broadcast on 24 August 1941, is accessible at http://www.ibiblio.org/pha/policy/1941/410824a.html.
27. On contacts between Lemkin and the early campaign for the recognition of the plight of the Ovaherero at the United Nations, see Krautwald, "Genocide and the Politics of Memory in the Decolonisation of Namibia", 12.
28. On Lemkin's efforts to this effect, see Segesser and Gessler, "Raphael Lemkin and the International Debate on the Punishment of War Crimes (1919–1948)"; Elder, "What You See before Your Eyes". Sands, *East West Street*, draws attention to the conflicting notions of genocide and crimes against humanity, the latter advocated and campaigned for in parallel by Hersch Lauterpacht. Given the centrality of the war-torn history of Lviv (formerly Lemberg), with the Jewish community forced to relocate from there as victims of antisemitism, this thrilling account offers background to the solidarity and empathy when witnessing the Russian invasion of Ukraine in 2022 under the pretext of "denazification".
29. Full text accessible at https://documents-dds-ny.un.org/doc/RESOLUTION/GEN/NR0/033/47/IMG/NR003347.pdf?OpenElement.
30. *Convention on the Prevention and Punishment of the Crime of Genocide*. Approved and proposed for signature and ratification or accession by General Assembly resolution 260 A (III) of 9 December 1948. In force on 12 January 1951, in accordance with article XIII. Full document at https://www.un.org/en/genocideprevention/documents/atrocity-crimes/Doc.1_Convention%20on%20the%20Prevention%20and%20Punishment%20of%20the%20Crime%20of%20Genocide.pdf. See also https://treaties.un.org/doc/publication/unts/volume%2078/volume-78-i-1021-english.pdf. See for a detailed report on the interactions leading to this pioneering resolution Lemkin, "Genocide as a Crime under International Law".
31. See Smith, *Less Than Human*.
32. Kamissek and Kreienbaum, "An Imperial Cloud?", 165.
33. Menger, "'Press the Thumb onto the Eye'".
34. Schubert, "The 'German Nation' and the 'Black Other'", 416.
35. Huttenbach, "Defining Genocide, Comparing Genocides", 17.
36. Ibid., 4.
37. Ibid., 5. For more detail see his article "Locating the Holocaust on the Genocide Spectrum".
38. Huttenbach, "From the Editor", 5.
39. Ibid., 6 (italics in the original).
40. Özsu, "Genocide as Fact and Form", 71 (italics in the original), quoting Lemkin, *Axis Rule in Occupied Europe*, 79. For the notion of genocide within the context of South West Africa/Namibia, see Kreienbaum, "Der Hererokrieg und die Genozidfrage".
41. Arendt, *The Origins of Totalitarian Rule*; see also Court, *Hannah Arendt's Response to the Crisis of Her Time*.

pp. [25–31] NOTES

42. Mitscherlich and Mitscherlich, *The Inability to Mourn*.
43. Horkheimer and Adorno, *Dialectic of Enlightenment*.
44. See Israel, *Radical Enlightenment*; *Enlightenment Contested*; and *Democratic Enlightenment*. See also Berman, *Enlightenment or Empire*.
45. Horkheimer and Adorno, *Dialectic of Enlightenment*.

3. THE GERMAN COLONIAL BRAND

1. Naranch, "Introduction", 1.
2. Geiger, "Afrikabilder in der Kritik".
3. Geiger, "Der deutsche Kolonialismus in aktuellen Lehrbüchern".
4. Albertini, *Moderne Kolonialgeschichte*. That the author is a Swiss historian should not count as an excuse. For the differences in treating the subject in the East and in the West with special reference to South West Africa, see Bürger, *Deutsche Kolonialgeschichte(n)*.
5. Grewe, "Das schwierige Erbe des Kolonialismus".
6. Mallinckrodt, Köstlbauer and Lentz, *Beyond Exceptionalism*.
7. See the historical documents in Gründer, *... da und dort ein junges Deutschland gründen*.
8. On the Welser dynasty and its business transactions in the colonisation of South America, see Häberlein, "Kaufleute, Höflinge und Humanisten"; Simmer, *Gold und Sklaven*; Denzer, *Die Konquista der Augsburger Welser-Gesellschaft in Südamerika (1528–1556)*; and, with special reference to the long-lasting amnesia of this involvement, Montenegro, "'The Welser Phantom'".
9. See the contributions on both the Welser and Fugger dynasties in Raphael-Hernandez and Wiegmink, *German Entanglements in Transatlantic Slavery*; and Raphael-Hernandez, *Deutschland und die Sklaverei*.
10. See Heyden, *Rote Adler an Afrikas Küste*; Weindl, "Die Kurbrandenburger im 'atlantischen System', 1650–1720".
11. Weber, "Deutschland, der atlantische Sklavenhandel und die Plantagenwirtschaft der Neuen Welt"; Hagedorn, *Bremen und die atlantische Sklaverei*.
12. See Zantop, *Colonial Fantasies*; Kundrus, *Phantasiereiche*.
13. For general assessments of their role during German colonial times, see the contributions in Bade, *Imperialismus und Kolonialmission*; and on their self-image as well as perception by others, Altena, *"Ein Häuflein Christen mitten in der Heidenwelt des dunklen Erdteils"*.
14. Gründer, *Christliche Mission und deutscher Imperialismus*, 343. It should be noted (as Gründer also does) that individual missionaries did not think and act alike. Many were protagonists of the "civilising mission", willing to eradicate everything resisting foreign rule by projecting their deterministic world view and own domestication of the inner nature on "their wards". Others were more critical of colonial practices and in particular the physical violence this involved.
15. For an early critical analysis of its role, see Loth, *Die christliche Mission in Südwestafrika*. For the first detailed overview of the role of local evangelists in their activities, see Milk, *"... Der im Sturm steht wie ein Kameldornbaum"*.

16. Ustorf, "Mission als Vorhut des Kolonialismus?" He quotes the first inspector of the Evangelische Missionsgesellschaft für Deutsch-Ostafrika, who at a missionary conference in 1885 articulated the formula "Jesus Christ—the greatest coloniser" ("Jesus Christus—der größte Kolonisator", ibid., 41).
17. See the comprehensive account by Bitterli, *Die "Wilden" und die "Zivilisierten"*; and the compilation of examples of travelogues over several centuries by Loth, *Reisen nach Nigritien*. For a shift in the narratives during the 18th and 19th century towards an increased popularisation of national interests in the colonisation of African territories, see Fiedler, *Zwischen Abenteuer, Wissenschaft und Kolonialismus*. Notably, Heinrich Barth was recognised as a relative exception to the dominant mid-19th-century perspectives by Marx, *Von Berlin nach Timbuktu*.
18. 109 of these were listed and analysed by Essner, *Deutsche Afrikareisende im 19. Jahrhundert*. These travels were often an early form of professional qualification for a career in academia or the military back home.
19. Unangst, "Men of Science and Action".
20. Harding, "Die Berliner Westafrikakonferenz von 1884/85 und der Hamburger Schnapshandel mit Westafrika", 31.
21. Hücking and Launer, *Aus Menschen Neger machen*, 63–72.
22. Gothsch, *Die deutsche Völkerkunde und ihr Verhältnis zum Kolonialismus*. See also contributions to Penny and Bunzl, *Worldly Provincialism*.
23. Honold, "Pfadfinder".
24. Gräbel, *Die Erforschung der Kolonien*.
25. See, among others, Nussbaum, *Vom "Kolonialenthusiasmus" zur Kolonialpolitik der Monopole*; Bendikat, *Organisierte Kolonialbewegung in der Bismarck-Ära*; and Denhardt, *Deutsche Kolonialgesellschaft, 1888–1918*.
26. See the programme of the Kolonialverein as published in the *Deutsche Kolonialzeitung*, no. 1, 1884. This was—like much else in colonial propaganda—a classic case of wishful thinking.
27. See chapter 2, but also Bauche, "Von der Unmöglichkeit, klare Grenzen zu ziehen".
28. For the colonial literature, see, among others, Benninghoff-Lühl, *Deutsche Kolonialromane, 1884–1914*; Schneider, "Um Scholle und Leben"; Warmbold, "Ein Stückchen neudeutsche Erd ..."; Pellatz, "Abenteuer Afrika"; for colonial propaganda among the youth, Bowersox, *Raising Germans in the Age of Empire*; and for the genre of film from the beginning of the 20th century to World War II, Fuhrmann, *Imperial Projections*.
29. See Thode-Arora, *Für fünfzig Pfennig um die Welt*, and "Hagenbeck"; Benninghoff-Lühl, "Die Ausstellung der Kolonialisierten"; Dreesbach, *Gezähmte Wilde*; and "Colonial Exhibitions, 'Völkerschauen' and the Display of the 'Other'"; Zedelmeier, "Das Geschäft mit dem Fremden"; Ames, "From the Exotic to the Everyday". The last also documents how some of these exhibitions laid the foundation for later theme parks (such as Disneyland); see Ames, *Carl Hagenbeck's Empire of Entertainments*. The topic has attained wider prominence as a subject in public media thanks to awareness campaigns by postcolonial initiatives, which succeeded in drawing attention to the relevance of such shows in local history.

30. Zimmerman, *Anthropology and Antihumanism in Imperial Germany*, 1. For a different perspective, see Penny, *Objects of Culture*, conceding to German anthropologists a far more cosmopolitan and liberal tradition. The role of ethnological museums, shifting the emphasis in their presentations from culture to race, is described by Laukötter, *Von der "Kultur" zur "Rasse"*; and "Das Völkerkundemuseum".
31. Wehler, *Bismarck und der Imperialismus*. For a summary of the debate on this label, see Kroboth, "Anhang: Der deutsche Kolonialismus im Spiegel der historischen Debatte". Another perspective stresses the era of colonial expansion as an ambition and step towards globalisation during imperialist times; see Laak, *Über alles in der Welt*. The notion of "social imperialism", which had lost currency by then, was reintroduced by Naranch and Eley, *German Colonialism in a Global Age*, and fruitfully discussed in the review essay by Smith, "Contexts of Colonialism".
32. Press, *Rogue Empires*.
33. See Förster, Mommsen and Robinson, *Bismarck, Europe, and Africa*; Eckert, *125 Jahre Berliner Afrika-Konferenz*.
34. Next to the British empire and France, these included Russia, whose expansion into large parts of neighbouring territories is often overlooked even today, when former colonies in the global South wrongly claim that Russia never colonised.
35. See, among others, the overview up to 2018 by Fitzpatrick, "Colonialism, Postcolonialism, and Decolonization". References include the published research from historians in the GDR. Their analyses of the African colonies is documented in Stoecker, *Drang nach Africa*. Research by contributors to this volume, in some cases starting as early as the late 1950s, benefited from access to the archives of the Reichskolonialamt in Potsdam (since then relocated to the Bundesarchiv in Koblenz). While some of the findings testify to a rather crude (and reductionist) Marxist theory and methodology, or at least use a jargon claiming so, many of the conclusions were based on and substantiated by archival, evidence-based material. The merits of the work of these scholars are unfairly dismissed as purely ideologically driven.
36. The special case of South West Africa, since 1990 the sovereign Republic of Namibia, is presented in much more depth and detail in chapter 5.
37. An attempt to enhance perspectives is Geiger and Melber, *Kritik des deutschen Kolonialismus*, where the chapters on the African colonies are (co-)authored by African scholars from these territories.
38. For more, see Todzi, *Unternehmen Weltaneignung*; Pieper, *Zucker, Schnaps und Nilpferdpeitsche*.
39. Nagl, "Seckenheim, Berlin, Buea, Windhoek".
40. Christopher, "One Man Fought 4 Wars on 3 Continents".
41. Schulte-Varendorff, *Kolonialheld für Kaiser und Führer*; Michels, *"Der Held von Deutsch-Ostafrika"*.
42. Lettow-Vorbeck, *Heia Safari!*
43. Documented with reference to the Boxer rebellion and the war against the Ovaherero and Nama, by Sobich and Bischoff, *Feinde werden*.
44. See Wempe, *Revenants of the German Empire;* and the chapter "Enter the Germans" in Pedersen, *The Guardians*.

NOTES

45. Kriel, "Heimat in the *Veld?*"
46. Lyon, "From Labour Elites to Garveyites".
47. Michels, *Schwarze deutsche Kolonialsoldaten*.
48. Hillebrecht and Melber, "Von den Deutschen verschleppt"; Zimmerer, *German Rule, African Subjects*, 52ff.
49. Gewald, "Mbadamassi of Lagos".
50. Fitzpatrick, *Purging the Empire*, 240ff.
51. This is a focus in the case studies of Qingdao, Samoa and South West Africa by Steinmetz, *The Devil's Handwriting*.
52. On the military culture unfolding, see especially Hull, *Absolute Destruction*, and Kuss, *Deutsches Militär auf kolonialen Kriegsschauplätzen*.
53. Auden, "Duala versus Germans in Cameroon"; Eckert, *Die Duala und die Kolonialmächte*.
54. Fitzpatrick, *The Kaiser and the Colonies*, 381.
55. Such as deliberately incorrect translations for purposes of misinformation, or the burning of seed to create the impression that the land was not fertile; see Gouaffo and Tsogang Fossi, "Kamerun: Ein deutsches Kapitel des globalen Imperialismus", 76.
56. Damara communities lived with and in-between the Ovaherero and Nama.
57. For more details and further literature, see Melber, "Economic and Social Transformation"; and Wallace, *A History of Namibia*, chapters 2–4.
58. Called in a vernacular *Namib* (meaning protection), it gave Namibia its name.
59. Press, *Blood and Diamonds*.
60. All this is well documented in Lüderitz, *Die Erschließung von Deutsch-Südwestafrika durch Adolf Lüderitz*.
61. On Witbooi's personality, see Dedering, "Hendrik Witbooi, the Prophet", and on his early interaction with the German colonial regime, Blackler, "From Boondoggle to Settlement Colony".
62. See Gewald, *Herero Heroes*; and "'I Was Afraid of Samuel, Therefore I Came to Sekgoma'".
63. Miescher, *Die Rote Linie*, 40ff.
64. Blackler, *An Imperial Homeland*.
65. On the ambivalences of Witbooi and Maharero as traditional leaders (in contrast to Marengo), see Hillebrecht, "Hendrik Witbooi and Samuel Maharero".
66. See Alexander, "Jakob Marengo and Namibian History"; and Masson, "A Fragment of Colonial History". In Germany, Marengo/Morenga was the title figure of a widely read novel, which introduced the general public to the German war against the local population; see Timm, *Morenga*.
67. Kreienbaum, *A Sad Fiasco*.
68. Sippel, "'Im Interesse des Deutschtums und der weissen Rasse'".
69. Sippel, "Recht und Emotion".
70. For its origins and further expansion, see the first two chapters in Moorsom, *Underdevelopment and Labour Migration*.
71. Lyon, "From Labour Elites to Garveyites".
72. Moorsom, "Migrant Workers and the Formation of SWANLA".

73. On the role of the police, see Muschalek, *Violence as Usual*. On the formation of the colonial state more generally (with specific reference to Togo), see Trotha, *Koloniale Herrschaft*. The continued extermination of the San is documented by Gordon and Douglas, *The Bushman Myth*; and Gordon, "Hiding in Full View".
74. See Wege, "Die Anfänge der Herausbildung einer Arbeiterklasse"; and "Zur sozialen Lage der Arbeiter Namibias".
75. Cooper, "The Institutionalization of Contract Labour in Namibia".
76. For the massive impact of the diamond economy on both the country and the German empire, see Press, *Blood and Diamonds*.
77. Hope, *Developmentalism, Dependency, and the State*, 23.
78. United Nations, *Report of the Committee on South West Africa*, 10 and 11. Quoted also in Hillebrecht, "Monuments—and What Else?" Notably, organised resistance against the regime was already in full swing. Namibians had been petitioning the United Nations since the late 1940s to demand independence from South Africa, and the first national anti-colonial liberation movement was founded three years after this speech.
79. See for details Wrigley, "The Military Campaigns against Germany's African Colonies", 50–52.
80. Quoted in Hope, *Developmentalism, Dependency, and the State*, 26.
81. See the contributions to Hayes, Silvester, Wallace and Hartmann, *Namibia under South African Rule*; and Kössler, "Historischer Wendepunkt, strukturelle Kontinuität".
82. Hücking and Launer, *Aus Menschen Neger machen*, 47f; Stoecker, "Die Annexionen von 1884/85", 30.
83. Austen, "Tradition, Invention and History".
84. Austen, "The Metamorphoses of Middlemen"; Austen and Derrick, *Middlemen of the Cameroons Rivers*, chapter 4.
85. Simo, "Colonization and Modernization", 100.
86. Full text with signatories accessible at *Black Central Europe*, https://blackcentraleurope.com/sources/1850–1914/treaty-of-protection-with-chiefs-of-cameroon-coast-1884/.
87. For the agreement and memorandum, see Rüger, "Die Duala und die Kolonialmacht 1884–1914".
88. Guaffo and Tsogang Fossi, "Kamerun: Ein deutsches Kapitel des globalen Imperialismus", 69; Van der Linden, *The Acquisition of Africa*, 194–196. Notably, paragraph 3 states: "the land cultivated by us now and the places where the towns are built on shall be the property of the present owners and their successors". The treaty text is accessible at https://afrolegends.com/2017/01/31/colonial-treaties-in-africa-the-germano-duala-treaty-of-12-july-1884/.
89. Austen, "The Metamorphoses of Middlemen", 12. For the 30 years of Duala interaction with the German colonial regime, see Austen, "Mythic Transformation and Historical Continuity".
90. For pioneering assessments of German colonialism in Cameroon in the two German states, see Stoecker, *Kamerun unter deutscher Kolonialherrschaft*; Hausen, *Deutsche Kolonialherrschaft in Afrika*; and Wirz, *Vom Sklavenhandel zum Kolonialhandel*.

91. Initial experiments with coffee turned out to be an economic failure and caused the loss of investment. Tobacco also did not secure an economic fortune. Cocoa became the booming export commodity, with rubber and kola nuts supplementing the agrobusiness emerging during the years to come.
92. Dr Y., "German Warfare in Africa".
93. Lock Priso's symbol of power, the *tangue* (a naval ram), was looted and is on display in the museum "Fünf Kontinente" in Munich. See Splettstösser, *Umstrittene Sammlungen*.
94. A detailed record of the numerous military encounters and other "punitive expeditions" (*Strafexpeditionen*) is offered by Hoffmann, *Okkupation und Militärverwaltung in Kamerun*. For the variety of strategies of local actors and their different forms of engagement with the German colonial regime, see several of the chapters in Fowler and Zeitlyn, *African Crossroads*.
95. The manifest clash of interests between economy and politics during the 1880s is described in Van der Linden, *The Acquisition of Africa*, chapter 7. See also Michels, *Imagined Power Contested*.
96. Stoecker, "Kamerun, 1885–1906", 59f.
97. This gruesome corporal punishment left huge open wounds on bodies. Not by coincidence an early anti-colonial intervention, originally published in 1897, referred in its title to this form of torture; see Aly, *Nilpferdpeitsche und Kultur*. The systematic use of corporal punishment as an integral part of German colonial rule is well documented through archival material in Müller, *Kolonien unter der Peitsche*.
98. Stoecker, "Kamerun, 1885–1906", 60.
99. Guaffo and Tsogang Fossi, "Kamerun: Ein deutsches Kapitel des globalen Imperialismus", 73f.
100. See Nganang, "Writing under Colonial Rule"; also Tsogang Fossi, "'Du bist wie ein Kücklein in mein Haus gekommen, Weisser ...'". Another exceptional case of collaboration is presented by Quinn, "Charles Atangana of Yaounde".
101. Hoffmann, *Okkupation und Militärverwaltung in Kamerun*, 16 and 17.
102. See details in Hücking and Launer, *Aus Menschen Neger machen*, 115–132.
103. Schaper, *Koloniale Verhandlungen*.
104. Bommarius, *Der gute Deutsche*, 36f.
105. Stoecker, "Kamerun, 1885–1906", 72f.
106. Otremba, "Stimmen der Auflehnung".
107. Gouaffo and Tsogang Fossi, "Kamerun: Ein deutsches Kapitel des globalen Imperialismus", 76; and Eckert, *Die Duala und die Kolonialmächte*, 98f.
108. Eckert, *Die Duala und die Kolonialmächte*, 141.
109. Aitken, "The Gravestone of a Cameroonian Prince (1891)". A history of these African students appears in Aitken and Rosenhaft, *Black Germany*; and Aitken, "Education and Migration".
110. Stoecker, "Kamerun, 1884–1905", 73f.
111. For some effects of such strategy on political parties in the Reichstag, see Lowry, "African Resistance and Center Party Recalcitrance".
112. Schaper, "Law and Colonial Order", 27.

113. Nyada, "Mpondo Akwa", 397.
114. Aitken and Rosenhaft, *Black Germany*, 34f.
115. For more on the following, see Nyanda, "Mpondo Akwa".
116. Nagl, *Grenzfälle*, 152.
117. Skwirblies, "Theatres of Colonialism", 100.
118. For Levi's remarkable plea in court, see Joeden-Forgey, *Mpundu Akwa*.
119. Skwirblies, "Theatres of Colonialism", 101.
120. Nyanda, "Mpondo Akwa", 396.
121. Kah and Kengo, "Coercion and Violence in German Labour Conscription in Cameroon, 1880s–1914".
122. See Stoecker, "Kamerun, 1906–1914".
123. Ibid., 147.
124. Ibid., 149.
125. For the Upper Cross River area of Cameroon, see Michels, *Imagined Power Contested*.
126. Adick and Mehnert, *Deutsche Missions- und Kolonialpädagogik in Dokumenten*, 429–460, have compiled archival material related to the German education and training of Alfred Bell, Tube Metom and Rudolf Manga Bell.
127. On King Rudolf Manga Bell and the particular case of colonial (in)justice, see especially Bommarius, *Der gute Deutsche*; Fitzpatrick, *The Kaiser and the Colonies*, chapter 13 ("Hanging a King"); Eyoum, Michels and Zeller, "Bonamanga"; and Hamann, *Prekäre koloniale Ordnung*, chapter IV.I.I ("Politik gegen die 'Gefahr' der Gleichheit in Duala").
128. The Social Democratic members of the Reichstag Hugo Haase and Paul Levi (the latter was also the advocate for Rosa Luxemburg).
129. The campaign demanding their rehabilitation forms part of chapter 4.
130. Fitzpatrick, *The Kaiser and the Colonies*, 372.
131. This follows Trüper, "Afrikaner in Berlin". See also Zeller and Michels, "Kamerunischer Nationalheld".
132. Bang and Balgah, "The Ramification of Cameroon's Anglophone Crisis".
133. Laumann, "A Historiography of German Togoland", 195.
134. Hüsgen, "Colonial Expeditions and Collecting".
135. Ibid., 5.
136. Kachim, "African Resistance to Colonial Conquest".
137. For more details see Aguigah, LeGall and Wagne, "Colonial Violence in the North of Togo".
138. Ibid.
139. Ibid., quoted in the English translation by the authors, from the letter of Köhler dated 22 February 1901 (Notes to K.A. 1035, German Federal Archives, R1001/4393, p. 160).
140. Yigbe, "Is Togo a Permanent Model Colony?" On the making of such perceptions, see Laumann, "Narratives of a 'Model Colony'".
141. For an overview, see Laumann, "A Historiography of German Togoland". On the image of the *Musterkolonie* in German colonial literature of the time, see Oloukpona-Yinnon, *Unter deutschen Palmen*. The most detailed work on Togo's

colonial realities, benefiting from access to the colonial archives, has been presented by Sebald, *Togo, 1884–1914*, summarised in shorter versions as *Die deutsche Kolonie Togo, 1884–1914*; "Togo, 1884–1900", and "Togo, 1900–1914".
142. For detailed statistics from 1884–5 to 1899, see Sebald, "Togo, 1884–1900", 77.
143. See Vera, "Die Kolonialpolizei als Instrument deutscher Herrschaftssicherung in Deutsch-Südwestafrika und Togo".
144. This figure is based on a calculation by Peter Sebald from documents of the colonial archives. The absence of German military forces and the small number of Europeans were also seen as motivating factors for an exceptional degree of brutality in "punitive" operations to achieve a chilling effect: Habermas, "Die deutsche Kolonie Togo", 3.
145. A term coined by Pesek, *Koloniale Herrschaft in Deutsch-Ostafrika*.
146. Trotha, "Das 'deutsche Nizza an Afrikas Westküste'".
147. Zurstrassen, *Ein Stück deutscher Erde schaffen*.
148. In the case of South West Africa, those in the colonial administration were at times internally divided, while the settlers had their own agendas and were not always in agreement with the colonial administration.
149. More details on the role of policing are to be found in Trotha, *Koloniale Herrschaft*, 41ff.
150. Sebald, *Die deutsche Kolonie Togo, 1884–1914*, 71 (with thanks to Dotsé Yigbe for alerting me to the source).
151. Trotha, "'One for Kaiser'", 535f.
152. For the role of power executed through sexual abuse as an integral part of German colonial rule, see Walther, "Sex, Race and Empire".
153. Habermas, *Skandal in Togo*; and "Der Kolonialskandal Atakpame".
154. For a general factual overview of the legal systems in the German colonies, see Hammen, "Kolonialrecht und Kolonialgerichtsbarkeit"; also Sippel, "Quellen des deutschen Kolonialrechts". For Cameroon, see Schaper, *Koloniale Verhandlungen*. An effort to contextualise and interpret the tensions and interactions between the colonial and the local African law systems is presented by Schaper, "Recht und Kolonialismus". For how colonial rules became the law of the rulers, escalating by means of juridical and physical acts of violence into genocidal practices, see, for South West Africa, Blackler, *An Imperial Homeland*. For the interplay between German and colonial jurisdiction, see Hanschmann, "Die Suspendierung des Konstitutionalismus im Herz der Finsternis".
155. Habermas, *Skandal in Togo*, 15.
156. Among other things, the scheme was based on the misperception that agriculture was a male affair, while women were those mainly in charge of cultivating the fields.
157. European colonialism has since the late 19th century not only been a matter of national competitions and rivalries, but, as the history of the International Colonial Institute (ICI) shows, also one of international cooperation, considering colonialism as trans-imperial policy; see Wagner, *Colonial Internationalism and the Governmentality of Empire*.

158. Zimmerman, *Alabama in Africa*, 248.
159. Habermas, *Skandal in Togo*, 210.
160. Zimmerman, "A German Alabama in Africa", 1363.
161. Sebald, "Togo, 1900–1914", 157.
162. Ibid., 160.
163. See Yigbe, "Deutsch-Togo und die Folgen", 87ff.
164. He had obtained a doctoral degree in philosophy on metaphysical questions in the work of Schopenhauer.
165. This is the emphasis in the political biography by Perras, *Carl Peters and German Imperialism, 1856–1918*.
166. Ibid., 49.
167. *German History in Documents and Images*, vol. 4. Sources for the German original and the English translation are provided there. See https://germanhistorydocs.ghi-dc.org/pdf/eng/623_Patent%20of%20Patronage_203.pdf.
168. Koponen, *Development for Exploitation*, 87. This was of course the same challenge colonialism faced in different degrees in all the claimed territories. A pioneering analysis of the establishment of colonial relations was presented by Iliffe, *A Modern History of Tanganyika*, and *Tanganyika under German Rule, 1905–1912*.
169. Considered of little use for economic interests in the colony not least due to his erratic behaviour, he was marginalised and by 1889 without employment.
170. Ground-breaking for East Africa is Pesek, *Koloniale Herrschaft in Deutsch-Ostafrika*.
171. Pierskalla, De Juan and Montgomery, "The Territorial Expansion of the Colonial State", 720.
172. See in particular Pesek, *Koloniale Herrschaft in Deutsch-Ostafrika*; "Die Grenzen des postkolonialen Staates in Deutsch-Ostafrika, 1890–1914"; and "Colonial Conquest and the Struggle for the Presence of the Colonial State in German East Africa, 1885–1903"; as well as LeGall and Mboro, "Deutsch-Ostafrika"; and more generally Kuss, *Deutsches Militär auf kolonialen Kriegsschauplätzen*. The shift in discourse is also documented in German travelogues on the region; see Unangst, "Changes in German Travel Writing about East Africa, 1884–1891".
173. Pierskalla, De Juan and Montgomery, "The Territorial Expansion of the Colonial State", 716.
174. For the early stages of German colonial encounters, see in particular Büttner, *Die Anfänge der deutschen Kolonialpolitik in Ostafrika*; Müller, *Deutschland—Zanzibar—Ostafrika*; Stoecker, "Deutsch-Ostafrika, 1885–1906"; Glassman, *Feasts and Riot*; and Akinola, "The East African Coastal Rising, 1888–1890".
175. Bade, "Antisklavereibewegung in Deutschland und Kolonialkrieg in Deutsch-Ostafrika".
176. For an exposure of this hypocritical pseudo-reasoning, see Unangst, "Manufacturing Crisis". Despite these solemnly declared goals, slavery remained a common practice until the end of German colonial rule.
177. Prinz, "Hermann von Wissmann als 'Kolonialpionier'".
178. Michels, "Der Askari".

NOTES

179. See Mann, *Mykoni ya damu*—"Hands of Blood".
180. Bückendorf, *"Schwarz-weiß-rot über Ostafrika"*, 445; see also Morlang, "'Finde ich keinen Weg, so bahne ich mir einen'".
181. Deutsch, *Emancipation without Abolition in German East Africa*.
182. On Nachtigal, see the parliamentary resolution by the AfD (in chapter 4).
183. "Das Wissmann-Denkmal im Kurpark von Bad Lauterberg", https://www.harzlife.de/bilder/wissmann-denkmal-bad-lauterberg.html.
184. Akinola, "The East African Coastal Rising", 628.
185. See Reyels, Ivanov and Weber-Sinn, *Humboldt Lab Tanzania*.
186. See Schneppen, "Der Helgoland-Sansibar-Vertrag von 1890"; on the consequences, see Fitzpatrick, *The Kaiser and the Colonies*, chapter 8 ("Swapping a Sultanate for an Island").
187. See Melber, "One Namibia, One Nation?"
188. On its distinct organisation and structure, also in comparison with South West Africa, see Bührer, *Die Kaiserliche Schutztruppe für Deutsch-Ostafrika*. Like several others, Bührer shows that the resort to extreme forms of violence by the colonial regime was more a sign of insecurity and weakness than of strength. For a wider discussion within the German local community over the boundaries to "White violence" in daily interactions, see Masters, "'The People Who Make Our Heads Spin'".
189. On the complexity of their identities, see Michels, *Schwarze deutsche Kolonialsoldaten*; Morlang, *Askari und Fitafita*; and Moyd, *Violent Intermediaries*.
190. The escalation is documented in Baer and Schröter, *Eine Kopfjagd*. See also Redmayne, "Mkwawa and the Hehe Wars". For an overall account of the interaction between the Wahehe and the German colonial regime, see Pizzo, "'To Devour the Land of Mkwawa'".
191. Bührer, "Die Hehe und die Schutztruppe in Deutsch-Ostafrika". The following summary account follows LeGall and Mboro, "Deutsch-Ostafrika", 103–107, who also give significant room to local African voices.
192. Pesek, "Colonial Conquest and the Struggle for the Presence of the Colonial State in German East Africa", 163.
193. LeGall and Mboro, "Deutsch-Ostafrika", 105; see also "Mtwa Mkwawa: Remembering the Dismembered", https://rememberinghumanremains.wordpress.com/mkwawa/.
194. For the meaning of this act of decapitation and the subsequent interactions for the return of the head, see Garsha, "The Head of Chief Mkwawa and the Transnational History of Colonial Violence"; chapter 4.2 ("The Story of the Mkwawa Head") in Stahn, *Confronting Colonial Objects*, 253–261; Bucher, "The Skull of Mkwawa and the Politics of Indirect Rule in Tanganyika"; and Brockmeyer, Edward and Stoecker, "The Mkwawa Complex". See also more broadly LeGall, "Remembering the Dismembered"; Garsha, "Expanding Vergangenheitsbewältigung?"; and Rushohora, "Desperate Mourning and Atrophied Representation".
195. The return has been filmed and broadcast as a 30-minute documentary ("Der Zahn des Häuptlings: Versöhnungsreise nach Tansania") on German television

on 6 October 2015. See https://programm.ard.de/?sendung=28111156 70241268.
196. Gewald, "Colonial Warfare".
197. See among others Baer and Schröter, *Eine Kopfjagd*, 89–92; and Perras, *Carl Peters and German Imperialism*.
198. LeGall and Mboro, "Deutsch-Ostafrika", 106f.
199. Escalona, "Mangi Meli".
200. For a historical background and differing local perspectives, see Rushohora, "An Archaeological Identity of the Majimaji".
201. See Gwassa, *The Outbreak and Development of the Maji Maji War*; Iliffe, "The Organization of the Maji Maji Rebellion"; Monson, "Relocating Maji Maji"; Wright, "Maji Maji Prophecy and Historiography"; Seeberg, *Der Maji-Maji Krieg gegen die deutsche Kolonialherrschaft*; Beez, *Geschosse zu Wassertropfen*; Becker and Beez, *Der Maji-Maji-Krieg in Deutsch-Ostafrika*; Giblin and Monson, *Maji Maji*; De Juan, "Extraction and Violent Resistance in the Early Phases of State Building"; Greenstein, "Making History"; and Schmidt, "(Re)negotiating Marginality".
202. Bachmann and Kemp, "300,000 Tanzanians Were Killed by Germany during the Maji-Maji Uprising".
203. Bachmann and Kemp, "Was Quashing the Maji-Maji Uprising Genocide?", 243.
204. Pierskalla, De Juan and Montgomery, "The Territorial Expansion of the Colonial State".
205. De Juan, "Extraction and Violent Resistance in the Early Phases of State Building", 315.
206. Yekani, *Koloniale Arbeit*.
207. For details, see Tetzlaff, *Koloniale Entwicklung und Ausbeutung*; Stoecker, "Deutsch-Ostafrika, 1906–1914".
208. Greiner, "Colonial Schemes and African Realities", 20.
209. Zimmerman, "'What Do You Really Want in German East Africa, Herr Professor?'" For a more general, less affirmative overview, see Laak, "Kolonien als 'Laborien der Moderne'?"
210. Gissibl, *The Nature of German Imperialism*.
211. For a general pioneering overview of medical research in the German colonies, see Eckart, *Medizin und Kolonialimperialismus*. There is a case study of malaria research in South West Africa by Esse, *Malaria in Südwest-Afrika*.
212. Eckart, "The Colony as Laboratory".
213. For a sober(ing) presentation of Koch's record, see Graw, "Robert Koch". For racist perceptions in colonial malaria research, see Bauche, *Medizin und Herrschaft*, and "Race, Class or Culture?"
214. See Schulte-Varendorff, *Kolonialheld für Kaiser und Führer*; Michels, *"Der Held von Deutsch-Ostafrika"*, and "Paul von Lettow-Vorbeck"; Pesek, *Das Ende eines Kolonialreiches*.
215. Schulte-Varendorff, "Der Erste Weltkrieg und die deutschen Kolonien in Afrika".
216. An entertaining but rather uncritical military history of Lettow-Vorbeck's war-

NOTES

fare is presented by Gaudi, *African Kaiser*, which seems more interested in how the German commander was able to fool the British than in the costs for the Africans—which shows how much perspectives matter.

217. Zeller, "Das Ende der deutschen Kolonialgeschichte".
218. Menger, "Abdulrazak Gurnah and the Afterlives of German Colonialism".
219. Boyd, *Zum Nachtisch Krieg*.
220. See in particular Gurnah, *Afterlives*.
221. Gardner, "Explainer: The Myth of the Noble Savage"; Senft, "'Noble Savages' and the 'Islands of Love'".
222. See Berghoff, Biess and Strasser, *Explorations and Entanglements*.
223. For more details on the South Sea "patchwork quilt", see Mückler, "Inselgruppen an der Peripherie", 114f.
224. Hardach, "Die deutsche Herrschaft in Mikronesien", 508.
225. See Wendt, "Die Südsee".
226. For a detailed overview, see Krug, *"Der Hauptzweck ist die Tötung von Kanaken"*.
227. Hiery, "Die deutsche Verwaltung Neuguineas, 1884–1914", 299.
228. Hempenstall, *Pacific Islanders under German Rule*, 213.
229. Ibid., 27.
230. Ibid., 32.
231. Campbell, "Resistance and Colonial Government", 56.
232. Droessler, *Coconut Colonialism*.
233. Hempenstall, *Pacific Islanders under German Rule*, 216 and 222.
234. See the detailed account by Morlang, *Rebellion in der Südsee*.
235. Details in Wendt, "Das Ende der deutschen Südsee".
236. Hempenstall and Mochida, *The Lost Man*, 1.
237. Moses, "The Solf Regime in Western Samoa", 56.
238. See Moyle, "'We Are Like Someone Completely Dead and Lack a Father, Your Excellency'".
239. Hempenstall, *Pacific Islanders under German Rule*, 68.
240. Fitzpatrick, "'Renegade' Resistance and Colonial Rule in German Samoa", 325.
241. Ibid.
242. Ibid., 328.
243. Ibid.
244. Ibid., 347.
245. There is a variety of spellings, using German or (different) Chinese terminology, and also some confusion of references to Qingdao/Tsingtao/Tsingtau as the city ("capital") and Jiaozhou/Kiautschou as the territory, which are often used synonymously. There are overviews in Geiger, "Das 'Pachtgebiet' Kiautschou, der 'Boxerkrieg' und die Folgen"; Lü, "Tstingtau"; and Kuss, "Die deutsche 'Musterkolonie' Qingdao".
246. Mühlhahn, *Herrschaft und Widerstand in der "Musterkolonie" Kiautschou*, 89–95.
247. The clashes between Christian missions and the local population were a regular occurrence at the time, and in Shandong anti-Christian combat units had been formed, which became the basis for the Boxer rebellion; Mühlhahn, *Herrschaft und Widerstand in der "Musterkolonie" Kiautschou*, 383–388.

248. *Stenographische Berichte über die Verhandlungen des Reichstags* [Stenographic Reports of Reichstag Proceedings], IX LP, 5th Session, vol. 1, Berlin, 1898, 60. In English translation in *German History in Documents and Images*, vol. 5; https://germanhistorydocs.ghi-dc.org/pdf/eng/607_Buelow_Place%20in%20the%20Sun_111.pdf.
249. The further bilateral interactions are documented in Leutner and Mühlhahn, *"Musterkolonie Kiautschou"*.
250. Ibid., 171.
251. Mühlhahn, *Herrschaft und Widerstand in der "Musterkolonie" Kiautschou*, 115.
252. For the historical background, see especially Esherick, *The Origins of the Boxer Uprising*, and the review essay by Liu, "Imperialism and the Chinese Peasants".
253. Xiang, *The Origin of the Boxer War*, 76. For a careful deconstruction of the dimensions as well as interpretations and the significance of the event in history, historical writing, memory and myth, see Cohen, *History in Three Keys*. For the external perspectives framing the Boxer War as a "conflict between civilisation and barbarism", see Klein, "The 'Yellow Peril'".
254. For different aspects, see the contributions to Leutner and Mühlhahn, *Kolonialkrieg in China*; and Kuss and Martin, *Das Deutsche Reich und der Boxeraufstand*.
255. Quoted in the English translation from *German History in Documents and Images*; https://ghdi.ghi-dc.org/sub_document.cfm?document_id=755. See also Klein, "Die Hunnenrede".
256. Harring, "German Reparations to the Herero Nation", 407.
257. Convention (II) with Respect to the Laws and Customs of War on Land, and its annexure: Regulations Concerning the Laws and Customs of War on Land. The Hague, 29 July 1899. Annexure to the Convention: Regulations Respecting the Laws and Customs of War on Land—Section II: On Hostilities—Chapter I: On Means of Injuring the Enemy, Sieges, and Bombardments—Regulations: Art. 23. https://ihl-databases.icrc.org/applic/ihl/ihl.nsf/Article.xsp?action=openDocument&documentId=14BF8E8D6537838EC12563CD00515E22.
258. Geiger, "Das 'Pachtgebiet' Kiautschou, der 'Boxerkrieg' und die Folgen", 131ff.
259. Mühlhahn, "A New Imperial Vision?"
260. Kuss, "Die deutsche 'Musterkolonie' Quingdao", 67ff.
261. These perspectives are introduced in Yuan, *Medizin und Kolonialismus*, 5–25. For a rather uncritical treatment, see Hiery and Hinz, *Alltagsleben und Kulturaustausch*. More critical explorations are presented in Leutner and Mühlhahn, *Deutsch-chinesische Beziehungen im 19. Jahrhundert*.
262. Groeneveld, "Far Away at Home in Qingdao", 75.
263. Lü, "Tsingtau", 217ff; Laak, "Kolonien als 'Laboratorien der Moderne'?".
264. Huang, *Quingdao*, 13.
265. Lü, "Tsingtau", 223ff.
266. See the contributions to Berman, Mühlhahn and Ngagang, *German Colonialism Revisited*; and Mühlhahn, *The Cultural Legacy of German Colonial Rule*.

NOTES

267. See the overview by Berman, Göttsche and Schüller, "Deutsche Kolonialgeschichte im Spiegel fremdsprachiger Literaturen".
268. Krautwald, "Branches of Memory", iii.
269. Volker, "The Legacy of the German Language in Papua New Guinea", 169. A similar positive assessment, conceding that Germans respected indigenous cultures and intervened little in existing societies, was made generally in the contributions to Hiery, *Die deutsche Südsee*. As suggested in a detailed review essay, this romanticising if not glorifying perspective may reflect more the affinity of the editor to the subject than a realistic assessment; Erckenbrecht, "Die wissenschaftliche Aufarbeitung der Kolonialzeit in der Südsee", 179. For a similar flaw, bestowing on German colonial policy more sensitivity than that of other colonial powers, see Hiery, *Das deutsche Reich in der Südsee*.
270. See Tapaleao, "Day NZ Took Samoa from Germany".
271. As pointed out by Wendt, "Das Ende der deutschen Südsee", 97
272. An exception might be Togo. As has been suggested, the roots of the close identification go back to the role of the missionary societies before official colonisation; see Yigbe, "Togo: Land einer anachronistischen Germanophilie". But there too the positive image cultivated towards Germany reveals strategic considerations, as shown by Sebald, "'Lust' und 'List' kolonialer Erinnerung".
273. Wendt, "Die Südsee". For the sexual connotations of such images, see the study of the novelist Hanns Heinz Ewers (1871–1943) by Poley, *Decolonization in Germany*.
274. See also Melber, *Namibia*, 16ff.
275. On the general debate over the introduction of *Kolonial-Deutsch* at the time, see Orosz, "Colonialism and the Simplification of Language".
276. This has especially been the case in Cameroon and Togo. See, for Togo: Sokolowsky, *Sprachenpolitik des deutschen Kolonialismus*; Adick, *Bildung und Kolonialismus in Togo*; Norris, *Die Umerziehung des Afrikaners*; for Cameroon: Boulleys, *Deutsch in Kamerun*; Ngatcha, *Der Deutschunterricht in Kamerun als Erbe des Kolonialismus*; and Gouaffo and Tsogang Fossi, "Kamerun: Spuren und Erinnerungen hundert Jahre nach der deutschen Kolonialzeit". The special role of German missionary societies in this process is documented by Adick and Mehnert, *Deutsche Missions- und Kolonialpädagogik in Dokumenten*. For a decolonial perspective on German in Togo, see Assemboni, Babka, Beck and Dunker, *Postkolonialität denken*.
277. Maitz and Volker, "Language Contact in the German Colonies", 2. But see also Engelberg, "The German Language in the South Seas".
278. Maitz and Volker, "Documenting Unserdeutsch". See also other contributions in Maitz and Volker, *Language Contact in the German Colonies*; and Volker, "The Legacy of the German Language in Papua New Guinea".
279. Derrick, "The 'Germanophone' Elite of Douala".
280. Stoecker, "Germanophilie und Hoffnung auf Hitler in Togo und Kamerun zwischen den Weltkriegen".
281. Several local scholars write and publish in German. See, for example, their country chapters in Geiger and Melber, *Kritik des deutschen Kolonialismus*.

NOTES

282. Piwowarczyk, "'Dangerous Liaisons'", 151.
283. Li, "Colonial Past and Present of Tsingtao Beer".
284. On the history of beer brewing in Namibia, see Van der Hoog, *Breweries, Politics and Identity*.
285. Van der Hoog, "Brewing Tensions". See also Kalb, "Reprinting the Past".
286. Ebert-Adeikis, "Wiesn weltweit".
287. Staff reporter, "Prost! To Oktoberfest".
288. BBC, "Togo Gets Tipsy on Bavarian Beer".
289. Diduk, "European Alcohol, History and the State in Cameroon".
290. Kirey, "Decolonizing German Colonial Sites in Dar es Salaam".
291. For a counter-narrative with reference to this aspect of the German legacy still in existence, see Heyl, *Namibische Gedenk- und Erinnerungsorte*; and Reitz and Mannitz, "Remembering Genocide in Namibia".
292. Ivory Tours, "Spuren deutscher Kolonien", https://www.ivory-tours.de/afrika-reisen/detailansicht/deutsche-kolonien-reise-afrika.html.
293. For more on this friendship, see Grill, *Wir Herrenmenschen*.
294. See the detailed eyewitness report by Kiessler, "'Josef ist der Größte'". The support by Strauss for a Bavarian enterprise in Lomé benefiting from subsidised meat processing was at the centre of a TV documentary, "Weißwürste am Äquator".
295. Brandt, "Franz-Josef Strauß". Rumours have it that he was not only hunting wildlife there, but also owned a farm.
296. For more details, see Lentz, "Erinnerungsräume öffnen", 100f.
297. Ibid., 97ff.
298. For a mapping of the colonial looting sprees, see Künkler, "Koloniale Gewalt und der Raub kultureller Objekte und menschlicher Überreste".
299. Schmitt-Egner, *Kolonialismus und Faschismus*, 108.
300. Essner, *Deutsche Afrikareisende im 19. Jahrhundert*, 32.
301. For an overview of protagonists of anti-colonial criticism at the time, see Klein-Arendt and Heyn, "'Glücklich das Volk, welches, gewollt oder ungewollt, keine Kolonien besitzt!'"; and Heyden, "Wider den Kolonialismus!"
302. *German History in Documents and Images*, vol. 4 (in English translation). Sources for the German original are provided there. See https://ghdi.ghi-dc.org/sub_document.cfm?document_id=1870.
303. Schlesinger, *Die Kolonialfrage in der Kommunistischen Internationale*, 22ff.
304. See, for example, Mergner, "Solidarität mit den 'Wilden'?"; and Roth, "Zwangsarbeit und Kolonialismus".
305. *Stenographische Berichte des Deutschen Reichstags*, 1 December 1906, 4057.
306. Kössler, "Socialism and Colonialism", 628.
307. *Stenographische Berichte des Deutschen Reichstags*, 19 March 1908, 4121.
308. *Stenographische Berichte des Deutschen Reichstages*, 6 March 1913, 4334.
309. For an early example of this approach and its arguments, often connected to the missionary societies, in which Friedrich Fabri is a prototype, see Bade, "Der Traum vom 'Export der sozialen Frage'".
310. See Schiefel, *Bernhard Dernburg*; and Naranch, "'Colonized Body', 'Oriental Machine'".

311. For an overview of the controversies over "best practices" in colonial policy, see Weinberger, *An den Quellen der Apartheid*, chapter 3, 96–133. Also instructive is Mogk, *Paul Rohrbach und das "Größere Deutschland"*.
312. See the biography by Epstein, *Matthias Erzberger and the Dilemma of German Democracy*.
313. This debate took place in parliament over three days in May 1912; see Roller, "'Wir sind Deutsche, wir sind Weiße und wollen Weiße bleiben'". See also more generally Schulte-Althoff, "Rassenmischung im kolonialen System".
314. Epstein, "Erzberger and the German Colonial Scandals", 663. For more examples of the clash in parliament between the openly dehumanising perspectives of the colonial hardliners and the reformers, see excerpts from the debates in Melber, "'Es sind doch auch Menschen!'"
315. For more detail and with further references, see Becker, "Die Hottentotten-Wahlen"; and Heyden, "Die 'Hottentottenwahlen' von 1907". See also chapter 6 ("The Hottentot Elections") in Short, *Magic Lantern Empire*.
316. This corresponded to English references to 'Hottentots' as a degrading name for the Cape San and Khoikhoi. See Hudson, "'Hottentots' and the Evolution of European Racism".
317. See, with particular reference to Bernstein, Hyrkkänen, *Sozialistische Kolonialpolitik*.
318. Ballod, "Die wissenschaftlichen Anschauungen über Kolonialpolitik", chapter 30, 11.
319. See Lange, *Hans Paasche*; Donat, *Hans Paasche*; Paasche, "Germany's Africa"; Fulbrook, *Dissonant Lives*, chapter 2: "Violence Abroad"; Nenguié, "Interkulturalität, Modernisierung und Nachhaltigkeit".
320. Paasche, *Die Forschungsreise des Afrikaners Lukanga Mukara ins innerste Deutschlands*.
321. Pellegrino and Böttcher, "Wer war Hans Paasche?"
322. See some of the chapters in Müller and Torp, *Das Deutsche Kaiserreich in der Kontroverse*.
323. See the contributions to Naranch and Eley, *German Colonialism in a Global Age*; as well as Short, *Magic Lantern Empire*.
324. Richter, *Aufbruch in die Moderne*.
325. See Conze, "Erinnerungskulturelle Rechtswende". For a summary of the immediate critical reactions to this "whitewashing" as "in tendency worrying historical-revisionist positions", see Simmerl, "Die hässlichen Seiten der Belle Époque".
326. Smith, "Contexts of Colonialism", 300.
327. Schmokel, *Dream of Empire*; see also Hildebrand, *Vom Reich zum Weltreich*; Linne, *Deutschland jenseits des Äquators?*; and Baranowski, *Nazi Empire, German Colonialism and Imperialism*. On a related matter, see Kum'a Ndumbe III, *Nationalsozialismus und Apartheid*.
328. Naranch, "Introduction", 5.
329. For examples of the cultural impact of German colonialism at home, see the contributions to Honold and Simons, *Kolonialismus als Kultur*. For the considerable role of postcards as mass media promoting and propagating the colonial

imagery, see Axster, *Koloniales Spektakel*; the summary overview by Axster, "Männlichkeit als Groteske"; as well as the review article by Yekani and Schaper, "Pictures, Postcards, Points of Contact". On colonial cinematography, see Fuhrmann, *Imperial Projections*; and on the colonial-racist projections in films of the Weimar Republic, see Nagl, *Die unheimliche Maschine*.
330. Klotz, "The Weimar Republic", 145.
331. Rüger, "Das Streben nach kolonialer Restitution in den ersten Nachkriegsjahren", 275.
332. Reed-Anderson, "Die Förderung des 'kolonialen Gedankens' durch kulturelle Akteure".
333. Zeller, "Symbolic Politics", 238. For more detail, see Zeller, *Kolonialdenkmäler und Geschichtsbewußtsein*, chapter 4: "Politik mit der Erinnerung, 1918–1945", 127–200.
334. Murphy, *The Heroic Earth*.
335. See the numerous examples in Heyden and Zeller, *Kolonialismus hierzulande*. For the medium of film, see the case study by Gordon and Mahoney, "Marching in Step".
336. See the contributions in Krobb and Martin, *Weimar Colonialism*.
337. Krobb and Martin, "Introduction: Coloniality in Post-Imperial Culture", 13f.
338. Ebert, *Koloniale Straßennamen*.
339. Sarè, "Abuses of German Colonial History". On colonialism as a subject for Nazi propaganda films, see also Hake, "Mapping the Native Body".
340. On this ambivalent relation, see Parr, "Koloniale Konstellationen von Heimat und Fremde". See also the account of colonialism and public culture in Nazi Germany by Sandler, *Empire in the Heimat*.
341. Wempe, *Revenants of the German Empire*, 12.
342. Grosse, "What Does German Colonialism Have to Do with National Socialism?", 119. See also Zimmerer, "The Birth of the *Ostland* out of the Spirit of Colonialism".
343. See as a precursor chapter 5.4 ("Science as Accomplice to Genocide") in Stahn, *Confronting Colonial Objects*, 272–277. This hunting spree has also been the (controversial) visual main focus and narrative in the 2023 cinema movie *Der vermessene Mensch* (Measures of Men).
344. See Campt, "Converging Spectres of an Other Within", 326ff. On the process and experiences of Africans and their offspring in Germany being "raced" (as part of the focus in the next section), see Nganang, "Autobiographies of Blackness in Germany".
345. See Kröner, *Von der Rassenhygiene zur Humangenetik*; Schmuhl, *The Kaiser Wilhelm Institute for Anthropology*; Weingart, Kroll and Bayertz, *Rasse, Blut und Gene*; Essner, "'Border-Line' im Menschenblut und Struktur rassistischer Rechtsspaltung"; and Bauche, "Die Figur des 'Mischling' in der deutschen Anthropologie (1900–1945)".
346. Ebner, *Nationalsozialistische Kolonialliteratur*.
347. Frenssen, *Peter Moors Fahrt nach Südwest*. Interestingly, a posthumous account of his work, while given in much detail, glosses over this novel, which pre-

sumably turned out to be his most popular; see Braun, "Gustav Frenssen in Retrospect". A similar oversight is found in Loewy, *Literatur unterm Hakenkreuz*, who does engage with both Grimm and Frenssen but omits any reference to this book. See in contrast Lehmann, "Fraternity, Frenzy, and Genocide in German War Literature, 1906–36".

348. Brehl, "Figures of Disintegration", 20. See also by the same author, *Vernichtung der Herero*; "Vernichtung als Arbeit an der Kultur"; and "Strategies of Exclusion"; as well as Noyes, "National Identity, Nomadism and Narration in Gustav Frenssen's *Peter Moor's Journey to Southwest Africa*", to mention only some of the engagements with this book.

349. Danish (Copenhagen, 1907), English (London, 1908), and Afrikaans (Pretoria, 1926).

350. By 1915 a fifth imprint brought the total to 182,000 copies. By 1944, 433,000 copies had been published. In addition, a 1927 textbook edition for schools had gone through three imprints, an edition by the Oberkommando der Wehrmacht was published as volume 34 in the *Soldatenbücherei* (Leipzig, 1942), another edition as volume 4 in the *Bücher des Frontarbeiters* (Berlin, Amsterdam, Prague, Vienna, 1943), with a final edition as *Schützengrabenliteratur* (Berlin, 1944) distributed in the trenches around Stalingrad.

351. See https://www.forum-marinearchiv.de/smf/index.php?topic=34794.0. A Google search shows numerous distributors offering different editions.

352. Titles include *Südafrikanische Novellen* (1913), *Die Olewagen Saga* (1918), *Das deutsche Südwester-Buch* (1929), *Der Richter in der Karu* (1930), *Der Zug des Hauptmanns von Erckert* (1932), *Lüderitzland* (1934), and the re-edited new compilation *Geschichten aus Südwestafrika* (1951). On the last-mentioned, see Nolden, "On Colonial Spaces and Bodies". For an engagement with both Frenssen and Grimm, see Parr, "The Relationship between Concepts of Home, Colonialism and Exoticism in the Works of Gustav Frenssen and Hans Grimm".

353. Grimm, *Volk ohne Raum*. A 1932 edition came to 1,353 pages. For a solid summary and contextualisation, see "Buchnotiz Martin Wellmann, 2003", http://www.polunbi.de/bibliothek/1926-grimm-volk.html.

354. Carsten, "'Volk ohne Raum'", 222.

355. Mentioned with praise by Jacob, *Anspruch und Wille*, 46. The collection with the revealing subtitle *Gesammelte Reden und Aufsätze aus dem kolonialen Kampfe* had a foreword by the former colonial governor Heinrich Schnee.

356. See Smith, "The Colonial Novel as Political Propaganda"; Wagner, "Volk ohne Raum"; Pakendorf, "'Volk ohne Raum'"; Kreutzer, "Deutsche Heimat und afrikanische Wahlheimat in Hans Grimms Roman '*Volk ohne Raum*'". For further critical engagements, see the literature in the profile "Hans Grimm" by Martin Wellmann, 2004, at http://www.polunbi.de/pers/grimm-01.html.

357. On Grimm's post-WWII continuities, not least through his activities at Haus Lippoldsberg, where the Klosterhaus Verlag (continued later by his daughter) republished his works, see Tourlamain, "In Defence of the Volk".

358. See the variety of contributions to the three volumes by Heyden and Zeller, *Kolonialmetropole Berlin*; *Macht und Anteil an der Weltherrschaft*; and *Kolonialismus hierzulande*.

359. See also the first three chapters in Schilling, *Postcolonial Germany*. Chapter 6 deals with a kind of private "message in a bottle", passing on colonial souvenirs and artefacts in privacy within families, thereby maintaining a sort of personal colonial memory. See also Schilling, "Imperial Heirlooms".
360. See for example Lorenz, "Die Ausstellung 'Das Sowjetparadies'".
361. Naranch, "Introduction", 9.
362. See Martin, *Schwarze Teufel, edle Mohren*.
363. See some of the chapters in the first part of AntiDiskriminierungsBüro Köln and cyberNomads, *The BlackBook*, and the following references.
364. "Fleeting Memories: Colonial Amnesia and Forgotten Figures" is the title of chapter 5 in Otele, *African Europeans*. It also recognises the role of several Africans in Germany since the late 19th century. For a comprehensive summary overview of the first generations of Africans in Germany, see Heyden, *Unbekannte Biographien*; and Aitken, "Black Germany".
365. For the early history, see some of the contributions to Honeck, Klimke and Kuhlmann-Smirnov, *Germany and the Black Diaspora*; and Kuhlmann-Smirnov, *Schwarze Europäer im Alten Reich*.
366. Loth, *Reisen nach Nigritien*, 65–70.
367. See Knauss, Wolfradt, Hofmann and Eberhard, *Auf den Spuren von Anton Wilhelm Amo*. Amo's year of death has not been established reliably. For a general historical account of Africans and African interlinkages with and influences in Europe and particularly Germany until 1945, see Martin, *Im Netz der Moderne*.
368. Trüper, "Afrikaner in Berlin".
369. Accessible at https://de.wikipedia.org/wiki/Datei:Doerstling_-_Preu%C3%9Fisches_Liebesgl%C3%BCck.jpg.
370. Kruse and Pieken, *Preußisches Liebesglück*. The 58-minute documentary with the same title was first televised in the same year. See https://programm.ard.de/TV/arte/preussisches-liebesglueck/eid_287246122962579.
371. For details of their composition and motives as well as references to further literature, see Aitken, "A Transient Presence". He recorded some 1,200 Africans living in Germany before 1914. Half of these were from the German colonies, mainly from Cameroon (about half) and Togo (about a quarter).
372. See Azamede, *Transkulturationen?*.
373. Aitken, "Forgotten Histories".
374. They were to a large extent from Cameroon. For details, see Aitken and Rosenhaft, *Black Germany*. For the "colonial encounter" experienced on both sides from then until the end of the Nazi regime, see some of the chapters in Bechhaus-Gerst and Klein-Arendt, *Die (koloniale) Begegnung*. For an overview from 1884 to 1950, see Oguntoye, *Eine afro-deutsche Geschichte;* and (until 1945) some of the chapters in Höpp, *Fremde Erfahrungen*. See also Reed-Anderson, *Re-writing the Footnotes; and, for 1920 to 1960,* Campt, Grosse and Lemke-Muniz de Faria, *"Blacks, Germans, and the Politics of Imperial Imagination"*.
375. *Deutsche Kolonialzeitung*, no. 38, 1912, 648.
376. For more details on the tragic family history, see Eyoum, Michels and Zeller, "Bonamanga".

377. See the examples mentioned by Aitken, "Black Germany", 8f and further references there; Bechhaus-Gerst, "Welche Farbe hat die Nation?"; Gerbing, *Afrodeutscher Aktivismus*, and "'Freier Mensch' oder 'deutscher Afrikaner'?"
378. Nagl, *Grenzfälle*. Nagl discovered only one case on record, of a person formerly classified as "native" who was awarded full German citizenship.
379. Joeden-Forgey, *Nobody's People*.
380. Lewerenz, "'Loyal Askari' and 'Black Rapist'".
381. See Aitken, "From Cameroon to Germany and Back via Moscow and Paris".
382. Messmer, "Erinnerung an AfrikanerInnen in Berlin".
383. https://www.demokratie-geschichte.de/koepfe/4155.
384. For more details, see Rosenhaft and Aitken, "Martin Dibobe"; Aitken and Rosenhaft, *Black Germany*, 199–202; Rüger, "Imperialismus, Sozialreformismus und antikoloniale demokratische Alternative"; Gerbing, *Afrodeutscher Aktivismus*.
385. See also El-Tayeb, *Schwarze Deutsche*. A focus on blackness and Nazi Germany is presented also in Lusane, *Hitler's Black Victims*.
386. Koller, "Frankfurt-Berlin-Rheinland".
387. Van Hoesen, "The Rhineland Controversy and Weimar Postcolonialism"; see also Pommerin, *"Sterilisierung der Rheinlandbastarde"*; and Roos, "Racist Hysteria to Pragmatic Rapprochement?", which highlights the political-strategic factors also influencing their treatment. Their fate was to some extent, though not in a life-threatening way, replicated by the treatment of the mothers and their children born as a result of the presence of Black (American) soldiers after World War II; see Roos, "Die 'farbigen Besatzungskinder' der zwei Weltkriege".
388. See the biography by Nejar, *Mach nicht so traurige Augen*; and Campt, *Other Germans*.
389. Prominent examples are the autobiographies of Theodor Wonja Michael (1925–2019), *Deutsch sein und schwarz dazu*, and of Hans-Jürgen Massaquoi (1926–2013), published in German and English as *Neger, Neger Schornsteinfeger*, and *Destined to Witness* and turned into a film; for a recent appraisal, see Mieder, "'Black is Beautiful'". Others growing up in Germany since the 1930s have added through their shared trauma to the awareness campaigns by Afro-Germans in self-organisation. From the 1980s they advanced their legitimate claims to be fully respected and recognised (more on this in the following chapter).
390. Gurnah, *Afterlives*, 274f. His life has been documented by Bechhaus-Gerst, *Treu bis in den Tod*.
391. See https://www.stolpersteine-berlin.de/en/biografie/263. On the *Stolpersteine*, see Apperly, "'Stumbling stones'"; and Östman, *The "Stolpersteine" and the Commemoration of Life*.
392. See for more details the official homepage at https://www.stolpersteine.eu/en/home.
393. Memarnia, "Stolpersteine für Schwarze Deutsche"; Gershon, "New Memorials in Berlin Honor the Holocaust's Overlooked Black Victims".
394. Hielscher, "Afrodeutsche unterm Hakenkreuz".
395. See, among others, Martin and Alonzo, *Zwischen Charleston und Stechschritt*.

396. Stoecker, *Afrikawissenschaften in Berlin von 1919 bis 1949*, and "Lehrer, Informanten, Studienobjekte"; Eckert, "Afrikanische Sprachen und Afrikanistik", and "Afrikawissenschaften in Deutschland".
397. See, for example, the chapters on "Das Schwarze Deutschland", in Heyden and Zeller, *Kolonialismus hierzulande*, 399ff, as well as the contributions in the part on "Afrikanische Migranten in der Reichs(kolonial)hauptstadt" in their volume *Kolonialmetropole Berlin*, 195ff; the chapters in the first two parts of Diallo and Zeller, *Black Berlin*, 31–130; and the last parts in Heyden, *Unbekannte Biographien*.
398. Thurman, "Review of Aitken", 2.

4. (POST-)COLONIAL (WEST) GERMANY

1. See, for example, Laak, *Imperiale Infrastruktur*.
2. Albrecht, *"Europa ist nicht die Welt"*.
3. Göttsche, *Remembering Africa*.
4. Schilling, "Imperial Heirlooms". This is also part of her profound analysis covering the German case in much more detail from a "memory culture" approach than this book can do. Schilling, *Postcolonial Germany*. For a comprehensive review, see Albrecht, "Review of *Postcolonial Germany*".
5. Poiger, "Imperialism and Empire in Twentieth-Century Germany", 124.
6. For a comparative perspective, see Bürger, *Deutsche Kolonialgeschichte(n)*. The much wider coverage of colonial topics in East German popular literature is recognised by Göttsche, *Remembering Africa*.
7. See Verber, "The Conundrum of Colonialism in Postwar Germany"; and Schilling, "Kolonialismus und Kalter Krieg".
8. Verber, "The Conundrum of Colonialism in Postwar Germany", 237.
9. For an overview, see Grau, "Aber das war eigentlich nach der Wende ..."; and, for a concrete example, Hamann and Schubert, "Zwischen anti-imperialistischem Anspruch und politischer Wirklichkeit".
10. For their archives, see http://www.argus.bstu.bundesarchiv.de/Bestaendeuebersicht/index.htm?kid=13791AEC-2C57-48CA-8803-1E057A454BB5. For a comparison of the Africa policy of both states, see Engel and Schleicher, *Die beiden deutschen Staaten in Afrika*.
11. See Kössler and Melber, "The West German Solidarity Movement with the Liberation Struggles in Southern Africa"; for a comparison of the solidarity in East and West with the struggle against apartheid in South Africa, see Bohne, Hüttner and Schade, *Apartheid No!*
12. Cornils, *"Denkmalsturz"*; Verber, "Building Up and Tearing Down the Myth of German Colonialism"; Jokinen, Manase and Zeller, *Stand und Fall*. For a more general overview on colonial monuments, see Zeller, *Kolonialdenkmäler und Geschichtsbewusstsein*; and Speitkamp, "Kolonialdenkmäler".
13. Conrad, "Rückkehr des Verdrängten?", 31.
14. Bauche, "On Overlaps, Solidarities, and Competitions", 50.
15. Rothberg, *Multidirectional Memory*.

NOTES   pp. [99–104]

16. Bauche, "On Overlaps, Solidarities, and Competitions", 50f, with reference to Attia, "Geteilte Erinnerungen", 81f. For a discussion of the linkages between colonialism and National Socialism as "entangled history", see the exchange between Attia and Rothberg, "Multidirectional Memory and *Verwobene Geschichte(n)*".
17. Wildenthal, "The Places of Colonialism in the Writing and Teaching of Modern German History", 9.
18. Manshard, "Deutsche Afrika-Gesellschaft".
19. "Freunde der früheren deutschen Schutzgebiete" was added in 1983 to its name. https://www.traditionsverband.de/.
20. Langer, "Die Statue im Kurpark".
21. Satzung, § 2. https://www.traditionsverband.de/download/pdf/Satzung_2019.pdf.
22. A detailed history is given by Brahm, *40 Jahre Vereinigung für Afrikawissenschaften in Deutschland (VAD), 1969–2009*.
23. See https://vad-ev.de/schrftenverzeichnis-der-vad/. The volume by Bley and Tetzlaff, *Afrika und Bonn*, is evidence of the partisan role played by the VAD.
24. Baumgart, "Die deutsche Kolonialherrschaft in Afrika", with the subtitle "Neue Wege der Forschung". The review essay refers to the studies by Bald, *Deutsch-Ostafrika 1900–1914*; Bley, *Kolonialherrschaft und Sozialstruktur in Deutsch-Südwestafrika*; Hausen, *Deutsche Kolonialherrschaft in Afrika*; and Tetzlaff, *Koloniale Entwicklung und Ausbeutung*—all except Bley (1968) published in 1970.
25. Baumgart, *Deutschland im Zeitalter des Imperialismus*, 82.
26. Paczensky, *"Die Weißen kommen"*.
27. Der Spiegel, "Das ist abenteuerlich".
28. See https://www.deutsche-afrika-stiftung.de/en/about/.
29. The influential role of the documentary and its creator Bernhard Grzimek (1909–1987) in strengthening a colonial approach to African wildlife management and nature conservation is explained by Gissibl and Paulmann, "'Serengeti darf nicht sterben'".
30. Berger, "Africa Addio".
31. Nowak, "Der Schock der Authentizität".
32. Ibid., 46ff.
33. Fuhrmann, "Zwischen kolonialer Wirklichkeit und kolonialer Legende", 462ff; and especially Michels, "Geschichtspolitik im Fernsehen".
34. https://www.fernsehserien.de/heia-safari.
35. Michels, "Geschichtspolitik im Fernsehen", 480.
36. Giordano in later reflections felt he was not sufficiently discriminating and had not recognised the longings, hopes, good intentions, eagerness, strains and sacrifices also at play on the German side; see https://www.dhm.de/zeughauskino/vorfuehrung/heia-safari-die-legende-von-der-deutschen-kolonialidylle-in-afrika-2777/.
37. For details on these, see Fuhrmann, "Zwischen kolonialer Wirklichkeit und kolonialer Legende", 464ff.
38. For more information, see https://www.iz3w.org/. Notably, the iz3w also

hosts the website *freiburg-postkolonial* (https://www.freiburg-postkolonial.de/). Established in 2006, it marks a milestone in local postcolonial initiatives and has operated since then as the most relevant project of its kind, setting an example followed by many others.
39. For many details, see https://www.issa-bonn.org/.
40. See Melber, *Namibia: Kolonialismus und Widerstand*; Melber, with Melber and Hillebrecht, *In Treue fest, Südwest!*; Bühler, *Der Namaaufstand gegen die deutsche Kolonialherrschaft in Namibia von 1904–1913;* Schneider, "Um Scholle und Leben"; Böhlke-Itzen, *Kolonialschuld und Entschädigung*.
41. Produced in informal settings by unpaid work, it was published for decades independently before joining a publisher: https://www.zeitschrift-peripherie.de/. By coincidence, its issue 165/166 (2022) has the thematic focus "DDR postkolonial".
42. Accessible at https://www.filmkraft.de/Filme/26/DIE-LIEBE-ZUM-IMPERIUM-/. For the book of the film, see Bald, Heller and Hundsdörfer, *Die Liebe zum Imperium*.
43. His numerous productions, often related to colonial history and current African topics, are listed on his *filmkraft* website: https://www.filmkraft.de/Filme/.
44. Paczensky, *Weiße Herrschaft*, 27.
45. Colonial insignia and other relics remain an important market, with collector items traded at high prices. Peter's Antiques in Swakopmund, for example, offers sought-after memorabilia mainly to German tourists (https://www.peters-antiques.com/).
46. Meaning that not all under Hitler was bad. Unemployment was reduced and the *Autobahn* was constructed.
47. Krüger, "Die 'guten' Seiten des #Kolonialismus".
48. With presentations published by Bruchhaus and Harding, *Hundert Jahre Einmischung in Afrika*.
49. Entwicklungspolitische Korrespondenz, *Deutscher Kolonialismus: Materialien zur Hundertjahrfeier 1984*; Hinz, Patemann and Meier, *Weiß auf schwarz*; Weiss and Mayer, *Afrika den Europäern!*; Melber, with Melber and Hillebrecht, *In Treue fest, Südwest!* A notable precursor was the coffee-table book by Timm, *Deutsche Kolonien*.
50. Ganslmayr and Paczensky, "Die geraubte Kultur". The anthropologist Herbert Ganslmayr (1937–1991) was from 1975 director of the Überseemuseum in Bremen and actively engaged in solidarity work. The museum frequently displayed exhibitions seeking to create awareness of Germany's colonial past and the need to decolonise in Germany too. He was convinced that ethnographic museums should provide information on the continued asymmetries and the situation in former colonies, and participated in early efforts in Bremen to support the struggle for Namibian independence. Because of his principled approach, he was much isolated and ostracised in the profession. He died while attending a UNESCO conference on restitution in Athens. The journalist Gert von Paczensky (1925–2014) was from the 1950s an outspoken advocate of anti-colonialism and a ruthless critic of colonialism; see especially *Die Weißen kommen*, republished as *Weiße Herrschaft*.

51. Setting the tone in advance were Graudenz and Schindler, *Die deutschen Kolonien*. Their colonial-apologetic propaganda was republished subsequently in several editions.
52. Steltzer, *Die Deutschen und ihr Kolonialreich*, 360 and 356.
53. Westphal, *Geschichte der deutschen Kolonien*, 327.
54. Ibid., 326.
55. Ibid., 327.
56. Bley, "Unerledigte deutsche Kolonialgeschichte", 12.
57. Gründer, *Geschichte der deutschen Kolonien*, 245.
58. Eckert and Wirz, "Wir nicht, die Anderen auch", 376.
59. Gründer and Hiery, *Die Deutschen und ihre Kolonien*, 24.
60. Osterhammel, *Kolonialismus*; Reinhard, *Kleine Geschichte des Kolonialismus*; Speitkamp, *Deutsche Kolonialgeschichte*; Eckert, *Kolonialismus*.
61. Conrad, "German Colonial History", 105. The author added to this survey his own overview: Conrad, *Deutsche Kolonialgeschichte* (republished several times), also in an English version as *German Colonialism*.
62. Conrad, "Colonizing the Nineteenth Century", 677.
63. Bundestagsfraktion Bündnis 90/Die Grünen, Ein Millennium Africa Renaissance Program, 55.
64. Ibid., 20.
65. Arndt, Thiel and Walther, *AfrikaBilder*; Arndt and Hornscheidt, *Afrika und die deutsche Sprache*; Arndt and Ofuatey-Alazard, *Wie Rassismus aus Wörtern spricht*.
66. See the overview by Göttsche, "Gegenwartsliteratur" (with many cross-references to other engagements), and, for the special case of Namibia, Arich-Gerz, *Namibias Postkolonialismen*.
67. Seyfried, *Herero*.
68. Göttsche, *Remembering Africa*, 412.
69. Ibid., 90.
70. Ibid., 89. For a similar drastic verdict, see Loimeier, "'Selten eine gute Figur'".
71. Hofmann, *Die weiße Massai*.
72. Hofmann, *Zurück aus Afrika*, and *Wiedersehen in Barsaloi*.
73. Hofmann, *Afrika meine Passion*. The implicit, not very subtle racism inherent in this narrative has been analysed by Reiniger, *Die große Liebe in einer fremden Welt*; and Maurer, *Fremdes im Blick, am Ort des Eigenen*.
74. Göttsche, *Remembering Africa*, 416.
75. Ibid., 413 and 419.
76. Göttsche, "Memory Studies", 118.
77. Göttsche, "Gegenwartsliteratur", 310.
78. See the detailed overview by Göttsche, "Erinnerung und Kritik des deutschen Kolonialismus in der Gegenwartsliteratur".
79. Loimeier, "Deutschland und die Literaturen Afrikas".
80. See UEPO, "Literaturpreis an Abdulrazak Gurnah", listing the titles, years and publishers.
81. See, among others, Mengiste, "Afterlives by Abdulrazak Gurnah"; and Pilling, "Afterlives by Abdulrazak Gurnah".

82. Rapp, "Hat die Identitätspolitik ihren ersten Nobelpreis?"
83. https://www.nobelprize.org/prizes/literature/2021/summary/.
84. https://twitter.com/ulfposh/status/1446072856132165635. The tweet was later deleted.
85. Quoted in *Der Spiegel*, "Literaturnobelpreis geht an Abdulrazak Gurnah".
86. Not to be mistaken as a full ministerial portfolio, it is nevertheless a highly influential position. The Federal Government Commissioner for Culture and the Media oversees an independent institution and reports directly to the office of the Chancellor. Grütters held the position in the government of Angela Merkel from 2013 to 2021. Her successor in the new government coalition was Claudia Roth (from December 2021).
87. Quoted in Deutsche Welle, "'Germany's Most Ambitious Cultural Project' Reveals Concept".
88. Kohl, Kramer, Möller, Sievernich and Völger, *Das Humboldt Forum und die Ethnologie*.
89. On this debate, see Zeller, "Weltkulturmuseum? Koloniale Schatzkammer?".
90. Zimmermann and Geissler, *Kolonialismus-Debatte*.
91. See, for example, Finkelstein, "Colonial Histories at the Humboldt Forum"; McGreevy, "Why Germany's Newly Opened Humboldt Forum Is So Controversial"; Trilling, "Has the Humboldt Forum Got It Horribly Wrong?"; and Wainwright, "Berlin's bizarre new museum".
92. Parzinger, "Von Chancen und Herausforderungen", 125.
93. Häntzschel, "Ein unlösbarer Widerspruch".
94. Quoted in the English translation from Thiemeyer, "Cosmopolitanizing Colonial Memories in Germany", 976.
95. Parzinger, "Wohlfeil wird es schnell".
96. Quoted in Schliess, "Is the Humboldt Forum Shying Away from Colonial History?".
97. Krause, "Eine Showtreppe für Wilhelm Zwo".
98. Sarr and Savoy, The Restitution of African Cultural Heritage.
99. Sarr and Savoy, *Zurückgeben*.
100. Teuwsen, "'Wir müssen nicht auf den nächsten Krieg warten, wir können die Sachen jetzt zurückgeben'".
101. Aly, *Das Prachtboot*.
102. Knöfel, "Rückgabe der deutschen Benin-Bronzen".
103. Quoted in Wainwright, "Berlin's bizarre new museum".
104. See El-Tayeb, "The Universal Museum".
105. See, among others, Eiser, "Ikone einer Debatte".
106. All quotes from "Grütters: Berliner Humboldt Forum ist Museum neuen Typs", *Zeit online*, 12 July 2021, https://www.zeit.de/news/2021-07/12/gruetters-berliner-humboldt-forum-ist-museum-neuen-typs?utm_referrer=https%3A%2F%2Fwww.google.com%2F.
107. Die Bundesregierung, *Im Wortlaut*.
108. Conze, "Erinnerungskulturelle Rechtswende"; for the Berlin Castle, see 91–92.
109. Bach, "Brand of Brothers?", 100.

110. http://www.no-humboldt21.de.
111. Apoh and Mehler, "Das Humboldt Forum und die Restitutionsdebatte", 58.
112. Wainwright, "Berlin's bizarre new museum".
113. Bach, "Brand of Brothers?", 108.
114. Bundespräsidialamt, Federal President Frank-Walter Steinmeier at the Inauguration of the Exhibitions of the Ethnological Museum and the Museum of Asian Art of the National Museums in Berlin on 22 September 2021, 7.
115. Steinmetz, "Das Humboldt Forum", 15f.
116. See for this Elsner and Brusius, "Memory Cultures 2.0 and Museums".
117. BDG Network, *The Black Diaspora and Germany*.
118. Della and Lehmann, "Afrodeutsche und eine Afrikapolitik".
119. See Pugach, *African Students in East Germany, 1949–1975*; and contributions to section 2 ("Navigating the GDR") in Burton, Dietrich, Harisch and Schenck, *Navigating Socialist Encounters*.
120. On the GDR realities, see Piesche, "Black and German?", and "Schwarz und Deutsch?"; Poutrus and Warda, "Ostdeutsche of Color". Biographical accounts of their upbringing—with different experiences of "othering"—are given in (on the negative side) Soost, *Heimkind—Neger—Pionier*; and (more positive) Zöllner, *Schokoladenkind*. See also "Rassismuserfahrungen im Osten", https://www.rassismusmonitor.de/kurzstudien/ostdeutsche-postmigrantinnen.
121. Fehrenbach, *Race after Hitler*; and Schroer, *Recasting Race after World War II*.
122. For a compassionate account with an annotated list of relevant literature, see Arp, "Zwischen den Welten"; see also Roos, "Die 'farbigen Besatzungskinder' der zwei Weltkriege"; Bechhaus-Gerst, "Welche Farbe hat die Nation?", 254–260; and Lemke Muniz de Faria, *Zwischen Fürsorge und Ausgrenzung*.
123. Gerunde, *Eine von uns*. For a review of her deeply moving history, see Mesghena in *Deutschlandfunk*.
124. Hügel-Marshall, *Daheim unterwegs*. For an engagement with her story, see Janson, "The Subject in Black and White".
125. More details at http://ika-huegel-marshall.com/ and https://en.wikipedia.org/wiki/Ika_H%C3%BCgel-Marshall#Autobiography.
126. For example Usleber, *Die Farben unter meiner Haut*, turns his pigmentation more into a personal problem than a societal one. For him, the word "home" is meaningless. This resonates with the German title of Ika Hügel-Marshall's account, "daheim unterwegs" (at home away). A biographical account of an upbringing in the 1970s is given by Mangold, *Das deutsche Krokodil*. His perspectives and way of engagement signal a new chapter in Afro-German engagement. See also Mangold, "Die Renaissance der Hautfarbe".
127. Hoeder, "Totgeschwiegen".
128. They have been given voice in the documentary *Schwarze Adler* (Black Eagles) of 2021. For a list of the protagonists, see https://www.schwarzeadler-film.com/die-protagonisten. The film received much praise in German media; see Schmitt, "TV-Doku 'Schwarze Adler'"; and Ahrens, "Der verletzte Stolz des Adlers".
129. Adu, "Racism on and off the Football Field".

130. See Fremgen, ... *Und wenn du dazu noch schwarz bist.*
131. On the organisational history, see the summary by Eleonore Wiedenroth-Coulibaly and Hadija-Haruna-Oelker on its home page https://isdonline.de/ueber-uns/#geschichte; and Wiedenroth-Coulibaly and Zinflou, "20 Jahre Schwarze Organisierung in Deutschland".
132. http://www.adefra.de/. See Ani, "Die Frau die Mut zeigt".
133. Oguntoye, Opitz and Schultz, *Farbe bekennen*, 14. The volume has subsequently been published in an English translation and there have been several new imprints.
134. Introduction of the editors, ibid., 10.
135. Ellen Wiedenroth, ibid., 166 and 170. On the notion of home (*Heimat*) and homelessness, see Mbombi, *Schwarze Deutsche und ihre sozialen Identitäten*.
136. On the forms of new self-organisation and the relevance of this book, see Bechhaus-Gerst, "Welche Farbe hat die Nation?", 261–263; and on the subsequent impact, see Florvil, *Mobilizing Black Germany*; and Lennox, *Remapping Black Germany*.
137. For a retrospective look at the three decades from the first meetings of ISD and an overview of some of the earlier historical experiences as well as current challenges, see the contributions to Bergold-Caldwell, Digoh, Haruna-Oelker, Nkwendja-Ngnoubamdjum, Ridha and Wiedenroth-Coulibaly, *Spiegelblicke*.
138. See Piesche, "Identität und Wahrnehmung in literarischen Texten Schwarzer deutscher Autorinnen der 90er Jahre"; and Kron, *Fürchte dich nicht, Bleichgesicht!*
139. See the examples in Godefridi, "'Schwarz sein in Deutschland'".
140. Kamta, *"Poesie des Überlebens"*. For many references and examples, see also Kron, "Afrikanische Diaspora und Literatur Schwarzer Frauen in Deutschland".
141. Ayim, *Blues in schwarz weiss*; *Nachtgesang*; and *Grenzenlos und unverschämt*.
142. Florvil, *Mobilizing Black Germany*, 117.
143. Ervedosa, "Das May-Ayim-Ufer in Berlin", which also details the controversial debates around the symbolic act.
144. https://www.demokratie-geschichte.de/koepfe/2372.
145. Kelly, *Sisters and Souls*; and *Sisters and Souls 2*; Hügel-Marshall, Prasad and Schultz, *May Ayim*. See also Florvil, "Seeing May Ayim through Her Friends' Eyes".
146. Schilling, "German Postcolonialism in Four Dimensions", 432. It might be worth a discussion if this should be phrased in a way giving full recognition to Black agency and the impact the Afro-German struggles for recognition have made.
147. See Kupka, "Schwarze Körper in weißen Kunsträumen".
148. More details at https://www.kulturstiftung-des-bundes.de/de/projekte/erbe_und_vermittlung/detail/dekoloniale.html. With the end of the five-year model project in 2024, a new colonialism remembrance concept (Erinnerungskonzept 'Kolonialismus' für Berlin) will be conceptualised in an open discussion process.
149. Dekoloniale Team, "Dekoloniale Erinnerungskultur in der Stadt". The volume

includes many more chapters of relevance to various aspects dealt with in this book. See also Kopp, "Ein Modellprojekt?"
150. https://www.museumsportal-berlin.de/de/ausstellungen/zurueckgeschaut-looking-back/.
151. The opening minutes of the 2023 cinema movie *Der vermessene Mensch* (Measures of Men) include the anthropological measurements taken from the members of the delegation from South West Africa during their presence for this event as a point of departure.
152. Memarnia, "Widerstand sichtbar machen".
153. For a thorough engagement and contextualisation, see Kuban "Wer schaut hier wen an?"
154. See the variety of topics and chapters in Vukadinovic, *Rassismus*.
155. United Nations, *Report of the Working Group of Experts on People of African Descent on Its Mission to Germany*, 12, at 52. On the degree of racism in Germany today, see Deutsches Zentrum für Integrations- und Migrationsforschung (DeZIM), *Rassistische Realitäten*. Many Afro-German experiences and perspectives are accessible in a dossier at the website *Heimatkunde*: https://heimatkunde.boell.de/de/dossier-schwarze-community-deutschland.
156. United Nations, *Report of the Working Group of Experts on People of African Descent on Its Mission to Germany*, 13, at 61.
157. United Nations, *Report of the Working Group of Experts on People of African Descent on Its Mission to Germany*, 13, at 57.
158. Committee on the Elimination of Racial Discrimination, *Concluding Observations on the Combined 23rd to 26th Reports of Germany*, 7.
159. While a closer engagement with this matter goes beyond the focus of this book, the fabrication of such inventions is deconstructed in some of the chapters in Böckmann, Gockel, Kössler and Melber, *Jenseits von Mbembe*.
160. Hyslop, "The Kaiser's Lost African Empire and the Alternative für Deutschland", 112.
161. On this reanimation with reference to past practices, see ibid., 108ff.
162. Ibid., 120.
163. For the context and in response, see Hira, "A Decolonial Critique of the Racist Case for Colonialism". For the significance of the concerted efforts by Gilley and a few others, see Brandon and Sarkar, "Labour History and the Case against Colonialism".
164. Gilley, "The Case for Colonialism: A Response to My Critics", 94.
165. Gilley, "The Case for German Colonialism", 1.
166. Ibid.
167. Ibid.
168. Ibid., 2.
169. Ibid., 6. For more on this event, see Heinze, "Colonial Revisionism in Germany".
170. Deutscher Bundestag, Drucksache 19/15784.
171. See Heinze, "A Technocratic Reformulation of Colonialism".
172. Teitel, "The Transitional Apology".

173. See for example Kössler and Melber, "Koloniale Amnesie".
174. Most prominently Bürger, *Deutsche Kolonialgeschichte(n)*.
175. Deutscher Bundestag, Drucksache 19/15784, 9–11.
176. Deutscher Bundestag, Drucksache 19/19914.
177. Deutscher Bundestag, Drucksache 20/3696.
178. For a recognition of his role in the formal proclamation of the German colonies of South West Africa, Cameroon and Togo, see chapter 3.
179. From the September 2021 preface of the revised and enlarged English version of the German book: Gilley, *In Defense of German Colonialism*.
180. Gilley, *Verteidigung des deutschen Kolonialismus*, full of distortions, misinterpretations and invectives aimed at his critics.
181. Gilley, "The Ethical Foundations of German Colonialism", 2.
182. Ibid., 4.
183. See chapter 4 in Kössler and Melber, *Völkermord und was dann?*
184. Parts of this section have benefited from Kössler and Melber, "Selective Commemoration".
185. Nooke, "Wir haben lange Zeit zu viel im Hilfsmodus gedacht".
186. For a somewhat critical assessment of the polarising effects of such campaigns, see Albrecht, "Negotiating Memories of German Colonialism".
187. Zeller, "Genozid und Gedenken". For more references, see chapter 5.
188. See, among others, Heyden and Zeller, *Kolonialismus hierzulande;* Hobuss and Lölke, *Erinnern verhandeln*; Zimmerer, *"Kein Platz an der Sonne";* Bechhaus-Gerst and Zeller, *Deutschland postkolonial?*; and further references in other chapters.
189. See Heyden and Zeller, *Kolonialmetropole Berlin*, and *Macht und Anteil an der Weltherrschaft*; Petersen, *Sønderjylland-Schleswig kolonial*; Grewe, Himmelsbach, Theisen and Wegmann, *Freiburg und der Kolonialismus*; Fechner and Schneider, *Fernes Hagen*; Zimmerer and Todzi, *Hamburg: Tor zur kolonialen Welt*; Bechhaus-Gerst, Michels and Fechner, *Nordrhein-Westfalen und der Imperialismus*. For examples of local initiatives, see Bahl, Pfeiffer, Ruhland, Rühlemann and Zölls, "München dekolonisieren"; Baum, "Bremen's Elefant"; Diallo and Zeller, *Berlin: Eine postkoloniale Metropole*.
190. On the challenges, see Zeller, "Weg vom Vergessen?"; and Kössler, "Zwischen kolonialer Amnesie und konstruktivem Engagement".
191. See https://www.museumsportal-berlin.de/en/museums/denkmal-fur-die-ermordeten-juden-europas-ort-der-information/.
192. For details of the initiative taken in the Berlin parliament, see Abgeordnetenhaus Berlin, Drucksache 18/2811.
193. See for details https://decolonize-berlin.de/de/koordinierungsstelle/; and Della, Diop, Kopp, Ofuatey-Alazard and Yeboah, "Gemeinsam und nachhaltig dekolonisieren"; Kopp, "Ein Modellprojekt?"; Ofuatey-Alazard and Della, "'Irritation ist notwendig, um uns von dem kolonialen Erbe zu befreien'".
194. See Ministerium für Wissenschaft, Forschung und Kunst Baden-Württemberg, "Aufarbeitung kolonialen Erbes mit der Namibia-Initiative", at https://mwk.baden-wuerttemberg.de/de/kunst-kultur/namibia-initiative.
195. Schleswig-Holsteinischer Landtag, Drucksache 19/2005; and Südschleswiger Wählerverband, "Der Kolonialismus ist Teil unserer Regionalgeschichte".

196. Todtmann, "An die Opfer erinnern". The same day a stone in commemoration of the victims of German colonialism was inaugurated by postcolonial initiatives in central Berlin.
197. Deutscher Bundestag, Drucksache 18/3013, 5.
198. Deutscher Bundestag, Plenarprotokoll 18/62, 5752 (C) and (D) and 5753 (a) and (B).
199. Bommarius, *Der gute Deutsche*.
200. https://markk-hamburg.de/en/ausstellungen/hey-hamburg-3/.
201. For the short appeal and the eight names (including also Christian Bommarius), see https://www.thorsten-blaufelder.de/2022/03/petition-zur-rehabilitierung-von-rudolf-duala-manga-bell-und-ngoso-din/.
202. Deutscher Bundestag, Drucksache 20/1827.
203. See, among others, Heissenbüttel, "Justizmord in der Kolonialzeit"; Dziedzic, "Der Fall Rudolf Manga Bell"; and Melber, "Erbärmliche Gesten".
204. As disclosed in an interview, see Schmidt, "Auf den Spuren des Urgroßvaters".
205. Federal Foreign Office, "Speech by Minister of State Katja Keul on the Occasion of a Wreath-Laying Ceremony at the Site of the Execution of Rudolf Manga Bell in Cameroon".
206. Klotz, "Rudolf Duala Manga Bell-Platz in Ulm eingeweiht".
207. Engomè "Emily" Dayas Bell (c.1881–1936) was the daughter of the English merchant Thomas Dayas and Tebedi Njanjo Eyum. See for more Eyoum, Michels and Zeller, "Bonamanga".
208. Connolly, "Campaigners celebrate changing of colonial street names in Berlin".
209. Klaproth, "Zwischen Jubel und Buhrufen".
210. Polifke, "Deshalb benennt Aalen Platz nach einem afrikanischen Prinzen".
211. Pfeffer and Wendt, *DuALA*.
212. Deutscher Bundestag, Petitionsausschuss, Petition 139208, https://epetitionen.bundestag.de/petitionen/_2022/_09/_20/Petition_139208.html.
213. "Wann wird Rudolf Duala Manga Bell rehabilitiert?" A Conversation with Jean-Pierre Félix-Eyoum, Radio Dreyeckland, 25 May 2023, at https://rdl.de/beitrag/wann-wird-rudolf-duala-manga-bell-rehabilitiert.
214. Garsha, "Expanding *Vergangenheitsbewältigung*?" See also chapter 1 and 5 with numerous further references.
215. See Kössler, *Namibia and Germany*, chapter 11.
216. See Kössler and Melber, *Völkermord und was dann?*, 74–81; Brehl, "Namibia im Deutschen Bundestag und in der Außenpolitik".
217. See Deutscher Bundestag, Plenarprotokoll 19/192, 24228 B-24241C.
218. Ibid., 24229D.
219. Agnieszka Brugger (Green Party), ibid., at 24229A.
220. Kathrin Vogler (Left Party), ibid., at 24235A.
221. Eva-Maria Schreiber (Left Party), ibid., at 24241A-B.
222. Volker Ulrich (CDU/CSU), ibid., at 24242A.
223. Bundespräsidialamt, Federal President Frank-Walter Steinmeier on the 75th Anniversary of the Liberation from National Socialism and the End of the Second World War in Europe, 2.

224. Ibid., 3 and 4.
225. Andress, *Cultural Dementia*, 106.
226. Terkessidis, *Wessen Erinnerung zählt?*, 191f.
227. Ibid., 199f, with reference to Young, "The Counter-Monument".

5. GERMANY AND NAMIBIA

1. Schilling, "Review Article", 403.
2. Bürger, *Deutsche Kolonialgeschichte(n)*, 278.
3. Partial exceptions are Förster, *Postkoloniale Erinnerungslandschaften*; and Kössler, *Namibia and Germany*, who include oral history and local perspectives on the subject. For a local project compiling such perspectives, see Biwa, "Stories of the Patchwork Quilt". For a variety of German and Namibian perspectives engaging with the shared history and the present, see Melber and Platt, *Koloniale Vergangenheit—postkoloniale Zukunft?*
4. Wallace, *A History of Namibia*, 181 (original emphasis).
5. Tjingaete, *The Weeping Graves of our Ancestors*, ii.
6. A competent summary overview with full references to the existing literature is given in Wallace, *A History of Namibia*, 131–203, including a chapter on "The Namibian War, 1904–8", 155–182.
7. Häussler and Eckl, *Lothar von Trotha in Deutsch-Südwestafrika, 1904–1905*. See also Eckl and Häussler, "Narratives of Genocide"; Weiler, "Insights into the Life and Mindset of a Genocidal Murderer"; and Rautenberg, "Genozid in Namibia".
8. This might explain why the order is not included in the official military history published as volume 1 ("Der Feldzug gegen die Herero") of *Die Kämpfe der deutschen Truppen in Südwestafrika* by the Kriegsgeschichtliche Abteilung 1 of the Große Generalstab (Berlin: Mittler & Sohn, 1906). It starts by declaring that the indigenous had carved out "a puny and meaningless existence" ("ein kümmerliches und inhaltsloses Dasein gefristet"), 1.
9. Quoted in English translation in Drechsler, *"Let Us Die Fighting"*, 156f. For more details on this document, see Gewald, "The Great General of the Kaiser".
10. See Siefkes, *Sprache, Glaube und Macht*, and "Discursive Traces of Genocide in Johannes Spiecker's Travel Diary (1905–1907)"; Melber, "Mission, Kolonialismus, Kultur und Entwicklung".
11. This proclamation is published as Appendix 1 in volume 2 ("Der Hottentottenkrieg") of *Die Kämpfe der deutschen Truppen in Südwestafrika* by the Kriegsgeschichtliche Abteilung 1 of the Große Generalstab (Berlin: Mittler & Sohn, 1907), 186.
12. See Hillebrecht and Melber, "Von den Deutschen verschleppt"; Zimmerer, *German Rule, African Subjects*, 55f.
13. Stapleton, *A History of Genocide in Africa*, 18.
14. Kreienbaum, "Guerilla Wars and Colonial Concentration Camps", and *A Sad Fiasco*. As has been observed, this risks downplaying the events by describing the mortality rates as an "unintentional by-product" of the conditions in the camps; see Severin, "Rezension".

NOTES pp. [140–145]

15. O'Sullivan, "Colonial Concentration Camps and Transnational Knowledge Transfers", 470.
16. See for example Eckl, "S'ist ein übles Land hier"; Zollmann, *Koloniale Herrschaft und ihre Grenzen*.
17. See Häussler and Trotha, "Brutalisierung 'von unten'".
18. Häussler, "From Destruction to Extermination", 62. See in more detail also Häussler, *The Herero Genocide*.
19. Leanza, "Colonial Trajectories", 376 and 386.
20. ǁGaroes, "A Forgotten Case of the ǂNukhoen / Damara People Added to Colonial German Genocidal Crimes in Namibia".
21. Gordon, "Hiding in Full View".
22. United Nations Economic and Social Council Commission on Human Rights, Sub-commission on Prevention of Discrimination and Protection of Minorities, Thirty-eighth session, Item 4 of the provisional agenda, E/CN.4/Sub.2/1985/6—Special Delivery, 2 July 1985. *Revised and Updated Report on the Question of the Prevention and Punishment of the Crime of Genocide*. Prepared by Benjamin Whitaker, 8. http://www.preventgenocide.org/prevent/UNdocs/whitaker/.
23. Menger, "'Press the Thumb onto the Eye'".
24. Grimshaw, "Britain's Response to the Herero and Nama Genocide, 1904–07".
25. As observed by Grimshaw (ibid., 56), the British ownership of the terrain was even overlooked in the comprehensive study by Erichsen, *"The Angel of Death Has Descended Violently among Them"*.
26. Quoted in Grimshaw, "Britain's Response to the Herero and Nama Genocide, 1904–07", 69. That this was a delicate balancing act ending in strained relations because of the negative impact this warfare and the violation of boundaries by German soldiers had in the Cape Colony is shown in Beckvold, "The Namibian War".
27. See Silvester and Gewald, *Words Cannot Be Found*. For extensive reviews of this somewhat controversial historical source, see Kössler, "Sjambok or Cane?"; and Adhikari, "Streams of Blood and Streams of Money". Some of the African eye-witness accounts published in the book are reproduced in Bridgman and Worley, "Genocide of the Hereros".
28. Hillebrecht, "'Certain Uncertainties'", 92.
29. Bridgman and Worley, "Genocide of the Hereros", 23.
30. Grimshaw, "Britain's Response to the Herero and Nama Genocide, 1904–07", 85.
31. Wallace, *A History of Namibia*, 181.
32. As quoted in Kundnani, *Eurowhiteness*, 80.
33. For the first detailed comparative study of its kind, see Bürger, *Deutsche Kolonialgeschichte(n)*.
34. Drechsler, *Südwestafrika unter deutscher Kolonialherrschaft*. For recognition of this pioneering work, see Vambe, "Whiteness, Power and Privilege?"
35. Bley, *Kolonialschuld und Sozialstruktur in Deutsch-Südwestafrika, 1894–1914*.
36. Schmitt-Egner, *Kolonialismus und Faschismus*.

37. Timm, *Morenga*. The novel served as the initial script for a film screened in 1985 in three parts on the state-owned German television channel with the same title and was the point of departure for its adaptation (and modification) as the 2023 cinema movie *Der vermessene Mensch*. For a retrospective personal reflection on the challenges of avoiding a colonial gaze, see Timm, "Jakob Morenga / Jacob Marengo".
38. Göttsche, *Remembering Africa*, 7.
39. Ibid., 70.
40. Among others Hinz, Patemann and Meier, *Weiß auf schwarz*; Melber, with Melber and Hillebrecht, *In Treue fest, Südwest!*; also Mamozai, *Herrenmenschen*; and Helbig and Helbig, *Mythos Deutsch-Südwest*.
41. Bürger, *Deutsche Kolonialgeschichte(n)*, 276.
42. See Rüdiger, *Die Namibia-Deutschen*; Wentenschuh, *Namibia und seine Deutschen*; Schmidt-Lauber, *Die abhängigen Herren*, and *"Die verkehrte Hautfarbe"*; Melber, *Namibia*, 13–22. For a detailed, rather uncritical but informed study of their historical role, see Hess and Becker, *Vom Schutzgebiet bis Namibia 2000*. In contrast, see Hillebrecht, "Monuments—and What Else?" For another critical reminder of German colonial remnants, see Heyl, *Namibische Gedenk- und Erinnerungsorte*.
43. Deutscher Bundestag, Plenarprotokoll 11/134, 9935–9941.
44. See Kössler and Melber, *Völkermord—und was dann?*, 40–68; Brehl, "Namibia im Deutschen Bundestag und in der Außenpolitik".
45. For an overview, see Jacob and Todzi, "Genocide and Violence". Somewhat surprisingly, the volume offers no chapter on or any detailed reference (except footnote 5 in this introduction) to the case of German South West Africa.
46. These include Krüger, *Kriegsbewältigung und Geschichtsbewußtsein*; Zimmerer, *Deutsche Herrschaft über Afrikaner*; Bühler, *Der Namaaufstand gegen die deutsche Kolonialherrschaft in Namibia von 1904–1913*; Kundrus, *Moderne Imperialisten*; Schneider, *"Um Scholle und Leben"*; Böhlke-Itzen, *Kolonialschuld und Entschädigung*; and Brehl, *Vernichtung der Herero*. Their findings were complemented by the analysis of Gewald, *Herero Heroes*; Lundtofte, *"'I Believe That the Nation as Such Must Be Annihilated'"*; Erichsen, *"The Angel of Death Has Descended Violently among Them"*; and Hull, *Absolute Destruction*; as well as the more popular non-fiction books by Olusoga and Erichsen, *The Kaiser's Holocaust*; and Sarkin, *Germany's Genocide of the Herero*. The latter two imply in their titles that the German Emperor was directly involved in the extermination strategy. Such a claim is not convincingly supported by factual evidence and promotes a perspective that the genocidal warfare was based on individual choices and not a systemic phenomenon. This is problematic, as colonial-apologetic advocates are eager to look for the tiniest windows of opportunity to discredit what they do not like— though it really does not matter if the Emperor was personally implicated. More importantly, he was not on record as objecting to such a strategy.
47. See Kössler and Melber, "Völkermord und Gedenken"; Zimmerer and Zeller, *Völkermord in Deutsch-Südwestafrika*; Förster, Henrichsen and Bollig, *Namibia— Deutschland*; Melber, *Genozid und Gedenken*; Böhlke-Itzen, *Kolonialschuld und*

Entschädigung. Subsequent in-depth scholarly engagements include, most prominently, Förster, *Postkoloniale Erinnerungslandschaften*; and Kössler, *Namibia and Germany*.
48. For a detailed overview, see Zeller, "Genozid und Gedenken".
49. See Heyden and Zeller, *Kolonialmetropole Berlin*; Kundrus, *Phantasiereiche*; Hobuss and Lölke, *Erinnern verhandeln*; Heyden and Zeller, *Kolonialismus hierzulande*; Perraudin and Zimmerer, *German Colonialism and National Identity*; Zimmerer, *"Kein Platz an der Sonne"*; Bechhaus-Gerst and Zeller, *Deutschland postkolonial?*
50. For her statement and the experiences afterwards, see Wieczorek-Zeul, *Welt bewegen*, 47–49.
51. More details are accessible on the website of the Namibian embassy in Germany: http://www.namibia-botschaft.de/aktuelles/717-namibian-german-special-initiative-programme-ngsip.html.
52. See Sarkin, *Colonial Genocide and Reparation Claims in the 21st Century*. See also Sarkin and Fowler, "Reparations for Historical Human Rights Violations".
53. Weidlich, "Reparations Motion Makes History". For details on the numerous initiatives of the Ovaherero from independence to 2014, see Melber, "Contested Notions of Genocide and Commemoration".
54. Wilson, "Remembering the Herero–Nama Genocide in Namibia".
55. A comprehensive compilation of articles on the subject is accessible at *freiburg-postkolonial*, https://www.freiburg-postkolonial.de/Seiten/anthropologische-schaedelsammlungen.htm. On the deeper meaning of the act with reference to the first return of skulls in 2011, see Kern, "Re-thinking the Agency of Human Remains".
56. Förster, Henrichsen, Stoecker and ǁEichab, "Re-individualising Human Remains from Namibia"; Faber-Jonker, *More Than Just an Object*; Henrichsen, "Demands for Restitution".
57. See Stoecker, Schnalke and Winkelmann, *Sammeln, Erforschen, Zurückgeben?* (with a chapter by Larissa Förster on the 2011 event); and Stoecker and Winkelmann, "Skulls and Skeletons from Namibia in Berlin"; see also Stoecker, "Knochen im Depot"; and Fründt and Förster, "Menschliche Überreste aus ehemals kolonisierten Gebieten in deutschen Institutionen". Since then, a further account of human remains from colonial contexts has been given by Oworu, Fuchs and Awale, *We Want Them Back*, and guidelines on how best to address the challenges have been presented by Winkelmann, Stoecker, Fründt and Förster, *Interdisziplinäre Provenienzforschung zu menschlichen Überresten aus kolonialen Kontexten*. For a general overview of cases and claims between 1970 and 2021, see Gram and Schoofs, "Germany's History of Returning Human Remains". Another recent volume offers a variety of restitution cases, including Namibian examples: Andratschke, Müller and Lembke, *Provenance Research on Collections from Colonial Contexts*.
58. See Grosse, *Kolonialismus, Eugenik und bürgerliche Gesellschaft in Deutschland, 1850–1918*; Glenn and Bunzl, *Worldly Provincialism*; Zimmermann, *Anthropology and Antihumanism in Imperial Germany*; Hanke, *Zwischen Auflösung und Fixierung*; and Bauche, "Von der Unmöglichkeit, klare Grenzen zu ziehen", and "Die Figur des 'Mischling' in der deutschen Anthropologie (1900–1945)".

59. Quoted from the English translation of the Federal Government's answer to the minor interpellation, (see fn. 61), 14.
60. Deutscher Bundestag, Drucksache 17/7741.
61. Deutscher Bundestag, Drucksache 17/8057. Published in an English translation at http://genocide-namibia.net/wp-content/uploads/2015/01/1708057_englische-Antwort.pdf.
62. From the English translation, 10f.
63. For a detailed illustrated report on the events both in Berlin and upon the return of the delegation to Windhoek, see Förster, "'These Skulls Are Not Enough'".
64. See, for more details, Office of University and Science Communications, Albert-Ludwigs-Universität Freiburg, "Repatriation of Skulls from Namibia", 4 March 2014. https://kommunikation.uni-freiburg.de/pm-en/2014/pm.2014-03-04.18-en. For a critical assessment of the background and history of the Freiburg collection, and also the fundamental contradictions and accompanying intricacies when human remains are returned on a government-to-government level, as well as a retrospective assessment of the 2011 act, see Kössler, "Imperial Skulduggery, Science and the Issue of Provenance and Restitution"; on the tension and divides that the return of the skulls has created between local customary rites, on the one hand, and the political morality of the Namibian and German governments, on the other, see Shigwedha, "The Return of Herero and Nama Bones from Germany", and "The Homecoming of Ovaherero and Nama Skulls"; as well as Pape, "Human Remains of Ovaherero and Nama".
65. As explained in earlier chapters, this is not a cabinet post. But the wording of the German press releases in English created such a misunderstanding in Namibian media.
66. German Embassy Windhoek, "Welcoming Speech Given by Minister of State Michelle Müntefering on 27 August 2018 at Villa Borsig in Berlin".
67. Federal Foreign Office, "Address by Minister of State Müntefering at the Restitution Ceremony of Human Remains to Namibia".
68. Kuteeue, "A Namibian people mark 1904 genocide".
69. Kahiruika, "Nam bars entry to skulls ceremony in Germany".
70. Staff reporter, "But what did they do to deserve that?"
71. https://www.lelamobile.com/content/76710/Namibia-will-continue-to-seek-reparations-on-genocide-Mbumba/.
72. German Embassy Windhoek, "Speech by Minister of State for International Cultural Affairs of the Federal Republic of Germany Michelle Müntefering on the Occasion of the 3rd Repatriation of Human Remains from Germany to Namibia on 31 August 2018 in Windhuk".
73. Beukes, "Müntefering's apology torn apart".
74. Chiringa, "Genocide: Germany says can't undo mistakes of the past".
75. AFP, "Germany to Return Human Remains from Namibian Genocide".
76. For a historical contextualisation and detailed account of the transfer with all the contradictory intricacies, see (by one of those in attendance) Kössler, "The Bible and the Whip".
77. Linden Museum, "Hendrik Witbooi's Family Bible and Whip". The announce-

ment shows that even the best intentions do not always protect one from a slip of the tongue, as it states that the artefacts were "acquired [sic] by German colonial troops".

78. Some video footage of the tour is posted here: https://www.youtube.com/watch?v=Td4-v-3RQXw.
79. Tjitemisa and Nuukala, "Geingob tells Germany to eat humble pie".
80. See Kössler, "Diversity in the Postcolonial State".
81. Kössler, "The Bible and the Whip", 16. For the contradictions concerning ongoing processes of genocidal dispossession within the confines of a central state, see Samudzi, "Looting the Archive".
82. Schwarz, "Germany to Loan Back 23 Looted Museum Pieces to Namibia".
83. Stiftung Preussischer Kulturbesitz, "Pressemitteilung".
84. Press Information Guide, "Confronting Colonial Pasts, Envisioning Creative Futures".
85. Ibid., 1.
86. The decision taken also included the authorisation to arrange for a return of objects to Tanzania, which were looted during the German colonial era.
87. Pollex, "Koloniale Raubkunst aus Deutschland geht zurück nach Namibia".
88. See Kössler and Melber, *Völkermord—und was dann?*, 69–74 and 80–84.
89. The whole exchange at the Government Press Conference of 10 July 2015 is documented in the very wording of an unofficial translation accessible at http://www.namibia-botschaft.de/images/stories/Aktuelles/Press_Conference_10_July_2015_Yes_it_was_genocide.pdf.
90. Zed Ngavirue (1933–2021) was active in the South West African National Union (SWANU) as the first national liberation movement. He made an academic career in exile before returning to Namibia in 1981 to work for an international mining company. At independence he became the Director General of the National Planning Commission and later served as ambassador to the EU and Belgium. He died of Covid-19 a few weeks after signing the Joint Declaration with Ruprecht Polenz.
91. Ruprecht Polenz (born 1946) served in 2000 briefly as the CDU Secretary General and was chairman of the German Parliament's Committee on Foreign Affairs between 2005 and 2013.
92. A resolution submitted on 31 May 2016 (Deutscher Bundestag, Drucksache 18/8613) was adopted on 2 June 2016 with only one vote against and one abstention. For details of the debate, see Deutscher Bundestag, "Antrag zum Völkermord an Armeniern beschlossen".
93. Deutscher Bundestag, Drucksache 20/4681.
94. Deutscher Bundestag, Drucksache 20/5228.
95. Kössler, "Die ausstehende Entschuldigung", 210.
96. United Nations, *Report of the Working Group of Experts on People of African Descent on Its Mission to Germany. Addendum: Mission to Germany: Comments by the State on the Report of the Working Group*, 4.
97. The devastating demographic consequences for the most-affected population groups in Namibia remain a non-issue in politics, since this might indicate that

without the genocide the ethnographic constellation and party-political affinities would have turned out very differently in the independent state.
98. Zollmann, "'Eine Frage von prinzipieller, weittragender Bedeutung für alle Zukunft'".
99. See Gibbs, "Who Still Owes What for the Two World Wars?"; Plucinska, "Germany Owes Poland over $850 Billion in WW2 Reparations"; Hasselbach and Romaniec, "Poland, Germany and the Shadow of World War II"; BBC, "Germany Takes Italy to UN Court over Nazi-Era Compensation Claims".
100. See Moses, *Genocide and Settler Society*; Moses and Stone, *Colonialism and Genocide*.
101. For their positions and those of some of their supporters, see Harring, *German Reparations to the Herero Nation*; Goldmann, "The Ovaherero and Nama Peoples v. Germany"; and the contributions in a reader compiled from presentations at events during a "Week of Justice" held in April 2019 in Windhoek and Swakopmund: Hackmack and Keller, *Colonial Repercussions*.
102. For the full text of the claim and the media responses, see the documents compiled and accessible at http://genocide-namibia.net/2017/01/05-01-2017-herero-und-nama-verklagen-deutschland-ovaherero-and-nama-file-lawsuit-in-new-york/.
103. Full text at http://genocide-namibia.net/2017/01/09-01-2017-pm-voelkermordklage-gegen-deutschland-ovaherero-und-nama-fordern-keine-individuellen-entschaedigungen/.
104. United Nations, *United Nations Declaration on the Rights of Indigenous Peoples*.
105. It was often stressed by both governments that the Namibian special envoy Dr Zed, as he was fondly called, was from the Ovaherero ethnic group.
106. See Pelz, "Genozid-Gespräche mit Namibia gehen in die Verlängerung".
107. Ibid.
108. https://www.dngev.de/.
109. Kaure, "Relations can improve, says German ambassador".
110. Photos were posted on the German Embassy's Twitter account at https://twitter.com/GermanEmbassyNA/status/1151370510414045187.
111. Nakale, "Political declaration on genocide draws closer".
112. Beukes, "German investors turned off".
113. Iikela, "Government committed to protecting property rights".
114. German Embassy Windhoek, "Speech of the President of the German Bundesrat Daniel Günther at the National Council of the Republic of Namibia on the Occasion of his Visit to Angola and Namibia".
115. Springer, "Günther vollzieht Gratwanderung".
116. Beukes, "German reparation offer 'not true'".
117. Oltermann, "Germany agrees to pay Namibia €1.1bn over historical Herero–Nama genocide".
118. Talmon, "The Genocide in Namibia".
119. Isilow, "Mixed Reactions in Africa as Germany Formally Recognizes 'Genocide' in Namibia".
120. Petersen and Nagtjiheue, "German genocide offer 'an insult'".

121. Nguherimo, "Genocide deal or not, the struggle continues".
122. Full title: *Joint Declaration by the Federal Republic of Germany and the Republic of Namibia*. *"United in Remembrance of Our Colonial Past, United in Our Will to Reconcile, United in Our Vision of the Future"*. Accessible at https://www.parliament.na/wp-content/uploads/2021/09/Joint-Declaration-Document-Genocide-rt.pdf.
123. Federal Foreign Office, "Foreign Minister Maas on the Conclusion of Negotiations with Namibia".
124. Statement by Heiko Maas, "Wir werden um Vergebung bitten", video online at *Der Spiegel*, 28 May 2021, https://www.spiegel.de/politik/deutschland/heiko-maas-ueber-deutschen-voelkermord-in-namibia-a-4039b424-a225-4998-bca6-7423acac1bd1.
125. Deutscher Bundestag, Plenarprotokoll 19/232, 29834 (C).
126. Ibid., 29838 (D).
127. Imani, Theurer and Kaleck, *The "Reconciliation Agreement"*, 1.
128. Ibid., 7.
129. Ibid., 4.
130. Language can be instructive and display patronising connotations that a colonial gaze is unaware of.
131. According to figures presented by the German Foreign Office, a total of 1.4 billion euros were allocated for development cooperation with Namibia between 1990 and 2020. Auswärtiges Amt, "Namibia: Beziehungen zu Deutschland".
132. Hibbeler, "Ein halbes Jahr danach".
133. Zawatka-Gerlach, "Neuer Etat wird am Donnerstag beschlossen".
134. Dahlkamp and Hammerstein, "Corona".
135. Sieben, "Berliner Flughafen BER vor der Eröffnung".
136. *Handelsblatt*, "Bahnkreise".
137. Deutsche Welle, "Namibia Genocide".
138. For more details see Melber, "Colonialism, Land, Ethnicity and Class", and "The Struggle Continues".
139. Tjirera, "Land Inequality in Namibia", 199.
140. Wietersheim, *This Land Is My Land!*
141. Resolutions of the Second National Land Conference, 30.
142. Brehl, "Namibia im Deutschen Bundestag und in der Außenpolitik", 57.
143. Imani, Theurer and Kaleck, *The "Reconciliation Agreement"*, 6.
144. Ibid., 2.
145. See, among others, Paulose and Rogo, "Addressing Colonial Crimes through Reparations"; Präfke, "The Herero People as the Subject of International Law?"; Goldmann, "'Ich bin ihr Freund und Kapitän'"; and Aboudounya, "Demanding Reparations for Colonial Genocide Using Historical Documents".
146. See Thomerson, *"German Reunification"*; and Doyle, "A Bitter Inheritance",
147. Elias, "The Doctrine of Intertemporal Law", 286. See also Wheatly, "Revisiting the Doctrine of Intertemporal Law"; and Arnauld, "How to Illegalize Past Injustice".

148. Weber and Weber, "Colonialism, Genocide and International Relations", 107.
149. Stahn, "Reckoning with Colonial Injustice", 823 and 829.
150. Harring, "German Reparations to the Herero Nation", 407.
151. Shelton, "The World of Atonement", 318. Also on customary international law of the time and the extermination war against the Ovaherero, see Cooper, "Reparations for the Herero Genocide".
152. Anderson, "Redressing Colonial Genocide under International Law", 1189.
153. Imani, Theurer and Kaleck, *The "Reconciliation Agreement"*, 6.
154. Roos and Seidl, "Im 'Südwesten' nichts Neues?"
155. Brehl, "Namibia im Deutschen Bundestag und in der Außenpolitik", 67–69.
156. Robel, *Verhandlungssache Genozid*, 388.
157. Bentley, "The Sorrow of Empire", 643. See also his monograph *Empires of Remorse*. For a general overview of political apologies by governments, see Zoodsma and Schaafsma, "Examining the 'Age of Apology'".
158. Imani and Theurer, "Reparationen für Kolonialverbrechen".
159. Kasuto and Kathindi, "Apology not accepted".
160. Tjitemisa, "Chiefs reject genocide reparations deal".
161. Al Jazeera, "Betrayal".
162. Angula, "Namibian Protesters Storm Parliament".
163. Quoted in Nebe and Ikela, "Namibia Debates German Genocide Deal".
164. Ngatjiheue, "'German and Namibian governments lack empathy'".
165. Bernadus Swartbooi, Contribution to the National Assembly Debate: On the Joint Declaration on the 1904–1905 Genocide between Germany and Namibia, 29 September. This speech as well as a few others is accessible on the website of the National Assembly at https://www.parliament.na/statement-on-genocide-apology-and-reparation/. Longer excerpts from the speeches of Swartbooi, Venaani, Alweendo and also Minister Calle Schlettwein are published in German in Melber and Platt, *Koloniale Vergangenheit—postkoloniale Zukunft?*
166. Quoted in Tjitemisa, "Parliament in session".
167. Tjitemisa, "Government poised to conclude genocide issue".
168. Tjitemisa, "Nujoma: N$ 18bn genocide deal woefully insignificant".
169. Hoffmann, "'Moral ist nicht weniger wert als Recht'".
170. Polenz, "Noch ein weiter Weg bis zur Aussöhnung", 127.
171. Koalitionsvertrag 2021–2025, *Mehr Fortschritt wagen*, 126 (see details in chapter 1).
172. Die Bundesregierung, *Im Wortlaut: Regierungspressekonferenz vom 26. Januar 2022*.
173. Deutscher Bundestag, Drucksache 20/2799.
174. Deutscher Bundestag, Drucksache 20/3236, 3.
175. Ibid., 3 and 5.
176. Ibid., 5 and 6.
177. Tendane, "Genocide deal racist, unconstitutional—Swartbooi"; Mumbuu, "Executive hijacked genocide talks—Swartbooi".
178. Bröll, "Lawyers clash with AG over genocide deal".
179. Mumbuu, "Kapofi digs into genocide, dungeons".

180. Deutscher Bundestag, Plenarprotokoll 20/59, 6621 C.
181. Ibid.
182. Boehme, "Reactive Remembrance".
183. Federal Foreign Office, "Speech by Minister of State Katja Keul at the Conference 'New Perspectives on German Colonial Rule—A Scholarship Programme for Cooperative Research'".
184. NBC, "Namibian Government Has Not Signed an Agreement with the German Government".
185. Tjitemisa, "Govt U-turns on genocide pact".
186. Mumbuu, "Namibia frets over revised genocide offer".
187. Bentley, "Colonial Apologies and the Problem of the Transgressor Speaking", 399.
188. Fragestunde im Deutschen Bundestag, 9 November 2022. The answer, composed of three sentences in eight lines (a copy of which is in my possession), stresses that both sides agree that the open questions will be clarified by means of *Nachverhandlungen* and not *Neuverhandlungen* (underlined in the original).
189. Respondents are the Speaker of the National Assembly, the State President, the Cabinet and the Attorney General. Case number HC-MD-CIV-MOT-REV-2023/00023. Available at ejustice.jud.na/ejustice/f/caseinfo/publicsearch. For an appraisal, see Theurer, "Litigating Reparations".
190. Theurer, "Minimum Legal Standards in Reparation Processes for Colonial Crimes", 1168.
191. Reference AL DEU 1/2023, accessible at spcommreports.ohchr.org/TMResultsBase/DownLoadPublicCommunicationFile?gId=27875.
192. Reference AL NAM 1/2023, accessible at spcommreports.ohchr.org/TMResultsBase/DownLoadPublicCommunicationFile?gId=27878.
193. For a comment, see Theurer, "Germany Has to Grant Reparations for Colonial Crimes".
194. AL DEU 1/2023 and AL NAM 1/2023, 8f.
195. Ibid., 10.
196. Republic of Namibia, Office of the Deputy Prime Minister and Minister of International Relations and Cooperation, Joint Communication from Special Procedures.
197. Permanent Mission of the Federal Republic of Germany to the Office of the United Nations and to the Other International Organizations Geneva, *Note Verbal*.
198. Theurer, "Minimum Legal Standards in Reparation Processes for Colonial Crimes", 1165.
199. Permanent Mission of the Federal Republic of Germany, to the Office of the United Nations and to the Other International Organizations Geneva, *Note Verbal*, 7f.
200. Ibid., 14.
201. Theurer, "Litigating Reparations".
202. Quoted in Beukes, "Apartheid worse than genocide, Geingob says".
203. Hembapu, "Uproar over Geingob's genocide remarks".

204. Joseph, "Nudo demands apology from president".
205. NTLA/OTA, "Open Letter to the Namibian Head of State: Dr Hage Geingob", 27 September 2023, 5 and 2.
206. Ndjebela, "Reparation talks".
207. Nakashole, "Venaani claims reparations agreement in closed-door negotiations".
208. https://twitter.com/GERonAfrica/status/1733441353764188578.
209. Bentley, "The Negotiated Apology", 1.
210. Theurer, "Minimum Legal Standards in Reparation Processes for Colonial Crimes", 1163.
211. Reflections on Restorative Justice Campaign for the Year 2023 by Gaob Johannes Isaack and Paramount Chief Mutjinde Katiua. Issued 31 December 2023, 3f.
212. Hackmack, "Repairing the Irreparable?", 5.
213. Van Wyk, "'Anything about Us, without Us, Is against Us'".
214. As an analysis of German media reports between 2001 and 2016 points out, the predominance of White male scholars among those who play an active role in sharing critical observations in public remains a significantly lopsided phenomenon: Wolff, *Post-/Koloniale Erinnerungsdiskurse in der Medienkultur*, 426.
215. Kössler, "Diversität und Erinnerung", 182. See also Hackmack, "Repairing the Irreparable?"
216. Kössler, "Postcolonial Asymmetry", 127.
217. Committee on the Elimination of Racial Discrimination, *Concluding Observations on the Combined 23rd to 26th reports of Germany*, 10.
218. Lenzerini, "Conclusive Notes", 622.
219. Dagdelen, "Völkermord zweiter Klasse?"
220. Wissenschaftliche Dienste, *Sachstand*.
221. Hackmack, "Repairing the Irreparable?", 4f.
222. Hamrick and Duschinski, "Enduring Injustice", 451.
223. Berat, "Genocide", 210.
224. Jason, "On the spot". For a list of the 23 Jewish non-state organisations attending the Conference on Jewish Material Claims Against Germany, see Protocol No. 2 of the Agreement signed between Israel and the Federal Republic of Germany in Luxembourg on 10 September 1952, https://treaties.un.org/doc/Publication/UNTS/Volume%20162/volume-162-I-2137-English.pdf.
225. Rechavia-Taylor and Moses, "The Herero and Nama Genocide, the Holocaust, and the Question of German Reparations", 3.
226. Coates, "The Case for Reparations".
227. Soyinka, *The Burden of Memory, the Muse of Forgiveness*.
228. Baldwin, *I Am Not Your Negro*.
229. Goldmann, "Why the Key to the Past Lies in the Future", 4.
230. Du Pisani, "Gerechtigkeit und Fairness in Verhandlungen".
231. Popp and Riedmann, "'Es ist, als hätten wir nie existiert'".
232. Quoted in Lawal, "How to Pay for Genocide".
233. Yerushalmi, *Zakhor*, 117.

6. CHALLENGING COLONIAL ASYMMETRIES AND BLIND SPOTS

1. Moses, "The Documenta, Indonesia and the Problem of Closed Universes".
2. Roth, "Kunst und Kultur sind frei", 28.
3. Andress, *Cultural Dementia*, 1.
4. Ibid., 1f.
5. Ibid., 5.
6. Ibid., 68.
7. Zimmerer, "Kolonialismus und kollektive Identität", 9.
8. Assmann, *Erinnerungsräume*, 133–140, and *Cultural Memory and Western Civilization*, 397.
9. An argument used by Bürger, *Deutsche Kolonialgeschichte(n)*, to dismiss the notion. For a similar argument, see Albrecht, "(Post-)colonial Amnesia?", and Schilling, *Postcolonial Germany*. Others again refer to a "conspiracy of silence" as an intended silence, see Rothermund, *Erinnerungskulturen post-imperialer Nationen*. For a new appraisal of the term in the specific context of the debate on Namibia, see Bürger and Rausch, "Ein 'vergessener' Völkermord?"
10. Herrmann, "Koloniale Amnesie?", 21.
11. See Bürger, *Deutsche Kolonialgeschichte(n)*, 264.
12. For a similar conclusion, see ibid., 276.
13. Renan, "What Is a Nation?", 3.
14. Ibid., 10.
15. Assmann, *Der lange Schatten der Vergangenheit*, 101.
16. Owuor, "Derelict Shards", 12 (italics in the original).
17. Krüger, "Koloniale Schuld und afrikanische Geschichte".
18. Assmann, *Der lange Schatten der Vergangenheit*, 108.
19. Ibid., 15f.
20. Möller, "Abschied von unserer Leiterinnerung".
21. Owuor, "Derelict Shards", 6.
22. Kössler, "Internationale Solidarität", 351.
23. The whole conversation can be followed here: https://www.youtube.com/watch?v=xIPsRR_MnaY.
24. Hackmack, "Repairing the Irreparable?", 5.
25. Wiedemann, *Den Schmerz der Anderen begreifen*, 78f.
26. Wiedemann, "Ohne Hierarchien des Gedenkens".
27. See Platt, "Gewalt, Trauma und Erinnerung".
28. Popp, "'Es ist, als hätten wir nie existiert'", 104.
29. Bulawayo, *We Need New Names*, 285.
30. Gurnah, *Gravel Heart*, 108.
31. Fitzpatrick, "Indigenous Australians and German Anthropology in the Era of 'Decolonization'", 709.
32. Bens and Zenker, "Sentiment", 104; see also Bens and Zenker, *Gerechtigkeitsgefühle*.
33. Wiedemann, *Den Schmerz der Anderen begreifen*, 11.
34. See Geiger, "Afrikabilder in der Kritik", and "Der deutsche Kolonialismus in aktuellen Lehrbüchern".

35. El-Tayeb, *Undeutsch*, 17.
36. Buruma, *Year Zero*.
37. Samudzi, "Reparative Futurities", 35 (italics in the original).
38. Stecklum, "A Joint Understanding on the Past?", 207f. See also Platt, "Gewalt, Trauma und Erinnerung".
39. Björkdahl and Kappler, "The Creation of Transnational Memory Spaces", 399.
40. Ibid.
41. Such as Katjivena, *Mama Penee*; Nguherimo, *Unburied, Unmarked*; and Utley, *The Lie of the Land*. On the last-mentioned, see Krishnamurthy, "Untold Tales and Occluded Histories".
42. Becker, "Writing Genocide". See, as examples, Serebrov, *Mama Namibia*; and Kubuitsile, *The Scattering*. On both, see Nandenga, "Reconstruction of Atrocities through Fiction in Namibia"; see also Abiatar and Krishnamurthy, "Herero–Nama Genocide as Historical Fiction".
43. Krishnamurthy and Tjiramanga, "Exploring Herero Genocide Survivor Narratives".
44. Such as Timm, *Morenga*; Brink, *The Other Side of Silence*; and Van den Berg, *Parts Unknown*.
45. See in particular Kleinschmidt, "Verstrickungen"; Henrichsen, "*Ovandoitji*"; Mühr, "Wer im Schatten sitzt ..."; Wietersheim, "Im Schatten des Genozids"; Schlettwein, "Das Schweigen der Ahnen"; and Trüper, *Zara oder das Streben nach Freiheit*.
46. Eley, "Empire by Land or Sea?", 38.
47. Rothberg, *Multidirectional Memory*.
48. See in particular the provocative polemic by Moses, "The German Catechism", and the comment by Fitzpatrick, "On the 'German Catechism'". For a collection of interventions, see New Fascism Syllabus, "The Catechism Debate".
49. For a general engagement with the subject, including special acknowledgement of and reference to the genocide committed in German South West Africa, see Howard-Hassmann, *Reparations to Africa*; and Lu, *Justice and Reconciliation in World Politics*.
50. Rausch, "'We're Equal to the Jews Who Were Destroyed'", 430.
51. Brusius, "Memory Cultures 2.0", 7.
52. Rothberg, "Lived Multidirectionality", 1322f.
53. Khan, "The Kaiser's Holocaust", 211 (italics in the original).
54. Ibid., 219.
55. Sznaider, *Fluchtpunkte der Erinnerung*, 162.
56. Legg, "A Plea for Commemorative Equality".
57. See the variety of topics in Zimmerer, *Erinnerungskämpfe*.
58. Schleiermacher and Schulz, "Koloniale Kanonenkugel zum Uni-Start".
59. The original poem in German is available in full at https://isdonline.de/das-erinnern/.

BIBLIOGRAPHY

Books

Adhikari, Mohamed (ed.), *Civilian-Driven Violence and the Genocide of Indigenous Peoples in Settler Societies* (Abingdon: Routledge, 2021).

———, *Destroying to Replace: Settler Genocides of Indigenous Peoples* (Cambridge, MA: Hackett, 2022).

——— (ed.), *Genocide on Settler Frontiers: When Hunter-Gatherers and Commercial Stock Farmers Clash* (Cape Town: UCT Press, 2014).

Adick, Christel, *Bildung und Kolonialismus in Togo: Eine Studie zu den Entstehungszusammenhängen eines europäisch geprägten Bildungswesens in Afrika am Beispiel Togos (1850–1914)* (Weinheim and Basel: Beltz, 1981).

Adick, Christel, and Mehnert, Wolfgang, with Christiani, Thea, *Deutsche Missions- und Kolonialpädagogik in Dokumenten: Eine kommentierte Quellensammlung aus den Afrikabeständen deutschsprachiger Archive, 1884–1914* (Frankfurt/Main: IKO, 2001).

Aitken, Robbie, and Rosenhaft, Eve, *Black Germany: The Making and Unmaking of a Diaspora Community, 1884–1960* (Cambridge: Cambridge University Press, 2013).

Albertini, Rudolf von (ed.), *Moderne Kolonialgeschichte* (Cologne and Berlin: Kiepenheuer & Witsch, 1970).

Albrecht, Monika, *"Europa ist nicht die Welt": (Post)Kolonialismus in Literatur und Geschichte der westdeutschen Nachkriegszeit* (Bielefeld: Aisthesis, 2008).

Altena, Thorsten, *"Ein Häuflein Christen mitten in der Heidenwelt des dunklen Erdteils": Zum Selbst- und Fremdverständnis protestantischer Missionare im kolonialen Afrika, 1884–1918* (Münster and New York: Waxmann, 2003).

Aly, Götz, *Das Prachtboot: Wie Deutsche die Kunstschätze der Südsee raubten* (Frankfurt/Main: Fischer, 2021).

——— (ed.), *Nilpferdpeitsche und Kultur: Eine Streitschrift aus dem Jahr 1897 über die Zivilisierung der Kolonien* (Berlin: Comimo, 2021).

Ames, Eric, *Carl Hagenbeck's Empire of Entertainments* (Seattle: University of Washington Press, 2008).

Andratschke, Claudia, Müller, Lars, and Lembke, Katja (eds.), *Provenance Research on Collections from Colonial Contexts: Principles, Approaches, Challenges* (Heidelberg: arthistoricum.net-ART-Books, 2023).

BIBLIOGRAPHY

Andress, David, *Cultural Dementia: How the West Has Lost Its History, and Risks Losing Everything Else* (London: Head of Zeus, 2018).

AntiDiskriminierungsBüro Köln, and cyberNomads (eds.), *The BlackBook: Deutschlands Häutungen* (Frankfurt/Main: IKO, 2004).

Apoh, Wazi, and Lundt, Bea (eds.), *Germany and Its West African Colonies: "Excavations" of German Colonialism in Post-colonial Times* (Münster: LIT, 2013).

Arendt, Hannah, *The Origins of Totalitarian Rule* (New York: Harcourt, Brace and Co., 1951).

Arich-Gerz, Bruno, *Namibias Postkolonialismen: Texte zu Gegenwart und Vergangenheiten in Südwestafrika* (Bielefeld: Aisthesis, 2008).

Arndt, Susan, and Hornscheidt, Antje (eds.), *Afrika und die deutsche Sprache: Ein kritisches Nachschlagewerk* (Münster: Unrast, 2004).

Arndt, Susan, and Ofuatey-Alazard, Nadja (eds.), *Wie Rassismus aus Wörtern spricht: (K)Erben des Kolonialismus im Wissensarchiv deutscher Sprache* (Münster: Unrast, 2011).

Arndt, Susan, Thiel, Heiko, and Walther, Ralf (eds.), *AfrikaBilder: Studien zu Rassismus in Deutschland* (Münster: Unrast, 2001).

Assemboni, Obi, Babka, Anna, Beck, Laura, and Dunker, Axel (eds.), *Postkolonialität denken: Spektren germanistischer Forschung in Togo* (Vienna: Praesens, 2017).

Assmann, Aleida, *Cultural Memory and Western Civilization: Functions, Media, Archives* (Cambridge: Cambridge University Press, 2011).

―――, *Der lange Schatten der Vergangenheit: Erinnerungskultur und Geschichtspolitik* (Munich: Beck, 2006).

―――, *Erinnerungsräume: Formen und Wandlungen des kulturellen Gedächtnisses* (Munich: Beck, 1999).

Austen, Ralph A., and Derrick, Jonathan, *Middlemen of the Cameroons Rivers: The Duala and Their Hinterland, c.1600–c.1960* (Cambridge and New York: Cambridge University Press, 1999).

Axster, Felix, *Koloniales Spektakel in 9x14 Bildpostkarten im Deutschen Kaiserreich* (Bielefeld: Transcript, 2014).

Ayim, May, *Blues in schwarz weiss: Gedichte* (Berlin: Orlanda, 1995).

―――, *Grenzenlos und unverschämt: Essays* (Berlin: Orlanda, 1997; Frankfurt/Main: Fischer 2002; Münster: Unrast, 2021).

―――, *Nachtgesang* (Berlin: Orlanda, 1997).

Azamede, Kokou, *Transkulturationen? Ewe-Christen zwischen Deutschland und Westafrika, 1884–1939* (Stuttgart: Steiner, 2009).

Bachmann, Klaus, *Genocidal Empires: German Colonialism in Africa and the Third Reich* (Berlin: Peter Lang, 2018).

Bade, Klaus J. (ed.), *Imperialismus und Kolonialmission: Kaiserliches Deutschland und koloniales Imperium* (Wiesbaden: Steiner, 1982).

Baer, Elizabeth R., *The Genocidal Gaze: From German Southwest Africa to the Third Reich* (Detroit: Wayne State University Press, 2017).

Baer, Martin, and Schröter, Olaf, *Eine Kopfjagd: Deutsche in Ostafrika; Spuren kolonialer Herrschaft* (Berlin: Ch. Links, 2001).

Bald, Detlev, *Deutsch-Ostafrika, 1900–1914: Eine Studie über Verwaltung, Interessengruppen und wirtschaftliche Erschließung* (Munich: Weltforum, 1970).

BIBLIOGRAPHY

Bald, Detlev, Heller, Peter, and Hundsdörfer, Volkhard, *Die Liebe zum Imperium: Ein Lesebuch zum Film; Deutschlands dunkle Vergangenheit in Afrika* (Bremen: Überseemuseum, 1978).

Baldwin, James, *I Am Not Your Negro* (London: Vintage, 2017).

Baranowski, Shelley, *Nazi Empire, German Colonialism and Imperialism from Bismarck to Hitler* (Cambridge: Cambridge University Press, 2011).

Bauche, Manuela, *Medizin und Herrschaft: Malariabekämpfung in Kamerun, Ostafrika und Ostfriesland (1890–1919)* (Frankfurt/Main and New York: Campus, 2017).

Bauman, Zygmunt, *Modernity and Ambivalence* (Cambridge: Polity Press, 1991).

———, *Modernity and the Holocaust* (Cambridge: Polity Press, 1989).

———, *Wasted Lives: Modernity and Its Outcasts* (Cambridge: Polity Press, 2003).

Baumgart, Winfried, *Deutschland im Zeitalter des Imperialismus (1890–1914): Grundkräfte, Thesen und Strukturen* (Frankfurt/Main, Berlin and Vienna: Ullstein, 1972)

BDG Network (ed.), *The Black Diaspora and Germany / Deutschland und die Schwarze Diaspora* (Münster: Edition Assemblage, 2018).

Bechhaus-Gerst, Marianne, *Treu bis in den Tod: Von Deutsch-Ostafrika nach Sachsenhausen; Eine Lebensgeschichte* (Berlin: Ch. Links, 2007).

Bechhaus-Gerst, Marianne, and Klein-Arendt, Reinhard (eds.), *Die (koloniale) Begegnung: AfrikanerInnen in Deutschland 1880–1945, Deutsche in Afrika 1880–1918* (Frankfurt/Main: Peter Lang, 2003).

Bechhaus-Gerst, Marianne, Michels, Stefanie, and Fechner, Fabian (eds.), *Nordrhein-Westfalen und der Imperialismus* (Berlin: Metropol, 2022).

Bechhaus-Gerst, Marianne, and Zeller, Joachim (eds.), *Deutschland postkolonial? Die Gegenwart der imperialen Vergangenheit* (Berlin: Metropol, 2018).

Becker, Felicitas, and Beez, Jigal (eds.), *Der Maji-Maji-Krieg in Deutsch-Ostafrika, 1905–1907* (Berlin: Ch. Links, 2005).

Beez, Jigal, *Geschosse zu Wassertropfen: Sozio-religiöse Aspekte des Maji-Maji-Krieges in Deutsch-Ostafrika (1905–1907)* (Cologne: Köppe, 2003).

Bendikat, Elfi, *Organisierte Kolonialbewegung in der Bismarck-Ära* (Heidelberg and Brazzaville: Kivouvou, 1984).

Benninghoff-Lühl, Sibylle, *Deutsche Kolonialromane, 1884–1914* (Bremen: Verlag des Übersee-Museums, 1983).

Bens, Jonas, and Zenker, Olaf, *Gerechtigkeitsgefühle: Zur affektiven und emotionalen Legitimität von Normen* (Bielefeld: Transcript, 2017).

Bentley, Tom, *Empires of Remorse: Narrative, Postcolonialism, and Apologies for Colonial Atrocity* (Oxford and New York: Routledge, 2016).

Berghoff, Hartmut, Biess, Frank, and Strasser, Ulrike (eds.), *Explorations and Entanglements: Germans in Pacific Worlds from the Early Modern Period to World War I* (New York and Oxford: Berghahn, 2019).

Bergold-Caldwell, Denise, Digoh, Laura, Haruna-Oelker, Hadija, Nkwendja-Ngnoubamdjum, Christelle, Ridha, Camilla, and Wiedenroth-Coulibaly, Eleonore (eds.), *Spiegelblicke: Perspektiven schwarzer Bewegung in Deutschland* (Berlin: Orlanda, 2016).

Berman, Nina, Mühlhahn, Klaus, and Nganang, Patrice (eds.), *German Colonialism*

BIBLIOGRAPHY

Revisited: African, Asian and Oceanic Experiences (Ann Arbor, MI: University of Michigan Press, 2014).

Berman, Russell A., *Enlightenment or Empire: Colonial Discourse in German Culture* (Lincoln: University of Nebraska Press, 1998).

Bitterli, Urs, *Die "Wilden" und die "Zivilisierten": Grundzüge einer Geistes- und Kulturgeschichte der europäisch-überseeischen Begegnung* (1976; 2nd edn, Munich: C.H. Beck, 1991).

Blackler, Adam A., *An Imperial Homeland: Forging German Identity in Southwest Africa* (Philadelphia: Pennsylvania State University Press, 2022).

Bley, Helmut, *Kolonialschuld und Sozialstruktur in Deutsch-Südwestafrika, 1894–1914* (Hamburg: Leibniz, 1968). Published in English as *South-West Africa under German Rule, 1894–1914* (London: Heinemann, 1971).

Bley, Helmut, and Tetzlaff, Rainer (eds.), *Afrika und Bonn: Versäumnisse und Zwänge deutscher Afrika-Politik* (Reinbek: Rowohlt, 1978).

Bloxham, Donald, and Moses, Dirk A. (eds.), *Genocide: Key Themes* (Oxford: Oxford University Press, 2022).

Böckmann, Matthias, Gockel, Matthias, Kössler, Reinhart, and Melber, Henning (eds.), *Jenseits von Mbembe: Geschichte, Erinnerung, Solidarität* (Berlin: Metropol, 2022).

Bodley, John H., *Victims of Progress* (Menlo Park, CA: Cummings Publishing, 1975).

Böhlke-Itzen, Janntje, *Kolonialschuld und Entschädigung: Der deutsche Völkermord an den Herero, 1904–1907* (Frankfurt/Main: Brandes & Apsel, 2004).

Bohne, Andreas, Hüttner, Bernd, and Schade, Anja (eds.), *Apartheid No! Facetten von Solidarität in der DDR und BRD* (Berlin: Rosa-Luxemburg-Stiftung, 2019).

Bommarius, Christian, *Der gute Deutsche: Die Ermordung Manga Bells in Kamerun, 1914* (Berlin: Berenber, 2015).

Boulleys, Vera Ebot, *Deutsch in Kamerun* (Bamberg: Collibri, 1998).

Bowersox, Jeff, *Raising Germans in the Age of Empire: Youth and Colonial Culture, 1871–1914* (Oxford: Oxford University Press, 2013).

Boyd, William, *Zum Nachtisch Krieg* (Reinbek: Rowohlt, 1986). Republished as *Der Eiskrem-Krieg* (Berlin: Bloomsbury, 2021). Originally published in English as *An Ice-Cream War* (London: Hamish Hamilton, 1982).

Brehl, Medardus, *Vernichtung der Herero: Diskurse der Gewalt in der deutschen Kolonialliteratur* (Munich: Fink, 2007).

Brink, André, *The Other Side of Silence* (London: Secker & Warburg, 2002). Published in German as *Die andere Seite der Stille* (Berlin: Osburg, 2008).

Bruchhaus, Eva-Maria, and Harding, Leonhard (eds.), *Hundert Jahre Einmischung in Afrika, 1884–1984* (Hamburg: Buske, 1986).

Bückendorf, Jutta, *"Schwarz-weiß-rot über Ostafrika!" Deutsche Kolonialpläne und afrikanische Realität* (Münster: LIT, 1997).

Bühler, Andreas Heinrich, *Der Namaaufstand gegen die deutsche Kolonialherrschaft in Namibia von 1904–1913* (Frankfurt/Main: IKO, 2003).

Bührer, Tanja, *Die Kaiserliche Schutztruppe für Deutsch-Ostafrika: Koloniale Sicherheitspolitik und transkulturelle Kriegführung, 1885 bis 1918* (Munich: Oldenbourg, 2011).

BIBLIOGRAPHY

Bulawayo, NoViolet, *We Need New Names* (London: Vintage, 2014).

Bürger, Christiane, *Deutsche Kolonialgeschichte(n): Der Genozid in Namibia und die Geschichtsschreibung der DDR und BRD* (Bielefeld: Transcript, 2017).

Burton, Eric, Dietrich, Anne, Harisch, Immanuel, and Schenck, Marcia C. (eds.), *Navigating Socialist Encounters: Moorings and (Dis)entanglements between Africa and East Germany during the Cold War* (Berlin: De Gruyter Oldenbourg, 2021).

Buruma, Ian, *Year Zero: A History of 1945* (London: Atlantic Books, 2013).

Büttner, Carl Gotthilf, *Die Anfänge der deutschen Kolonialpolitk in Ostafrika: Eine kritische Untersuchung anhand unveröffentlichter Quellen* (Berlin: Akademie-Verlag, 1959).

Campt, Tina, *Other Germans: Black Germans and the Politics of Race, Gender, and Memory in the Third Reich* (Ann Arbor, MI: University of Michigan Press, 2004).

Coetzee, J.M., *Waiting for the Barbarians* (Harmondsworth: Penguin, 1982).

Cohen, Paul A., *History in Three Keys: The Boxers as Event, Experience, and Myth* (New York: Columbia University Press, 1997).

Conrad, Sebastian, *Deutsche Kolonialgeschichte* (Munich: Beck, 2008).

———, *German Colonialism: A Short History* (Cambridge: Cambridge University Press, 2011).

Court, Anthony, *Hannah Arendt's Response to the Crisis of Her Time* (Amsterdam: Rozenberg 2008).

Dabag, Mihran, Gründer, Horst, and Ketelsen, Uwe-K. (eds.), *Kolonialismus: Kolonialdiskurs und Genozid* (Paderborn: Fink, 2004).

Denhardt, Imre Josef, *Deutsche Kolonialgesellschaft, 1888–1918: Ein Beitrag zur Organisationsgeschichte der deutschen Kolonialbewegung* (Wiesbaden: self-published, 2022).

Denzer, Jörg, *Die Konquista der Augsburger Welser-Gesellschaft in Südamerika (1528–1556): Historische Rekonstruktion, Historiografie und lokale Erinnerungskultur in Kolumbien und Venezuela* (Munich: Beck, 2003).

Deutsch, Jan-Georg, *Emancipation without Abolition in German East Africa, c.1884–1914* (Athens, OH: Ohio University Press, 2006).

Diallo, Oumar, and Zeller, Joachim, *Berlin: Eine postkoloniale Metropole; Ein historisch-kritischer Stadtrundgang im Bezirk Mitte*, edited by Verein Farafina e.V. (Berlin: Metropol, 2021; 2nd edn, 2024). Also published in English as *Berlin: A Postcolonial Metropolis; A Critical History Walking Tour of Central Berlin* (Berlin: Metropol, 2024).

——— (eds.), *Black Berlin: Die deutsche Metropole und ihre afrikanische Diaspora in Geschichte und Gegenwart* (Berlin: Metropol, 2013).

Donat, Helmut (ed.), *Hans Paasche: Ein Leben für die Zukunft* (Bremen: Donat, 2022).

Drechsler, Horst, *Südwestafrika unter deutscher Kolonialherrschaft: Der Kampf der Herero und Nama gegen den deutschen Imperialismus (1884–1915)* (Berlin: Akademie Verlag, 1966; 2nd edn, 1984). Published in English as *"Let Us Die Fighting": The Struggle of the Herero and Nama against German Imperialism (1884–1915)* (London: Zed, 1980).

Dreesbach, Anne, *Gezähmte Wilde: Die Zurschaustellung "exoticher" Menschen in Deutschland, 1870–1940* (Frankfurt/Main and New York: Campus, 2005).

Droessler, Holger, *Coconut Colonialism: Workers and the Globalization of Samoa* (Cambridge, MA: Harvard University Press, 2022).

BIBLIOGRAPHY

Duffield, Mark, and Hewitt, Vernon (eds.), *Empire, Development and Colonialism: The Past in the Present* (Woodbridge, UK: James Currey, 2009).

Ebert, Verena, *Koloniale Straßennamen: Benennungspraktiken im Kontext kolonialer Raumaneignung in der deutschen Metropole von 1884 bis 1945* (Berlin and Boston: De Gruyter, 2021).

Ebner, Timm, *Nationalsozialistische Kolonialliteratur: Koloniale und antisemitische Verräterfiguren "hinter den Kulissen des Welttheaters"* (Munich: Fink, 2016).

Eckart, Wolfgang U., *Medizin und Kolonialimperialismus: Deutschland, 1884–1945* (Paderborn and Munich: Ferdinand Schöningh, 1997).

Eckert, Andreas, *Die Duala und die Kolonialmächte: Eine Untersuchung zu Widerstand, Protest und Protonationalismus in Kamerun vor dem Zweiten Weltkrieg* (Münster and Hamburg: LIT, 1991).

———, *Kolonialismus* (Frankfurt/Main: Fischer, 2006).

Eckl, Andreas, *"S'ist ein übles Land hier": Zur Historiographie eines umstrittenen Kolonialkrieges; Tagebuchaufzeichnungen aus dem Herero-Krieg in Deutsch Südwestafrika 1904 von Georg Hillebrecht und Franz Ritter von Epp* (Cologne: Rüdiger Köppe, 2005).

Elden, Stuart, and Mendieta, Eduardo (eds.), *Reading Kant's Geography* (Albany, NY: State University of New York Press, 2011).

Elias, Norbert, *The Civilizing Process: Sociogenetic and Psychogenetic Investigations* (1994; rev. edn, Oxford: Blackwell, 2000).

———, *The Court Society* (Oxford: Blackwell, 1983).

El-Tayeb, Fatima, *Schwarze Deutsche: Der Diskurs um "Rasse" und nationale Identität, 1890–1933* (Frankfurt/Main: Campus, 2001).

———, *Undeutsch: Die Konstruktion des Anderen in der postmigrantischen Gesellschaft* (Bielefeld: Transcript, 2016).

Engel, Ulf, and Schleicher, Hans-Georg, *Die beiden deutschen Staaten in Afrika: Zwischen Konkurrenz und Koexistenz, 1949–1990* (Hamburg: Institut für Afrika-Kunde, 1998).

Entwicklungspolitische Korrespondenz (ed.), *Deutscher Kolonialismus: Materialien zur Hundertjahrfeier 1984* (Hamburg: Gesellschaft für entwicklungspolitische Bildungsarbeit, 1983).

Epstein, Klaus, *Matthias Erzberger and the Dilemma of German Democracy* (Princeton, NJ: Princeton University Press, 1959).

Erbar, Ralph, *Ein "Platz an der Sonne"? Die Verwaltungs- und Wirtschaftsgeschichte der deutschen Kolonie Togo, 1884–1914* (Stuttgart: Steiner, 1991).

Erichsen, Casper, *"The Angel of Death Has Descended Violently among Them": Concentration Camps and Prisoners-of-War in Namibia, 1904–08* (Leiden: African Studies Centre, 2005).

Esherick, Joseph W., *The Origins of the Boxer Uprising* (Berkeley: University of California Press, 1987).

Esse, Jan, *Malaria in Südwest-Afrika: Deutsche Kolonialmedizin, 1884–1915* (Berlin: Peter Lang, 2022).

Essner, Cornelia, *Deutsche Afrikareisende im 19. Jahrhundert: Zur Sozialgeschichte des Reisens* (Stuttgart: Steiner, 1985).

BIBLIOGRAPHY

Faber-Jonker, Leonor, *More Than Just an Object: A Material Analysis of the Return and Retention of Namibian Skulls from Germany* (Leiden: African Studies Centre, 2018).

Fechner, Fabian, and Schneider, Barbara (eds.), *Fernes Hagen: Kolonialismus und wir* (Hagen: Fernuniversität Hagen, 2021).

Fehrenbach, Heide, *Race after Hitler: Black Occupation Children in Postwar Germany and America* (Princeton, NJ: Princeton University Press, 2005).

Fiedler, Matthias, *Zwischen Abenteuer, Wissenschaft und Kolonialismus: Der deutsche Afrikadiskurs im 18. und 19. Jahrhundert* (Cologne: Böhlau, 2005).

Fischer, Eugen, *Die Rehobother Bastards und das Bastardisierungsproblem beim Menschen: Anthropologische und ethnographische Studien am Rehobother Bastardvolk in Deutsch-Südwest-Afrika* (Jena: G. Fischer, 1913).

Fitzpatrick, Matthew P., *The Kaiser and the Colonies: Monarchy in the Age of Empire* (Oxford: Oxford University Press, 2022).

———, *Purging the Empire: Mass Expulsions in Germany, 1871–1914* (Oxford: Oxford University Press, 2015).

Florvil, Tiffany N., *Mobilizing Black Germany: Afro-German Women and the Making of a Transnational Movement* (Champaign, IL: University of Illinois Press, 2020).

Förster, Larissa, *Postkoloniale Erinnerungslandschaften: Wie Deutsche und Herero in Namibia des Kriegs von 1904 gedenken* (Frankfurt/Main: Campus, 2010).

Förster, Larissa, Henrichsen, Dag, and Bollig, Michael (eds.), *Namibia—Deutschland: Eine geteilte Geschichte; Widerstand—Gewalt—Erinnerung* (Cologne: Rautenstrauch-Joest Museum für Völkerkunde; Wolfratshausen: Edition Minerva, 2004).

Förster, Stig, Mommsen, Wolfgang, and Robinson, Ronald (eds.), *Bismarck, Europe, and Africa: The Berlin Africa Conference 1884–1885 and the Onset of Partition* (London: Oxford University Press, for the German Historical Institute, 1988).

Foucault, Michel, *The Birth of the Clinic: An Archaeology of Medical Perception* (London and New York: Routledge, 1973; French original, 1963).

———, *Discipline and Punish: The Birth of the Prison* (New York: Pantheon, 1977; French original, 1975).

———, *Madness and Civilization: A History of Insanity in the Age of Reason* (New York: Vintage, 1965; French original, 1961).

———, *The Order of Things: An Archaeology of the Human Sciences* (New York: Pantheon, 1970; French original, 1966).

Fowler, Ian, and Zeitlyn, David (eds.), *African Crossroads: Intersections between History and Anthropology in Cameroon* (Providence, RI, and Oxford: Berghahn, 1996).

Francois, Etienne, and Schulze, Hagen (eds.), *Deutsche Erinnerungsorte*, 3 vols. (Munich: Beck, 2001).

Fredrickson, George M., *Racism: A Short History* (Princeton, NJ: Princeton University Press, 2002).

Fremgen, Gisela, *... Und wenn du dazu noch schwarz bist: Berichte schwarzer Frauen in der Bundesrepublik* (Bremen: CON, 1984).

Frenssen, Gustav, *Peter Moors Fahrt nach Südwest: Ein Feldzugsbericht* (Berlin: Grote, 1906).

Friedrichsmeyer, Sara, Lennox, Sara and Zantop, Susanne (eds.), *The Imperialist Imagination: German Colonialism and Its Legacy* (Ann Arbor, MI: University of Michigan Press, 1998).

BIBLIOGRAPHY

Fuhrmann, Wolfgang, *Imperial Projections: Screening the German Colonies* (New York and Oxford: Berghahn, 2015).

Fulbrook, Mary, *Dissonant Lives: Generations and Violence through the German Dictatorships* (Oxford: Oxford University Press, 2011).

Gaudi, Robert, *African Kaiser: General Paul von Lettow-Vorbeck and the Great War in Africa* (London: Hurst, 2017).

Gerbing, Stefan, *Afrodeutscher Aktivismus: Interventionen von Kolonisierten am Wendepunkt der Dekolonisierung Deutschlands 1919* (Frankfurt/Main: Peter Lang, 2010).

Gerunde, Harald, *Eine von uns: Als Schwarze in Deutschland geboren* (Wuppertal: Hammer, 2000).

Gewald, Jan-Bart, *Herero Heroes: A Socio-political History of the Herero of Namibia, 1890–1923* (Oxford: James Currey; Cape Town: David Philip; Athens, OH: Ohio University Press, 1999).

Giblin, James, and Monson, Jamie (eds.), *Maji Maji: Lifting the Fog of War* (Leiden: Brill, 2010).

Gilley, Bruce, *Verteidigung des deutschen Kolonialismus* (Lüdinghausen: Manuscriptum Verlagsbuchhandlung, 2021). Published in a revised edition in English as *In Defense of German Colonialism: And How Its Critics Empowered Nazis, Communists, and the Enemies of the West* (Washington, DC: Regnery Gateway, 2022).

Gissibl, Bernhard, *The Nature of German Imperialism: Conservation and the Politics of Wildlife in Colonial East Africa* (New York: Berghahn, 2016).

Glassman, Jonathon, *Feasts and Riot: Revelry, Rebellion, and Popular Consciousness on the Swahili Coast, 1856–1888* (London: James Currey; Portsmouth, NH: Heinemann, 1995).

Gordon, Robert, and Douglas, Stuart Sholto, *The Bushman Myth: The Making of a Namibian Underclass* (Boulder, CO: Westview Press, 2000).

Gothsch, Manfred, *Die deutsche Völkerkunde und ihr Verhältnis zum Kolonialismus: Ein Beitrag zur kolonialideologischen und kolonialpraktischen Bedeutung der deutschen Völkerkunde in der Zeit von 1870 bis 1975* (Baden-Baden: Nomos, 1983).

Göttsche, Dirk, *Remembering Africa: The Rediscovery of Colonialism in Contemporary German Literature* (Rochester, NY: Camden House; Woodbridge, UK: Boydell & Brewer, 2013).

Gräbel, Carsten, *Die Erforschung der Kolonien: Expeditionen und koloniale Wissenskultur deutscher Geographen, 1884–1919* (Bielefeld: Transcript, 2015).

Graudenz, Karlheinz, and Schindler, Hanns Michael, *Die deutschen Kolonien: Ihre Geschichte in Wort, Bild und Karte* (Munich: Südwest Verlag, 1981; several further editions since then).

Grewe, Bernd-Stefan, Himmelsbach, Markus, Theisen, Johannes, and Wegmann, Heiko, *Freiburg und der Kolonialismus: Vom Kaiserreich zum Nationalsozialismus* (Freiburg im Breisgau: Stadtarchiv, 2018).

Grill, Bartholomäus, *Wir Herrenmenschen: Unser rassistisches Erbe; Eine Reise in die deutsche Kolonialgeschichte* (Munich: Siedler, 2019).

Grimm, Hans, *Volk ohne Raum* (Munich: Albert Langen, 1926).

Grosse, Pascal, *Kolonialismus, Eugenik und bürgerliche Gesellschaft in Deutschland, 1850–1918* (Frankfurt/Main and New York: Campus, 2000).

BIBLIOGRAPHY

Gründer, Horst, *Christliche Mission und deutscher Imperialismus: Eine politische Geschichte ihrer Beziehungen während der deutschen Kolonialzeit (1884–1914) unter besonderer Berücksichtigung Afrikas und Chinas* (Paderborn: Ferdinand Schöningh, 1982).

——— (ed.), *... da und dort ein junges Deutschland gründen: Rassismus, Kolonien und kolonialer Gedanke vom 16. bis zum 20. Jahrhundert* (Munich: Deutscher Taschenbuch-Verlag, 1999).

———, *Geschichte der deutschen Kolonien* (Paderborn: Schöningh, 1985).

Gründer, Horst, and Thierry, Hermann Joseph (eds.), *Die Deutschen und ihre Kolonien: Ein Überblick* (Berlin: be.bra, 2017).

Gurnah, Abdulrazak, *Afterlives* (London: Bloomsbury, 2020).

———, *Gravel Heart* (London: Bloomsbury, 2017).

Gwassa, Gilbert Clement Kamana, *The Outbreak and Development of the Maji Maji War, 1905–1907* (Cologne: Köppe, 2005; posthumously published PhD of 1973, edited by Wolfgang Apelt with supplementary material by Wilhelm J.G. Möhlig).

Habermas, Rebekka, *Skandal in Togo: Ein Kapitel deutscher Kolonialherrschaft* (Frankfurt/Main: Fischer, 2016).

Hackmack, Judith, and Keller, Arite (eds.), *Colonial Repercussions: Namibia; 115 Years after the Genocide of the Ovaherero and Nama* (Berlin: European Center for Constitutional and Human Rights, 2019).

Hagedorn, Henning, *Bremen und die atlantische Sklaverei: Waren, Wissen und Personen, 1780–1860* (Baden-Baden: Nomos, 2023).

Hamann, Ulrike, *Prekäre koloniale Ordnung: Rassistische Konjunkturen im Widerspruch; Deutsches Kolonialregime, 1884–1914* (Bielefeld: Transcript, 2015).

Hanke, Christine, *Zwischen Auflösung und Fixierung: Zur Konstitution von "Rasse" und "Geschlecht" in der physischen Anthropologie um 1900* (Bielefeld: Transcript, 2007).

Hanke, Lewis, *Aristotle and the American Indians: A Study in Race Prejudice in the Modern World* (London: Hollis & Carter, 1959).

Harms, Volker (ed.), *Andenken an den Kolonialismus: Eine Ausstellung des Völkerkundlichen Instituts der Universität Tübingen* (Tübingen: Attempto, 1984).

Harvey, David, *Cosmopolitanism and the Geographies of Freedom* (New York: Columbia University Press, 2009).

Hausen, Karin, *Deutsche Kolonialherrschaft in Afrika: Wirtschaftsinteressen und Kolonialverwaltung in Kamerun vor 1914* (Zürich and Freiburg im Breisgau: Atlantis, 1970).

Häussler, Matthias, *The Herero Genocide: War, Emotion, and Extreme Violence in Colonial Namibia* (Oxford and New York: Berghahn Books, 2021). Originally published in German as *Der Genozid an den Herero: Krieg, Emotion und extreme Gewalt in "Deutsch-Südwestafrika"* (Weilerswist: Velbrück, 2018).

Häussler, Matthias, and Eckl, Andreas (eds.), *Lothar von Trotha in Deutsch-Südwestafrika, 1904–1905*, vol. I: *Das Tagebuch*; vol. II: *Das Fotoalbum* (Berlin: De Gruyter Oldenbourg, 2024).

Hayes, Patricia, Silvester, Jeremy, Wallace, Marion, and Hartmann, Wolfram (eds.), *Namibia under South African Rule: Mobility and Containment, 1915–46* (Oxford: James Currey; Windhoek: Out of Africa; Athens, OH: Ohio University Press, 1998).

BIBLIOGRAPHY

Helbig, Helga, and Helbig, Ludwig, *Mythos Deutsch-Südwest: Namibia und die Deutschen* (Weinheim and Basel: Beltz, 1983).

Hempenstall, Peter J., *Pacific Islanders under German Rule: A Study in the Meaning of Colonial Resistance* (Canberra: Australian National University Press, 1978; republished 2016).

Hempenstall, Peter J., and Mochida, Paula Tanaka, *The Lost Man: Wilhelm Solf in German History* (Wiesbaden: Harrassowitz, 2005).

Hess, Klaus A., and Becker, Klaus J. (eds.), *Vom Schutzgebiet bis Namibia 2000* (Göttingen and Windhoek: Klaus Hess Verlag, 2002).

Heyden, Ulrich van der, *Rote Adler an Afrikas Küste: Die brandenburgisch-preußische Kolonie Großfriedrichsburg in Westafrika* (1993; Berlin: Selignow-Verlag, 2001).

─────── (ed.), *Unbekannte Biographien: Afrikaner im deutschsprachigen Europa vom 18. Jahrhundert bis zum Ende des Zweiten Weltkrieges* (Berlin: Kai Homilius, 2008).

Heyden, Ulrich van der, and Zeller, Joachim (eds.), *Kolonialismus hierzulande: Eine Spurensuche in Deutschland* (Erfurt: Sutton, 2007).

─────── (eds.), *Kolonialmetropole Berlin: Eine Spurensuche* (Berlin: Berlin Edition, 2002).

─────── (eds.), *Macht und Anteil an der Weltherrschaft: Berlin und der deutsche Kolonialismus* (Münster: Unrast, 2005).

Heyl, Bernd, *Namibische Gedenk- und Erinnerungsorte: Postkolonialer Reisebegleiter in die deutsche Kolonialgeschichte* (Frankfurt/Main: Brandes & Apsel, 2021).

Hiery, Hermann Joseph, *Das Deutsche Reich in der Südsee (1900–1921): Eine Annäherung an die Erfahrungen verschiedener Kulturen* (Göttingen and Zürich: Vandenhoeck & Ruprecht, 1995).

─────── (ed.), *Die deutsche Südsee, 1884–1914: Ein Handbuch* (Paderborn: Schöningh, 2001).

Hiery, Hermann Joseph, and Hinz, Hans-Martin (eds.), *Alltagsleben und Kulturaustausch: Deutsche und Chinesen in Tsingtau, 1897–1914* (Wolfratshausen: Minerva, 1999).

Hildebrand, Klaus, *Vom Reich zum Weltreich: Hitler, NSDAP und koloniale Frage, 1919–1945* (Munich: Fink, 1969).

Hinz, Manfred O., Patemann, Helgard, and Meier, Arnim (eds.), *Weiß auf schwarz: 100 Jahre Einmischung in Afrika; Deutscher Kolonialismus und afrikanischer Widerstand* (Berlin: Elefanten Press, 1984; 2nd rev. edn, 1986).

Hobuss, Steffi, and Lölke, Ulrich (eds.), *Erinnern verhandeln: Kolonialismus im kollektiven Gedächtnis Afrikas und Europas* (Münster: Westfälisches Dampfboot, 2006; 2nd enlarged edn, 2007).

Hodge, Joseph M., Hödl, Gerald, and Kopf, Martina (eds.), *Developing Africa: Concepts and Practices in Twentieth-Century Colonialism* (Manchester: Manchester University Press, 2014).

Hoffmann, Florian, *Okkupation und Militärverwaltung in Kamerun: Etablierung und Institutionalisierung des kolonialen Gewaltmonopols, 1891–1914*, part 1 (Göttingen: Cuvillier, 2007).

Hofmann, Corinne, *Afrika meine Passion* (Munich: A1, 2011).

─────── , *Die weiße Massai* (Munich: A1, 1998; Munich: Knaur, 2000).

BIBLIOGRAPHY

———, *Wiedersehen in Barsaloi* (Munich: A1, 2005; Munich: Knaur, 2007).

———, *Zurück aus Afrika* (Munich: A1 2003; Munich: Knaur, 2004).

Honeck, Mischa, Klimke, Martin, and Kuhlmann-Smirnov, Anne (eds.), *Germany and the Black Diaspora: Points of Contact, 1250–1914* (New York: Berghahn, 2013).

Honold, Alexander, and Simons, Alexander (eds.), *Kolonialismus als Kultur: Literatur, Medien, Wissenschaft in der deutschen Gründerzeit des Fremden* (Tübingen and Basel: A. Francke, 2002).

Hope, Christopher, *Developmentalism, Dependency, and the State: Industrial Development and Economic Change in Namibia since 1900* (Basel: Basler Afrika Bibliographien, 2020).

Höpp, Gerhard (ed.), *Fremde Erfahrungen: Asiaten und Afrikaner in Deutschland, Österreich und in der Schweiz bis 1945* (Berlin: Das Arabische Buch, 1996).

Horkheimer, Max and Adorno, Theodor, *Dialectic of Enlightenment: Philosophical Fragments* (New York: Herder & Herder, 1972; rev. translation, Stanford: Stanford University Press, 2002). First published in German as *Dialektik der Aufklärung* (Amsterdam: Querido, 1947).

Howard-Hassmann, Rhoda E., with Lombardo, Anthony P., *Reparations to Africa* (Philadelphia: University of Pennsylvania Press, 2008).

Huang, Fu-teh, *Quingdao: Chinesen unter deutscher Herrschaft, 1897–1914* (Bochum: Project Verlag, 1999).

Hücking, Renate and Launer, Ekkehard, *Aus Menschen Neger machen: Wie sich das Handelshaus Woermann an Afrika entwickelt hat* (Hamburg: Galgenberg, 1986).

Hügel-Marshall, Ika, *Daheim unterwegs: Ein deutsches Leben* (Berlin: Orlanda, 1998; rev. edn, Münster: Unrast, 2020). Also published in English as *Invisible Woman: Growing Up Black in Germany* (New York: Continuum, 2001; new edn, Frankfurt/Main: Peter Lang, 2008).

Hügel-Marshall, Ika, Prasad, Nivedita, and Schultz, Dagmar (eds.), *May Ayim: Radikale Dichterin, sanfte Rebellin* (Münster: Unrast, 2021).

Hull, Isabel V., *Absolute Destruction: Military Culture and the Practices of War in Imperial Germany* (Ithaca, NY: Cornell University Press, 2005).

Hyrkkänen, Markku, *Sozialistische Kolonialpolitik: Eduard Bernsteins Stellung zur Kolonialpolitik und zum Imperialismus, 1882–1914; Ein Beitrag zur Geschichte des Revisionismus* (Helsinki: Societas Historica Finlandiae, 1986).

Iliffe, John, *A Modern History of Tanganyika* (Cambridge: Cambridge University Press, 1979).

———, *Tanganyika under German Rule, 1905–1912* (Cambridge: Cambridge University Press, 2009).

Israel, Jonathan Irvine, *Democratic Enlightenment: Philosophy, Revolution and Human Rights 1750–1790* (Oxford: Oxford University Press, 2011).

———, *Enlightenment Contested: Philosophy, Modernity, and the Emancipation of Man 1670–1752* (Oxford: Oxford University Press, 2006).

———, *Radical Enlightenment: Philosophy and the Making of Modernity* (Oxford: Oxford University Press, 2001).

Jacob, Ernst Gerhard, *Anspruch und Wille: Gesammelte Reden und Aufsätze aus dem kolonialen Kampfe* (Leipzig: Dieterich, 1937).

BIBLIOGRAPHY

Joeden-Forgey, Elisa von (ed.), *Mpundu Akwa: The Case of the Prince from Cameroon; The Newly Discovered Speech for the Defense by Dr. M. Levi* (Münster: LIT, 2002).

Jokinen, Hannimari, Manase, Flower, and Zeller, Joachim (eds.), *Stand und Fall: Das Wissmann-Denkmal zwischen kolonialer Weihestätte und postkolonialer Dekonstruktion* (Berlin: Metropol, 2022).

Kalb, Martin, *Environing Empire: Nature, Infrastructure and the Making of German Southwest Africa* (New York: Berghahn, 2022).

Kamta, Florentin Saha, *"Poesie des Überlebens": Vom Umgang mit der Krise der Identität in der afrodeutschen Literatur* (Würzburg: Königshausen & Neumann, 2015).

Katjivena, Uazuvara Ewald Kapombo, *Mama Penee: Transcending the Genocide* (Windhoek: UNAM Press, 2020).

Kelly, Natasha A. (ed.), *Sisters and Souls: Inspirationen durch May Ayim* (Berlin: Orlanda, 2015).

——— (ed.), *Sisters and Souls: Inspirationen durch May Ayim, 2* (Berlin: Orlanda, 2021).

Kinloch, Graham C., and Mohan, Raj P. (eds.), *Genocide: Approaches, Case Studies, and Responses* (New York: Algora Publishing, 2005).

Klein, Thoralf, and Schumacher, Frank (eds.), *Kolonialkriege: Militärische Gewalt im Zeichen des Imperialismus* (Hamburg: Hamburger Edition, 2006).

Knauss, Stefan, Wolfradt, Louis, Hofmann, Tim, and Eberhard, Jens (eds.), *Auf den Spuren von Anton Wilhelm Amo: Philosophie und der Ruf nach Interkulturalität* (Bielefeld: Transcript, 2021).

Knigge, Volkhard, and Frei, Norbert, with Schweitzer, Anett (eds.), *Verbrechen erinnern: Die Auseinandersetzung mit Holocaust und Völkermord* (Munich: Beck, 2002; Bundeszentrale für politische Bildung, 2005).

Kohl, Karl-Heinz, Kramer, Fritz, Möller, Johann Michael, Sievernich, Gereon, and Völger, Gisela, *Das Humboldt Forum und die Ethnologie* (Frankfurt/Main: Kula Verlag, 2019).

Koponen, Juhani, *Development for Exploitation: German Colonial Policies in Mainland Tanzania, 1884–1914* (Helsinki and Hamburg: LIT, 1995).

Koselleck, Reinhart, *Futures Past: On the Semantics of Historical Time* (Cambridge, MA: MIT Press, 1990; German original, 1985).

Kössler, Reinhart, *Namibia and Germany: Negotiating the Past* (Windhoek: UNAM Press; Münster: Westfälisches Dampfboot, 2015).

Kössler, Reinhart, and Melber, Henning, *Völkermord—und was dann? Die Politik deutsch-namibischer Vergangenheitsbearbeitung* (Frankfurt/Main: Brandes & Apsel, 2017).

Kreienbaum, Jonas, *A Sad Fiasco: Colonial Concentration Camps in Southern Africa, 1900–1908* (New York and Oxford: Berghahn Books, 2019). Published originally in German as *"Ein trauriges Fiasko": Koloniale Konzentrationslager im südliche Afrika, 1900–1908* (Hamburg: Hamburger Edition, 2015).

Krobb, Florian, and Martin, Elaine (eds.), *Weimar Colonialism: Discourses and Legacies of Post-imperialism in Germany after 1918* (Bielefeld: Aisthesis, 2014).

Kron, Stefanie, *Fürchte Dich nicht, Bleichgesicht! Perspektivenwechsel zur Literatur afrodeutscher Frauen* (Münster: Unrast, 1996).

BIBLIOGRAPHY

Kröner, Hans-Peter, *Von der Rassenhygiene zur Humangenetik: Das Kaiser-Wilhelm-Institut für Anthropologie, menschliche Erblehre und Eugenik nach dem Kriege* (Stuttgart: Gustav Fischer, 1998).

Krug, Alexander, *"Der Hauptzweck ist die Tötung von Kanaken": Die deutschen Strafexpeditionen in den Kolonien der Südsee, 1872–1914* (Tönning, Lübeck and Marburg: Der Andere Verlag, 2005).

Krüger, Gesine, *Kriegsbewältigung und Geschichtsbewußtsein: Realität, Deutung und Verarbeitung des deutschen Kolonialkriegs in Namibia, 1904–1907* (Göttingen: Vandenhoek & Ruprecht, 1999).

Kruse, Cornelia, and Pieken, Gorch, *Preußisches Liebesglück: Eine deutsche Familie aus Afrika* (Munich: Propyläen, 2007).

Kubuitsile, Lauri, *The Scattering* (Cape Town: Penguin, 2016).

Kuhlmann-Smirnov, Anne, *Schwarze Europäer im Alten Reich: Handel, Migration, Hof* (Göttingen: Vandenhoeck & Ruprecht/V&Runipress, 2013).

Kum'a Ndumbe III, *Nationalsozialismus und Apartheid: Rassenideologie und Geldgeschäfte in den Nord-Süd Beziehungen, 1913–1933* (Berlin: AfricAvenir and Exchange & Dialogue, 2006).

Kundnani, Hans, *Eurowhiteness: Culture, Empire and Race in the European Project* (London: Hurst, 2023).

Kundrus, Birte, *Moderne Imperialisten: Das Kaiserreich im Spiegel seiner Kolonien* (Vienna: Böhlau, 2003).

——— (ed.), *Phantasiereiche: Zur Kulturgeschichte des deutschen Kolonialismus* (Frankfurt/Main: Campus, 2003).

Kuss, Susanne, *Deutsches Militär auf kolonialen Kriegsschauplätzen: Eskalation von Gewalt zu Beginn des 20. Jahrhunderts* (Berlin: Ch. Links, 2010). Published in English as *German Colonial Wars and the Context of Military Violence* (Cambridge, MA: Harvard University Press, 2017).

Kuss, Susanne, and Martin, Bernd (eds.), *Das Deutsche Reich und der Boxeraufstand* (Munich: Iudicum, 2002).

Laak, Dirk van, *Imperiale Infrastruktur: Deutsche Planungen für die Erschließung Afrikas, 1880–1960* (Paderborn: Schöningh, 2004).

———, *Über alles in der Welt: Deutscher Imperialismus im 19. und 20. Jahrhundert* (Munich: Beck, 2005).

Lange, Werner, *Hans Paasche: Militant Pacifist in Imperial Germany* (Victoria, BC: Trafford, 2005). Originally published in German as *Hans Paasches Forschungsreise ins innerste Deutschlands* (Bremen: Donat, 1995).

Laukötter, Anja, *Von der "Kultur" zur "Rasse"—vom Objekt zum Körper? Völkerkundemuseen und ihre Wissenschaften zu Beginn des 20. Jahrhunderts* (Bielefeld: Transcript, 2007).

Lemke Muniz de Faria, Yara-Colette, *Zwischen Fürsorge und Ausgrenzung: Afrodeutsche "Besatzungskinder" im Nachkriegsdeutschland* (Berlin: Metropol, 2002).

Lemkin, Raphael, *Axis Rule in Occupied Europe* (Washington, DC: Carnegie Endowment for International Peace, 1944).

Lennox, Sara (ed.), *Remapping Black Germany: New Perspectives on Afro-German History, Politics and Culture* (Amherst, MA: University of Massachusetts Press, 2016).

Lettow-Vorbeck, Paul von, *Heia Safari! Deutschlands Kampf in Ostafrika* (Leipzig: Koehler, 1920).

BIBLIOGRAPHY

Leutner, Mechthild, and Mühlhahn, Klaus (eds.), *Deutsch-chinesische Beziehungen im 19. Jahrhundert: Mission und Wirtschaft in interkultureller Perspektive* (Münster: LIT, 2001).

——— (eds.), *Kolonialkrieg in China: Die Niederschlagung der Boxerbewegung, 1900–1901* (Berlin: Ch. Links, 2007).

———, *"Musterkolonie Kiautschou": Die Expansion des Deutschen Reiches in China; Deutsch-chinesische Beziehungen, 1897–1914; Eine Quellensammlung* (Berlin: Akademie Verlag, 1997).

Lindner, Ulrike, Möhring, Maren, Stein, Mark, and Stroh, Silke (eds.), *Hybrid Cultures, Nervous States: Britain and Germany in a (Post)Colonial World* (Amsterdam: Rodopi, 2010).

Lindqvist, Sven, *"Exterminate All the Brutes": One Man's Odyssey into the Heart of Darkness and the Origins of European Genocide* (New York: New Press, 1996; Swedish original, 1992).

Linne, Karsten, *Deutschland jenseits des Äquators? NS-Kolonialplanungen für Afrika* (Berlin: Ch. Links, 2008).

Loewy, Ernst, *Literatur unterm Hakenkreuz: Das Dritte Reich und seine Dichtung; Eine Dokumentation* (Frankfurt/Main: Europäische Verlagsanstalt, 1966).

Loth, Heinrich, *Die christliche Mission in Südwestafrika: Zur destruktiven Rolle der Rheinischen Missionsgesellschaft beim Prozeß der Staatsbildung in Südwestafrika (1842–1893)* (Berlin: Akademie-Verlag, 1963).

——— (ed.), *Reisen nach Nigritien: Bilder afrikanischer Vergangenheit* (Leipzig: Reclam, 1986).

Lu, Catherine, *Justice and Reconciliation in World Politics* (Cambridge: Cambridge University Press, 2017).

Lüderitz, C.A. (ed.), *Die Erschließung von Deutsch-Südwestafrika durch Adolf Lüderitz: Akten, Briefe und Denkschriften* (Oldenburg: Stalling, 1945).

Lusane, Clarence, *Hitler's Black Victims: The Historical Experiences of Afro-Germans, European Blacks, Africans, and African Americans in the Nazi Era* (New York and London: Routledge, 2002).

Mallinckrodt, Rebekka von, Köstlbauer, Josef, and Lentz, Sarah (eds.), *Beyond Exceptionalism: Traces of Slavery and the Slave Trade in Early Modern Germany, 1650–1850* (Berlin and Boston: De Gruyter, 2021).

Mamozai, Martha, *Herrenmenschen: Frauen im deutschen Kolonialismus* (Reinbek: Rowohlt, 1982).

Mangold, Ijoma, *Das deutsche Krokodil: Meine Geschichte* (Reinbek: Rowohlt 2017). Published in English as *The German Crocodile: A Literary Memoir* (Sutton: DAS Edition, 2021).

Mann, Erick J., *Mykoni ya damu—"Hands of Blood": African Mercenaries and the Politics of Conflict in German East Africa, 1888–1904* (Frankfurt/Main: Peter Lang, 2002).

Martin, Peter, *Schwarze Teufel, edle Mohren: Afrikaner in Geschichte und Bewußtsein der Deutschen* (Hamburg: Junius, 1993).

Martin, Peter, and Alonzo, Christine (eds.), *Zwischen Charleston und Stechschritt: Schwarze im Nationalsozialismus* (Munich: Dölling & Galitz, 2004).

Martin, Peter, with Alonzo, Christine, *Im Netz der Moderne: Afrikaner und Deutschlands gebrochener Aufstieg zur Macht* (Hamburg: Kovac, 2012).

BIBLIOGRAPHY

Marx, Christoph, *Von Berlin nach Timbuktu: Der Afrikaforscher Heinrich Barth; Biographie* (Göttingen: Wallstein, 2021).

Massaquoi, Hans-Jürgen, *Neger, Neger Schornsteinfeger: Meine Kindheit in Deutschland* (Munich: Fretz & Wasmuth, 1999). Published in English as *Destined to Witness: Growing Up Black in Nazi Germany* (New York: Harper Perennial, 1999).

Maurer, Elke Regina, *Fremdes im Blick, am Ort des Eigenen: Eine Rezeptionsanalyse von "Die weiße Massai"* (Herbolzheim: Centaurus, 2010).

Mbombi, Annette, *Schwarze Deutsche und ihre sozialen Identitäten: Eine empirische Studie zur Lebensrealität von Afrodeutschen und deren Bedeutung für die Entwicklung einer schwarzen und einer deutschen Identität* (Göttingen: Cuvillier, 2011).

Melber, Henning (ed.), *Genozid und Gedenken: Namibisch-deutsche Geschichte und Gegenwart* (Frankfurt/Main: Brandes & Apsel, 2005).

———, *Namibia: Gesellschaftspolitische Erkundungen seit der Unabhängigkeit* (Frankfurt/ Main: Brandes & Apsel, 2015; enlarged 2nd edn, 2017).

——— (ed.), *Namibia: Kolonialismus und Widerstand; Materialien für Unterricht und Bildungsarbeit* (Bonn: Informationsstelle Südliches Afrika, 1981).

———, *Understanding Namibia: The Trials of Independence* (London: Hurst, 2015).

Melber, Henning, and Platt, Kristin (eds.), *Koloniale Vergangenheit—postkoloniale Zukunft? Die deutsch-namibischen Beziehungen neu denken* (Frankfurt/Main: Brandes & Apsel, 2022).

Melber, Henning, with Melber, Mary, and Hillebrecht, Werner (eds.), *In Treue fest, Südwest! Eine ideologiekritische Dokumentation von der Eroberung Namibias über die deutsche Fremdherrschaft bis zur Kolonialapologie der Gegenwart* (Bonn: Informationsstelle Südliches Afrika, 1984).

Michael, Theodor Wonja, *Deutsch sein und schwarz dazu: Erinnerungen eines Afro-Deutschen* (Munich: dtv, 2013).

Michels, Eckard, *"Der Held von Deutsch-Ostafrika": Paul von Lettow-Vorbeck; Ein preußischer Kolonialoffizier* (Paderborn: Schoeningh, 2008).

Michels, Stefanie, *Imagined Power Contested: Germans and Africans in the Upper Cross River Area of Cameroon, 1887–1916* (Berlin and Münster: LIT, 2004).

———, *Schwarze deutsche Kolonialsoldaten: Mehrdeutige Repräsentationsräume und früher Kosmopolitismus in Afrika* (Bielefeld: Transcript, 2009).

Miescher, Giorgio, *Die Rote Linie: Die Geschichte der Veterinär- und Siedlungsgrenze in Namibia (1890er–1960er Jahre)* (Basel: Basler Afrika Bibliographien, 2013).

Milk, Hans-Martin, *"... der im Sturm steht wie ein Kameldornbaum": Die Evangelisten Namibias und ihre Geschichte* (Cologne: Rüdiger Köppe, 2019).

Mills, Sara, *Michel Foucault* (London and New York: Routledge, 2003).

Mitscherlich, Alexander, and Mitscherlich, Margarete, *The Inability to Mourn: Principles of Collective Behavior* (New York: Grove Press, 1975). Published originally in German as *Die Unfähigkeit zu trauern: Grundlagen kollektiven Verhaltens* (1967).

Mogk, Walter, *Paul Rohrbach und das "Größere Deutschland": Ethischer Imperialismus im Wilhelminischen Zeitalter; Ein Beitrag zur Geschichte des Kulturprotestantismus* (Munich: Goldmann, 1972).

Möhle, Heiko (ed.), *Branntwein, Bibeln und Bananen: Der deutsche Kolonialismus in Afrika; Eine Spurensuche* (Hamburg: Libertäre Assozation, 1999).

BIBLIOGRAPHY

Morlang, Thomas, *Askari und Fitafita: "Farbige" Söldner in den deutschen Kolonien* (Berlin: Ch. Links, 2008).

———, *Rebellion in der Südsee: Der Aufstand auf Ponape gegen die deutschen Kolonialherren, 1910/11* (Berlin: Ch. Links, 2010).

Moses, A. Dirk (ed.), *Genocide and Settler Society: Frontier Violence and Stolen Indigenous Children in Australian History* (New York and Oxford: Berghahn Books, 2005).

———, *The Problem of Genocide* (Cambridge: Cambridge University Press, 2021).

Moses, A. Dirk, and Stone, Dan (eds.), *Colonialism and Genocide* (Abingdon: Routledge, 2007).

Moyd, Michelle R., *Violent Intermediaries: African Soldiers, Conquest, and Everyday Colonialism in German East Africa* (Athens, OH: Ohio University Press 2014).

Mühlhahn, Klaus (ed.), *The Cultural Legacy of German Colonial Rule* (Berlin and Boston: De Gruyter Oldenbourg, 2017).

———, *Herrschaft und Widerstand in der "Musterkolonie" Kiautschou: Interaktionen zwischen China und Deutschland, 1897–1914* (Munich: Oldenbourg, 2000).

Müller, Fritz Ferdinand, *Deutschland—Zanzibar—Ostafrika: Geschichte einer deutschen Kolonialeroberung, 1884–1890* (Berlin: Rütten & Loening, 1959).

———, *Kolonien unter der Peitsche: Eine Dokumentation* (Berlin: Rütten & Loening, 1962).

Müller, Sven-Oliver, and Torp, Cornelius (eds.), *Das Deutsche Kaiserreich in der Kontroverse* (Göttingen: Vandenhoeck & Ruprecht, 2009).

Murphy, David Thomas, *The Heroic Earth: Geopolitical Thought in Weimar Germany, 1918–1933* (Kent, Ohio: Kent State University Press, 2019).

Muschalek, Marie, *Violence as Usual: Policing and the Colonial State in German Southwest Africa* (Ithaca, NY: Cornell University Press, 2019).

Nagl, Dominik, *Grenzfälle: Staatsangehörigkeit, Rassismus und nationale Identität unter deutscher Kolonialherrschaft* (Frankfurt/Main: Peter Lang, 2007).

Nagl, Tobias, *Die unheimliche Maschine: Rasse und Repräsentation im Weimarer Kino* (Munich: Edition Text + Kritik, 2009).

Naranch, Bradley, and Eley, Geoff (eds.), *German Colonialism in a Global Age* (Durham, NC: Duke University Press, 2014).

Nejar, Marie, *Mach nicht so traurige Augen, weil du ein Negerlein bist: Meine Jugend im Dritten Reich* (Reinbek: Rowohlt, 2007).

Nestvogel, Renate, and Tetzlaff, Rainer (eds.), *Afrika und der deutsche Kolonialismus: Zivilisierung zwischen Schnapshandel und Bibelstunde* (Berlin and Hamburg: Dietrich Reimer, 1987).

Ngatcha, Alexis, *Der Deutschunterricht in Kamerun als Erbe des Kolonialismus und seine Funktion in der postkolonialen Ära* (Frankfurt/Main: Peter Lang, 2002).

Nguherimo, Jephta U., *Unburied, Unmarked: The Untold Namibian Story of the Genocide of 1904–1908* (self-published, 2019).

Norris, Edward Graham, *Die Umerziehung des Afrikaners: Togo, 1895–1935* (Munich: Trickster, 1993).

Nussbaum, Manfred, *Vom "Kolonialenthusiasmus" zur Kolonialpolitik der Monopole: Zur deutschen Kolonialpolitik unter Bismarck, Caprivi, Hohenlohe* (Berlin: Akademie-Verlag, 1962).

BIBLIOGRAPHY

Oguntoye, Katharina, *Eine afro-deutsche Geschichte: Zur Lebenssituation von Afrikanern und Afro-Deutschen in Deutschland von 1884 bis 1950* (Berlin: Hoho-Verlag Hoffmann, 1997).

Oguntoye, Katharina, Opitz, May, and Schultz, Dagmar (eds.), *Farbe bekennen: Afrodeutsche Frauen auf den Spuren ihrer Geschichte* (Berlin: Orlanda, 1986). Published in English as Opitz, May, Oguntoye, Katharina, and Schultz, Dagmar (eds.), *Showing Our Colors: Afro-German Women Speak Out* (London: Open Letters, 1992).

Oloukpona-Yinnon, Adjaï Paulin, *Unter deutschen Palmen: Die "Musterkolonie" Togo im Spiegel deutscher Kolonialliteratur (1884–1914)* (Frankfurt/Main: IKO, 1998).

Olusoga, David, and Erichsen, Casper W., *The Kaiser's Holocaust: Germany's Forgotten Genocide and the Colonial Roots of Nazism* (London: Faber & Faber, 2010).

Osterhammel, Jürgen, *Kolonialismus: Geschichte, Formen, Folgen* (Munich: Beck, 1995).

Östman, Lars, *The "Stolpersteine" and the Commemoration of Life: Death and Government. A Philosophical Archaeology* (Frankfurt/Main: Peter Lang, 2018).

Otele, Olivette, *African Europeans: An Untold History* (London: Hurst, 2020).

Paasche, Hans, *Die Forschungsreise des Afrikaners Lukanga Mukara ins innerste Deutschlands* (Werther: Fackelreither-Verlag, 1921).

Paczensky, Gert von, *"Die Weißen kommen"* (Hamburg: Hoffmann und Campe, 1970). Revised version published as *Weiße Herrschaft: Eine Geschichte des Kolonialismus* (Frankfurt/Main: Fischer, 1979).

Pedersen, Susan, *The Guardians: The League of Nations and the Crisis of Empire* (Oxford: Oxford University Press, 2015).

Penny, H. Glenn, *Objects of Culture: Ethnology and Ethnographic Museums in Imperial Germany* (Chapel Hill, NC: University of North Carolina Press, 2001).

Penny, H. Glenn, and Bunzl, Matti (eds.), *Worldly Provincialism: German Anthropology in the Age of Empire* (Ann Arbor, MI: University of Michigan Press, 2003).

Perras, Arne, *Carl Peters and German Imperialism, 1856–1918: A Political Biography* (Oxford: Oxford University Press, 2004).

Perraudin, Michael, and Zimmerer, Jürgen, with Heady, Katy (eds.), *German Colonialism and National Identity* (London and New York: Routledge, 2011).

Pesek, Michael, *Das Ende eines Kolonialreiches: Ostafrika im Ersten Weltkrieg* (Frankfurt/Main: Campus, 2010).

———, *Koloniale Herrschaft in Deutsch-Ostafrika: Expeditionen, Militär und Verwaltung seit 1880* (Frankfurt/Main: Campus, 2005).

Petersen, Marco L. (ed.), *Sønderjylland-Schleswig kolonial: Das kulturelle Erbe des Kolonialismus in der Region zwischen Eider und Königsau* (Odense: Syddansk Universitetsforlag, 2018).

Pieper, Dietmar, *Zucker, Schnaps und Nilpferdpeitsche: Wie hanseatische Kaufleute Deutschland zur Kolonialherrschaft trieben* (Munich: Piper, 2023).

Poley, Jared, *Decolonization in Germany: Weimar Narratives of Colonial Loss and Foreign Occupation* (Bern: Peter Lang, 2005).

Poliakov, Léon, *The Aryan Myth: A History of Racist and Nationalist Ideas in Europe* (New York: Basic Books, 1971).

Pommerin, Reiner, *"Sterilisierung der Rheinlandbastarde": Das Schicksal einer farbigen deutschen Minderheit, 1918–1937* (Düsseldorf: Droste, 1979).

BIBLIOGRAPHY

Press, Steven, *Blood and Diamonds: Germany's Imperial Ambitions in Africa* (Cambridge, MA: Harvard University Press, 2021).

———, *Rogue Empires: Contracts and Conmen in Europe's Scramble for Africa* (Cambridge, MA: Harvard University Press, 2017).

Pugach, Sara, *African Students in East Germany, 1949–1975* (Ann Arbor, MI: University of Michigan Press, 2022).

Pugach, Sara, Pizzo, David, and Blackler, Adam (eds.), *After the Imperialist Imagination: Two Decades of Research on Global Germany and Its Legacies* (Oxford: Peter Lang, 2020).

Raphael-Hernandez, Heike, *Deutschland und die Sklaverei: Die lange Vorgeschichte des Rassismus* (Berlin: Ch. Links, 2022).

Raphael-Hernandez, Heike, and Wiegmink, Pia (eds.), *German Entanglements in Transatlantic Slavery* (London: Routledge, 2020; originally published as a special issue of *Atlantic Studies*, 14, no. 4, 2017).

Reinhard, Wolfgang, *Kleine Geschichte des Kolonialismus* (Stuttgart: Kröner, 1996).

Reiniger, Franziska, *Die große Liebe in einer fremden Welt: Die Inszenierungen von Schwarzsein und Weißsein in gegenwärtigen Afrikaromanen am Beispiel Corinne Hofmanns "Die weiße Massai"* (Saarbrücken: VDM Verlag, 2008).

Reyels, Lili, Ivanov, Paola, and Weber-Sinn, Kristin (eds.), *Humboldt Lab Tanzania: Objects from the Colonial Wars in the Ethnologisches Museum, Berlin; Tanzanian–German Perspectives* (Berlin: Reimer, 2018).

Richter, Hedwig, *Aufbruch in die Moderne: Reform und Massenpolitisierung im Kaiserreich* (Frankfurt/Main: Suhrkamp, 2021).

Ritz, Hans, *Die Sehnsucht nach der Südsee: Bericht über einen europäischen Mythos* (Göttingen: Muriverlag, 1983).

Robel, Yvonne, *Verhandlungssache Genozid: Zur Dynamik geschichtspolitischer Deutungskämpfe* (Paderborn: Fink, 2013).

Rothberg, Robert, *Multidirectional Memory: Remembering the Holocaust in the Age of Decolonization* (Stanford, CA: Stanford University Press, 2009). Published in German as *Multidirektionale Erinnerung: Holocaustgedenken im Zeitalter der Dekolonisierung* (Berlin: Metropol, 2021).

Rothermund, Dietmar (ed.), *Erinnerungskulturen post-imperialer Nationen* (Baden-Baden: Nomos, 2015).

Rüdiger, Klaus H., *Die Namibia-Deutschen: Geschichte einer Nationalität im Werden* (Stuttgart: Steiner, 1993).

Sandler, Willeke, *Empire in the Heimat: Colonialism and Public Culture in the Third Reich* (Oxford: Oxford University Press, 2018).

Sands, Phillipe, *East West Street: On the Origins of Genocide and Crimes against Humanity* (London: Weidenfeld & Nicolson, 2016).

Sarkin, Jeremy, *Colonial Genocide and Reparation Claims in the 21st Century: The Socio-legal Context of Claims under International Law by the Herero against Germany for Genocide in Namibia, 1904–1908* (Westport, CT: Praeger, 2009).

———, *Germany's Genocide of the Herero: Kaiser Wilhelm II, His General, His Settler, His Soldiers* (Rochester, NY: Boydell & Brewer; London: James Currey, 2011).

Sarr, Felwine, and Savoy, Bénédicte, *Zurückgeben: Über die Restitution afrikanischer Kulturgüter* (Berlin: Matthes & Seitz, 2019).

BIBLIOGRAPHY

Schaller, Dominik, and Zimmerer, Jürgen (eds.), *The Origins of Genocide: Raphael Lemkin as a Historian of Mass Violence* (London: Routledge 2009).

Schaper, Ulrike, *Koloniale Verhandlungen: Gerichtsbarkeit, Verwaltung und Herrschaft in Kamerun, 1884–1916* (Frankfurt/Main and New York: Campus, 2012).

Scheurmann, Erich, *Der Papalagi: Die Reden des Südseehäuptlings Tuiavii aus Tiavea* (Buchenbach: Felsen-Verlag, 1920).

———, *Zweierlei Blut: Ein Südsee-Roman* (Munich: Ludendorffs Verlag, 1936).

Schiefel, Werner, *Bernhard Dernburg, 1865–1937: Kolonialpolitiker und Bankier im wilhelminischen Deutschland* (Zürich: Atlantis, 1974).

Schilling, Britta, *Postcolonial Germany: Memories of Empire in a Decolonized Nation* (Oxford: Oxford University Press, 2014).

Schlesinger, Rudolf, *Die Kolonialfrage in der Kommunistischen Internationale* (Frankfurt/Main: Europäische Verlagsanstalt, 1970).

Schmidt-Lauber, Brigitta, *Die abhängigen Herren: Deutsche Identität in Namibia* (Münster and Hamburg: LIT, 1993).

———, *"Die verkehrte Hautfarbe": Ethnizität deutscher Namibier als Alltagspraxis* (Berlin and Hamburg: Reimer, 1998).

Schmitt-Egner, Peter, *Kolonialismus und Faschismus: Eine Studie zur historischen und begrifflichen Genesis faschistischer Bewußtseinsformen am deutschen Beispiel* (Gießen and Lollar: Achenbach, 1975).

Schmokel, Wolfe W., *Dream of Empire: German Colonialism, 1919–1945* (New Haven, CT: Yale University Press, 1964). Published in German as *Der Traum vom Reich: Der deutsche Kolonialismus zwischen, 1919 und 1945* (Gütersloh: Mohn, 1967).

Schmuhl, Hans-Walter, *The Kaiser Wilhelm Institute for Anthropology, Human Heredity, and Eugenics, 1927–1945: Crossing Boundaries* (Dordrecht: Springer, 2008)

Schneider, Rosa B., *"Um Scholle und Leben": Zur Konstruktion von "Rasse" und Geschlecht in der deutschen kolonialen Afrikaliteratur um 1900* (Frankfurt/Main: IKO, 2003).

Schroer, Timothy L., *Recasting Race after World War II: Germans and African Americans in American-Occupied Germany* (Boulder, CO: University Press of Colorado, 2007).

Schulte-Varendorff, Uwe, *Kolonialheld für Kaiser und Führer: General Lettow-Vorbeck* (Berlin: Ch. Links, 2006).

Sebald, Peter, *Die deutsche Kolonie Togo, 1884–1914: Auswirkungen einer Fremdherrschaft* (Berlin: Ch. Links, 2013; slightly modified shorter version of the 1988 volume).

———, *Togo, 1884–1914: Eine Geschichte der deutschen "Musterkolonie" auf der Grundlage amtlicher Quellen* (Berlin: Akademie-Verlag, 1988).

Seeberg, Karl-Martin, *Der Maji-Maji Krieg gegen die deutsche Kolonialherrschaft: Historische Ursprünge nationaler Identität in Tansania* (Berlin: Reimer, 1989).

Serebrov, Mari, *Mama Namibia* (Windhoek: Wordweaver, 2013).

Seyfried, Gerhard, *Herero* (Berlin: Eichborn, 2003).

Short, John Phillip, *Magic Lantern Empire: Colonialism and Society in Germany* (Ithaca, NY: Cornell University Press, 2012).

Siefkes, Martin, *Sprache, Glaube und Macht: Die Aufzeichnungen des Johannes Spiecker in Deutsch-Südwestafrika zur Zeit des Herero–Nama Aufstands* (Würzburg: Königshausen & Neumann, 2013).

BIBLIOGRAPHY

Silvester, Jeremy, and Gewald, Jan-Bart (eds.), *Words Cannot Be Found: German Colonial Rule in Namibia; An Annotated Reprint of the 1918 Blue Book* (Leiden: Brill, 2003).

Simmer, Götz, *Gold und Sklaven: Die Provinz Venezuela während der Welser-Verwaltung (1528–1556)* (Berlin: Verlag Wissenschaft und Technik, 2000).

Smith, David Livingston, *Less Than Human: Why We Demean, Enslave, and Exterminate Others* (New York: St. Martin's Press, 2011).

Sobich, Frank Oliver, and Bischoff, Sebastian, *Feinde werden: Zur nationalen Konstruktion existenzieller Gegnerschaft; Drei Fallstudien* (Berlin: Metropol, 2015).

Sokolowsky, Celia, *Sprachenpolitik des deutschen Kolonialismus: Deutschunterricht als Mittel imperialer Herrschaftssicherung in Togo (1884–1914)* (Stuttgart: Ibidem, 2004).

Soost, Detlef D., *Heimkind—Neger—Pionier: Mein Leben* (Reinbek: Rowohlt, 2005).

Soyinka, Wole, *The Burden of Memory, the Muse of Forgiveness* (Oxford: Oxford University Press, 1998).

Speitkamp, Winfried, *Deutsche Kolonialgeschichte* (Stuttgart: Reclam, 2005).

Splettstösser, Anne, *Umstrittene Sammlungen: Vom Umgang mit kolonialem Erbe aus Kamerun in ethnologischen Museen; Die Fälle Tange/Schiffschnabel und Ngonnso/ Schalenträgerfigur in Deutschland und Kamerun* (Göttingen: Universitätsverlag, 2019).

Stahn, Carsten, *Confronting Colonial Objects: Histories, Legalities, and Access to Culture* (Oxford: Oxford University Press, 2023).

Stapleton, Timothy J., *A History of Genocide in Africa* (Santa Barbara, CA: Praeger, 2017).

Steinmetz, George, *The Devil's Handwriting: Precoloniality and the German Colonial State in Qingdao, Samoa, and Southwest Africa* (Chicago: University of Chicago Press, 2007).

Steltzer, Hans Georg, *Die Deutschen und ihr Kolonialreich* (Frankfurt/Main: Societäts-Verlag, 1984).

Stoecker, Helmuth (ed.), *Drang nach Afrika: Die deutsche koloniale Expansionspolitik und Herrschaft in Afrika von den Anfängen bis zum Verlust der Kolonien* (Berlin: Akademie-Verlag, 2nd rev. edn, 1991).

―――― (ed.), *Kamerun unter deutscher Kolonialherrschaft*, 2 vols. (Berlin: Rütten & Loening, 1960; Deutscher Verlag der Wissenschaften, 1968).

Stoecker, Holger, *Afrikawissenschaften in Berlin von 1919 bis 1949: Zur Geschichte und Topographie eines wissenschaftlichen Netzwerkes* (Stuttgart: Steiner, 2008).

Stoecker, Holger, Schnalke, Thomas, and Winkelmann, Andreas (eds.), *Sammeln, Erforschen, Zurückgeben? Menschliche Gebeine aus der Kolonialzeit in akademischen und musealen Sammlungen* (Berlin: Ch. Links, 2013).

Sznaider, Natan, *Fluchtpunkte der Erinnerung: Über die Gegenwart von Holocaust und Kolonialismus* (Munich: Hanser, 2022).

Táíwò, Olúfémi, *Against Decolonisation: Taking African Agency Seriously* (London: Hurst, 2022).

Terkessidis, Mark, *Wessen Erinnerung zählt? Koloniale Vergangenheit und Rassismus Heute* (Hamburg: Hoffmann & Campe, 2019).

Tetzlaff, Rainer, *Koloniale Entwicklung und Ausbeutung: Wirtschafts- und Sozialgeschichte Deutsch-Ostafrikas, 1885–1914* (Berlin: Duncker & Humblot, 1970).

BIBLIOGRAPHY

Thode-Arora, Hilke, *Für fünfzig Pfennig um die Welt: Die Hagenbeckschen Völkerschauen* (Frankfurt/Main: Campus, 1989).

Timm, Uwe, *Deutsche Kolonien* (Munich: AutorenEdition, 1981; Cologne: Kiepenheuer & Witsch, 1986).

———, *Morenga* (Gütersloh: AutorenEdition, 1978; Reinbek: Rowohlt, 1981, with several more editions, the latest Munich: dtv, 2020). Published in English under the same title (New York: New Directions, 1978, with several editions following).

Tjingaete, Rukee, *The Weeping Graves of Our Ancestors* (Windhoek: Capital Press, c.2014; rev. edn, 2017).

Todorov, Tzvetan, *The Conquest of America: The Question of the Other* (New York: Harper & Row, 1984; French original, 1982).

Todzi, Kim Sebastian, *Unternehmen Weltaneignung: Der Woermann-Konzern und der deutsche Kolonialismus, 1837–1916* (Hamburg: Wallstein, 2023).

Trotha, Trutz von, *Koloniale Herrschaft: Zur soziologischen Theorie der Staatsentstehung am Beispiel des "Schutzgebietes Togo"* (Tübingen: Mohr Siebeck, 1994).

Trüper, Ursula, *Zara oder das Streben nach Freiheit: Eine koloniale Familiengeschichte in Schwarz-Weiß* (Cologne: Bastei Lübbe, 2022).

Unangst, Matthew, *Colonial Geography: Race and Space in German East Africa, 1884–1905* (Toronto: University of Toronto Press, 2022).

Urena Valerio, Lenny A., *Colonial Fantasies, Imperial Realities: Race Science and the Making of Polishness on the Fringes of the German Empire, 1840–1922* (Athens, OH: Ohio University Press, 2019).

Usleber, Thomas, *Die Farben unter meiner Haut: Autobiografische Aufzeichnungen* (Frankfurt/Main: Brandes & Apsel, 2002).

Utley, Jasper D., *The Lie of the Land* (Windhoek: UNAM Press, 2017).

Van den Berg, Zirk, *Parts Unknown* (Cape Town: Kwela, 2018).

Van der Hoog, Tycho, *Breweries, Politics and Identity: The History behind Namibia's Beer* (Basel: Basler Afrika Bibliographien, 2019).

Van der Linden, Mieke, *The Acquisition of Africa (1870–1914): The Nature of International Law* (Boston: Brill, 2016).

Vukadinovic, Vojin Sasa (ed.), *Rassismus. Von der frühen Bundesrepublik bis zur Gegenwart* (Berlin: De Gruyter Oldenbourg, 2023).

Wagner, Florian, *Colonial Internationalism and the Governmentality of Empire, 1893–1982* (Cambridge: Cambridge University Press, 2022).

Wallace, Marion, with Kinahan, John, *A History of Namibia: From the Beginning to 1990* (London: Hurst, 2011).

Warmbold, Joachim, *"Ein Stückchen neudeutsche Erd …": Deutsche Kolonial-Literatur* (Frankfurt/Main: Haag & Herchen, 1982).

Wehler, Hans-Ulrich, *Bismarck und der Imperialismus* (Cologne: Kiepenheuer & Witsch, 1969).

Weinberger, Gerda, *An den Quellen der Apartheid* (Berlin: Akademie Verlag, 1975).

Weingart, Peter, Kroll, Jürgen, and Bayertz, Kurt, *Rasse, Blut und Gene: Geschichte der Eugenik und Rassenhygiene in Deutschland* (Frankfurt/Main: Suhrkamp, 1988).

Weiss, Ruth, and Mayer, Hans, *Afrika den Europäern! Von der Berliner Kongokonferenz 1884 ins Afrika der neuen Kolonisation* (Wuppertal: Peter Hammer, 1984).

BIBLIOGRAPHY

Wempe, Sean Andrew, *Revenants of the German Empire: Colonial Germans, Imperialism and the League of Nations* (New York: Oxford University Press, 2019).

Wentenschuh, Walter G., *Namibia und seine Deutschen: Geschichte und Gegenwart der deutschen Sprachgruppe im Südwesten Afrikas* (Göttingen: Klaus Hess, 1995).

Westphal, Wilfried, *Geschichte der deutschen Kolonien* (Munich: Bertelsmann, 1984).

Wieczorek-Zeul, Heidemarie, *Welt bewegen: Erfahrungen und Begegnungen* (Berlin: Vorwärts Buch, 2007).

Wiedemann, Charlotte, *Den Schmerz der Anderen begreifen: Holocaust und Weltgedächtnis* (Berlin: Propyläen, 2022).

———, *Der lange Abschied von der weißen Dominanz* (Munich: dtv, 2019).

Wietersheim, Erika von, *This Land Is My Land! Motions and Emotions around Land in Namibia* (Windhoek: Friedrich-Ebert-Stiftung, 2008; 2nd rev. edn, 2021).

Williams, David, *Condorcet and Modernity* (Cambridge: Cambridge University Press, 2004).

Winkelmann, Andreas, Stoecker, Holger, Fründt, Sarah, and Förster, Larissa, *Interdisziplinäre Provenienzforschung zu menschlichen Überresten aus kolonialen Kontexten: Eine methodische Arbeitshilfe des Deutschen Zentrums Kulturgutverluste, des Berliner Medizinhistorischen Museums der Charité und von ICOM Deutschland* (Heidelberg: arthistoricum.net, 2022).

Wirz, Albert, *Vom Sklavenhandel zum Kolonialhandel: Wirtschaftsräume und Wirtschaftsformen in Kamerun vor 1914* (Zürich and Freiburg im Breisgau: Atlantis, 1973).

Wolff, Kaya de, *Post-/Koloniale Erinnerungsdiskurse in der Medienkultur: Der Genozid an den Ovaherero und Nama in der deutschsprachigen Presse von 2001 bis 2016* (Bielefeld: Transcript, 2021).

Wünsche, Dietlind, *Feldpostbriefe aus China: Wahrnehmungs- und Deutungsmuster deutscher Soldaten zur Zeit des Boxeraufstandes, 1900–1901* (Berlin: Ch. Links, 2008).

Xiang, Lanxin, *The Origin of the Boxer War: A Multinational Study* (London: Routledge, 2003).

Yekani, Minu Haschemi, *Koloniale Arbeit: Rassimus, Migration und Herrschaft in Tansania (1885–1914)* (Frankfurt/Main: Campus, 2019).

Yerushalmi, Yosef Hayim, *Zakhor: Jewish History and Jewish Memory* (Seattle: University of Washington Press, 1996).

Yuan, Weiman, *Medizin und Kolonialismus: Deutsche Darstellung von chinesischer Medizin vom Opiumkrieg bis zum Ersten Weltkrieg* (Berlin and Boston: De Gruyter, 2021).

Zantop, Susanne, *Colonial Fantasies: Conquest, Family, and Nation in Precolonial Germany, 1770–1870* (Durham, NC: Duke University Press, 1997). Published in German as *Kolonialphantasien im vorkolonialen Deutschland (1770–1870)* (Berlin: Erich Schmidt, 1999).

Zeigerer, Merle, *Kriegsberichterstatter in den deutschen Kolonialkriegen in Asien und Afrika: Augenzeugen, Anstifter, Komplizen?* (Kiel: Solivagus, 2016).

Zeller, Joachim, *Kolonialdenkmäler und Geschichtsbewusstsein: Eine Untersuchung der kolonialdeutschen Erinnerungskultur* (Frankfurt/Main: IKO, 2000).

Zimmerer, Jürgen, *Deutsche Herrschaft über Afrikaner: Staatlicher Machtanspruch und Wirklichkeit im kolonialen Namibia* (Münster: LIT, 2001). Published in English as *German Rule, African Subjects: State Aspirations and the Reality of Power in Colonial Namibia* (New York: Berghahn, 2021).

BIBLIOGRAPHY

——— (ed.), *Erinnerungskämpfe: Neues deutsches Geschichtsbewusstsein* (Ditzingen: Reclam, 2023).

——— (ed.), *"Kein Platz an der Sonne": Erinnerungsorte der deutschen Kolonialgeschichte* (Frankfurt/Main and New York: Campus, 2013; Bonn: Bundeszentrale für politische Bildung, 2014).

———, *Von Windhuk nach Auschwitz? Beiträge zum Verhältnis von Kolonialismus und Holocaust* (Berlin: De Gruyter, 2011). Published in English with a new preface as *From Windhoek to Auschwitz: Reflections on the Relationship between Colonialism and National Socialism* (Berlin: De Gruyter, 2024).

Zimmerer, Jürgen, and Todzi, Kim Sebastian (eds.), *Hamburg: Tor zur kolonialen Welt; Erinnerungsorte der (post-)kolonialen Globalisierung* (Göttingen: Wallstein, 2021).

Zimmerer, Jürgen, and Zeller, Joachim (eds.), *Völkermord in Deutsch-Südwestafrika: Der Kolonialkrieg (1904–1908) in Namibia und seine Folgen* (Berlin: Ch. Links, 2003; Augsburg: Weltbild, 2011; 3rd rev. edn, 2016). Published in English as *Genocide in German South-West Africa: The Colonial War of 1904–1908 and Its Aftermath* (Monmouth, UK: Merlin Press, 2008).

Zimmerman, Andrew, *Alabama in Africa: Booker T. Washington, the German Empire and Globalization of the New South* (Princeton, NJ: Princeton University Press, 2010).

———, *Anthropology and Antihumanism in Imperial Germany* (Chicago: University of Chicago Press, 2001).

Zimmermann, Olaf, and Geissler, Theo (eds.), *Kolonialismus-Debatte: Bestandsaufnahme und Konsequenzen* (Berlin: Deutscher Kulturrat, 2019).

Zollmann, Jakob, *Koloniale Herrschaft und ihre Grenzen: Die Kolonialpolizei in Deutsch Südwestafrika, 1894–1915* (Göttingen: Vandenhoeck & Ruprecht, 2010).

Zöllner, Abini, *Schokoladenkind: Meine Familie und andere Wunder* (Reinbek: Rowohlt, 2003).

Zurstrassen, Bettina, *Ein Stück deutscher Erde schaffen: Koloniale Beamte in Togo, 1884–1914* (Frankfurt/Main: Campus, 2008).

Chapters in Books

Abiatar, Festus, and Krishnamurthy, Sarala, "Herero–Nama Genocide as Historical Fiction: A New Historical Analysis of *Mama Namibia*, *The Scattering*, and *The Lie of the Land*", in Krishnamurthy, Sarala, Mlambo, Nelson, and Vale, Helen (eds.), *Writing Namibia: Coming of Age* (Basel: Basler Afrika Bibliographien, 2022).

Aitken, Robbie, "Education and Migration: Cameroonian Schoolchildren and Apprentices in Germany, 1884–1914", in Honeck, Mischa, Klimke, Martin, and Kuhlmann, Anne (eds.), *Germany and the Black Diaspora: Points of Contact, 1250–1914* (New York: Berghahn, 2013).

———, "Forgotten Histories: Recovering the Precarious Lives of African Servants in imperial Germany", in Garrido, Felipe Espinoze, Koegler, Caroline, Nyangulu, Deborah, and Stein, Mark U. (eds.), *Locating African European Studies: Interventions—Intersections—Coalitions* (London: Routledge, 2019).

———, "Surviving in the Metropole: The Struggle for Work and Belonging amongst African Colonial Migrants in Weimar Germany", in Bressey, Caroline,

BIBLIOGRAPHY

and Adi, Hakim (eds.), *Belonging in Europe: The African Diaspora and Work* (Oxford: Routledge, 2011).

Albrecht, Monika, "(Post-)colonial Amnesia? German Debates on Colonialism and Decolonization in the Post-war Era", in Perraudin, Michael, and Zimmerer, Jürgen, with Heady, Katy (eds.), *German Colonialism and National Identity* (London and New York: Routledge, 2011).

Ames, Eric, "From the Exotic to the Everyday: The Ethnographic Exhibitions in Germany", in Schwartz, Vanessa R., and Przyblyski, Jeanenne M. (eds.), *The Nineteenth Century Visual Culture Reader* (New York and London: Routledge, 2004).

Ani, Ekpenyong, "Die Frau, die Mut zeigt: Der Verein ADEFRA; Schwarze Deutsche Frauen/Schwarze Frauen in Deutschland e.V.", in AntiDiskriminierungsBüro Köln and cyberNomads (eds.), *The BlackBook: Deutschlands Häutungen* (Frankfurt/Main: IKO, 2004).

Attia, Iman, "Geteilte Erinnerungen: Global- und beziehungsgeschichtliche Perspektiven auf Erinnerungspolitik", in Attia, Iman, Köbsell, Swantje, and Prasad, Nivedita (eds.), *Dominanzkultur reloaded: Neue Texte zu gesellschaftlichen Machtverhältnissen und ihren Wechselwirkungen* (Bielefeld: Transcript, 2015).

Attikpoe, Kodjo, "Folgenschwere Konstrukte: Beobachtungen zu Afrika-Bildern in weißen Köpfen", in Böhler, Katja, and Hoeren, Jürgen (eds.), *Afrika: Mythos und Zukunft* (Freiburg im Breisgau: Herder, 2003).

Austen, Ralph A., "Mythic Transformation and Historical Continuity: The Duala of Cameroon and German Colonialism, 1884–1914", in Fowler, Ian, and Zeitlyn, David (eds.), *African Crossroads: Intersections between History and Anthropology in Cameroon* (Providence, RI, and Oxford: Berghahn, 1996).

Axster, Felix, "Licht und Schatten? Zur Debatte um Holocaust und koloniale Gewaltverbrechen", in Böckmann, Matthias, Gockel, Matthias, Kössler, Reinhart, and Melber, Henning (eds.), *Jenseits von Mbembe: Geschichte, Erinnerung, Solidarität* (Berlin: Metropol, 2022).

Bahl, Eva, Pfeiffer, Zara, Ruhland, Katharina, Rühlemann, Martin W., and Zölls, Philip, "München dekolonisieren: Von kleinen Schritten und überschaubaren Erfolgen", in Bechhaus-Gerst, Marianne, and Zeller, Joachim (eds.), *Deutschland postkolonial? Die Gegenwart der imperialen Vergangenheit* (Berlin: Metropol, 2018).

Ballod, Carl, "Die wissenschaftlichen Anschauungen über Kolonialpolitik", in *Die Entwicklung der deutschen Volkswirtschaftslehre im neunzehnten Jahrhundert* (Leipzig: Duncker & Humblot, 1908).

Bauche, Manuela, "Die Figur des 'Mischling' in der deutschen Anthropologie (1900–1945)", in Böckmann, Matthias, Gockel, Matthias, Kössler, Reinhart, and Melber, Henning (eds.), *Jenseits von Mbembe: Geschichte, Erinnerung, Solidarität* (Berlin: Metropol, 2022).

———, "Von der Unmöglichkeit, klare Grenzen zu ziehen: Rassismus und Medizin in den deutschen Kolonien", in Foroutan, Naika, Geulen, Christian, Illmer, Susanne, Vogel, Klaus, and Wernsig, Susanne (eds.): *Das Phantom Rasse: Zur Geschichte und Wirkungsmacht von Rassismus* (Vienna and Cologne: Böhlau, 2018).

Bechhaus-Gerst, Marianne, "Welche Farbe hat die Nation? Afrodeutsche (Gegen-)Stimmen", in Bechhaus-Gerst, Marianne, and Zeller, Joachim (eds.), *Deutschland postkolonial? Die Gegenwart der imperialen Vergangenheit* (Berlin: Metropol, 2018).

BIBLIOGRAPHY

Becker, Frank, "Die Hottentotten-Wahlen (1907)", in Zimmerer, Jürgen (ed.), *"Kein Platz an der Sonne". Erinnerungsorte der deutschen Kolonialgeschichte* (Frankfurt/Main and New York: Campus, 2013).

Benninghoff-Lühl, Sibylle, "Die Ausstellung der Kolonialisierten: Völkerschauen von 1874–1932", in Harms, Volker (ed.), *Andenken an den Kolonialismus: Eine Ausstellung des Völkerkundlichen Instituts der Universität Tübingen* (Tübingen: Attempto, 1984).

Bens, Jonas, and Zenker, Olaf, "Sentiment", in Slaby, Jan, and Van Scheve, Christian (eds.), *Affective Societies: Key Concepts* (London: Routledge, 2019).

Berman, Nina, Göttsche, Dirk, and Schüller, Thorsten, "Deutsche Kolonialgeschichte im Spiegel fremdsprachiger Literaturen", in Göttsche, Dirk, Dunker, Axel, and Dürbeck, Gabriele (eds.), *Handbuch Postkolonialismus und Literatur* (Stuttgart: Metzler, 2017).

Biwa, Memory, "Stories of the Patchwork Quilt: An Oral History Project of the Nama–German War in Southern Namibia", in Du Pisani, André, Kössler, Reinhart, and Lindeke, William A. (eds.), *The Long Aftermath of War: Reconciliation and Transition in Namibia* (Freiburg: Arnold Bergstraesser Institute, 2010).

Bley, Helmut, "Unerledigte deutsche Kolonialgeschichte", in Entwicklungspolitische Korrespondenz (ed.), *Deutscher Kolonialismus: Materialien zur Hundertjahrfeier 1984* (Hamburg: Gesellschaft für entwicklungspolitische Bildungsarbeit, 1983).

Brehl, Medardus, "Namibia im Deutschen Bundestag und in der Außenpolitik", in Melber, Henning, and Platt, Kristin (eds.), *Koloniale Vergangenheit—postkoloniale Zukunft? Die deutsch-namibischen Beziehungen neu denken* (Frankfurt/Main: Brandes & Apsel, 2022).

———, "Strategies of Exclusion: The Genocide of the Herero in German Colonial Discourse", in Kinloch, Graham C., and Mohan, Raj P. (eds.), *Genocide: Approaches, Case Studies, and Responses* (New York: Algora Publishing, 2005).

Bridgman, Jon, and Worley, Leslie J., "Genocide of the Hereros", in Totten, Samuel, Parsons, William S., and Charny, Israel W. (eds.), *Century of Genocide: Eyewitness Accounts and Critical Views* (New York and London: Garland, 1997).

Bührer, Tanja, "Die Hehe und die Schutztruppe in Deutsch-Ostafrika: Die Schlacht bei Rugaro, 1891", in Walter, Dierk, and Kundrus, Birthe (eds.), *Waffen Wissen Wandel: Anpassung und Lernen in transkulturellen Erstkonflikten* (Hamburg: Hamburger Edition, 2012).

Cain, Horst, "Tuiavi's Papalagi", in Duerr, Hans Peter (ed.), *Authentizität und Betrug in der Ethnologie* (Frankfurt/Main: Suhrkamp, 1987).

Campt, Tina, Grosse, Pascal, and Lemke-Muniz de Faria, Yara-Colette, "Blacks, Germans, and the Politics of Imperial Imagination", in Friedrichsmeyer, Sara, Lennox, Sara, and Zantop, Susanne (eds.), *The Imperialist Imagination: German Colonialism and Its Legacy* (Ann Arbor, MI: University of Michigan Press, 1998).

Cornils, Ingo, "*Denkmalsturz*: The German Student Movement and German Colonialism", in Perraudin, Michael, and Zimmerer, Jürgen, with Heady, Katy (eds.), *German Colonialism and National Identity* (London and New York: Routledge, 2011).

Dağdelen, Sevim, "Völkermord zweiter Klasse? Koloniale Kontinuitäten im deutsch-namibischen 'Versöhnungsabkommen'", in Melber, Henning, and Platt, Kristin

BIBLIOGRAPHY

(eds.), *Koloniale Vergangenheit—postkoloniale Zukunft? Die deutsch-namibischen Beziehungen neu denken* (Frankfurt/Main: Brandes & Apsel, 2022).

Dekoloniale Team, "Dekoloniale Erinnerungskultur in der Stadt", in Brücke-Museum, Stiftung Deutsches Technikmuseum Berlin, Stiftung Stadtmuseum Berlin, Bystron, Daniela, and Fäser, Anne (eds.), *Das Museum dekolonisieren?* (Bielefeld: Transcript, 2022).

Della, Tahir, and Lehmann, Bebero, "Afrodeutsche und eine Afrikapolitik: Zwischen kritischer Aufarbeitung und kolonialen Kontinuitäten", in Melber, Henning (ed.), *Deutschland und Afrika: Anatomie eines komplexen Verhältnisses* (Frankfurt/Main: Brandes & Apsel, 2019).

Dülffer, Jost, "Kolonialismus ohne Kolonien: Deutsche Kolonialpläne, 1938", in Knipping, Franz, and Müller, Klaus-Jürgen (eds.), *Machtbewußtsein in Deutschland am Vorabend des Zweiten Weltkrieges* (Paderborn: Schöningh, 1984).

Eckert, Andreas, "Afrikanische Sprachen und Afrikanistik", in Tenorth, Heinz-Elmar, with Hess, Volker, and Hoffmann, Dieter (ed.), *Geschichte der Universität unter den Linden, 1810–2010*, vol. 5: *Transformation der Wissensordnung* (Berlin: Akademie-Verlag, 2010).

———, "Afrikawissenschaften in Deutschland: Eine historische Perspektive", in Melber, Henning (ed.), *Deutschland und Afrika: Anatomie eines komplexen Verhältnisses* (Frankfurt/Main: Brandes & Apsel, 2019).

Eckert, Andreas, and Wirz, Albert, "Wir nicht, die Anderen auch: Deutschland und der Kolonialismus", in Conrad, Sebastian, and Randeria, Shalini (eds.), *Jenseits des Eurozentrismus* (Frankfurt/Main and New York: Campus 2002).

Eley, Geoff, "Empire by Land or Sea? Germany's Imperial Imaginary, 1840–1945", in Naranch, Bradley, and Eley, Geoff (eds.), *German Colonialism in a Global Age* (Durham, NC: Duke University Press, 2014).

Engelberg, Stefan, "The German Language in the South Seas: Language Contact and the Influence of Language Politics and Language Attitudes", in Siebel-Achenbach, Sebastian, Liebscher, Grit, John, David G., Skidmore, James M., and Schulze, Mathias (eds.), *German Diasporic Experiences: Identity, Migration and Loss* (Waterloo, Ontario: Wilfrid Laurier University Press, 2008).

Engert, Stefan, "Germany–Namibia: The Belated Apology to the Herero", in Daase, Christoph, Engert, Stefan, Horelt, Michel-André, Rennert, Judith, and Strassner, Renate (eds.), *Apology and Reconciliation in International Relations: The Importance of Being Sorry* (Abingdon: Routledge, 2016).

Ervedosa, Clara, "Das May–Ayim-Ufer in Berlin", in Zimmerer, Jürgen (ed.), *"Kein Platz an der Sonne": Erinnerungsorte der deutschen Kolonialgeschichte* (Frankfurt/Main and New York: Campus, 2013).

Essner, Cornelia, "'Border-Line' im Menschenblut und Struktur rassistischer Rechtsspaltung: Koloniales Kaiserreich und 'Drittes Reich'", in Brumlik, Micha, Meinl, Susanne, and Renz, Werner (eds.), *Gesetzliches Unrecht: Rassistisches Recht im 20. Jahrhundert* (Frankfurt/Main and New York: Campus, 2005).

Fründt, Sarah, and Förster, Larissa, "Menschliche Überreste aus ehemals kolonisierten Gebieten in deutschen Institutionen: Historische Entwicklungen und zukünftige Perspektiven", in Bechhaus-Gerst, Marianne, and Zeller, Joachim

BIBLIOGRAPHY

(eds.), *Deutschland postkolonial? Die Gegenwart der imperialen Vergangenheit* (Berlin: Metropol, 2018).

Fuhrmann, Wolfgang, "Zwischen kolonialer Wirklichkeit und kolonialer Legende: Die deutsche Kolonialherrschaft in Film- und Fernsehproduktionen", in Bechhaus-Gerst, Marianne, and Zeller, Joachim (eds.), *Deutschland postkolonial? Die Gegenwart der imperialen Vergangenheit* (Berlin: Metropol, 2018).

Ganslmayr, Herbert, and Paczensky, Gert von, "Die geraubte Kultur", in Hinz, Manfred O., Patemann, Helgard, and Meier, Arnim (eds.), *Weiß auf schwarz: 100 Jahre Einmischung in Afrika; Deutscher Kolonialismus und afrikanischer Widerstand* (Berlin: Elefanten Press, 1984; 2nd rev. edn, 1986).

Geiger, Wolfgang, "Afrikabilder in der Kritik", in Geiger, Wolfgang, and Melber, Henning (eds.), *Kritik des deutschen Kolonialismus: Postkoloniale Sicht auf Erinnerung und Geschichtsvermittlung* (Frankfurt/Main: Brandes & Apsel, 2021).

———, "Das 'Pachtgebiet' Kiautschou, der 'Boxerkrieg' und die Folgen", in Geiger, Wolfgang, and Melber, Henning (eds.), *Kritik des deutschen Kolonialismus: Postkoloniale Sicht auf Erinnerung und Geschichtsvermittlung* (Frankfurt/Main: Brandes & Apsel, 2021).

———, "Der deutsche Kolonialismus in aktuellen Lehrbüchern: Eine kritische Analyse", in Geiger, Wolfgang, and Melber, Henning (eds.), *Kritik des deutschen Kolonialismus: Postkoloniale Sicht auf Erinnerung und Geschichtsvermittlung* (Frankfurt/Main: Brandes & Apsel, 2021).

Gerbing, Stefan, "'Freier Mensch' oder 'deutscher Afrikaner'? Politische Interventionen zwischen Novemberrevolution und Weimarer Republik", in Diallo, Oumar, and Zeller, Joachim (eds.), *Black Berlin: Die deutsche Metropole und ihre afrikanische Diaspora in Geschichte und Gegenwart* (Berlin: Metropol, 2013).

Gissibl, Bernhard, and Paulmann, Johann, "'Serengeti darf nicht sterben'", in Zimmerer, Jürgen (ed.), *"Kein Platz an der Sonne": Erinnerungsorte der deutschen Kolonialgeschichte* (Frankfurt/Main and New York: Campus, 2013).

Gordon, Robert, and Mahoney, Dennis, "Marching in Step: German Youth and Colonial Cinema", in Ames, Eric, Klotz, Marcia, and Wildenthal, Lora (eds.), *Germany's Colonial Pasts* (Lincoln, NE: University of Nebraska Press, 2005).

Göttsche, Dirk, "Erinnerung und Kritik des deutschen Kolonialismus in der Gegenwartsliteratur", in Bechhaus-Gerst, Marianne, and Zeller, Joachim (eds.), *Deutschland postkolonial? Die Gegenwart der imperialen Vergangenheit* (Berlin: Metropol, 2018).

———, "Gegenwartsliteratur", in Göttsche, Dirk, Dunker, Axel, and Dürbeck, Gabriele (eds.), *Handbuch Postkolonialismus und Literatur* (Stuttgart: Metzler, 2017).

———, "Kamerun: Spuren und Erinnerungen hundert Jahre nach der deutschen Kolonialzeit", in Bechhaus-Gerst, Marianne, and Zeller, Joachim (eds.), *Deutschland postkolonial? Die Gegenwart der imperialen Vergangenheit* (Berlin: Metropol, 2018).

———, "Memory Studies", in Göttsche, Dirk, Dunker, Axel, and Dürbeck, Gabriele (eds.), *Handbuch Postkolonialismus und Literatur* (Stuttgart: Metzler, 2017).

Gouaffo, Albert, and Tsogang Fossi, Richard, "Kamerun: Ein deutsches Kapitel des globalen Imperialismus", in Geiger, Wolfgang, and Melber, Henning (eds.), *Kritik*

BIBLIOGRAPHY

des deutschen Kolonialismus: Postkoloniale Sicht auf Erinnerung und Geschichtsvermittlung (Frankfurt/Main: Brandes & Apsel, 2021).

Grau, Ines, "'Aber das war eigentlich nach der Wende …': Von Brüchen und Kontinuitäten rassistischer Erfahrungen mosambikanischer ArbeitsmigrantInnen in der DDR bis in die Gegenwart", in Institut für Demokratie und Zivilgesellschaft (ed.), *Wissen schafft Demokratie: Tagungsband zur Online-Fachtagung "Gesellschaftlicher Zusammenhalt & Rassismus"* (Jena: Institut für Demokratie und Zivilgesellschaft, 2022).

Grewe, Bernd-Stefan, "Das schwierige Erbe des Kolonialismus", in Bechhaus-Gerst, Marianne, and Zeller, Joachim (eds.), *Deutschland postkolonial? Die Gegenwart der imperialen Vergangenheit* (Berlin: Metropol, 2018).

Grosse, Pascal, "What Does German Colonialism Have to Do with National Socialism?", in Ames, Eric, Klotz, Marcia, and Wildenthal, Lora (eds.), *Germany's Colonial Pasts* (Lincoln, NE: University of Nebraska Press, 2005).

———, "Zwischen Privatheit und Öffentlichkeit: Kolonialmigration in Deutschland, 1900–1940", in Kundrus, Birthe (ed.), *Phantasiereiche: Der deutsche Kolonialismus in kulturgeschichtlicher Perspektive* (Frankfurt/Main: Campus, 2003).

Hake, Sabine, "Mapping the Native Body: On Africa and the Colonial Film in the Third Reich", in Friedrichsmeyer, Sara, Lennox, Sara, and Zantop, Susanne (eds.), *The Imperialist Imagination: German Colonialism and Its Legacy* (Ann Arbor, MI: University of Michigan Press, 1998).

Hardach, Gerd, "Die deutsche Herrschaft in Mikronesien", in Hiery, Hermann J. (ed.), *Die deutsche Südsee, 1884–1914: Ein Handbuch* (Paderborn: Schöningh, 2001).

Harding, Leonhard, "Die Berliner Westafrikakonferenz von 1884/85 und der Hamburger Schnapshandel mit Westafrika", in Nestvogel, Renate, and Tetzlaff, Rainer (eds.), *Afrika und der deutsche Kolonialismus: Zivilisierung zwischen Schnapshandel und Bibelstunde* (Berlin and Hamburg: Dietrich Reimer, 1987).

Henrichsen, Dag, "*Ovandoitji*: Geteilte und gespaltene Archive", in Melber, Henning, and Platt, Kristin (eds.), *Koloniale Vergangenheit—postkoloniale Zukunft? Die deutsch-namibischen Beziehungen neu denken* (Frankfurt/Main: Brandes & Apsel, 2022).

Heyden, Ulrich van der, "Die 'Hottentottenwahlen' von 1907", in Zimmerer, Jürgen, and Zeller, Joachim (eds.), *Völkermord in Deutsch-Südwestafrika: Der Kolonialkrieg (1904–1908) in Namibia und seine Folgen* (Berlin: Ch. Links, 2003; Augsburg: Weltbild, 2011; 3rd rev. edn, 2016). Published in English as *Genocide in German South-West Africa: The Colonial War of 1904–1908 and Its Aftermath* (London: Merlin Press, 2008).

Hiery, Hermann Joseph, "Die deutsche Verwaltung Neuguineas, 1884–1914", in Hiery, Hermann Joseph (ed.), *Die deutsche Südsee, 1884–1914: Ein Handbuch* (Paderborn: Schöningh, 2001).

Hillebrecht, Werner, "Hendrik Witbooi and Samuel Maharero: The Ambiguity of Heroes", in Jeremy Silvester (ed.), *Re-viewing Resistance in Namibia History* (Windhoek: University of Namibia Press, 2015).

———, "Monuments—and What Else? The Controversial Legacy of German Colonialism in Namibia", in Mühlhahn, Klaus (ed.), *The Cultural Legacy of German Colonial Rule* (Berlin and Boston: De Gruyter Oldenbourg, 2017).

BIBLIOGRAPHY

Hillebrecht, Werner, and Melber, Henning, "Von den Deutschen verschleppt: Spurensicherung", in Mbumba, Nangolo, Patemann, Helgard, and Katjivena, Uazuvara (eds.), *Ein Land, eine Zukunft: Namibia auf dem Weg in die Unabhängigkeit* (Wuppertal: Hammer, 1988).

Honold, Alexander, "Pfadfinder: Zur Kolonisierung des geographischen Raumes", in Geppert, Alexander C.T., Jensen, Uffa, and Weinhold, Jörn (eds.), *Ortsgespräche: Raum und Kommunikation im 19. und 20. Jahrhundert* (Bielefeld: Transcript, 2005).

Jacob, Frank, and Todzi, Kim Sebastian, "Genocide and Violence: An Introduction", in Jacob, Frank, and Todzi, Kim Sebastian (eds.), *Genocidal Violence: Concepts, Forms, Impact* (Berlin: De Gruyter, 2023).

Janson, Deborah, "The Subject in Black and White: Afro-German Identity Formation in Ika Hügel-Marshall's Autobiography *Daheim unterwegs: Ein deutsches Leben*", in *Women in German Yearbook: Feminist Studies in German Literature and Culture*, vol. 21, 2005.

Kalb, Martin, "Reprinting the Past: Persisting German Settler Narratives in Namibia Today", in Huang, Yu-ting, and Weaver-Hightower, Rebecca (eds.), *Archiving Settler Colonialism: Culture, Space and Race* (London and New York: Routledge, 2019).

Keim, Wiebke, "Colonialism, National-Socialism and the Holocaust: An Essay on Modern Ways of Dealing with Deviance", in Sitas, Ari, Keim, Wiebke, Damodaran, Sumangala, Trimikiniotis, Nicos, and Garba, Faisal, *Gauging and Engaging Deviance, 1600–2000* (Delhi: Tulika Press, 2014).

Klein, Thoralf, "Die Hunnenrede (1900)", in Zimmerer, Jürgen (ed.), *"Kein Platz an der Sonne": Erinnerungsorte der deutschen Kolonialgeschichte* (Frankfurt/Main and New York: Campus, 2013).

Klein-Arendt, Reinhard, and Heyn, Susanne, "'Glücklich das Volk, welches gewollt oder ungewollt, keine Kolonien besitzt!' Kolonialkritik in Deutschland zwischen 1750 und 1933", in Heyden, Ulrich van der, and Zeller, Joachim (eds.), *Kolonialismus hierzulande: Eine Spurensuche in Deutschland* (Erfurt: Sutton, 2007).

Kleinschmidt, Horst, "Verstrickungen: Eine Familie auf der Suche nach sich selbst", in Melber, Henning, and Platt, Kristin (eds.), *Koloniale Vergangenheit—postkoloniale Zukunft? Die deutsch-namibischen Beziehungen neu denken* (Frankfurt/Main: Brandes & Apsel, 2022).

Klotz, Marcia, "The Weimar Republic: A Postcolonial State in a Still-Colonial World", in Ames, Eric, Klotz, Marcia, and Wildenthal, Lora (eds.), *Germany's Colonial Pasts* (Lincoln, NE: University of Nebraska Press, 2005).

Koller, Christian, "Frankfurt-Berlin-Rheinland: Vom ethnologischen 'Material' zur 'schauerlichen Gefahr'; Afrikanische Kriegsgefangene und Besatzungssoldaten in Deutschland (1870–1945)", in Heyden, Ulrich van der, and Zeller, Joachim (eds.), *Kolonialismus hierzulande: Eine Spurensuche in Deutschland* (Erfurt: Sutton, 2007).

Kößler, Reinhart, "Diversität und Erinnerung: Zur Auseinandersetzung um die Konsequenzen des kolonialen Völkermordes (1904–1908) in Namibia", in Bogner, Artur, Kößler, Reinhart, Korff, Rüdiger, and Melber, Henning (eds.), *Die Welt aus der Perspektive der Entwicklungssoziologie: Festschrift für Dieter Neubert* (Baden-Baden: Nomos, 2020).

BIBLIOGRAPHY

———, "Historischer Wendepunkt, strukturelle Kontinuität: Der Erste Weltkrieg im Süden Afrikas und die Folgen für Namibia", in Bechhaus-Gerst, Marianne, and Zeller, Joachim (eds.), *Deutschland postkolonial? Die Gegenwart der imperialen Vergangenheit* (Berlin: Metropol, 2018).

———, "Internationale Solidarität: Chancen und Grenzen gemeinsamen Gedenkens im Schatten der Völkermorde des 20. Jahrhunderts", in Böckmann, Matthias, Gockel, Matthias, Kössler, Reinhart, and Melber, Henning (eds.), *Jenseits von Mbembe: Geschichte, Erinnerung, Solidarität* (Berlin: Metropol, 2022).

———, "Postcolonial Asymmetry: Coping with the Consequences of Genocide between Namibia and Germany", in Albrecht, Monika (ed.), *Postcolonialism Cross-examined: Multidirectional Perspectives on Imperial and Colonial Pasts and the Neocolonial Present* (London: Routledge, 2019).

———, "Socialism and Colonialism", in Van der Linden, Marcel (ed.), *The Cambridge History of Socialism*, vol. 2 (Cambridge: Cambridge University Press, 2023).

———, "Zwischen kolonialer Amnesie und konstruktivem Engagement: Postkoloniale Asymmetrien", in Melber, Henning (ed.), *Deutschland und Afrika: Anatomie eines komplexen Verhältnisses* (Frankfurt/Main: Brandes & Apsel, 2019).

Kössler, Reinhart, and Melber, Henning, "Selective Commemoration: Coming to Terms with German Colonialism", in Louis, Tatjana, Molope, Mokgadi, and Peters, Stefan (eds.), *Dealing with the Past in Latin America, Southern Africa and Germany* (Baden-Baden: Nomos, 2021).

———, "Völkermord und Gedenken: Der Genozid an den Herero und Nama in Deutsch-Südwestafrika, 1904–1908", in Fritz Bauer Institut (ed.), *Völkermord und Kriegsverbrechen in der ersten Hälfte des 20. Jahrhunderts: Jahrbuch 2004 zur Geschichte und Wirkung des Holocaust* (Frankfurt/Main and New York, Campus, 2004).

———, "The West German Solidarity Movement with the Liberation Struggles in Southern Africa: A (Self-)critical Retrospective", in Engel, Ulf, and Kappel, Robert (eds.), *Germany's Africa Policy Revisited: Interests, Images and Incrementalism* (2002; rev. edn, Münster: LIT, 2006).

Kreutzer, Leo, "Deutsche Heimat und afrikanische Wahlheimat in Hans Grimms Roman '*Volk ohne Raum*': Zur Dekolonisierung eines 'Kolonialismus ohne Kolonien'", in Hobuss, Steffi, and Lölke, Ulrich (eds.), *Erinnern verhandeln: Kolonialismus im kollektiven Gedächtnis Afrikas und Europas* (Münster: Westfälisches Dampfboot, 2006; 2nd rev. edn, 2007).

Krishnamurthy, Sarala, and Tjiramanga, Alexandra, "Exploring Herero Genocide Survivor Narratives", in Krishnamurthy, Sarala, Mlambo, Nelson, and Vale, Helen (eds.), *Writing Namibia. Coming of Age* (Basel: Basler Afrika Bibliographien, 2022).

Krobb, Florian, and Martin, Elaine, "Introduction: Coloniality in Post-Imperial Culture", in Krobb, Florian, and Martin, Elaine (eds.), *Weimar Colonialism: Discourses and Legacies of Post-Imperialism in Germany after 1918* (Bielefeld: Aisthesis, 2014).

Kroboth, Rudolf, "Anhang: Der deutsche Kolonialismus im Spiegel der historischen Debatte", in Harms, Volker (ed.), *Andenken an den Kolonialismus: Eine Ausstellung des Völkerkundlichen Instituts der Universität Tübingen* (Tübingen: Attempto, 1984).

BIBLIOGRAPHY

Kundrus, Birthe, "Colonialism, Imperialism, National Socialism: How Imperial Was the Third Reich?", in Naranch, Bradley, and Eley, Geoff (eds.), *German Colonialism in a Global Age* (Durham, NC: Duke University Press, 2014).

Kuss, Susanne, "Die deutsche 'Musterkolonie' Qingdao (1897–1914)", in Bechhaus-Gerst, Marianne, and Zeller, Joachim (eds.), *Deutschland postkolonial? Die Gegenwart der imperialen Vergangenheit* (Berlin: Metropol, 2018).

Laak, Dirk van, "Kolonien als 'Laborien der Moderne'?", in Conrad, Sebastian, and Osterhammel, Jürgen (eds.), *Das Kaiserreich transnational: Deutschland in der Welt, 1871–1914* (Göttingen: Vandenhoeck & Ruprecht, 2004).

Laukötter, Anja, "Das Völkerkundemuseum", in Zimmerer, Jürgen (ed.), *"Kein Platz an der Sonne": Erinnerungsorte der deutschen Kolonialgeschichte* (Frankfurt/Main and New York: Campus, 2013).

Laumann, Dennis, "Narratives of a 'Model Colony': German Togoland in Written and Oral Histories", in Perraudin, Michael, and Zimmerer, Jürgen, with Heady, Katy (eds.), *German Colonialism and National Identity* (London and New York: Routledge, 2011).

LeGall, Yann, and Mboro, Mnyaka Sururu, "Deutsch-Ostafrika: Ein permanenter Kriegszustand", in Geiger, Wolfgang, and Melber, Henning (eds.), *Kritik des deutschen Kolonialismus: Postkoloniale Sicht auf Erinnerung und Geschichtsvermittlung* (Frankfurt/Main: Brandes & Apsel, 2021).

Lehmann, Jörg, "Fraternity, Frenzy, and Genocide in German War Literature, 1906–36", in Perraudin, Michael, and Zimmerer, Jürgen, with Heady, Katy (eds.), *German Colonialism and National Identity* (London and New York: Routledge, 2011).

Lentz, Carola, "Erinnerungsräume öffnen, Erinnerungsgemeinschaften verbinden: Der Umgang mit kolonialem Erbe als Herausforderung für das Goethe-Institut", in Melber, Henning, and Platt, Kristin (eds.), *Koloniale Vergangenheit—postkoloniale Zukunft? Die deutsch-namibischen Beziehungen neu denken* (Frankfurt/Main: Brandes & Apsel, 2022).

Lenzerini, Federico, "Conclusive Notes: Defining Best Practices and Strategies for Maximizing the Concrete Chances of Reparation for Injuries Suffered by Indigenous Peoples", in Lenzerini, Federico (ed.), *Reparations for Indigenous Peoples: International and Comparative Perspectives* (Oxford: Oxford University Press, 2008).

Lerp, Dörte, and Lewerenz, Susann, "Getrennte Geschichten: Der Kolonialismus im Deutschen Historischen Museum", in Geiger, Wolfgang, and Melber, Henning (eds.), *Kritik des deutschen Kolonialismus: Postkoloniale Sicht auf Erinnerung und Geschichtsvermittlung* (Frankfurt/Main: Brandes & Apsel, 2021).

Lewerenz, Susann, "'Loyal Askari' and 'Black Rapist': Two Images in the German Discourse on National Identity and Their Impact on the Lives of Black People in Germany, 1918–45", in Perraudin, Michael, and Zimmerer, Jürgen, with Heady, Katy (eds.), *German Colonialism and National Identity* (London and New York: Routledge, 2011).

Lim, Jie-Hyun, "Postcolonial Reflections in the Mnemonic Confluence of the Holocaust, Stalinist Crimes, and Colonialism", in Lim, Jie-Hyun, and Rosenhaft, Eve (eds.), *Mnemonic Solidarity: Global Interventions* (Cham: Palgrave Macmillan, 2021).

BIBLIOGRAPHY

Lindner, Ulrike, "'An Inclination towards a Policy of Extermination'? German and British Discourse on Colonial Wars during High Imperialism", in Rash, Felicity, and Horan, Geraldine (eds.), *The Discourse of British and German Colonialism: Convergence and Competition* (London: Routledge, 2020).

Loimeier, Manfred, "Deutschland und die Literaturen Afrikas: Eine vergleichende Perspektive", in Melber, Henning (ed.), *Deutschland und Afrika: Anatomie eines komplexen Verhältnisses* (Frankfurt/Main: Brandes & Apsel, 2019).

Lü, Yixu, "Tstingtau", in Zimmerer, Jürgen (ed.), *"Kein Platz an der Sonne": Erinnerungsorte der deutschen Kolonialgeschichte* (Frankfurt/Main and New York: Campus, 2013).

Lundtofte, Henrik, "'I Believe That the Nation as Such Must Be Annihilated': The Radicalization of the German Suppression of the Herero Rising in 1904", in Jensen, Steven L.B. (ed.), *Genocide: Cases, Comparisons and Contemporary Debates* (Copenhagen: Danish Centre for Holocaust and Genocide Studies, 2003).

Melber, Henning, "Contested Notions of Genocide and Commemoration: The Case of the Herero in Namibia", in Eltringham, Nigel, and McLean, Pam (eds.), *Remembering Genocide* (Oxford: Routledge, 2014).

———, "Economic and Social Transformation in the Process of Colonisation: Society and State before and during German Colonial Rule", in Keulder, Christiaan (ed.), *State, Society and Democracy: A Reader in Namibian Politics* (Windhoek: Gamsberg Macmillan, 2000; Windhoek: Konrad-Adenauer-Stiftung, 2010).

———, "'Es sind doch auch Menschen!' Die Kolonisierten aus der Sicht deutscher Reichstagsabgeordneter", in Mbumba, Nangolo, Patemann, Helgard, and Katjivena, Uazuvara (eds.), *Ein Land, eine Zukunft: Namibia auf dem Weg in die Unabhängigkeit* (Wuppertal: Hammer, 1988).

———, "Kontinuität totaler Herrschaft: Völkermord und Apartheid in 'Deutsch-Südwestafrika'; Zur kolonialen Herrschaftspraxis im Deutschen Kaiserreich", in Benz, Wolfgang (ed.), *Jahrbuch für Antisemitismusforschung*, vol. 1 (Frankfurt/Main: Campus, 1992).

———, "The Struggle Continues: Namibia's Enduring Land Question", in Mazwi, Freedom, Mudimo, George Tonderai, and Helliker, Kirk (eds.), *Capital Penetration and the Peasantry in Southern and Eastern Africa: Neoliberal Restructuring* (Cham: Springer, 2022).

Mergner, Gottfried, "Solidarität mit den 'Wilden'? Das Verhältnis der deutschen Sozialdemokratie zu den afrikanischen Widerstandskämpfen in den ehemaligen deutschen Kolonien um die Jahrhundertwende", in Van Holthoon, Frits, and Van der Linden, Marcel (eds.), *Internationalism in the Labour Movement, 1830–1940* (Leiden: Brill, 1988).

Michaels, Eckard, "Paul von Lettow-Vorbeck", in Zimmerer, Jürgen (ed.), *"Kein Platz an der Sonne": Erinnerungsorte der deutschen Kolonialgeschichte* (Frankfurt/Main and New York: Campus, 2013).

Michels, Stefanie, "Der Askari", in Zimmerer, Jürgen (ed.), *"Kein Platz an der Sonne": Erinnerungsorte der deutschen Kolonialgeschichte* (Frankfurt/Main and New York: Campus, 2013).

BIBLIOGRAPHY

Mills, Charles W., "White Ignorance", in Sullivan, Shannon, and Tuana, Nancy (eds.), *Race and Epistemologies of Ignorance* (Albany, NY: State University of New York Press, 2007).

Morlang, Thomas, "'Finde ich keinen Weg, so bahne ich mir einen': Der umstrittene 'Kolonialheld' Hermann von Wissmann", in Heyden, Ulrich van der, and Zeller, Joachim (eds.), *Macht und Anteil an der Weltherrschaft: Berlin und der deutsche Kolonialismus* (Münster: Unrast, 2005).

Moses, A. Dirk, "Empire, Colony, Genocide: Keywords and the Philosophy of History", in Moses, A. Dirk (ed.), *Empire, Colony, Genocide: Conquest, Occupation, and Subaltern Resistance in World History* (New York and Oxford: Berghahn, 2008).

———, "Raphael Lemkin, Culture, and the Concept of Genocide", in Bloxham, David, and Moses, A. Dirk (eds.), *The Oxford Handbook of Genocide Studies* (Oxford: Oxford University Press, 2010).

Mückler, Hermann, "Inselgruppen an der Peripherie: Die deutschen Südsee-Kolonien", in Geiger, Wolfgang, and Melber, Henning (eds.), *Kritik des deutschen Kolonialismus: Postkoloniale Sicht auf Erinnerung und Geschichtsvermittlung* (Frankfurt/Main: Brandes & Apsel, 2021).

Mühlhahn, Klaus, "A New Imperial Vision? The Limits of German Colonialism in China", in Naranch, Bradley, and Eley, Geoff (eds.), *German Colonialism in a Global Age* (Durham, NC: Duke University Press, 2014).

Mühr, Stephan, "Wer im Schatten sitzt ...", in Melber, Henning, and Platt, Kristin (eds.), *Koloniale Vergangenheit—postkoloniale Zukunft? Die deutsch-namibischen Beziehungen neu denken* (Frankfurt/Main: Brandes & Apsel, 2022).

Nagl, Dominik, "Seckenheim, Berlin, Buea, Windhoek: Die imperiale Weitläufigkeit des Theodor Seitz", in Gissibl, Bernhard, and Niederau, Katharina (eds.), *Imperiale Weitläufigkeit und ihre Inszenierungen: Theodor Bumiller, Mannheim und der deutsche Kolonialismus um 1900* (Göttingen: Vandenhoeck & Ruprecht, 2021).

Naranch, Bradley, "Introduction: German Colonialism Made Simple", in Naranch, Bradley, and Eley, Geoff (eds.), *German Colonialism in a Global Age* (Durham, NC: Duke University Press, 2014).

Nganang, Patrice, "Autobiographies of Blackness in Germany", in Ames, Eric, Klotz, Marcia, and Wildenthal, Lora (eds.), *Germany's Colonial Pasts* (Lincoln, NE: University of Nebraska Press, 2005).

———, "Writing under Colonial Rule", in Mühlhahn, Klaus (ed.), *The Cultural Legacy of German Colonial Rule* (Berlin and Boston: De Gruyter Oldenbourg, 2017).

Nolden, Thomas, "On Colonial Spaces and Bodies: Hans Grimm's *Geschichten aus Südwestafrika*", in Friedrichsmeyer, Sara, Lennox, Sara, and Zantop, Susanne (eds.), *The Imperialist Imagination: German Colonialism and Its Legacy* (Ann Arbor, MI: University of Michigan Press, 1998).

Noyes, John K., "National Identity, Nomadism and Narration in Gustav Frenssen's *Peter Moor's Journey to Southwest Africa*", in Friedrichsmeyer, Sara, Lennox, Sara, and Zantop, Susanne (eds.), *The Imperialist Imagination: German Colonialism and Its Legacy* (Ann Arbor, MI: University of Michigan Press, 1998).

Orosz, Kenneth J., "Colonialism and the Simplification of Language: Germany's *Kolonial-Deutsch* Experiment", in Perraudin, Michael, and Zimmerer, Jürgen, with

BIBLIOGRAPHY

Heady, Katy (eds.), *German Colonialism and National Identity* (London and New York: Routledge, 2011).

Otremba, Katrin, "Stimmen der Auflehnung: Antikoloniale Haltungen in afrikanischen Petitionen an das Deutsche Reich", in Warnke, Ingo H. (ed.), *Deutsche Sprache und Kolonialismus* (Berlin and New York: De Gruyter, 2009).

Pakendorf, Gunther, "'Volk ohne Raum'", in Heyden, Ulrich van der, and Zeller, Joachim (eds.), *Kolonialismus hierzulande: Eine Spurensuche in Deutschland* (Erfurt: Sutton, 2007).

Parr, Rolf, "Koloniale Konstellationen von Heimat und Fremde: Wie Heimat und Fremde im Rückblick miteinander verschmelzen", in Bönisch, Dana, Runia, Jil, and Zehschnetzler, Hanna (eds.), *Heimat Revisited: Kulturwissenschaftliche Perspektiven auf einen umstrittenen Begriff* (Berlin and Boston: De Gruyter, 2020).

Parzinger, Hermann, "Von Chancen und Herausforderungen: Das Humboldt Forum im neuen Berliner Schloss", in Zimmermann, Olaf, and Geissler, Theo (eds.), *Kolonialismus-Debatte: Bestandsaufnahme und Konsequenzen* (Berlin: Deutscher Kulturrat, 2019).

Pellatz, Susanne, "Abenteuer Afrika: Kolonialerziehung in der Jugendlektüre der Kaiserzeit (1871–1918)", in *Jahrbuch für Historische Bildungsforschung*, vol. 8 (Bad Heilbrunn: Verlag Julius Klinkhardt, 2002).

Pesek, Michael, "Colonial Conquest and the Struggle for the Presence of the Colonial State in German East Africa, 1885–1903", in Rockel, Stephen J., and Halpern, Rick (eds.), *Inventing Collateral Damage: Civilian Casualties, War, and Empire* (Toronto: Between the Lines, 2009).

———, "Die Grenzen des postkolonialen Staates in Deutsch-Ostafrika, 1890–1914", in Chatriot, Alain, and Gosewinkel, Dieter (eds.), *Figurationen des Staates in Deutschland und Frankreich, 1870–1945* (Munich: Oldenbourg, 2006).

Piesche, Peggy, "Black and German? East German Adolescents before 1989: A Retrospective View of a 'Non-existent Issue' in the GDR", in Adelson, Leslie A. (ed.), *The Cultural After-life of East Germany: New Transnational Perspectives* (Washington, DC: American Institute for Contemporary German Studies, 2002)

———, "Identität und Wahrnehmung in literarischen Texten Schwarzer deutscher Autorinnen der 90er Jahre", in Gelbin, Cathy S., Konuk, Kader, and Piesche, Peggy (eds.), *Aufbrüche: Kulturelle Produktionen von Migrantinnen, Schwarzen und jüdischen Frauen in Deutschland* (Königstein: Helmer, 1999).

Platt, Kristin, "Gewalt, Trauma und Erinnerung: Zum Umgang mit Völkermord", in Melber, Henning, and Platt, Kristin (eds.), *Koloniale Vergangenheit—postkoloniale Zukunft? Die deutsch-namibischen Beziehungen neu denken* (Frankfurt/Main: Brandes & Apsel, 2022).

Polenz, Ruprecht, "Noch ein weiter Weg bis zur Aussöhnung", in Melber, Henning, and Platt, Kristin (eds.), *Koloniale Vergangenheit—postkoloniale Zukunft? Die deutsch-namibischen Beziehungen neu denken* (Frankfurt/Main: Brandes & Apsel, 2022).

Roller, Kathrin, "'Wir sind Deutsche, wir sind Weiße und wollen Weiße bleiben': Reichstagsdebatten über koloniale 'Rassenmischung'", in Heyden, Ulrich van der, and Zeller, Joachim (eds.), *Kolonialmetropole Berlin: Eine Spurensuche* (Berlin: Berlin Edition, 2002).

BIBLIOGRAPHY

Rosenhaft, Eve, and Aitken, Robbie, "Martin Dibobe", in Heyden, Ulrich van der (ed.), *Unbekannte Biographien: Afrikaner im deutschsprachigen Europa vom 18. Jahrhundert bis zum Ende des Zweiten Weltkrieges* (Berlin: Kai Homilius, 2008).

Roth, Karl Heinz, "Zwangsarbeit und Kolonialismus: Das Beispiel Deutschland", in Höfer, Bruni, Dietrich, Heinz, and Meyer, Klaus (eds.), *Das Fünfhundertjährige Reich: Emanzipation und lateinamerikanische Identität* (Frankfurt/Main: Medico International, 1990).

Rüger, Adolf, "Das Streben nach kolonialer Restitution in den ersten Nachkriegsjahren", in Stoecker, Helmuth (ed.), *Drang nach Afrika: Die deutsche koloniale Expansionspolitik und Herrschaft in Afrika von den Anfängen bis zum Verlust der Kolonien* (Berlin: Akademie-Verlag, 2nd rev. edn, 1991).

———, "Die Duala und die Kolonialmacht, 1884–1914: Eine Studie über die historischen Ursprünge des afrikanischen Antikolonialismus", in Stoecker, Helmuth (ed.), *Kamerun unter deutscher Kolonialherrschaft* (Berlin: Deutscher Verlag der Wissenschaften, 1968).

Sankoh, Osman A., "'Ich setze mich nicht neben einen N …': Alltagserfahrungen eines Afrikaners in Deutschland", in Böhler, Katja, and Hoeren, Jürgen, *Afrika: Mythos und Zukunft* (Freiburg im Breisgau: Herder, 2003)

Sarè, Constant Kpao, "Abuses of German Colonial History: The Character of Carl Peters as Weapon for *Völkisch* and National Socialist Discourses; Anglophobia, Anti-semitism and Aryanism", in Perraudin, Michael, and Zimmerer, Jürgen, with Heady, Katy (eds.), *German Colonialism and National Identity* (London and New York: Routledge, 2011).

Schilling, Britta, "Kolonialismus und Kalter Krieg: Unabhängigkeitsgeschenke und die materielle Politik der Erinnerung (1949–1968)", in Bechhaus-Gerst, Marianne, and Zeller, Joachim (eds.), *Deutschland postkolonial? Die Gegenwart der imperialen Vergangenheit* (Berlin: Metropol, 2018).

Schlettwein, Sylvia, "Das Schweigen der Ahnen", in Melber, Henning, and Platt, Kristin (eds.), *Koloniale Vergangenheit—postkoloniale Zukunft? Die deutsch-namibischen Beziehungen neu denken* (Frankfurt/Main: Brandes & Apsel, 2022).

Schneppen, Heinz, "Der Helgoland-Sansibar-Vertrag von 1890", in Heyden, Ulrich van der, and Zeller, Joachim (eds.), *Kolonialismus hierzulande: Eine Spurensuche in Deutschland* (Erfurt: Sutton, 2007).

Schulte-Varendorff, Uwe, "Der Erste Weltkrieg und die deutschen Kolonien in Afrika: Der Anfang vom Ende eines Kolonialtraums", in Bechhaus-Gerst, Marianne, and Zeller, Joachim (eds.), *Deutschland postkolonial? Die Gegenwart der imperialen Vergangenheit* (Berlin: Metropol, 2018).

Sebald, Peter, "'Lust' und 'List' kolonialer Erinnerung: Togo, 2005", in Hobuss, Steffi, and Lölke, Ulrich (eds.), *Erinnern verhandeln: Kolonialismus im kollektiven Gedächtnis Afrikas und Europas* (Münster: Westfälisches Dampfboot, 2006; 2nd rev. edn, 2007).

———, "Togo, 1884–1900", in Stoecker, Helmuth (ed.), *Drang nach Afrika: Die deutsche koloniale Expansionspolitik und Herrschaft in Afrika von den Anfängen bis zum Verlust der Kolonien* (Berlin: Akademie-Verlag, 2nd rev. edn, 1991).

———, "Togo, 1900–1914", in Stoecker, Helmuth (ed.), *Drang nach Afrika: Die*

BIBLIOGRAPHY

deutsche koloniale Expansionspolitik und Herrschaft in Afrika von den Anfängen bis zum Verlust der Kolonien (Berlin: Akademie-Verlag, 2nd rev. edn, 1991).

Senft, Gunter, "'Noble Savages' and the 'Islands of Love': Trobriand Islanders in 'Popular Publications'", in Wassmann, Jürg (ed.), *Pacific Answers to Western Hegemony: Cultural Practices of Identity Construction*. (London: Routledge, 1998).

Shigwedha, Vilho Amukwaya, "The Return of Herero and Nama Bones from Germany: The Victims' Struggle for Recognition and Recurring Genocide Memories in Namibia", in Dreyfus, Jean-Marc, and Anstett, Élisabeth (eds.), *Human Remains in Society: Curation and Exhibition in the Aftermath of Genocide and Mass Violence* (Manchester: Manchester University Press, 2018).

Simo, David, "Colonization and Modernization: The Legal Foundation of the Colonial Enterprise; A Case Study of German Colonization in Cameroon", in Ames, Eric, Klotz, Marcia, and Wildenthal, Lora (eds.), *Germany's Colonial Pasts* (Lincoln, NE: University of Nebraska Press, 2005).

Sippel, Harald, "'Im Interesse des Deutschtums und der weissen Rasse'": Behandlung und Rechtswirkungen von 'Rassenmischehen' in den Kolonien Deutsch-Ostafrika und Deutsch-Südwestafrika", *Jahrbuch für afrikanisches Recht*, vol. 9 (Cologne: Köppe, 1995).

———, "Quellen des deutschen Kolonialrechts", in Eckert, Andreas, and Krüger, Gesine (eds.), *Lesarten eines globalen Prozesses: Quellen und Interpretationen zur Geschichte der europäischen Expansion* (Münster: LIT, 1998).

Speitkamp, Winfried, "Kolonialdenkmäler", in Zimmerer, Jürgen (ed.), *"Kein Platz an der Sonne": Erinnerungsorte der deutschen Kolonialgeschichte* (Frankfurt/Main and New York: Campus, 2013).

Stecklum, Clara, "A Joint Understanding on the Past? Challenges and Prospects of Reconciliation between Germany and the Ovaherero and Nama from an Emotions Perspective", in Ohnesorge, Hendrik W., Heidbrink, Christiane, and Gu, Xuewu (eds.), *Mächte, Menschen und Diskurse: Neue Perspektiven auf internationale Herausforderungen*, vol. 1. emPOWER Papers (Bonn: Center for Global Studies, 2022).

Stoecker, Helmuth, "Deutsch-Ostafrika, 1885–1906", in Stoecker, Helmuth (ed.), *Drang nach Afrika: Die deutsche koloniale Expansionspolitik und Herrschaft in Afrika von den Anfängen bis zum Verlust der Kolonien* (Berlin: Akademie-Verlag, 2nd rev. edn, 1991).

———, "Deutsch-Ostafrika, 1906–1914", in Stoecker, Helmuth (ed.), *Drang nach Afrika: Die deutsche koloniale Expansionspolitik und Herrschaft in Afrika von den Anfängen bis zum Verlust der Kolonien* (Berlin: Akademie-Verlag, 2nd rev. edn, 1991).

———, "Die Annexionen von 1884/85", in Stoecker, Helmuth (ed.), *Drang nach Afrika. Die deutsche koloniale Expansionspolitik und Herrschaft in Afrika von den Anfängen bis zum Verlust der Kolonien* (Berlin: Akademie-Verlag, 2nd rev. edn, 1991).

———, "Germanophilie und Hoffnung auf Hitler in Togo und Kamerun zwischen den Weltkriegen", in Heine, Peter, and Heyden, Ulrich van der (eds.), *Studien zur Geschichte des deutschen Kolonialismus in Afrika: Festschrift zum 60. Geburtstag von Peter Sebald* (Pfaffenweiler: Centaurus, 1995).

———, "Kamerun, 1885–1906", in Stoecker, Helmuth (ed.), *Drang nach Afrika:*

BIBLIOGRAPHY

Die deutsche koloniale Expansionspolitik und Herrschaft in Afrika von den Anfängen bis zum Verlust der Kolonien (Berlin: Akademie-Verlag, 2nd rev. edn, 1991).

———, "Kamerun, 1906–1914", in Stoecker, Helmuth (ed.), *Drang nach Afrika: Die deutsche koloniale Expansionspolitik und Herrschaft in Afrika von den Anfängen bis zum Verlust der Kolonien* (Berlin: Akademie-Verlag, 2nd rev. edn, 1991).

Stoecker, Holger, "Knochen im Depot: Namibische Schädel in anthropologischen Sammlungen aus der Kolonialzeit", in Zimmerer, Jürgen (ed.), *"Kein Platz an der Sonne": Erinnerungsorte der deutschen Kolonialgeschichte* (Frankfurt/Main and New York: Campus, 2013).

———, "Lehrer, Informanten, Studienobjekte: Afrikanische Sprachlektoren im Berlin der Zwischenkriegsjahre", in Diallo, Oumar, and Zeller, Joachim (eds.), *Black Berlin: Die deutsche Metropole und ihre afrikanische Diaspora in Geschichte und Gegenwart* (Berlin: Metropol, 2013).

Struck, Wolfgang, "The Persistence of Fantasies: Colonialism as Melodrama on German Television", in Perraudin, Michael, and Zimmerer, Jürgen, with Heady, Katy (eds.), *German Colonialism and National Identity* (London and New York: Routledge, 2011).

Teitel, Rudi, "The Transitional Apology", in Barkan, Elazar, and Karn, Alexander (eds.), *Taking Wrongs Seriously: Apologies and Reconciliation* (Stanford, CA: Stanford University Press, 2006).

Thode-Arora, Hilke, "Hagenbeck: Tierpark und Völkerschau", in Zimmerer, Jürgen (ed.), *"Kein Platz an der Sonne": Erinnerungsorte der deutschen Kolonialgeschichte* (Frankfurt/Main and New York: Campus, 2013).

Timm, Uwe, "Jakob Morenga / Jacob Marengo", in Melber, Henning, and Platt, Kristin (eds.), *Koloniale Vergangenheit—postkoloniale Zukunft? Die deutsch-namibischen Beziehungen neu denken* (Frankfurt/Main: Brandes & Apsel, 2022).

Trotha, Trutz von, "'One for Kaiser': Beobachtungen zur politischen Soziologie der Prügelstrafe am Beispiel des 'Schutzgebietes Togo'", in Heine, Peter, and Heyden, Ulrich van der (eds.), *Studien zur Geschichte des deutschen Kolonialismus in Afrika: Festschrift zum 60. Geburtstag von Peter Sebald* (Pfaffenweiler: Centaurus, 1995).

Tsogang Fossi, Richard, "'Du bist wie ein Kücklein in mein Haus gekommen, Weisser …': Intermediale Erinnerung an eine transnationale Männerfreundschaft im kolonialen Kamerun", in Gouaffo, Albert, and Michels, Stefanie (eds.), *Koloniale Verbindungen—transkulturelle Erinnerungstopografien: Das Rheinland in Deutschland und das Grasland Kameruns* (Bielefeld: Transcript, 2019).

Ustorf, Werner, "Mission als Vorhut des Kolonialismus? Das Beispiel der Norddeutschen Mission", in Nestvogel, Renate, and Tetzlaff, Rainer (eds.), *Afrika und der deutsche Kolonialismus: Zivilisierung zwischen Schnapshandel und Bibelstunde* (Berlin and Hamburg: Dietrich Reimer, 1987).

Vambe, Maurice Taonezvi, "Whiteness, Power and Privilege? A Critique of a Western Account of the Herero and Nama Genocide in Horst Drechsler's *Let Us Die Fighting*", in Krishnamurthy, Sarala, Mlambo, Nelson, and Vale, Helen (eds.), *Writing Namibia: Coming of Age* (Basel: Basler Afrika Bibliographien, 2022).

Van der Westhuizen, Christi, "Apology as a Pathway out of White Unknowing", in Judge, Melanie, and Smythe, Dee (eds.), *Apologies: Critical Writings on Apology from South Africa* (Bristol: Bristol University Press, 2022).

BIBLIOGRAPHY

Van Hoesen, Brett M., "The Rhineland Controversy and Weimar Postcolonialism", in Naranch, Bradley, and Eley, Geoff (eds.), *German Colonialism in a Global Age* (Durham, NC: Duke University Press, 2014).

Vera, Antonio, "Die Kolonialpolizei als Instrument kolonialer Herrschaftssicherung in Deutsch-Südwestafrika und Togo", in Vera, Antonio (ed.), *Die Polizei im Fokus von Wissenschaft und Forschung: Polizeiwissenschaftliche Studien aus soziologischer, ökonomischer, philosophischer und historischer Perspektive* (Münster: Deutsche Hochschule der Polizei—Hochschulverlag, 2015).

Verber, Jason, "Building Up and Tearing Down the Myth of German Colonialism: Colonial *Denkmale* and *Mahnmale* after 1945", in Niven, Bill, and Paver, Chloe (eds.), *Memorialization in Germany since 1945* (Basingstoke: Palgrave Macmillan, 2010).

Volker, Craig Alan, "The Legacy of the German Language in Papua New Guinea", in Mühlhahn, Klaus (ed.), *The Cultural Legacy of German Colonial Rule* (Berlin and Boston: De Gruyter Oldenbourg, 2017).

Wendt, Reinhard, "Das Ende der deutschen Südsee", in Bechhaus-Gerst, Marianne, and Zeller, Joachim (eds.), *Deutschland postkolonial? Die Gegenwart der imperialen Vergangenheit* (Berlin: Metropol, 2018).

———, "Die Südsee", in Zimmerer, Jürgen (ed.), *"Kein Platz an der Sonne": Erinnerungsorte der deutschen Kolonialgeschichte* (Frankfurt/Main and New York: Campus, 2013).

Wiedenroth-Coulibaly, Ellen, and Zinflou, Sascha, "20 Jahre Schwarze Organisierung in Deutschland: Ein Abriss", in AntiDiskriminierungsBüro Köln and cyberNomads (eds.), *The BlackBook: Deutschlands Häutungen* (Frankfurt/Main: IKO, 2004).

Wietersheim, Erika von, "Im Schatten des Genozids: Gedanken einer deutschsprachigen Namibierin", in Melber, Henning, and Platt, Kristin (eds.), *Koloniale Vergangenheit—postkoloniale Zukunft? Die deutsch-namibischen Beziehungen neu denken* (Frankfurt/Main: Brandes & Apsel, 2022).

Wright, Marcia, "Maji Maji Prophecy and Historiography", in Anderson, David M., and Johnson, Douglas H. (eds.), *Revealing Prophets: Prophecy in East African History* (London: James Currey; Athens, OH: Ohio University Press, 1995).

Yigbe, Dotsé, "Deutsch-Togo und die Folgen", in Geiger, Wolfgang, and Melber, Henning (eds.), *Kritik des deutschen Kolonialismus: Postkoloniale Sicht auf Erinnerung und Geschichtsvermittlung* (Frankfurt/Main: Brandes & Apsel, 2021).

———, "Is Togo a Permanent Model Colony?", in Mühlhahn, Klaus (ed.), *The Cultural Legacy of German Colonial Rule* (Berlin and Boston: De Gruyter Oldenbourg, 2017).

———, "Togo: Land einer anachronistischen Germanophilie?", in Bechhaus-Gerst, Marianne, and Zeller, Joachim (eds.), *Deutschland postkolonial? Die Gegenwart der imperialen Vergangenheit* (Berlin: Metropol, 2018).

Zedelmeier, Helmut, "Das Geschäft mit dem Fremden: Völkerschauen im Kaiserreich", in Freytag, Nils, and Petzold, Dominik (eds.), *Das "lange" 19. Jahrhundert: Alte Fragen und neue Perspektiven* (Munich: Herbert Utz Verlag, 2007).

Zeller, Joachim, "Das Ende der deutschen Kolonialgeschichte: Der Einzug Lettow-Vorbecks und seiner 'Heldenschar' in Berlin", in Heyden, Ulrich van der, and

BIBLIOGRAPHY

Zeller, Joachim (eds.), *Kolonialmetropole Berlin: Eine Spurensuche* (Berlin: Berlin Edition, 2002).

———, "Genozid und Gedenken: Ein dokumentarischer Überblick", in Melber, Henning (ed.), *Genozid und Gedenken: Namibisch-deutsche Geschichte und Gegenwart* (Frankfurt/Main: Brandes & Apsel, 2015).

———, "Symbolic Politics: Notes on the Colonial German Culture of Remembrance", in Zimmerer, Jürgen, and Zeller, Joachim (eds.), *Genocide in German South-West Africa: The Colonial War of 1904–1908 and Its Aftermath* (Monmouth, UK: Merlin Press, 2008).

———, "Weg vom Vergessen? (Post)Koloniale Erinnerungskultur in Deutschland", in Melber, Henning (ed.), *Deutschland und Afrika: Anatomie eines komplexen Verhältnisses* (Frankfurt/Main: Brandes & Apsel, 2019).

———, "Weltkulturmuseum? Koloniale Schatzkammer? Das Berliner Humboldt Forum in der Krise: Plädoyer für eine radikale Ehrlichkeit", in Bechhaus-Gerst, Marianne, and Zeller, Joachim (eds.), *Deutschland postkolonial? Die Gegenwart der imperialen Vergangenheit* (Berlin: Metropol, 2018).

Zeller, Joachim, and Michels, Stefanie, "Kamerunischer Nationalheld—treuer Diener und Soldat: Mebenga m'Ebono alias Martin Paul Samba", in Heyden, Ulrich van der (ed.), *Unbekannte Biographien: Afrikaner im deutschsprachigen Raum vom 18. Jahrhundert bis zum Ende des Zweiten Weltkrieges* (Berlin: Kai Homilius, 2008)

Zimmerer, Jürgen, "The Birth of the *Ostland* out of the Spirit of Colonialism: A Postcolonial Perspective on the Nazi Policy of Conquest and Extermination", in Moses, Dirk A., and Stone, Dan (eds.), *Colonialism and Genocide* (Abingdon: Routledge, 2007).

———, "Kolonialismus und kollektive Identität: Erinnerungsorte der deutschen Kolonialgeschichte", in Zimmerer, Jürgen (ed.), *"Kein Platz an der Sonne": Erinnerungsorte der deutschen Kolonialgeschichte* (Frankfurt/Main and New York: Campus, 2013).

Zollmann, Jakob, "From Windhuk to Auschwitz: Old Wine in New Bottles?", in Hartmann, Wolfram (ed.), *Nuanced Considerations: Recent Voices in Namibian–German Colonial History* (Windhoek: Orumbonde Press, 2019).

Journal Articles

Aboudounya, Seebal, "Demanding Reparations for Colonial Genocide Using Historical Documents: Do the Herero of Namibia Have Legal Evidence to Support Their Demand for German Reparations?", *Journal of Namibian Studies*, 32 (2022), 145–163.

Adhikari, Mohamed, "'Streams of Blood and Streams of Money': New Perspectives on the Annihilation of the Herero and Nama Peoples of Namibia, 1904–1908", *Kronos*, 34, 1 (2008), 303–320.

———, "'We Will Utterly Destroy Them … and We Will Go In and Possess the Land': Reflections on the Role of Civilian-Driven Violence in the Making of Settler Genocides", *Acta Academica*, 52, 1 (2020), 142–164.

BIBLIOGRAPHY

Aikins, Joshua Kwesi, Bremberger, Teresa, Gyamerah, Daniel, and Aikins, Muna AnNisa, "Afrozensus: Intersektionale Analysen zu Anti-Schwarzem Rassismus in Deutschland", *Aus Politik und Zeitgeschichte*, 72, 12 (2022), 26–34.

Aitken, Robbie, "Black Germany: Zur Entstehung einer schwarzen Community in Deutschland", *Aus Politik und Zeitgeschichte*, 72, 12 (2022), 4–10.

———, "From Cameroon to Germany and Back via Moscow and Paris: The Political Career of Joseph Bilé (1892–1959), Performer, 'Negerarbeiter' and Comintern Activist", *Journal of Contemporary History*, 43, 4 (2008), 597–616.

———, "A Transient Presence: Black Visitors and Sojourners in Imperial Germany, 1884–1914", *Immigrants and Minorities*, 34, 3 (2016), 233–255.

Akinola, G. A., "The East African Coastal Rising, 1888–1890", *Journal of the Historical Society of Nigeria*, 7, 4 (1975), 609–630.

Albrecht, Monika, "Negotiating Memories of German Colonialism: Reflections on Current Forms of Non-governmental Memory Politics", *Journal of European Studies*, 47, 2 (2017), 203–218.

Alexander, Neville E., "Jakob Marengo and Namibian History", *Social Dynamics: A Journal of African Studies*, 7, 1 (1981), 1–7.

Anderson, Rachel, "Redressing Colonial Genocide under International Law: The Hereros' Cause of Action against Germany", *California Law Review*, 93, 4 (2005), 1155–1189.

Apoh, Wazi, and Mehler, Andreas, "Das Humboldt Forum und die Restitutionsdebatte", *WeltTrends*, 29, 179 (2021), 54–58.

Arnauld, Andreas von, "How to Illegalize Past Injustice: Reinterpreting the Rules of Intertemporality", *European Journal of International Law*, 32, 2 (2021), 401–432.

Attia, Iman, and Rothberg, Michael, "Multidirectional Memory and *Verwobene Geschichte(n)* [Entangled Histories]", *Transit*, 12, 1 (2019), 46–54.

Austen, Ralph A., "Duala versus Germans in Cameroon: Economic Dimensions of a Political Conflict", *Revue francais d'histoire d'outre-mer*, 64, 237 (1977), 477–497.

———, "The Metamorphoses of Middlemen: The Duala, Europeans, and the Cameroon Hinterland, ca. 1800—ca. 1960", *International Journal of African Historical Studies*, 16, 1 (1983), 1–24.

———, "Tradition, Invention and History: The Case of the Ngondo (Cameroon)", *Cahiers d'études africaines*, 32, 2 (1992), 285–309.

Bach, Jonathan, "Brand of Brothers? The Humboldt Forum and the Myths of Innocence", *German Politics and Society*, 39, 135 (2021), 100–111.

Bachmann, Klaus, and Kemp, Gerhard, "Was Quashing the Maji-Maji Uprising Genocide? An Evaluation of Germany's Conduct through the Lens of International Criminal Law", *Holocaust and Genocide Studies*, 35, 2 (2021), 235–249.

Bade, Klaus J., "Antisklavereibewegung in Deutschland und Kolonialkrieg in Deutsch-Ostafrika, 1888–1890: Bismarck und Friedrich Fabri", *Geschichte und Gesellschaft*, 3, 1 (1977), 31–58.

———, "Der Traum vom 'Export der sozialen Frage' durch imperiale Expansion und koloniale Auswanderung: Der Fall Friedrich Fabri", *Historical Social Research*, Supplement 30 (2018 [1975/2005]), 95–114.

BIBLIOGRAPHY

Bajohr, Frank, and O'Sullivan, Rachel, "Holocaust, Kolonialismus und NS-Imperialismus: Forschung im Schatten einer polemischen Debatte", *Vierteljahreshefte für Zeitgeschichte*, 70, 1 (2022), 191–202.

Bang, Henry Ngenyam, and Balgah, Roland Azibo, "The Ramification of Cameroon's Anglophone Crisis: Conceptual Analysis of a Looming 'Complex Disaster Emergency'", *Journal of International Humanitarian Action*, 7, 1 (2022) 6, https://doi.org/10.1186/s41018-022-00114-1.

Bauche, Manuela, "On Overlaps, Solidarities, and Competition", *German Historical Institute London Bulletin*, 44, 2 (2022), 45–57.

———, "Race, Class or Culture? The Construction of the European in Colonial Malaria Control", *Comparativ*, 25, 5/6 (2015), 116–136.

Baumgart, Winfried, "Die deutsche Kolonialherrschaft in Afrika: Neue Wege der Forschung", *Vierteljahrschrift für Sozial- und Wirtschaftsgeschichte*, 58, 4 (1971), 468–481.

Becker, Heike, "Writing Genocide: Fiction, Biography and Oral History of the German Colonial Genocide in Namibia, 1904–1908", *Matatu: Journal for African Culture and Society*, 50, 2 (2018), 361–395.

Beckvold, Christopher H., "The Namibian War: Challenges to the Anglo-German Relationship in Southern Africa", *Southern Journal for Contemporary History*, 46, 1 (2021), 159–182.

Bentley, Tom, "Colonial Apologies and the Problem of the Transgressor Speaking", *Third World Quarterly*, 39, 3 (2018), 399–417.

———, "The Negotiated Apology: 'Double Ventriloquism' in Addressing Historical Wrongs", *Global Studies Quarterly*, 2, 4 (2022), 1–11, https://doi.org/10.1093/isagsq/ksac056.

———, "The Sorrow of Empire: Rituals of Legitimation and the Performative Contradictions of Liberalism", *Review of International Studies*, 41, 3 (2015), 623–645.

Berat, Lynn, "Genocide: The Namibian Case against Germany", *Peace International Law Review*, 5, 1 (1993), 165–210.

Björkdahl, Annika, and Kappler, Stefanie, "The Creation of Transnational Memory Spaces: Professionalization and Commercialization", *International Journal of Politics, Culture, and Society*, 32, 3 (2019), 383–401.

Blackler, Adam A., "From Boondoggle to Settlement Colony: Hendrik Witbooi and the Evolution of Germany's Imperial Project in Southwest Africa, 1884–1894", *Central European History*, 50, 4 (2017), 449–470.

Boehme, Franziska, "Reactive Remembrance: The Political Struggle over Apologies and Reparations between Germany and Namibia for the Herero Genocide", *Journal of Human Rights*, 19, 2 (2020), 238–255.

Brandon, Pepjin, and Sarkar, Aditya, "Labour History and the Case against Colonialism", *International Review of Social History*, 64, 1 (2019), 73–109.

Braun, Frank X., "Gustav Frenssen in Retrospect", *Monatshefte*, 39, 7 (1947), 449–462.

Brehl, Medardus, "Figures of Disintegration: 'Half-castes' and 'Frontiersmen' in German Colonial Literature on South West Africa", *Journal of Namibian Studies*, 12 (2012), 7–27.

BIBLIOGRAPHY

———, "Vernichtung als Arbeit an der Kultur: Kolonialdiskurs, kulturelles Wissen und der Völkermord an den Herero", *Zeitschrift für Genozidforschung*, 2, 2 (2000), 8–28.

Brockmeyer, Bettina, Edward, Frank, and Stoecker, Holger, "The Mkwawa Complex: A Tanzanian–European History about Provenance, Restitution and Politics", *Journal of Modern European History*, 18, 2 (2020), 117–139.

Brusius, Mirjam Sarah, "Memory Cultures 2.0: From *Opferkonkurrenz* to Solidarity: Introduction", *German Historical Institute London Bulletin*, 44, 2 (2022), 3–20.

Bucher, Jesse, "The Skull of Mkwawa and the Politics of Indirect Rule in Tanganyika", *Journal of Eastern African Studies*, 10, 2 (2016), 284–302.

Bürger, Christiane, and Rausch, Sahra, "Ein 'vergessener' Völkermord? Der Begriff der 'kolonialen Amnesie' als erinnerungspolitisches Instrument in der Auseinandersetzung mit dem Genozid an den OvaHerero und Nama: Konjunktur, Funktionen und Grenzen", *Zeitschrift für Genozidforschung*, 20, 2 (2022), 267–289.

Campbell, I. C., "Resistance and Colonial Government: A Comparative Study of Samoa", *Journal of Pacific History*, 40, 1 (2005), 45–69.

Campt, Tina M., "Converging Spectres of an Other Within: Race and Gender in Prewar Afro-German History", *Callaloo*, 26, 2 (2003), 322–341.

Carsten, Francis L., "'Volk ohne Raum'", *Journal of Contemporary History*, 2, 2 (1967), 221–227.

Conrad, Sebastian, "Colonizing the Nineteenth Century", *Central European History*, 51, 4 (2018), 674–678.

———, "German Colonial History: New Trends and Perspectives", *Mondo Contemporaneo: Rivista di Storia*, 3, 3 (2007), 105–115.

———, "Rückkehr des Verdrängten? Erinnerung an den Kolonialismus in Deutschland, 1919–2019", *Aus Politik und Zeitgeschichte*, 69, 40/41 (2019), 28–33.

Conze, Eckart, "Erinnerungskulturelle Rechtswende: 150 Jahre 1871 und der Deutungskampf ums Kaiserreich", *Blätter für deutsche und internationale Politik*, 12 (2021), 85–95.

Cooper, Allan D., "The Institutionalization of Contract Labour in Namibia", *Journal of Southern African Studies*, 25, 1 (1999), 121–138.

———, "Reparations for the Herero Genocide: Defining the Limits of International Litigation", *African Affairs*, 106, 422 (2006), 113–126.

Dedering, Tilman, "Compounds, Camps, Colonialism", *Journal of Namibian Studies*, 12 (2012), 29–46.

———, "Hendrik Witbooi, the Prophet", *Kleio*, 25, 1 (1993), 54–78.

De Juan, Alexander, "Extraction and Violent Resistance in the Early Phases of State Building: Quantitative Evidence from the 'Maji Maji' Rebellion, 1905–1907", *Comparative Political Studies*, 49, 3 (2016), 291–323.

Derrick, Jonathan, "The 'Germanophone' Elite of Douala under the French Mandate", *Journal of African History*, 21 (1980), 255–267.

Diduk, Susan, "European Alcohol, History, and the State in Cameroon", *African Studies Review*, 36, 1 (1993), 1–42.

BIBLIOGRAPHY

Doyle, Jonathan J., "A Bitter Inheritance: East German Real Property and the Supreme Constitutional Court's 'Land Reform' Decision of April 23, 1991", *Michigan Journal of International Law*, 18 (1992), 832–864.

Du Pisani, André, "Gerechtigkeit und Fairness in Verhandlungen: Völkermord und Reparationen", *Peripherie*, 41, 162/163 (2021), 328–341.

Eckart, Wolfgang U., "The Colony as Laboratory: German Sleeping Sickness Campaigns in German East Africa and in Togo, 1900–1914", *History and Philosophy of the Life Sciences*, 24, 1 (2002), 69–89.

Eckl, Andreas, and Häussler, Matthias, "Narratives of Genocide: Lothar von Trotha's Written and Photographic Legacy; A Critical Edition in Preparation", *Journal of Namibian Studies*, 28 (2020), 93–102.

Eiser, Isabel, "Ikone einer Debatte: Eine Rezeptionsgeschichte der 'Benin-Bronzen'", *Aus Politik und Zeitgeschichte*, 71, 32–33 (2021), 34–39.

Elder, Tanya, "What You See before Your Eyes: Documenting Raphael Lemkin's Life by Exploring His Archival Papers, 1900–1959", *Journal of Genocide Research*, 7, 4 (2005), 469–499.

Elias, T.O., "The Doctrine of Intertemporal Law", *American Journal of International Law*, 74, 2 (1980), 285–307.

Elsner, Jás, and Brusius, Mirjam Sarah, "Memory Cultures 2.0 and Museums", *German Historical Institute London Bulletin*, 44, 2 (2022), 99–111.

El-Tayeb, Fatima, "The Universal Museum: How the New Germany Built Its Future on Colonial Amnesia", *Nka: Journal of Contemporary African Art*, 46 (2020), 72–82.

Epstein, Klaus, "Erzberger and the German Colonial Scandals, 1905–1910", *English Historical Review*, 74, 293 (1959), 637–663.

Erckenbrecht, Corinna, "Die wissenschaftliche Aufarbeitung der deutschen Kolonialzeit in der Südsee: Kritische Bemerklungen zum Handbuch 'Die deutsche Südsee, 1884–1914'", *Anthropos*, 97, 1 (2002), 163–179.

Escalona, Victor Maria, "Mangi Meli: Rufe aus dem Depot", *iz3w*, 390 (2022), 41–42.

Eyoum, Jean-Pierre Félix, Michels, Stefanie, and Zeller, Joachim, "Bonamanga: Eine kosmopolitische Familiengeschichte", *Mont Cameroun: Afrikanische Zeitschrift für interkulturelle Studien zum deutschsprachigen Raum*, 2 (2005), 11–48.

Fitzpatrick, Matthew P., "Colonialism, Postcolonialism, and Decolonization", *Central European History*, 51 (2018), 83–89.

———, "Indigenous Australians and German Anthropology in the Era of 'Decolonization'", *Historical Journal*, 63, 3 (2020), 686–709.

———, "The Pre-history of the Holocaust? The Sonderweg and Historikerstreit Debates and the Abject Colonial Past", *Central European History*, 41, 3 (2008), 477–503.

———, "'Renegade' Resistance and Colonial Rule in German Samoa", *Journal of Pacific History*, 58, 4 (2023), 325–347.

Förster, Larissa, Henrichsen, Dag, Stoecker, Holger, and ǁEichab, Hans Axas, "Re-individualising Human Remains from Namibia: Colonialism, Grave Robbery and Intellectual History", *Human Remains and Violence*, 4, 2 (2018), 45–66.

Garsha, Jeremiah J., "Expanding *Vergangenheitsbewältigung*? German Repatriation of

BIBLIOGRAPHY

Colonial Artefacts and Human Remains", *Journal of Genocide Research*, 22, 1 (2020), 46–61.

Gewald, Jan-Bart, "Colonial Warfare: Hehe and World War I, the Wars besides Maji Maji in South-Western Tanzania", *African Historical Review*, 40, 2 (2008), 1–27.

———, "The Great General of the Kaiser", *Botswana Notes and Records*, 26 (1994), 67–76.

———"'I Was Afraid of Samuel, Therefore I Came to Sekgoma': Herero Refugees and Patronage Politics in Ngamiland, Bechuanaland Protectorate, 1890–1914", *Journal of African History*, 43, 2 (2002), 211–234.

———, "Mbadamassi of Lagos: A Soldier for King and Kaiser, and a Deportee to German South West Africa", *African Diaspora*, 2 (2009), 103–124.

Gilley, Bruce, "The Case for Colonialism: A Response to My Critics", *Acad. Quest*, 35, 1 (2022), 89–126.

Gordon, Robert, "Hiding in Full View: The 'Forgotten' Bushman Genocides in Namibia", *Genocide Studies and Prevention*, 4, 1 (2009), 29–57.

Greenstein, Elijah, "Making History: Historical Narratives of the Maji Maji", *Penn History Review*, 12, 2 (2010), 60–77.

Greiner, Andreas, "Colonial Schemes and African Realities: Vernacular Infrastructure and the Limits of Road Building in German East Africa", *Journal of African History*, 63, 3 (2022), 328–347.

Groeneveld, Sabina, "Far Away at Home in Qingdao (1897–1914)", *German Studies Review*, 39, 1 (2016), 65–79.

Häberlein, Mark, "Kaufleute, Höflinge und Humanisten: Die Augsburger Welser-Gesellschaft und die Eliten des Habsburgerreiches in der ersten Hälfte des 16. Jahrhunderts", *Zeitschrift für Historische Forschung*, 43, 4 (2016), 667–702.

Habermas, Rebekka, "Der Kolonialskandal Atakpame: Eine Mikrogeschichte des Globalen", *Historische Anthropologie*, 17, 3 (2013), 295–319.

———, "Restitutionsdebatten, koloniale Aphasie und die Frage, was Europa ausmacht", *Aus Politik und Zeitgeschichte*, 69, 40/41 (2019), 17–22.

Hahmann, Andree, "Rassismus in der Klassischen Deutschen Philosophie?", *Deutsche Zeitschrift für Philosophie*, 70, 4 (2022), 641–662.

Hamann, Raja-Léon, and Schubert, Jan Daniel, "Zwischen anti-imperialistischem Anspruch und politischer Wirklichkeit: Die Reproduktion kolonialrassistischer Strukturen in dem Amo-Forschungsprojekt der 1960er Jahre und der Statue 'Freies Afrika' in Halle a.d. Saale", *Peripherie: Politik Ökonomie Kultur*, 165/166 (2022), 129–153.

Hammen, Horst, "Kolonialrecht und Kolonialgerichtsbarkeit in den deutschen Schutzgebieten: Ein Überblick", *Verfassung und Recht in Übersee*, 32, 2 (1999), 191–209.

Hamrick, Ellie, and Duschinski, Haley, "Enduring Injustice: Memory Politics and Namibia's Genocide Reparations Movement", *Memory Studies*, 11, 4 (2018), 437–454.

Hanschmann, Felix, "Die Suspendierung des Konstitutionalismus im Herz der Finsternis: Recht, Rechtswissenschaft und koloniale Expansion des Deutschen Reiches", *Kritische Justiz*, 45, 2 (2012), 144–162.

BIBLIOGRAPHY

Harring, Sidney L., "German Reparations to the Herero Nation: An Assertion of Herero Nationhood in the Path of Namibian Development?", *West Virginia Law Review*, 104 (2002), 393–417.

Häussler, Matthias, "From Destruction to Extermination: Genocidal Escalation in Germany's War against the Herero, 1904", *Journal of Namibian Studies*, 10 (2011), 55–81.

Häussler, Matthias, and Trotha, Trutz von, "Brutalisierung 'von unten': Kleiner Krieg, Entgrenzung der Gewalt und Genozid im kolonialen Deutsch-Südwestafrika", *Mittelweg*, 36, 2 (2012), 57–89.

Henrichsen, Dag, "Demands for Restitution: A Recent Phenomenon? Early Histories of Human Remains Violations in Namibia", *Contemporary Journal of African Studies*, 7, 1 (2020), 38–46.

Heyden, Ulrich van der, "Wider den Kolonialismus! Antikoloniale Haltungen in der deutschen Geschichte von Mitte der 1880er-Jahre bis zum Beginn der 1930er-Jahre: Ein Überblick", *Zeitschrift für Religions- und Geistesgeschichte*, 70, 3 (2018), 224–253.

Hillebrecht, Werner, "'Certain Uncertainties' or Venturing Progressively into Colonial Apologetics?", *Journal of Namibian Studies*, 1 (2007), 73–95.

Hudson, Nicholas, "'Hottentots' and the Evolution of European Racism", *Journal of European Studies*, 34, 4 (2004), 308–332.

Hüsgen, Jan, "Colonial Expeditions and Collecting: The Context of the 'Togo-Hinterland Expedition' of 1894–1895", *Journal for Art Market Studies*, 4, 1 (2020), https://www.fokum-jams.org/index.php/jams/article/view/100/184.

Huttenbach, Henry R., "From the Editor: Genocide in a Global Context; The Next Assignment", *Journal of Genocide Research*, 5, 1 (2003), 5–7.

———, "Locating the Holocaust on the Genocide Spectrum: Towards a Methodology of Categorization", *Holocaust and Genocide*, 3, 3 (1988), 289–303.

Hyslop, Jonathan, "The Kaiser's Lost African Empire and the Alternative für Deutschland: Colonial Guilt-Denial and Authoritarian Populism in Germany", *Historia*, 66, 2 (2021), 101–124.

Iliffe, John, "The Organization of the Maji Maji Rebellion", *Journal of African History*, 8, 3 (1967), 495–512.

Imani, Sarah, and Theurer, Karina, "Reparationen für Kolonialverbrechen: Die ambivalente Rolle des Rechts am Beispiel der Verhandlungen zwischen Deutschland und Namibia", *Zeitschrift für Friedens- und Konfliktforschung*, 11, 2 (2022), 209–227.

Kachim, Joseph Udimal, "African Resistance to Colonial Conquest: The Case of the Konkomba Resistance to German Occupation of Northern Togoland, 1896–1901", *Asian Journal of Humanities and Social Studies*, 1, 3 (2013), https://ir.ucc.edu.gh/xmlui/handle/123456789/6756.

Kah, Henry Kam, and Kengo, Emmanuel E., "Coercion and Violence in German Labour Conscription in Cameroon, 1880s–1914", *Brazilian Journal of African Studies*, 7, 14 (2022), 11–30.

Kamissek, Christoph, and Kreienbaum, Jonas, "An Imperial Cloud? Conceptualising Interimperial Connections and Transimperial Knowledge", *Journal of Modern European History*, 14, 2 (2016), 164–182.

BIBLIOGRAPHY

Khan, Khatija Bibi, "The Kaiser's Holocaust: The Coloniality of German's Forgotten Genocide of the Nama and Herero of Namibia", *African Identities*, 10, 3 (2012), 211–220.

Kössler, Reinhart, "Die ausstehende Entschuldigung: Zum Umgang des offiziellen Deutschland mit dem Völkermord in Deutsch-Südwestafrika (Namibia), 1904–1908", *KonfliktDynamik*, 12, 3 (2023), 203–211.

———, "Diversity in the Postcolonial State: The Case of the Return of Looted Heirlooms from Germany to Namibia in 2019", *Nuovi Autoritarismi e Demokrazie: Dritto, Instituzioni, Societa*, 1, 2 (2019), 109–124.

———, "From Genocide to Holocaust? Structural Parallels and Discourse Continuities", *Afrika Spectrum*, 40, 2 (2005), 309–317.

———, "Imperial Skulduggery, Science and the Issue of Provenance and Restitution: The Fate of Namibian Skulls in the Alexander Ecker Collection in Freiburg", *Human Remains and Violence*, 4, 2 (2018), 27–44.

———, "'Sjambok or Cane?' Reading the Blue Book", *Journal of Southern African Studies*, 30, 3 (2004), 703–708.

———, "Two Modes of Amnesia: Complexity in Postcolonial Namibia", *Acta Academica*, 47, 1 (2015), 138–160.

Kpao Sarè, Constant, "Carl Peters and the German East Africa: Between Myth, Colonial Literature, and Prussianism", *Vingtième siècle: Revue d'histoire*, 94, 2 (2007), 149–165.

Krautwald, Fabian, "Genocide and the Politics of Memory in the Decolonisation of Namibia", *Journal of Southern African Studies*, 48, (2022), https://doi.org/10.1080/03057070.2022.2127587.

Kreienbaum, Jonas, "Der Hererokrieg und die Genozidfrage: Ein Überblick über die neueren Forschungen", *Zeitschrift für Genozidforschung*, 20, 2 (2022), 254–266.

———, "Guerilla Wars and Colonial Concentration Camps: The Exceptional Case of German South West Africa (1904–1908)", *Journal of Namibian Studies*, 11 (2012), 83–101.

Krell, David Farrell, "The Bodies of Black Folk: From Kant and Hegel to Du Bois and Baldwin", *Boundary 2*, 27, 3 (2000), 103–134.

Kriel, Lie, "Heimat in the *Veld*? German Afrikaners of Missionary Descent and Their Imaginings of Women and Home", *Geschichte und Gesellschaft*, 41, 2 (2015), 228–256.

Krishnamurthy, Sarala, "Untold Tales and Occluded Histories: Jasper Utley's *The Lie of the Land* as an Illustrative Nama Genocide Narrative", *Matatu: Journal for African Culture and Society*, 50, 2 (2018), 396–406.

Kühne, Thomas, "Colonialism and the Holocaust: Continuities, Causations, and Complexities", *Journal of Genocide Research*, 15, 3 (2013), 339–362.

Kundrus, Birthe, "From the Herero to the Holocaust? Some Remarks on the Current Debate", *Afrika Spectrum*, 40, 2 (2005), 299–308.

Kupka, Mahret Ifeoma, "Schwarze Körper in weißen Kunsträumen", *Aus Politik und Zeitgeschichte*, 72, 12 (2022), 35–41.

Laumann, Dennis, "A Historiography of German Togoland, or the Rise and Fall of a 'Model Colony'", *History in Africa*, 30 (2003), 195–211.

BIBLIOGRAPHY

Leanza, Matthias, "Colonial Trajectories: On the Evolution of the German Protectorate of Southwest Africa", *Comparativ*, 30, 3/4 (2020), 372–386.

Lederer, Klaus, "Wie viel Blut klebt an der Kunst? Von der Dekolonisierung der Museen zur Dekolonisierung der Politik", *Blätter für deutsche und internationale Politik*, 64, 1 (2019), 111–119.

Legg, Harry, "A Plea for Commemorative Equality: The Holocaust, Factual Specificity, and Commemorative Prioritisation", *Journal of Genocide Research* (2022), DOI: 10.1080/14623528.2022.2159737.

Lemkin, Raphael, "Genocide", *American Scholar*, 15, 2 (1946), 227–230.

———, "Genocide: A Modern Crime", *Free World*, 4 (1945), 39–43.

———, "Genocide as a Crime under International Law", *American Journal of International Law*, 41, 1 (1947), 145–151.

Liu, Kwang-Chjing, "Imperialism and the Chinese Peasants: The Background of the Boxer Uprising", *Modern China*, 15, 1 (1989), 102–116.

Loimeier, Manfred, "'Selten eine gute Figur': Belletristische Literatur über die Deutschen und ihren Kolonialismus in Afrika", *iz3w*, 277 (2004), 44–46.

Lorenz, Oliver, "Die Ausstellung 'Das Sowjetparadies': Nationalsozialistische Propaganda und kolonialer Diskurs", *Revue d'Allemagne et des pays de langue allemande*, 48, 1 (2016), 121–139.

Lowry, John S., "African Resistance and Center Party Recalcitrance in the Reichstag Colonial Debates of 1905–06", *Central European History*, 39, 2 (2006), 244–269.

Lyon, William Blakemore, "From Labour Elites to Garveyites: West African Migrant Labour in Namibia, 1892–1925", *Journal of Southern African Studies*, 47, 1 (2021), 37–55.

Madley, Benjamin, "From Africa to Auschwitz: How German South West Africa Incubated Ideas and Methods Adopted and Developed by the Nazis in Eastern Europe", *European History Quarterly*, 35 (2005), 429–464.

———, "Patterns of Frontier Genocide, 1803–1910", *Journal of Genocide Research*, 6, 2 (2004), 167–192.

Maitz, Peter, and Volker, Craig Allan, "Documenting Unserdeutsch: Reversing Colonial Amnesia", *Journal of Pidgin and Creole Languages*, 32, 2 (2017), 365–397.

———, "Language Contact in the German Colonies: Introduction", in Maitz, Peter, and Volker, Craig Allan (eds.), *Language Contact in the German Colonies: Papua New Guinea and Beyond*. Special Issue 2017 of *Language and Linguistics in Melanesia: Journal of the Linguistic Society of Papua New Guinea*, 1–8.

——— (eds.), *Language Contact in the German Colonies: Papua New Guinea and Beyond*. Special Issue 2017 of *Language and Linguistics in Melanesia: Journal of the Linguistic Society of Papua New Guinea*.

Mangold, Ijoma, "Die Renaissance der Hautfarbe", *Aus Politik und Zeitgeschichte*, 72, 12 (2022), 42–46.

Manshard, Walter, "Deutsche Afrika-Gesellschaft", *Journal of Modern African Studies*, 3, 4 (1965), 607–608.

Martinez Mateo, Marina, and Stubenrauch, Heiko, "'Rasse' und Naturteleologie bei Kant: Zum Rassismusproblem der Vernunft", *Deutsche Zeitschrift für Philosophie*, 70, 4 (2022), 619–640.

BIBLIOGRAPHY

Masson, J. R., "A Fragment of Colonial History: The Killing of Jakob Marengo", *Journal of Southern African Studies*, 21, 2 (1995), 247–256.

Melber, Henning, "Colonialism, Land, Ethnicity and Class: Namibia after the Second National Land Conference", *Africa Spectrum*, 54, 1 (2019), 73–86.

———, "How to Come to Terms with the Past: Revisiting the German Colonial Genocide in Namibia", *Afrika Spectrum*, 40, 1 (2005), 139–148.

———, "Mission, Kolonialismus, Kultur und Entwicklung: Die Reise von Missionsinspektor Spiecker durch Deutsch-Südwestafrika (1905–1907)", *Stichproben: Vienna Journal of African Studies*, 14, 26 (2014), 167–176.

———, "One Namibia, One Nation? The Caprivi as a Contested Territory", *Journal of Contemporary African Studies*, 27, 4 (2009), 463–481.

Menger, Tom, "'Press the Thumb onto the Eye': Moral Effect, Extreme Violence and the Transimperial Notions of British, German, and Dutch Colonial Warfare, ca. 1890–1914", *Itinerario*, 46, 1 (2022), 84–108.

Michels, Eckhard, "Geschichtspolitik im Fernsehen: Die WDR-Dokumentation 'Heia Safari' von 1966–67 über Deutschlands Kolonialvergangenheit", *Vierteljahrshefte für Zeitgeschichte*, 56, 3 (2008), 467–492.

Mieder, Wolfgang, "'Black Is Beautiful': Hans-Jürgen Massaquoi's Proverbial Autobiography *Destined to Witness* (1999)", *Proverbium*, 39 (2022), 173–223.

Monson, Jamie, "Relocating Maji Maji: The Politics of Alliance and Authority in the Southern Highlands of Tanzania, 1870–1918", *Journal of African History*, 39, 1 (1998), 95–120.

Montenegro, Giovanna, "'The Welser Phantom': Apparitions of the Welser Venezuela Colony in Nineteenth- and Twentieth-Century German Cultural Memory", *Transit*, 11, 2 (2018), 21–53.

Moorsom, Richard, "Migrant Workers and the Formation of SWANLA, 1900–1926", *South African Labour Bulletin*, 4, 1/2 (1978), 107–115.

Moses, John A., "The Solf Regime in Western Samoa: Ideal and Reality", *New Zealand Journal of History*, 6, 1 (1972), 42–56.

Moyle, Richard, "'We Are Like Someone Completely Dead and Lack a Father, Your Excellency': Bandsmen Sucking Up and Blowing Out in German Samoa", *World of Music*, 8, 2 (2019), 13–26.

Naranch, Bradley D., "'Colonized Body', 'Oriental Machine': Debating Race, Railroads, and the Politics of Reconstruction in Germany and East Africa, 1906–1910", *Central European History*, 33, 3 (2000), 299–338.

Nenguié, Pierre Kodjio, "Interkulturalität, Modernisierung und Nachhaltigkeit: Eine postkoloniale Lektüre von Hans Paasches Werk", *Monatshefte*, 103, 1 (2011), 36–59.

Nowak, Kai, "Der Schock der Authentizität: Der Filmskandal um *Africa Addio* (1966) und antikolonialer Protest in der Bundesrepublik", *Werkstatt Geschichte*, 69 (2015), 37–53.

Nyada, Germain, "Mpondo Akwa Nya Bonambela (1875–1914), or, How to Shape Colonial Amnesia", *Djiboul*, 2, 3 (2022), 386–399.

O'Sullivan, Rachel, "Colonial Concentration Camps and Transnational Knowledge Transfers", *Patterns of Prejudice*, 54, 4 (2020), 469–471.

BIBLIOGRAPHY

Özsu, Umut, "Genocide as Fact and Form", *Journal of Genocide Research*, 22, 1 (2020), 62–71.

Paasche, Karin Ilona, "Germany's Africa: A Literary and Historical Disconnect", *Procedia: Social and Behavioral Sciences*, 192 (2015), 398–407.

Pape, Elise, "Human Remains of Ovaherero and Nama: Transnational Dynamics in Post-genocidal Restitutions", *Human Remains and Violence*, 4, 2 (2018), 90–106.

Parr, Rolf, "The Relationship between Concepts of Home, Colonialism and Exoticism in the Works of Gustav Frenssen and Hans Grimm", *Journal of Namibian Studies*, 16 (2014), 61–82.

Paulose, Regina Menachery, and Rogo, Ronald Gordon, "Addressing Colonial Crimes through Reparations: The Mau Mau, Herero and Nama", *State Crime*, 7, 2 (2018), 369–388.

Pierskalla, Jan, De Juan, Alexander, and Montgomery, Max, "The Territorial Expansion of the Colonial State: Evidence from German East Africa, 1890–1909", *British Journal of Political Science*, 49, 2 (2019), 711–737.

Piwowarczyk, Darius J., "'Dangerous Liaisons': Whiteness and Private Relations between German Colonial Officials and Indigenous Women in German Togo and Their Political Consequences", *Prace Etnograficzne*, 50 (2022), 137–156.

Poiger, Uta G., "Imperialism and Empire in Twentieth-Century Germany", *History and Memory*, 17, 1/2 (2005), 117–143.

Poutrus, Patrice G., and Warda, Katharina, "Ostdeutsche of Color: Schwarze Geschichte(n) der DDR und Erfahrungen nach der deutschen Einheit", *Aus Politik und Zeitgeschichte*, 72, 12 (2022), 19–25.

Prinz, Claudia, "Hermann von Wissmann als 'Kolonialpionier'", *Peripherie*, 118/119 (2010), 315–336.

Quinn, Frederick, "Charles Atangana of Yaoundé", *Journal of African History*, 21, 4 (1980), 485–495.

Rausch, Sahra, "'We're Equal to the Jews Who Were Destroyed. [...] Compensate Us, Too': An Affective (Un)remembering of Germany's Colonial Past?", *Memory Studies*, 15, 2 (2022), 418–435.

Redmayne, Alison, "Mkwawa and the Hehe Wars", *Journal of African History*, 9, 3 (1968), 409–436.

Roos, Julia, "Die 'farbigen Besatzungskinder' der zwei Weltkriege", *Aus Politik und Zeitgeschichte*, 72, 12 (2022), 11–18.

———, "Racist Hysteria to Pragmatic Rapprochement? The German Debate about Rhenish 'Occupation Children', 1920–30", *Contemporary European History*, 22, 2 (2013), 155–180.

Roos, Ulrich, and Seidl, Timo, "Im 'Südwesten' nichts Neues? Eine Analyse der deutschen Namibiapolitik als Beitrag zur Rekonstruktion der außenpolitischen Identität des deutschen Nationalstaates", *Zeitschrift für Friedens- und Konfliktforschung*, 4, 2 (2015), 182–224.

Rothberg, Michael, "Lived Multidirectionality: '*Historikerstreit 2.0*' and the Politics of Holocaust Memory", *Memory Studies*, 15, 6 (2022), 1316–1329.

Rüger, Adolf, "Imperialismus, Sozialreformismus und antikoloniale demokratische Alternative: Zielvorstellungen von Afrikanern in Deutschland im Jahre 1919", *Zeitschrift für Geschichtswissenschaft*, 23, 11 (1975), 1293–1308.

BIBLIOGRAPHY

Rushohora, Nancy, "An Archaeological Identity of the Majimaji: Toward an Historical Archeology of Resistance to German Colonization in Southern Tanzania", *Archeologies*, 11, 2 (2015), 246–271.

———, "Desperate Mourning and Atrophied Representation: A Tale of Two Skulls", *African Historical Review*, 51, 1 (2019), 25–45.

Samudzi, Zoé, "Looting the Archive: German Genocide and Incarcerated Skulls", *Social and Health Sciences*, 19, 2 (2021), 1–21 (published online).

———, "Reparative Futurities: Thinking from the Herero and Nama Genocide", *The Funambulist*, 5, 30 (2020), 30–35.

Sarkin, Jeremy, and Fowler, Carly, "Reparations for Historical Human Rights Violations: The International and Historical Dimensions of the Alien Torts Claims Act Genocide Case of the Herero of Namibia", *Human Rights Review*, 9, 3 (2008), 331–360.

Schaller, Dominik, "Colonialism and Genocide: Raphael Lemkin's Concept of Genocide and Its Application to European Rule in Africa", *Development Dialogue*, 50 (2008), 95–123.

Schaper, Ulrike, "Law and Colonial Order: Legal Policy in German Cameroon between Civilising and Public Peace", *Comparativ*, 19, 1 (2009), 17–33.

———, "Recht und Kolonialismus: Heuristische und methodische Überlegungen zu Quellenbeständen am Beispiel der deutschen Kolonie Kamerun", *Werkstatt Geschichte*, 68 (2015), 79–95.

Schilling, Britta, "German Postcolonialism in Four Dimensions: A Historical Perspective", *Postcolonial Studies*, 18, 4 (2015), 427–439.

———, "Imperial Heirlooms: The Private Memory of Colonialism in Germany", *Journal of Imperial and Commonwealth History*, 41, 4 (2013), 663–682.

———, "Review Article: German Colonialism in Africa", *English Historical Review*, 84, 567 (2019), 390–403.

Schmidt, Heike, "(Re)negotiating Marginality: The Maji Maji War and Its Aftermath in Southwestern Tanzania, ca. 1905–1916", *International Journal of African Historical Studies*, 43, 1 (2010), 27–62.

Schnee, Heinrich, "Die koloniale Schuldlüge", *Süddeutsche Monatshefte*, 21, 4 (1924), 91–152.

Schubert, Michael, "The 'German Nation' and the 'Black Other': Social Darwinism and the Cultural Mission in German Colonial Discourse", *Patterns of Prejudice*, 45, 5 (2011), 399–416.

Schulte-Althoff, Franz-Josef, "Rassenmischung im kolonialen System: Zur deutschen Kolonialpolitik im letzten Jahrzehnt vor dem Ersten Weltkrieg", *Historisches Jahrbuch* 105 (1985), 52–94.

Schwarzer, Anke, "Das verdrängte Verbrechen: Plädoyer für eine Dekolonialisierung der Bundesrepublik", *Blätter für deutsche und internationale Politik*, 63, 6 (2018), 85–92.

Segesser, Daniel Marc, and Gessler, Myriam, "Raphael Lemkin and the International Debate on the Punishment of War Crimes (1919–1948)", *Journal of Genocide Research*, 7, 4 (2005), 453–68.

Shelton, Dinah, "The World of Atonement: Reparations for Historical Injustices", *Netherlands International Law Review*, 50, 3 (2003), 289–325.

BIBLIOGRAPHY

Shigwedha, Vilho Amukwaya, "The Homecoming of Ovaherero and Nama Skulls: Overriding Politics and Injustice", *Human Remains and Violence*, 4, 2 (2018), 67–89.

Siefkes, Martin, "Discursive Traces of Genocide in Johannes Spiecker's Travel Diary (1905–1907)", *Journal of Namibian Studies*, 16 (2014), 83–114.

Sippel, Harald, "Recht und Emotion: 'German Angst' und das Verwaltungshandeln in Deutsch-Südwestafrika", *Recht in Afrika*, 21, 2 (2018), 208–233.

Smith, Woodrow D., "The Colonial Novel as Political Propaganda: Hans Grimm's *Volk ohne Raum*", *German Studies Review*, 6, 2 (1983), 215–235.

———, "Contexts of Colonialism", *History and Theory*, 55, 2 (2016), 290–301.

Stahn, Carsten, "Reckoning with Colonial Injustice: International Law as Culprit and as Remedy?", *Leiden Journal of International Law*, 33 (2020), 823–835.

Steyn, Melissa, "The Ignorance Contract: Recollections of Apartheid Childhoods and the Construction of Epistemologies of Ignorance", *Identities*, 19, 1 (2012), 8–25.

Stoecker, Holger, and Winkelmann, Andreas, "Skulls and Skeletons from Namibia in Berlin: Results of the Charité Human Remains Project", *Human Remains and Violence*, 4, 2 (2018), 5–26.

Theurer, Karina, "Minimum Legal Standards in Reparation Processes for Colonial Crimes: The Case of Namibia and Germany", *German Law Journal*, 24, 7 (2023), 1146–1168.

Thiemeyer, Thomas, "Cosmopolitanizing Colonial Memories in Germany", *Critical Inquiry*, 45, 4 (2019), 967–990.

Thomerson, Michael J., "German Reunification: The Privatization of Socialist Property on East Germany's Path to Democracy", *Georgia Journal of International and Comparative Law*, 21 (1991), 123–143.

Tjirera, Ellison, "Land Inequality in Namibia: White Indifference, Elite Capture and Policy Inadequacies", *Namibian Journal of Social Justice*, 2 (2022), 197–203.

Tourlamain, Guy, "In Defence of the Volk: Hans Grimm's *Lippoldsberger Dichtertage* and *Völkisch* Continuity in Germany before and after the Second World War", *Oxford German Studies*, 39, 3 (2010), 228–249.

Trotha, Trutz von, "Das 'deutsche Nizza an Afrikas Westküste': Zur politischen Soziologie der kolonialen Hauptstadt am Beispiel Lomés der Jahre 1897–1914", *Sociologus*, 49, 1 (1999), 98–118.

Unangst, Matthew, "Changes in German Travel Writing about East Africa, 1884–1891", *Colloquia Germanica*, 46, 2 (2016), 266–283.

———, "Manufacturing Crisis: Anti-slavery 'Humanitarianism' and Imperialism in East Africa, 1888–1890", *Journal of Imperial and Commonwealth History*, 48, 5 (2020), 805–825.

———, "Men of Science and Action: The Celebrity of Explorers and German National Identity, 1870–1895", *Central European History*, 50, 3 (2017), 305–327.

Van der Hoog, Tycho Alexander, "Brewing Tensions: The Colonial Gaze of the German–Namibian Publishing Industry", *Africa Spectrum*, 57, 3 (2022), 264–281.

Vasel, Johann Justus, "'In the Beginning, There Was No Word …'", *European Journal of International Law*, 29, 4 (2019), 1053–1056.

BIBLIOGRAPHY

Volk, Sabine, "Patriotic History in Postcolonial Germany, Thirty Years after 'Reunification'", *Journal of Genocide Research*, 24, 2 (2022), 276–287.

Wagner, Hans-Ulrich, "Volk ohne Raum: Zur Geschichte eines Schlagwortes", *Sprachwissenschaft*, 17, 1 (1992), 68–109.

Walther, Daniel J., "Sex, Race and Empire: White Male Sexuality and the 'Other' in Germany's Colonies, 1894–1914", *German Studies Review*, 33, 1 (2010), 45–71.

Weber, Heloise, and Weber, Martin, "Colonialism, Genocide and International Relations: The Namibian–German Case and Struggles for Restorative Relations", *European Journal of International Relations*, 26, S1 (2020), 91–115.

Weber, Klaus, "Deutschland, der atlantische Sklavenhandel und die Plantagenwirtschaft der Neuen Welt (15. bis 19. Jahrhundert)", *Journal of Modern European History*, 7, 1 (2009), 37–67.

Wege, Fritz, "Die Anfänge der Herausbildung einer Arbeiterklasse in Südwestafrika unter der deutschen Kolonialwirtschaft", *Jahrbuch für Wirtschaftsgeschichte*, 10, 1 (1969), 183–222.

———, "Zur sozialen Lage der Arbeiter Namibias unter der deutschen Kolonialherrschaft in den Jahren vor dem Ersten Weltkrieg", *Jahrbuch für Wirtschaftsgeschichte*, 12, 3 (1971), 201–218.

Weiskott, Eric, "Futures Past: Prophecy, Periodization, and Reinhart Koselleck", *New Literary History*, 52, 1 (2021), 169–188.

Wheatley, Steven, "Revisiting the Doctrine of Intertemporal Law", *Oxford Journal of Legal Studies*, 41, 2 (2021), 484–509.

Wildenthal, Lora, "The Places of Colonialism in the Writing and Teaching of Modern German History", *European Studies Journal*, 16, 2 (1999), 9–23.

Wilson, Paul, "Remembering the Herero–Nama Genocide in Namibia", *African Arts*, 56, 1 (2023), 62–81.

Wrigley, G. M., "The Military Campaigns against Germany's African Colonies", *Geographical Review*, 5, 1 (1918), 44–65.

Yekani, Minu Haschemi, and Schaper, Ulrike, "Pictures, Postcards, Points of Contact: New Approaches to Cultural Histories of German Colonialism", *German History*, 35, 4 (2017), 603–623.

Young, James E., "The Counter-Monument: Memory against Itself in Germany Today", *Critical Inquiry*, 18, 2 (1992), 267–296.

Zambrana, Rocio, "Schlechte Angewohnheiten: Gewohnheit, Müßiggang und Rasse bei Hegel", *Deutsche Zeitschrift für Philosophie*, 70, 4 (2022), 663–684.

Zimmerman, Andrew, "A German Alabama in Africa: The Tuskegee Expedition to German Togo and the Transnational Origins of West African Cotton Growers", *American Historical Review*, 110, 5 (2005), 1362–1398.

———, "'What Do You Really Want in German East Africa, Herr Professor?' Counterinsurgency and the Science Effect in Colonial Tanzania", *Comparative Studies in Society and History*, 48, 2 (2006), 419–461.

Zollmann, Jakob, "'Eine Frage von prinzipieller, weittragender Bedeutung für alle Zukunft': Deutsche Entschädigungsleistungen infolge des Herero-Kriegs, 1904–1914", *Zeitschrift für Genozidforschung*, 20, 2 (2022), 238–253.

Zoodsma, Marieke, and Schaafsma, Juliette, "Examining the 'Age of Apology':

BIBLIOGRAPHY

Insights from the Political Apology Database", *Journal of Peace Research*, 59, 3 (2022), 436–448.

Theses

Adu, Alexander, "Racism on and off the Football Field: Racism and the Responses to Racism in German Football from the Predigital Era to the Present". MA thesis, Uppsala University, 2022.

Böcker, Julia Franziska Maria, "'In the face of such "unspeakable truths", would it not be better to simply, silently, bow down?' Fragen juristischer, politischer und ethischer Aufarbeitung des Völkermords an den Herero und Nama". Master's thesis, University of Hamburg, 2019.

Garsha, Jeremiah J., "The Head of Chief Mkwawa and the Transnational History of Colonial Violence, 1898–2019". PhD dissertation, Wolfson College, Cambridge, 2019.

Godefridi, Isabelle, "'Schwarz sein in Deutschland': Identitätssuche in der interkulturellen Literatur aus dem deutsch-afrikanischen Kulturraum". Master's thesis, Université Catholique de Louvain, 2016–2017.

Grimshaw, Daniel, "Britain's Response to the Herero and Nama Genocide, 1904–07: A Realist Perspective on Britain's Assistance to Germany during the Genocide in German South-West Africa". Master's thesis, Uppsala University, 2014.

Joeden-Forgey, Elisa von, "Nobody's People: Colonial Subjects, Race Power and the German State, 1884–1945". PhD dissertation, University of Pennsylvania, 2004.

Kern, Michaela, "Re-thinking the Agency of Human Remains: Haunting and the Struggle for Justice in the Restitution Process of Herero and Nama Skulls in 2011". Master's thesis, Utrecht University, 2017.

Krautwald, Fabian, "Branches of Memory: Colonialism and the Making of the Historical Imagination in Namibia and Tanzania, 1914–1969". PhD dissertation, Princeton University, 2022.

LeGall, Yann (with Mnyaka Sururu Mboro, Hester J. Booysen, and Serafino Liduino), "Remembering the Dismembered: African Human Remains and Memory Cultures in and after Repatriation". PhD dissertation, University of Potsdam, 2019.

Masters, Ryan, "'The People Who Make Our Heads Spin': White Violence in German East Africa". PhD dissertation, University of Toronto, 2019.

Nandenga, Anna Ndishakena, "Reconstruction of Atrocities through Fiction in Namibia: An Evaluation of Mari Serebrov's *Mama Namibia* and Lauri Kubuitsile's *The Scattering*". MA thesis, University of Namibia, April 2019.

Pizzo, David, "'To Devour the Land of Mkwawa': Colonial Violence and the German Hehe War in East Africa c.1884–1914". PhD dissertation, University of North Carolina at Chapel Hill, 2007.

Reed-Anderson, Paulette, "Die Förderung des 'kolonialen Gedankens' durch kulturelle Akteure: Die deutsche Behörde für koloniale Angelegenheiten in Berlin während der Weimarer Republik (1919–1931)". PhD dissertation, Humboldt University, Berlin, 2019.

BIBLIOGRAPHY

Skwirblies, Lisa, "Theatres of Colonialism: Theatricality, Coloniality, and Performance in the German Empire, 1884–1914". PhD dissertation, University of Warwick, 2017.

Van Wyk, Bayron, "'Anything about Us, without Us, Is against Us': An Ethnography of the Genocide Reparations and Decolonial Movements in Namibia". MA thesis, University of the Western Cape, 2022.

Verber, Jason, "The Conundrum of Colonialism in Postwar Germany". PhD dissertation, University of Iowa, 2010.

Other Texts

Abgeordnetenhaus Berlin, Drucksache 18/2811, 26 June 2020 ("Berlin übernimmt Verantwortung für seine koloniale Vergangenheit"). https://www.parlament-berlin.de/ados/18/Kult/vorgang/k18-0196-v.pdf.

AFP, "Germany to Return Human Remains from Namibian Genocide", *Daily Maverick*, 29 August 2018. https://www.dailymaverick.co.za/article/2018-08-29-germany-to-return-human-remains-from-namibian-genocide/.

Aguigah, Elias, LeGall, Yann, and Wagne, Jeanne-Ange, "Colonial Violence in the North of Togo and the Plunder of Biema Asabiè's Belongings", Staatliche Kunstsammlungen Dresden, *Voices*, 19 January 2023. https://voices.skd.museum/en/voices-mag/colonial-violence-in-the-north-of-togo-and-the-plunder-of-biema-asabies-belongings/.

Ahrens, Peter, "Der verletzte Stolz des Adlers", *Der Spiegel*, 15 March 2021. https://www.spiegel.de/sport/fussball/amazon-doku-ueber-schwarze-fussballer-in-deutschland-der-verletzte-stolz-des-adlers-a-df1045ed-76bb-48ac-aebf-13f7ee051e0b.

Aitken, Robbie, "The Gravestone of a Cameroonian Prince (1891)", *Black Central Europe*. https://blackcentraleurope.com/sources/1850-1914/a-princes-gravestone-1891/.

Albrecht, Monika, "Review of *Postcolonial Germany: Memories of Empire in a Decolonized Nation*", (review no. 1677), *Reviews in History*, 23 October 2014. https://reviews.history.ac.uk/review/1677.

Al Jazeera, "Betrayal: Namibian Opposition MPs Slam Germany Genocide Deal", 8 June 2021. https://www.aljazeera.com/news/2021/6/8/betrayal-namibian-opposition-lawmakers-slam-germany-genocide-deal.

———, "Germany Returns 20 Benin Bronzes to Nigeria, Noting 'Dark Past'", 21 December 2022. https://www.aljazeera.com/news/2022/12/21/germany-returns-nigerian-bronzes-notes-its-dark-past.

Angula, Vitalio, "Namibian Protesters Storm Parliament, Criticize German Genocide Compensation", *VOA News*, 24 September 2021. https://www.voanews.com/a/namibian-protesters-storm-parliament-criticize-german-genocide-compensation/6244568.html.

Arp, Doris, "Zwischen den Welten: Besatzungskinder in Deutschland nach 1945", *Deutschlandfunk*, 24 October 2020. https://www.deutschlandfunkkultur.de/besatzungskinder-in-deutschland-nach-1945-zwischen-den-104.html.

BIBLIOGRAPHY

Auswärtiges Amt, "Joint Declaration on the Return of Benin Bronzes and Bilateral Museum Cooperation", Berlin, 1 July 2022. https://www.auswaertiges-amt.de/blob/2540404/8a42afe8f5d79683391f8188ee9ee016/220701-benin-bronzen-polerkl-data.pdf.

―――, "Namibia: Beziehungen zu Deutschland", 22 December 2021. https://www.auswaertiges-.amt.de/de/aussenpolitik/laender/namibia-node/bilateral/208320.

Axster, Felix, "Männlichkeit als Groteske. Koloniale (Un-)Ordnung auf Bildpostkarten um 1900", *Themenportal Europäische Geschichte*, 2017. https://www.europa.clio-online.de/Portals/_Europa/documents/B2017/E_Axster_Kolonialpostkarten.pdf.

Bachmann, Klaus, and Kemp, Gerhard, "300,000 Tanzanians Were Killed by Germany during the Maji-Maji Uprising: It Was Genocide and Should Be Called That", *The Conversation*, 17 November 2023. https://theconversation.com/300000-tanzanians-were-killed-by-germany-during-the-maji-maji-uprising-it-was-genocide-and-should-be-called-that-217712.

Baum, Berklee, "Bremen's Elefant: Memorialisation, Politics, and Memory Surrounding German Colonialism", *Contested Histories*, Occasional Paper IX, March 2022. https://contestedhistories.org/wp-content/uploads/Occasional-Paper-IX_Bremens-Elefant_March–2022.pdf.

BBC, "Germany Takes Italy to UN Court over Nazi-Era Compensation Claims", 30 April 2022. https://www.bbc.com/news/world-europe-61285285.

―――, "Togo Gets Tipsy on Bavarian Beer", 4 November 2011. https://www.bbc.com/news/av/world-africa-15594600.

Brahm, Felix, *40 Jahre Vereinigung für Afrikawissenschaften in Deutschland (VAD), 1969–2009*. https://vad-ev.de/wp-content/uploads/2022/07/FelixBrahm-40JahreVAD.pdf.

Bundespräsidialamt, Federal President Frank-Walter Steinmeier on the 75th Anniversary of the Liberation from National Socialism and the End of the Second World War in Europe at the Central Memorial of the Federal Republic of Germany to the Victims of War and Tyranny (Neue Wache) in Berlin on 8 May 2020. https://www.bundespraesident.de/SharedDocs/Downloads/DE/Reden/2020/05/200508-75-Jahre-Ende-WKII-Englisch.pdf?__blob=publicationFile.

―――, Federal President Frank-Walter Steinmeier at the Inauguration of the Exhibitions of the Ethnological Museum and the Museum of Asian Art of the National Museums in Berlin on 22 September 2021. https://www.bundespraesident.de/SharedDocs/Downloads/DE/Reden/2021/09/210922-Humboldt-Forum-Englisch.pdf;jsessionid=498F158220D8375094BCA8FDCA676D76.1_cid370?__blob=publicationFile.

―――, Federal President Frank-Walter Steinmeier on the Occasion of the Visit to the Maji Maji Memorial Museum and Talks with Descendants of Chief Songea Mbano on 1 November 2023 in Songea/Tanzania. https://www.bundespraesident.de/SharedDocs/Downloads/DE/Reden/2023/11/231101-Songea-Maji-Maji-Museum-Englisch2.pdf?__blob=publicationFile&v=1.

Bundestagsfraktion Bündnis 90/Die Grünen (ed.), Ein Millennium Africa Renaissance

BIBLIOGRAPHY

Program: Afrikanische Vision für eine selbstbestimmte Entwicklung. Dokumentation der Anhörung vom 8. April 2001 in Berlin.

Christopher, Kurt, "One Man Fought 4 Wars on 3 Continents and Helped Create the Nazi Party", *History Collection*, 26 July 2017. https://historycollection.com/one-man-fought-germany-4-wars-3-continents-helped-create-nazi-party/.

Coates, Ta-Nehisi, "The Case for Reparations", *The Atlantic*, June 2014. https://www.theatlantic.com/magazine/archive/2014/06/the-case-for-reparations/361631/.

Committee on the Elimination of Racial Discrimination, *Concluding Observations on the Combined 23rd to 26th Reports of Germany*, 8 December 2023, CERD/C/DEU/CO/23–26 (advance unedited version). https://tbinternet.ohchr.org/_layouts/15/treatybodyexternal/Download.aspx?symbolno=CERD%2FC%2FDEU%2FCO%2F23–26&Lang=en.

Dahlkamp, Jürgen, and Hammerstein, Konstantin von, "Corona: So will Jens Spahn unbrauchbare Masken im Wert von einer Milliarde Euro verschwinden lassen", *Der Spiegel*, 4 June 2021. https://www.spiegel.de/politik/deutschland/corona-so-will-jens-spahn-unbrauchbare-masken-im-wert-von-einer-milliarde-euro-loswerdena-22872107-0002-0001-0000-000177779146.

Della, Tahir, Diop, Ibou, Kopp, Christian, Ofuatey-Alazard, Nadja, and Yeboah, Anna, "Gemeinsam und nachhaltig dekolonisieren", *Politik & Kultur*, Dossier "20 Jahre Kulturstiftung des Bundes", Berlin 2022, 57+59. https://www.kulturstiftung-des-bundes.de/fileadmin/user_upload/content_stage/stiftung/PuK_Dossier_Kulturstiftung-des-Bundes.pdf.

Der Spiegel, "Das ist abenteuerlich", 24 November 1974. https://www.spiegel.de/politik/das-ist-abenteuerlich-a-15d59e04-0002-0001-0000-000041599389.

———, "Literaturnobelpreis geht an Abdulrazak Gurnah", 7 October 2021. https://www.spiegel.de/kultur/literatur/nobelpreis-fuer-literatur-geht-an-abdulrazak-gurnah-a-6cda9b2a-1249-46e2-8259-4949f18573f6.

Deutscher Bundestag, "Antrag zum Völkermord an Armeniern beschlossen", 2 June 2016. https://www.bundestag.de/webarchiv/textarchiv/2016/kw22-de-armenier-423826.

———, Ausschuss für Kultur und Medien, Protokoll-Nr. 20/20. Wortprotokoll, 28 November 2022. https://www.bundestag.de/resource/blob/927758/dd5cf-915c00827f74a49c044a63507ea/Protokoll_20-data.pdf.

———, Drucksache 17/7741, 14 November 2011 ("Umstände der Rückführung von Gebeinen von Opfern deutscher Kolonialverbrechen nach Namibia und die Entschuldigungs- und Versöhnungsfrage"). https://dserver.bundestag.de/btd/17/077/1707741.pdf.

———, Drucksache 17/8057, 1 December 2011 ("Antwort der Bundesregierung"). http://genocide-namibia.net/wp-content/uploads/2015/01/1708057_Antwort.pdf.

———, Drucksache 18/3013, 31 October 2014 ("Fragen für die Fragestunde der 62. Sitzung des Deutschen Bundestags"). https://dserver.bundestag.de/btd/18/030/1803013.pdf.

———, Drucksache 18/8613, 31 May 2016 ("Erinnerung und Gedenken an den

BIBLIOGRAPHY

Völkermord an den Armeniern und anderen christlichen Minderheiten in den Jahren 1915 und 1916"). https://dserver.bundestag.de/btd/18/086/1808613.pdf.

———, Drucksache 19/5130, 18 October 2018 ("Kulturpolitische Aufarbeitung der deutschen Kolonialzeit"). https://dserver.bundestag.de/btd/19/051/1905130.pdf.

———, Drucksache 19/15784, 11 December 2019 (Antrag, "Die deutsche Kolonialzeit kulturpolitisch differenziert aufarbeiten"). https://dipbt.bundestag.de/dip21/btd/19/157/1915784.pdf.

———, Drucksache 19/19914, 12 June 2020 (Antrag, "Restitution von Sammlungsgut aus kolonialem Kontext stoppen"). https://dserver.bundestag.de/btd/19/199/1919914.pdf.

———, Drucksache 20/1827, 13 May 2022 ("Mögliche Rehabilitierung von Manga Bell und Ngoso Din als Opfer kolonialistischer Justizmorde"). https://dserver.bundestag.de/btd/20/018/2001827.pdf.

———, Drucksache 20/2799, 19 July 2022 (Kleine Anfrage, "Die deutsch-namibischen Beziehungen und das sogenannte Versöhnungsabkommen"). https://dserver.bundestag.de/btd/20/027/2002799.pdf.

———, Drucksache 20/3236, 31 August 2022 (Antwort der Bundesregierung, "Die deutsch-namibischen Beziehungen und das sogenannte Versöhnungsabkommen"). https://dserver.bundestag.de/btd/20/032/2003236.pdf.

———, Drucksache 20/3696, 28 September 2022 (Antrag, "Einrichtung einer unabhängigen Beratenden Gustav-Nachtigal-Kommission für Kulturgut aus kolonialem Kontext"). https://dserver.bundestag.de/btd/20/036/2003696.pdf.

———, Drucksache 20/4681, 29 November 2022 ("Holodomor in der Ukraine: Erinnern—Gedenken—Mahnen"). https://dserver.bundestag.de/btd/20/046/2004681.pdf.

———, Drucksache 20/5228, 18 January 2023 ("Anerkennung und Gedenken an den Völkermord an den Êzidinnen und Êziden 2014"). https://dserver.bundestag.de/btd/20/052/2005228.pdf.

———, Plenarprotokoll 18/62, 5 November 2015. https://dserver.bundestag.de/btp/18/18062.pdf.

———, Plenarprotokoll 19/192, Stenografischer Bericht, 19 November 2020, 24228 B-24241C https://dserver.bundestag.de/btp/19/19192.pdf.

———, Plenarprotokoll 19/232, Stenografischer Bericht, 9 June 2021. https://dserver.bundestag.de/btp/19/19232.pdf.

———, Plenarprotokoll 20/59, Stenografischer Bericht, 12 October 2022. https://dserver.bundestag.de/btp/20/20059.pdf.

Deutsche Welle, "'Germany's Most Ambitious Cultural Project' Reveals Concept", 11February2016.https://www.dw.com/en/humboldt-forum-germanys-most-ambitious-cultural-project-reveals-concept/a-36234628.

———, "Namibia Genocide: Mbumba Says Germany's Payment Is 'Not Enough'", 5June2021.https://www.dw.com/en/namibia-genocide-mbumba-says-germanys-payment-is-not-enough/a-57785288.

Deutsches Zentrum für Integrations- und Migrationsforschung (DeZIM), *Rassistische*

BIBLIOGRAPHY

Realitäten: Wie setzt sich Deutschland mit Rassismus auseinander? Auftaktstudie zum Nationalen Diskriminierungs- und Rassismusmonitor (NaDiRa), Berlin: DeZIM, 2022. https://www.rassismusmonitor.de/fileadmin/user_upload/NaDiRa/CATI_Studie_Rassistische_Realit%C3%A4ten/DeZIM-Rassismusmonitor-Studie_Rassistische-Realit%C3%A4ten_Wie-setzt-sich-Deutschland-mit-Rassismus-auseinander.pdf.

Die Bundesregierung, *Im Wortlaut: Rede von Kulturstaatsministerin Monika Grütters bei der Eröffnung des Humboldt-Forums für das Publikum am 20. Juli 2021 in Berlin*. https://www.bundesregierung.de/breg-de/suche/rede-von-kulturstaatsministerin-gruetters-bei-der-eroeffnung-des-humboldt-forums-fuer-das-publikum-am-20-juli-2021-in-berlin-1944562.

———, *Im Wortlaut: Regierungspressekonferenz vom 26. Januar 2022*. https://www.bundesregierung.de/breg-de/suche/regierungspressekonferenz-vom-26-januar-2022–2001390.

———, *Koalitionsvertrag vom 12. März 2018*. https://www.bundesregierung.de/breg-de/service/archiv/alt-inhalte/koalitionsvertrag-vom-12-maerz-2018-975210.

———, *Ressortgemeinsame Strategie zur Unterstützung von "Vergangenheitsarbeit und Versöhnung (Transitional Justice)" im Kontext von Krisenprävention, Konfliktbewältigung und Friedensförderung*. Berlin: Auswärtiges Amt 2019.

Dreesbach, Anne, "Colonial Exhibitions, 'Völkerschauen' and the Display of the 'Other'", *European History Online* (EGO), Leibniz Institute of European History (IEG), Mainz, 3 May 2012.

Dr Y., "German Warfare in Africa: 1884 Bombings in Kamerun and the Defiance of Kum'a Mbappé", *African Heritage*, 3 April 2019. https://afrolegends.com/tag/kuma-mbappe/.

Ebert, Roger, "Africa Addio", 25 April 1967. https://www.rogerebert.com/reviews/africa-addio-1967.

Ebert-Adeikis, Romy, "Wiesn weltweit (3): Ein Prosit auf den Mix in Namibia", *hallo-münchen-de*, 25 September 2021. https://www.hallo-muenchen.de/hallo-serie/wiesn-weltweit-so-laeuft-das-windhoek-oktoberfest-in-namibia-ab-91000650.html.

Eckert, Andreas, *125 Jahre Berliner Afrika-Konferenz: Bedeutung für Geschichte und Gegenwart*. Hamburg: GIGA German Institute of Global and Area Studies, GIGA Focus, no. 12, 2009. https://www.ssoar.info/ssoar/bitstream/handle/document/27459/ssoar-2009-eckert-125_jahre_berliner_afrika-konferenz.pdf;jsessionid=54CC59307115948FAAB53C6820C34344?sequence=1.

Federal Foreign Office, "Address by Minister of State Müntefering at the Restitution Ceremony of Human Remains to Namibia", 29 August 2018. https://www.auswaertiges-amt.de/en/newsroom/news/muentefering-namibia/2131566.

———, "Foreign Minister Maas on the Conclusion of Negotiations with Namibia", 28 May 2021. https://www.auswaertiges-amt.de/en/newsroom/news/-/2463598.

———, "Speech by Foreign Minister Annalena Baerbock on the Occasion of the Return of the Benin Bronzes to Nigeria", 20 December 2022. https://www.

BIBLIOGRAPHY

auswaertiges-amt.de/en/newsroom/news/baerbock-return-of-benin-bronzes-to-nigeria/2570334.

———, "Speech by Minister of State Katja Keul at the Conference 'New Perspectives on German Colonial Rule—A Scholarship Programme for Cooperative Research'", 17 October 2022. https://www.auswaertiges-amt.de/en/newsroom/news/-/2558984.

———, "Speech by Minister of State Katja Keul on the Occasion of a Wreath-Laying Ceremony at the Site of the Execution of Rudolf Manga Bell in Cameroon", 2 November 2022. https://www.auswaertiges-amt.de/en/newsroom/news/-/2561510.

Federal Government, *Interministerial Strategy to Support "Dealing with the Past and Reconciliation (Transitional Justice)" in the Context of Preventing Crises, Resolving Conflicts and Building Peace* (Berlin: German Federal Foreign Office, 2019).

Finkelstein, Emi, "Colonial Histories at the Humboldt Forum", *Europe Now Journal*, 28 April 2020. https://europenowjournal.org/2020/04/27/colonial-histories-at-the-humboldt-forum/.

Fitzpatrick, Matt, "On the 'German Catechism'", *New Fascism Syllabus*, 27 May 2021. http://newfascismsyllabus.com/opinions/on-the-german-catechism/.

Florvil, Tiffany, "Seeing May Ayim through Her Friends' Eyes", *Black Perspectives*, 13 June 2022. https://www.aaihs.org/seeing-may-ayim-through-her-friends-eyes/.

Förster, Larissa, "'These Skulls Are Not Enough': The Repatriation of Namibian Human Remains from Berlin to Windhoek in 2011", *darkmatter*, 11, 18 November 2013. https://web.archive.org/web/20210126224618/http://www.darkmatter101.org/site/2013/11/18/these-skulls-are-not-enough-the-repatriation-of-namibian-human-remains-from-berlin-to-windhoek-in-2011/.

Gardner, Helen, "Explainer: The Myth of the Noble Savage", *The Conversation*, 25 February 2016. https://theconversation.com/explainer-the-myth-of-the-noble-savage-55316.

Garises, Lee, "The Damara and the Genocide. A Call for Recognition and Restitution", Rosa Luxemburg Stiftung Southern Africa, Johannesburg 2022. https://www.rosalux.co.za/our-work/the-damara-and-the-genocide.

Garoes, Tshukhoe M., "A Forgotten Case of the ǂNukhoen / Damara People Added to Colonial German Genocidal Crimes in Namibia: We Cannot Fight the Lightning during the Rain", *Future Pasts* Working Papers, no. 11, December 2021. https://www.futurepasts.net/fpwp11-garoes-2021.

German Embassy Windhoek, "Speech by Minister of State for International Cultural Affairs of the Federal Republic of Germany Michelle Müntefering on the Occasion of the 3rd Repatriation of Human Remains from Germany to Namibia on 31 August 2018 in Windhuk". https://windhuk.diplo.de/na-en/aktuelles/-/2131686.

———, "Speech of the President of the German Bundesrat Daniel Günther at the National Council of the Republic of Namibia on the Occasion of his Visit to Angola and Namibia", 16 July 2019. https://windhuk.diplo.de/na-en/aktuelles/-/2233464.

BIBLIOGRAPHY

———, "Welcoming Speech Given by Minister of State Michelle Müntefering on 27 August 2018 at Villa Borsig in Berlin". https://windhuk.diplo.de/na-en/aktuelles/-/2130590.

Gershon, Livia, "New Memorials in Berlin Honor the Holocaust's Overlooked Black Victims", *Smithsonian Magazine*, 3 December 2021. https://www.smithsonianmag.com/smart-news/berlin-memorials-honor-black-holocaust-victims-180979156/.

Gibbs, Alexandra, "Who Still Owes What for the Two World Wars?", *CNBC*, 18 March 2015. https://www.cnbc.com/2015/03/18/who-still-owes-what-for-the-two-world-wars.html.

Gilley, Bruce, "The Case for German Colonialism", Paper presented in the German Parliament on 11 December 2019. https://www.researchgate.net/publication/338555799_The_Case_for_German_Colonialism.

———, "The Ethical Foundations of German Colonialism", Paper presented at the Conference "Ethics & Empire IV: The Modern Period", Christ Church, University of Oxford, 30 June–1 July 2022. https://www.researchgate.net/publication/360919744_The_Ethical_Foundations_of_German_Colonialism.

Goldmann, Matthias, "'Ich bin ihr Freund und Kapitän': Die deutsch-namibische Entschädigungsfrage im Spiegel intertemporaler und interkultureller Völkerrechtskonzepte", Max Planck Institute for Comparative Public Law and International Law, MPIL Research Paper Series, No. 2020–29. https://papers.ssrn.com/sol3/papers.cfm?abstract_id=3672406.

———, "The Ovaherero and Nama Peoples v. Germany: Declaration of Matthias Goldmann before the SDNY Court", 25 April 2018. https://papers.ssrn.com/sol3/papers.cfm?abstract_id=3169852.

———, "Why the Key to the Past Lies in the Future: The Dispute about Reparations for Namibia", *Verfassungsblog on Matters Constitutional*, 20 August 2020. https://verfassungsblog.de/why-the-key-to-the-past-lies-in-the-future/.

Gram, Rikke, and Schoofs, Zoe, "Germany's History of Returning Human Remains and Objects from Colonial Contexts: An Overview of Successful Cases and Unsettled Claims between 1970 and 2021". Magdeburg: Deutsches Zentrum für Kulturgutverluste, 28 November 2022 (Working Paper 3/2022).

Graw, Jill, "Robert Koch: Menschenexperimente unter der Sonne Afrikas?", *Geschichte lernen*, 7 September 2020. https://www.geschichte-lernen.net/robert-koch/.

Habermas, Rebekka, "Die deutsche Kolonie Togo", *Göttingen kolonial* (undated, c.2019). https://www.goettingenkolonial.uni-goettingen.de/index.php/orte/die-deutschen-kolonien/togo.

Hackmack, Judith, "Repairing the Irreparable? Tackling the Long-Term Effects of German Colonialism in Germany and Namibia", Policy Paper, Berlin: ECCHR, October 2022. https://www.ecchr.eu/en/publication/repairing-the-irreparable-tackling-the-long-term-effects-of-german-colonialism-in-germany-namibia/.

Harring, Sydney, *German Reparations to the Herero Nation: An Assertion of Herero Nationhood in the Path of Namibian Development*. City University of New York, CUNY Academic Works, 2002. https://academicworks.cuny.edu/cgi/viewcontent.cgi?article=1249&context=cl_pub.

BIBLIOGRAPHY

Hasselbach, Christoph, and Romaniec, Rosalia, "Poland, Germany and the Shadow of World War II", *Deutsche Welle*, 31 August 2019. https://www.dw.com/en/poland-germany-and-the-shadow-of-world-war-ii/a-50221515.

Heinze, Robert, "Colonial Revisionism in Germany", *Africa Is a Country*, 22 January 2020. https://africasacountry.com/2020/01/colonial-revisionism-in-germany.

———, "A Technocratic Reformulation of Colonialism", *Africa Is a Country*, 21 January 2019. https://africasacountry.com/2019/01/a-technocratic-reformulation-of-colonialism.

Heissenbüttel, Dietrich, "Justizmord in der Kolonialzeit: Rudolf, der gute Deutsche", *Kontext: Wochenzeitung*, no. 580, 11 May 2022. https://www.kontextwochenzeitung.de/schaubuehne/580/rudolf-der-gute-deutsche-8172.html.

Hernandez, Bonar Ludwig, *The Las Casas–Sepúlveda Controversy: 1550/51*. Undated. http://userwww.sfsu.edu/epf/2001/hernandez.html.

Herrmann, Sabine, "Koloniale Amnesie? 100 Jahre Archiv zur Geschichte der deutschen Kolonien", *Archive zur Kolonialgeschichte*, 18 June 2019. https://www.bundesarchiv.de/DE/Content/Publikationen/Aufsaetze/aufsatz-s-herrmann-koloniale-amnesie.pdf?__blob=publicationFile.

Hibbeler, Birgit, "Ein halbes Jahr danach: Die Spendenflut nach dem Tsunami", *Deutsches Ärzteblatt*, 27, 102 (2005). https://www.aerzteblatt.de/archiv/47554/Ein-halbes-Jahr-danach-Die-Spendenflut-nach-dem-Tsunami.

Hielscher, Hans, "Afrodeutsche unterm Hakenkreuz: 'Besondere Kennzeichen: Neger'", *Der Spiegel*, 25 June 2019. https://www.spiegel.de/geschichte/afrodeutsche-im-nationalsozialismus-a-1270980.html.

Hira, Sandew, "A Decolonial Critique of the Racist Case for Colonialism", *Decolonial International Network*, 22 September 2017. https://din.today/wp-content/uploads/2017/09/The-Racist-case-for-colonialism.pdf.

Hoeder, Ciani-Sophia, "Totgeschwiegen", *Süddeutsche Zeitung Magazin*, 9 July 2020. https://sz-magazin.sueddeutsche.de/willkommen-bei-mir/geschichte-afrodeutsch-88967.

Hoffmann, Heiner, "'Moral ist nicht weniger wert als Recht'", *Der Spiegel*, 9 October 2021. https://www.spiegel.de/ausland/ruprecht-polenz-ueber-das-versoehnungsabkommen-nach-dem-voelkermord-an-den-nama-und-herero-a-57c8c649-6a5d-415c-9044-3c5a2973ce07.

———, "'Wir erleben den Beginn einer großen Dekolonisierungsbewegung'", *Der Spiegel*, 18 December 2023. https://www.spiegel.de/ausland/wiedergutmachung-fuer-sklaverei-kolonialzeit-erleben-den-beginn-einer-grossen-dekolonisierungsbewegung-a-f8d0395f-cdc3-4eea-b1b5-2b852720a229.

Huttenbach, Henry R., "Defining Genocide, Comparing Genocides: Dilemmas and Solutions of a Methodological Quandary", Working Paper, Yale Center for International and Area Studies, New Haven, CT, undated (c.2001). https://gsp.yale.edu/sites/default/files/defining_genocide_comparing_genocides.pdf.

Imani, Sarah and Theurer, Karina, "The German–Namibian 'Reconciliation Agreement'", *Zeitgeister: International Perspectives from Culture and Society*, Goethe Institut, undated (2021). https://www.goethe.de/prj/zei/en/pos/22326696.html.

Imani, Sarah, Theurer, Karina, and Kaleck, Wolfgang, *The "Reconciliation Agreement"*:

BIBLIOGRAPHY

A Lost Opportunity. Berlin: European Center for Constitutional and Human Rights, June 2021. https://www.ecchr.eu/fileadmin/Hintergrundberichte/ECCHR_GER_NAM_Statement.pdf.

Isilow, Hassan, "Mixed Reactions in Africa as Germany Formally Recognizes 'Genocide' in Namibia", *Anadolu Agency*, 28 May 2021. https://www.aa.com.tr/en/africa/mixed-reactions-in-africa-as-germany-formally-recognizes-genocide-in-namibia/2257660.

Joint Declaration by the Federal Republic of Germany and the Republic of Namibia: "United in Remembrance of our Colonial Past, United in Our Will to Reconcile, United in Our Vision of the Future". https://www.parliament.na/wp-content/uploads/2021/09/Joint-Declaration-Document-Genocide-rt.pdf.

Kiessler, Richard, "'Josef ist der Größte'", *Der Spiegel*, no. 21, 1983. https://www.spiegel.de/politik/josef-ist-der-groesste-a-fe4ec6fb-0002-0001-0000-000014019665.

Kirey, Reginald E., "Decolonizing German Colonial Sites in Dar es Salaam: The Case of Hermann von Wissmann and the Askari Monument", *Zeitgeschichte-online*, 10September2021.https://zeitgeschichte-online.de/geschichtskultur/decolonizing-german-colonial-sites-dar-es-salaam.

Klein, Thoralf, "The 'Yellow Peril'", *European History Online (EGO)*, published by the Leibniz Institute of European History (IEG), Mainz, 15 October 2015. https://d-nb.info/1125549890/34.

Klotz, Jürgen, "Rudolf Duala Manga Bell-Platz in Ulm eingeweiht", *SWR aktuell*, 8 October 2022. https://www.swr.de/swraktuell/baden-wuerttemberg/ulm/rudolf-duala-manga-bell-platz-wird-eingeweiht-100.html.

Knöfel, Ulrike, "Rückgabe der deutschen Benin-Bronzen: 'Ich wehre mich dagegen, alles in einen Unrechtskontext zu stellen'", *Der Spiegel*, 26 August 2022. https://www.spiegel.de/kultur/rueckgabe-der-benin-bronzen-ich-wehre-mich-dagegen-alles-in-einen-unrechtskontext-zu-stellen-a-3064a884-4897-43ae-91a5-ea050144d813.

Koalitionsvertrag 2021–2025 zwischen SPD, Bündnis 90/Die Grünen und FDP, *Mehr Fortschritt wagen: Bündnis für Freiheit, Gerechtigkeit und Nachhaltigkeit*. https://www.bundesregierung.de/resource/blob/974430/1990812/04221173eef9a6720059cc353d759a2b/2021-12-10-koav2021-data.pdf.

Koldehoff, Stefan, "Kommentar zu Benin-Bronzen: Diese Rückgabe kann nur ein Anfang sein". *Deutschlandfunk*, 20 December 2022. https://www.deutschlandfunk.de/kommentar-beninbronzen-rueckgabe-kann-nur-ein-anfang-sein-100.html.

Kölnische Gesellschaft für Christlich-Jüdische Zusammenarbeit (ed.), *100 Jahre deutscher Rassismus: Katalog und Arbeitsbuch*. Cologne: Kölnische Gesellschaft für Christlich-Jüdische Zusammenarbeit, 1988.

Kopp, Christian, "Ein Modellprojekt? Dekoloniale Erinnerungskultur in der Stadt", *Politik & Kultur*, no. 12, December 2022/January 2023. https://politikkultur.de/inland/ein-modellprojekt/.

Kössler, Reinhart, "The Bible and the Whip: Entanglements around the Restitution of Robbed Heirlooms", Arnold Bergstraesser Institut, ABI Working Paper

BIBLIOGRAPHY

No. 12, May 2019. https://www.arnold-bergstraesser.de/en/the-bible-and-the-whip-entanglements-surrounding-the-restitution-of-looted-heirlooms.

Kössler, Reinhart, and Melber, Henning, "Koloniale Amnesie: Zum Umgang mit der deutschen Kolonialvergangenheit", *Standpunkte* 9/2018 (Berlin: Rosa Luxemburg Stiftung, 2018). https://www.rosalux.de/fileadmin/rls_uploads/pdfs/Standpunkte/Standpunkte_9-2018.pdf.

Kron, Stefanie, "Afrikanische Diaspora und Literatur Schwarzer Frauen in Deutschland", Heinrich Böll Stiftung, *Heimatkunde*, Migrationspolitisches Portal, 18 February 2009. https://heimatkunde.boell.de/de/2009/02/18/afrikanische-diaspora-und-literatur-schwarzer-frauen-deutschland.

Krüger, Gesine, "Die 'guten' Seiten des #Kolonialismus", *Geschichte der Gegenwart*, 27 March 2019. https://geschichtedergegenwart.ch/die-guten-seiten-des-kolonialismus/.

———, "Koloniale Schuld und afrikanische Geschichte: Es ist Zeit für einen neuen historischen Blick auf das koloniale Afrika", *Geschichte der Gegenwart*, 6 June 2018. https://geschichtedergegenwart.ch/koloniale-schuld-und-afrikanische-geschichte-es-ist-zeit-fuer-einen-neuen-historischen-blick-auf-das-koloniale-afrika/.

Kuban, Josephine, "Wer schaut hier wen an? Die Ausstellung 'zurückGESCHAUT' im Museum Treptow in Berlin", *Visual History*, 28 June 2021. https://visual-history.de/2021/06/28/wer-schaut-hier-wen-an/.

Kundnani, Hans, "'Eurowhiteness': Europe's Civilisational Turn", *Green European Journal*, 4 December 2023. https://www.greeneuropeanjournal.eu/eurowhiteness-europes-civilisational-turn/.

Künkler, Eva, "Koloniale Gewalt und der Raub kultureller Objekte und menschlicher Überreste: Eine systematische Übersicht zu Militärgewalt und sogenannten Strafexpeditionen in deutschen Kolonialgebieten in Afrika (1884–1919)", Magdeburg: Deutsches Zentrum Kulturgutverluste, Working Paper 2/2022. https://perspectivia.net/publikationen/wpk/kuenkler_gewalt.

Lawal, Shola, "How to Pay for Genocide: Namibian Victims of German Colonialism Want a Say", *Al Jazeera*, 23 December 2013. https://www.aljazeera.com/features/2023/12/23/how-to-pay-for-genocide-the-cost-of-germanys-colonial-crimes-in-namibia.

Li, Gabriel, "Colonial Past and Present of Tsingtao Beer", *pandaily*, 14 September 2019. https://pandaily.com/colonial-past-and-present-of-tsingtao-beer/.

Linden Museum, "Hendrik Witbooi's Family Bible and Whip". https://www.lindenmuseum.de/en/sehen/rueckblick/hendrik-witboois-family-bible.

Mallon, Frederik, "Benin-Bronzen: Baerbock hat absolut recht, ihre Hater blamieren sich", *Der Volksverpetzer*, 22 December 2022. https://www.volksverpetzer.de/faktencheck/benin-bronzen-baerbock-hat-recht/.

McGreevy, Nora, "Why Germany's Newly Opened Humboldt Forum Is So Controversial", *Smithsonian Magazine*, 23 July 2021. https://www.smithsonianmag.com/smart-news/germany-controversial-humboldt-forum-180978251/.

Menger, Tom, "Abdulrazak Gurnah and the Afterlives of German Colonialism", *AfricaIsaCountry*, 13 January 2022. https://africasacountry.com/2022/01/abdulrazak-gurnah-and-the-afterlives-of-german-colonialism-in-east-africa.

BIBLIOGRAPHY

Mesghena, Mekonnen, "Harald Gerunde: Eine von uns; Als Schwarze in Deutschland geboren", *Deutschlandfunk*, 4 December 2020. https://www.deutschlandfunk.de/harald-gerunde-eine-von-uns-als-schwarze-in-deutschland-100.html.

Möller, Johann Michael, "Abschied von unserer Leiterinnerung: Im Schatten des Humboldt Forums findet ein Selbstentkernungsversuch statt", *Politik & Kultur*, no. 10, October 2021. https://www.kulturrat.de/themen/texte-zur-kulturpolitik/abschied-von-unserer-leiterinnerung/.

Moorsom, Richard, *Underdevelopment and Labour Migration: The Contract Labour System in Namibia*. Bergen: Chr. Michelsen Institute, 1997. https://open.cmi.no/cmi-xmlui/bitstream/handle/11250/2435915/WP%201997_10%20Richard%20Moorsom-07112007_1.pdf?sequence=2&isAllowed=y.

Moradi, Fazil, "'Restitution' of Looted African Art Just Continues Colonial Policies: Much More Is at Stake", *The Conversation*, 13 October 2022. https://theconversation.com/restitution-of-looted-african-art-just-continues-colonial-policies-much-more-is-at-stake-191386.

Moses, Dirk, "The Documenta, Indonesia and the Problem of Closed Universes", *New Fascism Syllabus*, 24 July 2022. http://newfascismsyllabus.com/contributions/the-documenta-indonesia-and-the-problem-of-closed-universes/?fbclid=IwAR2jk8D3cdUaYTuGKetf57-_8ts240XEz06lnFtnHWH4UQyf_UFj5mggZNQ&fs=e&s=cl.

———, "The German Catechism", *Geschichte der Gegenwart*, 23 May 2021. https://geschichtedergegenwart.ch/the-german-catechism/.

Nagel, Jürgen G., "Koloniale Herrschaft in Togo: Eine Episode aus dem Hinterland der deutschen Kolonie Togo", *Themenportal Europäische Geschichte*, 2011. www.europa.clio-online.de/essay/id/fdae-1555.

NBC, "Namibian Government Has Not Signed an Agreement with the German Government", 27 October 2022. https://nbcnews.na/node/98498.

Nebe, Cai, and Ikela, Sakeus, "Namibia Debates German Genocide Deal", *Deutsche Welle*, 21 September 2021. https://www.dw.com/en/namibia-debates-german-genocide-deal/a-59243358.

New Fascism Syllabus, "The Catechism Debate". http://newfascismsyllabus.com/category/opinions/the-catechism-debate/.

Ofuatey-Alazard, Nadja, and Della, Tahir, "'Irritation ist notwendig, um uns von dem kolonialen Erbe zu befreien'", *Politik & Kultur*, no. 12, December 2022/January 2023. https://politikkultur.de/inland/irritation-ist-notwendig-um-uns-von-dem-kolonialen-erbe-zu-befreien/.

Oworu, Adel, Fuchs, Merel, and Awale, Anab (eds.), *We Want Them Back: Scientific Report on the Presence of Human Remains from Colonial Contexts in Berlin*. Coordination Office of Decolonize Berlin e. V., February 2022. https://decolonize-berlin.de/wp-content/uploads/2022/02/We-Want-Them-Back_english-web.pdf.

Owuor, Yvonne Adhiambo, "Derelict Shards and The Roaming of Colonial Phantoms", Keynote Address at the International Conference "Colonialism as Shared History. Past, Present, Future", 7–9 October 2019, Berlin. https://www.theelephant.info/long-reads/2020/11/06/derelict-shards-the-roaming-of-colonial-phantoms/?print=pdf.

BIBLIOGRAPHY

Parzinger, Hermann, "Wohlfeil wird es schnell", *Cicero online*, 9 September 2017. https://www.cicero.de/kultur/humboldt-forum-berlin-wohlfeil-wird-es-schnell.

Pellegrino, Antonia, and Böttcher, Kirsten, "Wer war Hans Paasche? Verleger Helmut Donat im Gespräch", *Bayern 2*, 8 September 2020. https://www.br.de/radio/bayern2/sendungen/radiotexte/verleger-helmut-donat-ueber-hans-paasche-und-lukanga-mukara-100.html.

Pelz, Daniel, "Genozid-Gespräche mit Namibia gehen in die Verlängerung", *Deutsche Welle*, Fokus Afrika, 28 July 2017. http://www.dw.com/de/genozid-gespr%C3%A4che-mit-namibia-gehen-in-die-verl%C3%A4ngerung/a-39873655.

Pérez Ramirez, Maria Leonor, *Survey on Human Remains from Colonial Contexts Held in Museum and University Collections in Germany*. Berlin: Kulturstiftung der Länder, 2023. https://www.cp3c.org/dealing_with_human_remains/Pérez_Ramírez-KSL_2023_Survey_on_Human_Remains.pdf.

Permanent Mission of the Federal Republic of Germany to the Office of the United Nations and to the Other International Organizations Geneva, *Note Verbal*. Ref: Pol-10 552.00 NAM, Note No.: 159/2023, 1 June 2023. spcommreports.ohchr.org/TMResultsBase/DownLoadFile?gId=37548.

Pfeffer, Matthias, and Wendt, Georg, *DuALA: Eine Handreichung für den Schulunterricht*. Stadt Aaalen, 2023. https://www.aalen.de/bell.

Piesche, Peggy, "Schwarz und deutsch? Eine ostdeutsche Jugend vor 1989: Retrospektive auf ein 'nichtexistentes' Thema in der DDR", Heinrich Böll Stiftung, *Heimatkunde*, Migrationspolitisches Portal (undated). https://heimatkunde.boell.de/de/2006/05/01/schwarz-und-deutsch-eine-ostdeutsche-jugend-vor-1989-retrospektive-auf-ein.

Plucinska, Joanna, "Germany Owes Poland over $850 Billion in WW2 Reparations: Senior Lawmaker", *Reuters*, 26 April 2019. https://www.reuters.com/article/us-poland-germany-reparations-idUSKCN1S215R.

Polifke, Frank, "Deshalb benennt Aalen Platz nach einem afrikanischen Prinzen", *SWR aktuell*, 21 July 2022. https://www.swr.de/swraktuell/baden-wuerttemberg/ulm/gemeinderat-wuerdigt-rudolf-duala-manga-bell-100.html.

Pollex, Charlotte, "Koloniale Raubkunst aus Deutschland geht zurück nach Namibia", 26 June 2022. https://www.daserste.de/information/wissen-kultur/ttt/koloniale-raubkunst-100.html.

Popp, Maximilian, and Riedmann, Bernhard, "'Es ist als hätten wir nie existiert'", *Der Spiegel*, no. 45, 5 November 2022. https://www.spiegel.de/ausland/namibia-wie-deutsche-siedler-vom-voelkermord-profitierten-a-7ac7f948-cd5c-48c3-8036-5f7dd035e90d.

Präfke, Jonas, "The Herero People as the Subject of International Law? Implications for Reparation Claims Based on the Herero Genocide", *Law Review at Johns Hopkins*, Spring 2019. https://www.jhlawreview.org/herero-genocide-jonas-prafke.

Press Information Guide, "Confronting Colonial Pasts, Envisioning Creative Futures", Windhoek, 23 May 2022. https://www.museums.com.na/images/Namibian_CCP_ECF_Project_Press_Release_May_2022.pdf.

BIBLIOGRAPHY

Rapp, Tobias, "Hat die Identitätspolitik ihren ersten Nobelpreis?", *Der Spiegel* online, 7 October 2021. https://www.spiegel.de/kultur/abdulrazak-gurnah-hat-die-identitaetspolitik-hat-ihren-ersten-nobelpreis-a-a767fe03-0f23-45bb-a88a-bd0a4fdadb1b.

Rautenberg, Marius, "Genozid in Namibia: So dachte der erste deutsche Völkermörder", *National Geographic*, 1 June 2022. https://www.nationalgeographic.de/geschichte-und-kultur/2022/06/genozid-in-namibia-so-dachte-der-erste-deutsche-voelkermoerder.

Rechavia-Taylor, Howard, and Moses, Dirk, "The Herero and Nama Genocide, the Holocaust, and the Question of German Reparations", E-International Relations, 27 August 2021. https://www.e-ir.info/2021/08/27/the-herero-and-nama-genocide-the-holocaust-and-the-question-of-german-reparations/.

Reed-Anderson, Paulette, Rewriting the Footnotes: Berlin and the African Diaspora. Berlin: Ausländerbeauftragte des Senats, 2000.

Reitz, Núrel Bahi, and Mannitz, Sabine, "Remembering Genocide in Namibia", PRIF Working Papers, 53 (Frankfurt/Main: Hessische Stiftung Friedens- und Konfliktforschung, 2021). https://www.hsfk.de/publikationen/publikationssuche/publikation/remembering-genocide-in-namibia.

Renan, Ernest, "What Is a Nation?" Text of a conference paper delivered at the Sorbonne on March 11th, 1882, in Ernest Renan, *Qu'est-ce qu'une nation?* (Paris: Presses-Pocket, 1992; translated by Ethan Rundell). http://ucparis.fr/files/9313/6549/9943/What_is_a_Nation.pdf.

Republic of Namibia, Office of the Deputy Prime Minister and Minister of International Relations and Cooperation, Joint Communication from Special Procedures, 30 May 2023. spcommreports.ohchr.org/TMResultsBase/DownLoadFile?gId=37541.

Resolutions of the Second National Land Conference, 1 to 5 October 2018. http://www.mlr.gov.na/documents/20541/638917/Second+National+Land+Conference+Resolutions+2018.pdf/15b498fd-fdc6-4898-aeda-91fecbc74319.

Roth, Claudia, "Kunst und Kultur sind frei: Im Gespräch mit Hans Jenssen", *Politik & Kultur*, Dossier "20 Jahre Kulturstiftung des Bundes", Berlin, 2022, 27–28. https://www.kulturstiftung-des-bundes.de/fileadmin/user_upload/content_stage/stiftung/PuK_Dossier_Kulturstiftung-des-Bundes.pdf.

Sarr, Felwine, and Savoy, Bénédicte, The Restitution of African Cultural Heritage: Toward a New Relational Ethics. November 2018. https://drive.google.com/file/d/1jetudXp3vued-yA8gvRwGjH6QLOfss4-/view.

Schleswig-Holsteinischer Landtag, Drucksache 19/2005, "Antwort der Landesregierung auf die Große Anfrage der Abgeordneten des SSW", 18 February 2020. https://www.landtag.ltsh.de/infothek/wahl19/drucks/02000/drucksache-19-02005.pdf.

Schliess, Gero, "Is the Humboldt Forum Shying Away from Colonial History?", *Deutsche Welle*, 14 August 2017. https://www.dw.com/en/is-berlins-humboldt-forum-shying-away-from-colonial-history/a-40082234.

Schmidt, Gerold, "Auf den Spuren des Urgroßvaters", *Südlink-Magazin*, 13 September 2022. https://www.inkota.de/news/auf-den-spuren-des-urgrossvaters.

BIBLIOGRAPHY

Schult, Christoph, "Rückgabe von Benin-Bronzen: 'Deutschland ist ein Vorbild für die Welt'", *Der Spiegel*, 20 December 2022. https://www.spiegel.de/kultur/benin-bronzen-annalena-baerbock-und-claudia-roth-geben-kunst-an-nigeria-zurueck-a-24521eb2-4a9e-4936-b979-09392cf12bbd.

Schwarz, Tobias, "Germany to Loan Back 23 Looted Museum Pieces to Namibia", *eNCA*, 24 May 2022. https://www.enca.com/news/germany-loan-back-23-looted-museum-pieces-namibia.

Severin, Jan, "Rezension zu: Kreienbaum, Jonas, '"Ein trauriges Fiasko": Koloniale Konzentrationslager im südlichen Afrika 1900–1908. Hamburg, 2015'", *H-Soz-Kult*, 28 July 2017. www.hsozkult.de/publicationreview/id/rezbuecher24393.

Sieben, Peter, "Berliner Flughafen BER vor der Eröffnung: Eine Chronik des Scheiterns", *Ingenieur.de*, 21 October 2020. https://www.ingenieur.de/technik/fachbereiche/luftfahrt/ber-flughafen-berlin.

Steinmetz, George, "Das Humboldt Forum: Eine immanente Kritik", *Soziopolis: Gesellschaft beobachten*, 6 October 2023. https://www.soziopolis.de/das-humboldt-forum.html.

Stiftung Preussischer Kulturbesitz, "Pressemitteilung: Exemplarische Partnerschaft zwischen SPK und Museums Association of Namibia geht in nächste Phase", Berlin, 24 May 2022. https://www.preussischer-kulturbesitz.de/pressemitteilung/artikel/2022/05/23/exemplarische-partnerschaft-zwischen-spk-und-museums-association-of-namibia-geht-in-naechste-phase.html.

———, "Rückgabe nach Namibia und Tansania: Stiftungsrat macht Weg frei", 27 June 2022. https://www.preussischer-kulturbesitz.de/news-detail/artikel/2022/06/27/rueckgaben-nach-namibia-und-tansania-stiftungsrat-macht-weg-frei.html.

Südschleswiger Wählerverband, "Der Kolonialismus ist Teil unserer Regionalgeschichte", 18 June 2020. https://www.ssw.de/dk/emner/der-kolonialismus-ist-teil-unserer-regionalgeschichte.pdf.

Talmon, Stefan, "The Genocide in Namibia: Genocide in a Historical-Political or Legal Sense?", *GPIL: German Practice in International Law*, 23 September 2017. https://gpil.jura.uni-bonn.de/2017/09/genocide-namibia-genocide-historical-political-legal-sense/.

Theurer, Karina, "Germany Has to Grant Reparations for Colonial Crimes: UN Special Rapporteurs Get Involved Right on Time", *Völkerrechtsblog*, 2 May 2023. https://voelkerrechtsblog.org/germany-has-to-grant-reparations-for-colonial-crimes/.

———, "Litigating Reparations: Will Namibia Be Setting Standards?", *Völkerrechtsblog*, 25 January 2023. https://voelkerrechtsblog.org/litigating-reparations/.

Thurman, Kira, "Review of Aitken, Robbie; Rosenhaft, Eve, *Black Germany: The Making and Unmaking of a Diaspora Community, 1884–1960*", H-German, H-Net Reviews, 22 February 2016. https://networks.h-net.org/node/112955/pdf.

Trilling, Daniel, "Has the Humboldt Forum Got It Horribly Wrong?", *Apollo Magazine*, 21 January 2022. https://www.apollo-magazine.com/humboldt-forum-berlin-ethnographic-collections/.

UEPO, "Literaturpreis an Abdulrazak Gurnah: Keine Übersetzungen lieferbar",

BIBLIOGRAPHY

8 October 20221. https://uepo.de/2021/10/08/literatur-nobelpreis-an-abdulrazak-gurnah-keine-uebersetzungen-lieferbar/.

United Nations, *Report of the Committee on South West Africa*. General Assembly, Official records. Twelfth Session, Supplement no. 12 (A/3626), 1957. https://digitallibrary.un.org/record/712995?ln=en.

———, *Report of the Working Group of Experts on People of African Descent on Its Mission to Germany*. General Assembly, 15 August 2017, A/HRC/36/60/Add. 2. https://digitallibrary.un.org/record/1304263?ln=en.

———, *Report of the Working Group of Experts on People of African Descent on Its Mission to Germany. Addendum: Mission to Germany: Comments by the State on the Report of the Working Group*. General Assembly, 21 August 2017, A/HRC/36/60/A. https://www.ohchr.org/en/documents/comments-state/report-working-group-experts-people-african-descent-its-mission-germany.

———, *United Nations Declaration on the Rights of Indigenous Peoples*. March 2008. http://www.un.org/esa/socdev/unpfii/documents/DRIPS_en.pdf.

Weiler, Julia, "Insights into the Life and Mindset of a Genocidal Murderer", Ruhr Universität Bochum, 9 March 2022. https://news.rub.de/english/2022-03-09-colonial-history-insights-life-and-mindset-genocidal-murderer.

Weindl, Andrea, "Die Kurbrandenburger im 'atlantischen System', 1650–1720", Universität Köln, Arbeitspapiere zur Lateinamerikaforschung, 2001. https://lateinamerika.phil-fak.uni-koeln.de/fileadmin/sites/aspla/bilder/arbeitspapiere/weindl.pdf.

Wiedemann, Charlotte, "Ohne Hierarchien des Gedenkens", *südlink*, no. 201, September 2022, 14–15.

Wissenschaftliche Dienste, Deutscher Bundestag, *Dokumentation. Zur kolonialen Vergangenheit Deutschlands in Namibia: Geschichte—Erinnerungskultur—Aufarbeitung*. Deutscher Bundestag 2013. https://www.bundestag.de/resource/blob/405272/fc16f05eb5fea3b4da9ece62b7c3abef/wd-1-069-13-pdf-data.pdf.

———, *Sachstand: Zur völkerrechtlichen Zulässigkeit von freiwilligen Entschädigungszahlungen an Herero und Nama in Namibia*. Deutscher Bundestag, WD 2—3000—067/21, 11 October 2021. https://www.bundestag.de/resource/blob/868674/e1e537a1e84079ffdfbdda1995dee0ad/WD-2-067-21-pdf-data.pdf.

Newspaper Articles

Apperly, Eliza, "'Stumbling stones': a different vision of Holocaust remembrance", *The Guardian*, 18 February 2019.

Beukes, Jemima, "Apartheid worse than genocide, Geingob says", *Namibian Sun*, 20 September 2023.

———, "German investors turned off", *Namibian Sun*, 16 July 2019.

———, "German reparation offer 'not true'", *Namibian Sun*, 8 January 2020.

———, "Müntefering's apology torn apart", *Namibian Sun*, 3 September 2018.

Böhm, Andrea, "Europas Angst, sich zu entschuldigen", *Die Zeit*, 2 November 2023.

Brandt, Hans, "Franz-Josef Strauß: 'Ich bin ein Südwester'", *die tageszeitung*, 30 January 1988.

BIBLIOGRAPHY

Bröll, Claudia, "Lawyers clash with AG over genocide deal", *Namibian Sun*, 8 November 2022.

Chiringa, Kelvin, "Genocide: Germany says can't undo mistakes of the past", *The Villager*, 3 September 2018.

Connolly, Kate, "Campaigners celebrate changing of colonial street names in Berlin", *The Guardian*, 2 December 2022.

Dziedzic, Paul, "Der Fall Rudolf Manga Bell", *Neues Deutschland*, 18 May 2022.

Handelsblatt / Wirtschaftswoche, "Bahnkreise: Stuttgart 21 wird mehr als doppelt so teuer wie geplant", 27 January 2022.

Häntzschel, Jörg, "Ein unlösbarer Widerspruch", *Süddeutsche Zeitung*, 21 July 2017.

———, "Humboldt-Forum Berlin: Fragwürdiges Konzept", *Süddeutsche Zeitung*, 15 September 2022.

Hembapu, Otniel, "Uproar over Geingob's genocide remarks", *New Era*, 26 September 2023.

Iikela, Sakeus, "Government committed to protecting property rights", *The Namibian*, 17 July 2019.

Jason, Loide, "On the spot: Muinjangue on party politics, Covid-19 and reparations", *New Era*, 11 February 2022.

Johnson, Dominic, "Ein Signal, aber noch keine Politik", *die tageszeitung*, 2 November 2023.

Joseph, Elizabeth, "Nudo demands apology from president", *Namibian Sun*, 25 September 2023.

Kahiruika, Ndanki, "Nam bars entry to skulls ceremony in Germany", *The Namibian*, 24 August 2018.

Kasuto, Tujoromajo, and Kathindi, Andrew, "Apology not accepted: Rukoro as OTA denounces deal", *Windhoek Observer*, 29 May 2021.

Kaure, Adolf, "Relations can improve, says German ambassador: Germany willing to shake hands", *Windhoek Express*, 16 June 2019.

Klaproth, Franka, "Zwischen Jubel und Buhrufen: Straßenumbenennung in Wedding", *Berliner Zeitung*, 3 December 2022.

Krause, Tilman, "Eine Showtreppe für Wilhelm Zwo", *Die Welt*, 2 September 2017.

Kuteeue, Petrus, "A Namibian people mark 1904 genocide: German minister issues an apology", *Boston Globe*, 15 August 2004.

Langer, Bernd, "Die Statue im Kurpark", *Neues Deutschland*, 2 November 2022.

Melber, Henning, "Erbärmliche Gesten", *die tageszeitung*, 25 May 2022.

Memarnia, Susanne, "Stolpersteine für Schwarze Deutsche: 'Sterilisiert und ins Lager gesteckt'", *die tageszeitung*, 27 August 2021.

———, "Widerstand sichtbar machen", *die tageszeitung*, 22 October 2021.

Mengiste, Maaza, "Afterlives by Abdulrazak Gurnah review: Living through colonialism", *The Guardian*, 30 September 2020.

Messmer, Susanne, "Erinnerung an AfrikanerInnen in Berlin: Ingenieur, Performer, Kommunist", *die tageszeitung*, 21 April 2022.

Mumbuu, Edward, "Executive hijacked genocide talks—Swartbooi", *New Era*, 22 September 2022.

———, "Kapofi digs into genocide, dungeons", *New Era*, 9 September 2022.

BIBLIOGRAPHY

———, "Namibia frets over revised genocide offer", *New Era*, 4 November 2022.

Nakale, Albertine, "Political declaration on genocide draws closer", *New Era*, 16 July 2019.

Nakashole, Puyelpawa, "Venaani claims reparations agreement in closed-door negotiations", *The Namibian*, 9 November 2023.

Ndjebela, Toivo, "Reparation talks: Namibia pushes Germany on three fronts", *Namibian Sun*, 20 October 2023.

Ngatjiheue, Charmaine, "'German and Namibian governments lack empathy'", *The Namibian*, 29 September 2021.

Nguherimo, Jephta U., "Genocide deal or not, the struggle continues", *The Namibian*, 28 May 2021.

Nooke, Günter, "Wir haben lange Zeit zu viel im Hilfsmodus gedacht", *Berliner Zeitung*, 7 October 2018.

Oltermann, Philip, "Germany agrees to pay Namibia €1.1bn over historical Herero–Nama genocide", *The Guardian*, 28 May 2021.

———, "Germany returns 21 Benin bronzes to Nigeria—amid frustration at Britain", *The Guardian*, 20 December 2022.

Petersen, Shelleygan, and Nagtjiheue, Charmaine, "German genocide offer 'an insult'", *The Namibian*, 28 May 2021.

Pilling, David, "Afterlives by Abdulrazak Gurnah: Forgotten Africa", *Financial Times Weekend*, 22 October 2020.

Rogers, Thomas, Lassa, Rahila, and Marshall, Alex, "How Germany changed its mind, and gave the Benin Bronzes back", *New York Times*, 20 December 2022.

Schleiermacher, Uta, and Schulz, Bert, "Koloniale Kanonenkugel zum Uni-Start", *die tageszeitung*, 19 July 2022.

Schmitt, Daniel, "TV-Doku 'Schwarze Adler': Zwischen Stolz und Hass", *Frankfurter Rundschau*, 26 April 2021.

Selz, Christian, "Krokodilstränen", *Junge Welt*, 2 November 2023.

Simmerl, Georg, "Die hässlichen Seiten der Belle Époque", *Süddeutsche Zeitung*, 31 March 2021.

Springer, Marc, "Günther vollzieht Gratwanderung", *Allgemeine Zeitung*, 17 July 2019.

Staff reporter, "But what did they do to deserve that?", *New Era*, 31 August 2018.

———, "Prost! To Oktoberfest", *New Era*, 28 October 2022.

Tapaleao, Vaimoana, "Day NZ took Samoa from Germany", *NZ Herald*, 28 August 2014.

Tendane, Sophie, "Genocide deal racist, unconstitutional—Swartbooi", *The Namibian*, 22 September 2022.

Teuwsen, Per, "'Wir müssen nicht auf den nächsten Krieg warten, wir können die Sachen jetzt zurückgeben'", *Neue Zürcher Zeitung*, 15 October 2018.

Tjitemisa, Kuzeeko, "Chiefs reject genocide reparations deal", *New Era*, 27 May 2021.

———, "Government poised to conclude genocide issue—Kapofi", *New Era*, 3 December 2021.

———, "Govt U-turns on genocide pact: Namibia seeks N$ 18bn deal renegotiation", *New Era*, 28 October 2022.

BIBLIOGRAPHY

———, "Nujoma: N$ 18bn genocide deal woefully insignificant", *New Era*, 12 May 2022.

———, "Parliament in session: Alweendo troubled by 'divisive' genocide debate", *New Era*, 28 October 2021.

Tjitemisa, Kuzeeko, and Nuukala, Emmency, "Geingob tells Germany to eat humble pie", *New Era*, 1 March 2019.

Todtmann, Feliks, "An die Opfer erinnern", *die tageszeitung*, 8 August 2014.

Trüper, Ursula, "Afrikaner in Berlin", *die tageszeitung*, 6 May 2000.

Wainwright, Oliver, "Berlin's bizarre new museum: A Prussian palace rebuilt for €680m", *The Guardian*, 9 September 2021.

Weidlich, Brigitte, "Reparations motion makes history", *The Namibian*, 20 September 2006.

Zawatka-Gerlach, Ulrich, "Neuer Etat wird am Donnerstag beschlossen: Berliner Wirtschaft kritisiert den Doppelhaushalt", *Der Tagesspiegel*, 12 December 2019.

INDEX

Aalen, 132
Abuja, 7–8, 9, 11
Abushiri, 62
Action Third World, 103–4
Adam Mohamed, Mahjub bin, 95
ADEFRA (ADEFRA e. V.—Schwarze Frauen in Deutschland, or Black Women in Germany), 117
Adenauer, Konrad, 144
Adorno, Theodor, 26
AfD (Alternative für Deutschland), 6, 101, 134, 198
   case of, 121–7
   colonialism, debates on, 132–3
Africa Addio (also released as *Africa: Blood and Guts*) (Jacopetti and Prosperi) (documentary film), 102–3
Africa, 2, 9, 17, 55, 59, 102, 105, 119, 123, 138
   coalition agreement, 3–7
   colonial Germany, Africans in, 91–6
   Europe's colonial and imperialist expansion, 188–9
   German election, 81–7
   internal liberation, 133–4
   Manga Bell and Ngoso Din, rehabilitation of, 128–33
   monograph, 108–9
   overseas territories, ownership of, 30–4
African exoticism, 108

African Society of Germany, 32
African Society, 81
African, Development, Cultural and Postcolonial Studies, 99
Afrika heute (Africa Today) (magazine), 100–1
Afrikafonds budget, 81
Afro-Asiatic Solidarity Committee, 98–9
Afro-German movement, 116
Afro-Germans. *See* Black Germans
Afterlives (Gurnah), 95, 110
Aitken, Robbie, 93
Akwa Duala, 47–8
Akwa, Dika Mpondo (King Akwa), 43–4, 47, 48, 49, 51
Alabama, 57
Algeria, 1
Alien Tort Statute, 157
Alternative für Deutschland (AfD). *See* AfD (Alternative für Deutschland)
Alweendo, Tom, 171
Amo, Anton Wilhelm, 92
Andress, David, 11–12, 134, 186–7
Angra Pequena (Lüderitz Bay), 37
Anne Frank Educational Centre, 191
Anti-Apartheid Movement (1974–1994), 104
anti-Semitism, 4, 81
ARD (TV channel), 103
Arendt, Hannah, 24–5, 145
ArtWorld (magazine), 113

INDEX

Asian Art Museum, 111
Askari child soldier, 95
Askari monument, 80
Askaris, 61, 67–8
Association of Elected Officials of African Descent, 118
"Atakpame scandal", 56
Atlantic Ocean, 37
Australia, 71, 78, 157
Ayim, May. *See* Opitz, May

Bad Lauterberg, 62, 100
Baden-Württemberg, 128, 131
Baerbock, Annalena, 7–8, 11
Bagamoyo, 61
Baldwin, James, 183
Ballod, Carl, 86
Bamum, 45
Bauman, Zygmunt, 20
Baumgart, Winfried, 101
Bavarian Federal State, 80
Bavarian–Togolese Society, 80
Bebel, August, 64, 82–3, 85
Bechuanaland (Botswana), 40, 62–3, 139
Beijing, 74
Belgium, 68
Bell family, 36, 47, 49–51, 93
Bell, Ndumbé Lobé, 43–4
"benevolent paternalism", 85
Benin Bronzes, 6–10, 13, 113, 125
Benin kingdom, 7, 125
Benin, 53
Bentley, Tom, 169–70, 174, 178
Berlin Africa Conference, 33–4
Berlin-Charlottenburg, 92
Berlin City Museum Foundation, 119
Berlin Conference (1884–1885), 60, 145
Berlin Conference (1984), 105
Berlin Ethnological Museum, 54, 154
Berlin Mission, 31
Berlin-Mitte, 131
"Berlin Postcolonial", 158
Berlin Senate, 119
Berlin Senator for Culture and Social Cohesion, 118

Berlin Wall, 145
Berlin, 4, 9, 47, 55, 62, 67, 76, 93, 94, 107, 111, 113–19, 128, 150–2, 170, 178, 198
  negotiating genocide, 154–61
Berlin, Treaty of, 69
Berlin-Dahlem, 197
Biema dynasty, 54
Bilé, Joseph Ekwe, 94
Bismarck Archipelago, 69, 113
Bismarck, Otto von (Chancellor), 33, 38, 47, 59–61, 81
Black Germans
  AfD, case of, 121–7
  racism, 115–21
Black German Initiative (Initiative Schwarzer Deutscher/ISD), 117
Blue Book, 143
Boehme, Franziska, 173
Böhm, Andrea, 10
Bonn, 104
Booth, William, 19
Botswana, 174
Boxer War, 74–6
Brandenburg African Company, 30
Brandenburg colony, 92
Brandenburg Gate, 67
Brandt, Willy, 159
Bredekamp, Horst, 112
Bremen, 32, 37
Brink, André, 109
Britain, 7, 19, 69, 70
British colonial power, 43
British Foreign Office, 142
Brussels, 157
Bulawayo, NoViolet, 192–3
Bülow, Bernhard von, 33, 73–44, 85–6
Bundestag, 6, 103
Burundi, 68

Cabinet Technical Committee, 158
Cameroon, 34–5, 41, 53, 55–6, 58–9, 63, 79, 80, 93, 94, 105, 140
  colonisation of, 43–52
  Manga Bell and Ngoso Din, rehabilitation of, 128–32

INDEX

Cape Colony, 140, 142–3
Cape of Good Hope, 143
Caprivi Strip, 63
Carl Peters (film), 95
Caroline Islands group, 71
Carolines, 71
CDU–Green Party, 118
Centre Party (Zentrum), 85
Chaga, 64–5
Chamberlain, Houston Stuart, 20
Charité Human Remains Project, 148
Charles III, King of the United Kingdom, 10
Chernobyl, 112
Chialo, Joe, 118
Chicago, 90–1
China, 73–6, 138
Christian Democratic Union (CDU), 3, 6, 103, 198
Christian Social Union (CSU), 3, 6, 80
Churchill, Winston, 21
civilisation, 15, 16, 83, 84, 86
  European, 6
  Western, 192
"civilising mission", 12, 22, 32, 67, 84, 89, 93, 100, 105
  decolonisation, 24–7
Club of German Mixed-Bloods (Club der deutschen Mischlinge), 79
Coates, Ta-Nehisi, 183
Cold War, 98, 116
Cologne, 76
"Colonial Legacy", 5
Columbus, Christopher, 17–18
"Commemoration and Memory", 3
Committee on the Elimination of Racial Discrimination, 121
Compensation Bill, 181
Condorcet, Marquis de, 18
"Confronting Colonial Pasts, Envisioning Creative Futures", 153–4
"Conquest of Paradise", 17
Convention for the Prevention and Punishment of the Crime of Genocide, 22
Covid-19, 164, 170

Critical Theory, 26
Critical Whiteness Studies, 12
Culture, Minister of, 113

Dağdelen, Sevim, 6, 172, 174–5, 181
Dahomey slaves, 45
Damara community, 141, 142, 161, 172
Dar es Salaam, 61, 80
Darwin, Charles, 20
Darwinism, 59
"das erinnern" (Otoo), 198
Declaration on the Rights of Indigenous Peoples, 158
Decolonial Memory Culture in the City, 119
decolonisation, 6–7, 11, 24–7, 137, 145, 194
Deido, King (Jim Ekwalla/Epee Ekwalla Deido), 47
Demnig, Gunter, 95
Der Spiegel (Magazine), 127
Dernburg, Bernhard, 85
Deutsche Marks, 41
Deutsch-Südwest, 40
"development policy", 97
Dibobe, Martin, 94
Dido, 43
Die Grundlagen des 19. Jahrhunderts (Chamberlain), 20
Die Kirchdorfer, 80
Die Liebe zum Imperium (Love of empire) (documentary) (Heller), 104
Die Tageszeitung (newspaper), 128
Die weiße Massai (The white Massai), 108
Die Welt (newspaper), 110
Douala, 36, 79
Douala Bell, Jean-Yves Eboumbou, 131–2
Douala People, 43
Duala, 47, 50, 129
dualism, 17

East Africa, 55, 58–68, 75, 78, 82–3, 99, 102, 105, 110, 138

INDEX

East African coast, 61
East African territories, 78
East African war, 86
East Asia Squadron, 73
East Berlin, 111
East German (GDR) state, 3
East German dictatorship (*SED-Diktatur*), 4
East Germany, 98, 111, 135, 144
Eastern Europe, 21, 91
Eastern European states, 156
Education, Arts and Culture, Minister for, 153
Egypt, 92
Eichhorn, 84
el Cher, Gustav Sabac, 92
Elgin, Lord, 143
Emily, 131
Epp, Franz Ritter von, 34
Erdoğan, Tayyip, 155
Erzberger, Matthias, 85
Essay on the Inequality of Human Races (Gobineau), 20
Ethnological Museum, 54, 62, 111
Europe, 9, 50, 112, 133–4, 137, 188, 197
  decolonisation, 24–7
  enlightenment, dark side of, 16–20
  foreign territory, empires, 34–7
  overseas territories, ownership of, 30–4
  violence and extinction, 20–4
  white oppression and exploitation, 10–13
European Center for Constitutional and Human Rights (ECCHR), 163, 166–7, 168–9
European colonialism, 8
European imperialism, 15
"Eurowhiteness", 12
Ewe communities, 53
Ewe school, 93
Eyadéma, Gnassingbé, 80

Farbe bekennen (Lorde), 117
FDP. *See* Liberal Party (FDP)

Federal Agency for Civic Education, 1
Federal Council (Bundesrat), 159
Federal Foreign Office, 150, 178
Federal Government Commissioner for Culture, 185
Federal Republic of Germany (FRG), 29, 98
Federal State President, 10
Feldzugsbericht (field campaign report) (Frenssen), 90–1
Félix-Eyoum, Jean-Pierre, 130
First East Prussian Grenadier Regiment, 92
Fischer, Joseph (Joschka), 147, 169
Fitzpatrick, Matthew, 36, 72
Foreign and Commonwealth Office, 143
Foundations of the Nineteenth Century (Chamberlain), 20
France, 50, 53, 112–13, 186
France24 (news network), 177
Frankfurt University of Applied Sciences, 191
Fredericks, Chief David, 157
Fredericks, Cornelius, 198
Free University of Berlin, 197
Freiburg, 103–4
French colonial power, 43
French Congo, 50
French Revolution, 18
Frenssen, Gustav, 90
Freud, 99
Fugger, Jakob, 30

GDR Committee for Solidarity, 98
Geingob, Hage, 153, 160, 177
Genocide Convention, 156
genocide, 2, 6, 41–2, 65, 72, 123–4, 127–8, 136–7, 140–2, 176–80, 180–2, 186, 191
  colonialism, parliamentary debates on, 132–3
  colonialism, violence and extinction, 20–4
  enlightenment, dark Side of, 16–20
  human remains and looted artefacts, return of, 148–54

324

INDEX

Joint Declaration, 161–6
long denial, 144–8
Namibian disagreements, 170–2
negotiating genocide, 154–61
power, coloniality of, 196–8
reparations and intertemporality, 166–70
Sonderweg, 142–4
"writing genocide", 195
German Africa Foundation (DAS), 102
German African Society (DAG), 100–2
German Colonial Exhibition, 119
German Colonial Society, 32, 93, 144
German Colonial Union, 32
German Cultural Council, 5–6, 111, 189
German Democratic Republic (GDR), 29, 98–9, 114–15, 144, 167, 187, 191
German Development Cooperation, 147, 164
German East Africa Company (DOAG), 60–1, 66
German Federal Archives, 187
German Federal Cultural Foundation, 119
German Federal Government, 150
German flag, 38, 43, 59
German government, 128, 132, 135, 143, 147, 149–50, 154–5, 160–3, 165–6, 171, 174
  Benin Bronzes, 7–10
  coalition agreement, 3–7
  colonialism, violence and extinction, 20–4
German Historical Museum, 92
German lager beer, 79
German naval infantry, 45
German policy, 13
German Protestant Church, 151
German Research Foundation, 148
German Society for South West Africa, 38
German South Seas, 78
German South West Africa, 21, 31, 135, 142

AfD, case of, 121–7
German Trading and Plantation Society of Hamburg for the South Sea Islands (DHPG), 69
German–Namibian agreement, 6
German–Namibian Joint Declaration, 190–1
German–Namibian relations, 150
German-Namibian Society, 159
German–Nigerian agreement, 125
Gerstenmaier, Eugen, 103
Ghana, 30, 80, 92
Gibeon, 153
Gilley, Bruce, 122, 126
Giordano, Ralph, 103
globalisation, 16, 115
Gobineau, Joseph Arthur Comte de, 20
Goethe Institute, 80–1, 130
Gold Coast, 53, 58
Goldmann, Matthias, 183–4
Gotha, 92
Gottschalk, 145
Göttsche, Dirk, 108–9
"grand coalition", 3
Gravel Heart (Gurnah), 193
Great Britain, 53, 60, 62, 143
Great Friedrichsburg, 30
Greece, 156
Green Party, 3, 5–6, 107, 128, 133, 147, 179
Gregorius, 92
Greiner, Andreas, 66
Grill, Bartholomäus, 127
Grimm, Hans, 90–1
Grundl, Erhard, 6
Grütters, Monika, 6, 111, 113–14
Günther, Daniel, 159–60
Gurnah, Abdulrazak Abdulrazak, 68, 95, 193, 110

Hacker, Thomas, 6
Hackmack, Judith, 181–2
Hague Convention (1899), 75, 168
Halle, 92
Hamburg, 32, 62, 129

325

INDEX

Chamber of Commerce, 43
Hamburger Nachrichten (German newspaper), 48
"Hanging Peters", 64
Harz, 62
Hausa, 58
Hegel, Georg Wilhelm Friedrich, 19
Heia Safari (documentary) (Giordano), 103, 104–5
Heligoland–Zanzibar, Treaty of, 62–3
Heller, Peter, 104
Hempenstall, Peter, 71
Henke, 84
Herero, 139–40
Herzog, Roman, 159
Hickory, 43
Hickorytown (Bonabéri), 44
Hishoono, Naita, 191
Hitler, Adolf, 106
  See also Nazism
Hohenzollern dynasty, 111
Holocaust, 1, 12, 98–9, 121, 144, 182–3, 185, 186, 189, 194, 196–7
  Holocaust Studies, 146
  memorial, 128
  violence and extinction, 20–4
Hong Kong, 73
Horkheimer, Max, 26
Hornkranz, 39, 152
Hügel-Marshall, Ika (Erika), 116
Humboldt Forum, 111–15, 164, 186, 189–90
Humboldt University, 111
Humboldt, Alexander von, 111
"100 Köpfe der Demokratie" (100 heads of democracy), 94
Huttenbach, Henry, 23–4
Hyslop, Jonathan, 121–2

Iltis (German naval vessel), 76
Imperial Colonial Office, 51, 85, 187
Imperial Navy Office, 74
In Darkest England and the Way Out (manifesto), 19
Independent Social Democratic Party (USPD), 86

Information Centre Southern Africa (Informationsstelle Südliches Afrika/ISSA), 104
Information Centre Third World (Informationszentrum Dritte Welt/ Iz3w), 104
Informationsdienst Südliches Afrika (from 1994 as *afrika süd*), 104
International Military Tribunal, 182
Islamic State, 155
Italy, 156

J.C. Godeffroy & Sohn, 68–9
Jacopetti, 102
Jagodja, 64
James Allen, Ferdinand, 95
Japan, 1, 72, 73
Jena, 92
Jiaozhou, Bay of, 74
Joeden-Forgey, Elisa von, 94
Johnson, Dominic, 10
Joint Declaration, 5, 161–6, 169, 172–5, 178, 181–2, 183

*Kaiserreich*i, 2, 9, 33, 34–5, 38, 44, 88, 105, 196–7
Kampmann, Bärbel, 116
Kant, Immanuel, 19
Kapofi, Frans, 173
Katjiua, Mutjinde, 192
Kenya, 10
Kenyan coast, 110
Keul, Katja, 130–1, 173–4
Khan, Khatija, 197
Kiautschou, Bay of, 73
Kiepenheuer & Witsch, 109
Koblenz, 187
Koch, Robert, 67, 106
Köhler, Governor, 54
Konkomba communities, 53
Koob, Markus, 133
Kössler, Reinhart, 84, 153, 155, 180
Kostedde, Erwin, 117
Kreuzberg, 118
Krobb, Florian, 88
Kru, 35, 58

INDEX

Krüger, Gesine, 105
Kundnani, Hans, 12
Kunene, 37

Lamarck, Jean-Baptiste, 20
Landless People's Movement (LPM), 171, 173, 175
Lans, 76
Las Casas, Bartholomé de, 16–17, 20
Laumann, Dennis, 52–3
Leanza, Matthias, 141
"lease agreement", 61
Lederer, Klaus, 9, 11
Left Party, 130, 133, 149, 172, 181
Legislative Assembly of South West Africa, 143
Leipzig, 54
Lemkin, Raphael, 21–2
Lenzerini, Federico, 181
Lettow-Vorbeck, Paul von, 34, 67–8, 75
Liberal Party (FDP), 5, 198
Liberia, 58, 94
Liebert, Governor Eduard von, 63, 64
Liebknecht, Karl, 86
Linden Museum, 54, 152
Linné, Carl von, 18
"lion of Africa", 34
Lomé, 80
London, 8–9, 64, 142
Lord's Prayer, 147, 151
Lorde, Audre, 117
Lüderitz Bay, 41, 140, 142
Lüderitz, Adolph, 37–8, 43, 58, 59
Lüderitzland, 37
Luf island, 113
Luipert, Sima, 184
Luxemburg, Rosa, 86

m'Ebono, Mebenga. *See* Zampa, Martin Paul (Samba)
Maas, Heiko, 162–3
Macron, Emmanuel, 112
Maharero, Samuel, 40, 138
Maji Maji Memorial Museum, 9–10
Maji Maji war, 65

"Makunganya". *See* Omari, Hassan bin
Manga Bell Square, 131–2
Manga Bell, Emily Duala, 198
Manga Bell, Marilyn Douala
    rehabilitation of, 128–32
Manga Bell, Ndumbe, 47, 81
Manga Bell, Richard, 93
Manga Bell, Rudolf Duala, 51–2, 93
    rehabilitation of, 128–32
    See also Ngoso Din, Adolf
Mangi Sina, 65
Marengo, Jakob, 40, 139–40
Marshall Islands, 69
Marshalls, 71
Martin Brown, Hagar, 95
Martin, Elaine, 88
"master race", 117
May–Ayim-Ufer, 118
Mbano, Songea, 10
Mbumba, Nangolo, 152, 164, 174
McCarthyism, 121
McEachrane, Michael, 11
Media in the Office of the Chancellor, 185
Meli, 65
Micronesia, 69, 71
Mill, John Stuart, 19
Mkwawa, 63–4
Mohamed Husen, Bayume, 95
Mohamed, Lai, 7
Moosdorf, Matthias, 6
Morenga (novel) (Timm), 104
Morenga, Jacob, 145
Morocco, 50
Morocco–Congo Treaty, 50
Moses, Dirk, 182
Moshi, 65
Mpondo, Prince, 48
Muinjangue, Esther, 170–1, 182
Müller, Michael, 6
Multidirectional Memory (Rothberg), 196
Munich Studio Theatre, 81
Müntefering, Michelle, 150–2
Museum Island, 111, 115
Museum Treptow, 119
"Musterkolonie", 70

INDEX

Nachtigal, Gustav, 38, 43, 53, 62, 125
Nachtigalplatz, 131
Nama agency, 151
Nama community, 35, 37, 40, 65, 85, 123, 139–41, 142–3, 163, 171–3, 175, 177
   negotiating genocide, 154–61
   victim groups, solution, 179–84
Nama Traditional Leaders Association (NTLA), 157, 173, 175–7, 179
Namibia, 2, 4, 5–7, 78, 97, 108, 124, 127–8, 197–8
   colonialism, debates on, 132–3
   colonialism, perspective on, 142–4
   German colonial intervention, 136–7
   German–Namibian Joint Declaration, 190–1
   German–Namibian negotiations, 135–6
   Germany's denial, 144–8
   human remains and looted artefacts, return of, 148–54
   Joint Declaration, 161–6
   Namibian disagreements, 170–2
   negotiating genocide, 154–61
   reconciliation agreement, 172–9
   reparations and intertemporality, 166–70
   victim groups, solution, 179–84
   warfare, 138–42
Namibian Breweries, 79
Namibian Council of Churches, 151
Namibian High Court, 175
Namibian–German Special Initiative Programme, 147
Namibian–German War, 181
Nandi-Ndaitwah, Netumbo, 178
Naranch, Bradley, 91
National Assembly, 170
National Land Conference, 165
National Museum of Namibia, 154
National Unity Democratic Organisation (NUDO), 147, 170–77
Nauru, 71

Nazi Germany, 35, 88–90, 95–6
Nazi regime, 97–8, 120, 121–2, 144, 190, 196
   Benin Bronzes, 7–10
   coalition agreement, 3–7
   colonial Germany, Africans in, 91–6
   colonialism, scholars on, 87–91
   decolonisation, 24–7
   enlightenment, dark Side of, 16–20
   foreign territory, empires, 34–7
   overseas territories, ownership of, 30–4
   white oppression and exploitation, 10–13
   See also Hitler, Adolf
Nazism, 121–2
Ndumbe, Martha, 95
Netherlands, 1
"New Berlin Conference", 107
New Guinea (Kaiser Wilhelmsland), 69
New Guinea Company, 69, 71
New South, 57
New York, 157, 177
New Zealand, 71, 78
Ngavirue, Zed, 152, 155, 159, 170
Ngoni warriors, 10
Ngoso Din, Adolf, 51–2, 81, 93–4
   rehabilitation of, 128–32
Nigeria, Obasanjo of, 107
Nigeria
   Benin Bronzes, 7–10
   See also Africa
Nigerian ambassador, 107
Njoya, Sultan Ibrahim, 45–6
No Humboldt 21, 114
Nooke, Günter, 127
Nora Schimming Promenade, 197–8
North America, 32
North German Mission, 31
Northern Rhodesia, 62–3
northern Solomon Islands, 69
northern Togoland, 53
NTLA. *See* Nama Traditional Leaders Association (NTLA)

INDEX

NUDO. *See* National Unity Democratic Organisation (NUDO)
Nujoma, Sam, 171–2
Nuremberg, 182

O'Sullivan, Rachel, 140
Ohamakari, 151
Oktoberfest, 79
"Old Africans" (*Alte Afrikaner*), 97, 100–1
Omari, Hassan bin, 61, 62
On the Origin of Species (Darwin), 20
Opitz, May, 117
Orange River, 37, 41
Other Side of Silence, The (Brink), 109
Otoo, Sharon Dodua, 198
Out of Africa (Hollywood movie), 108
Ovaherero communities, 37, 39–40, 65, 90, 123, 129, 138–42, 147, 151–2, 170–2
  negotiating genocide, 154–61
  victim groups, solution, 179–84
Ovaherero Genocide Foundation, 171
Ovaherero Genocide, 157
Ovaherero Paramount, 192
Ovaherero Paramount Chief, 170
Ovaherero Traditional Authority (OTA), 157, 175–7, 173, 179
Ovaherero/Ovambanderu and Nama Council for Dialogue on the 1904–1908 Genocide (ONCD 1904–1908), 158
Ovambo, 41
Ovamboland, 37, 41
Owuor, Yvonne, 188–9

Paasche, Hans, 86–7
Pacific Islands, 68–72, 76
Paczensky, Gert von, 104
Papua New Guinea, 78–9, 113
Paris Institute of Political Studies (Sciences Po), 177
Parzinger, Hermann, 112–13, 154
People's Palace, 111
Peripherie: Politik-Ökonomie-Kultur. See Peripherie: Zeitschrift für Politik und Ökonomie in der Dritten Welt (Periphery: Journal of Politics and Economy in the Third World) (journal)
Peripherie: Zeitschrift für Politik und Ökonomie in der Dritten Welt (Periphery: Journal of Politics and Economy in the Third World) (journal), 104
Permanent Mandates Commission, 35
Peter Moors Fahrt nach Südwest (Peter Moor's Journey to South West) (Frenssen), 90
Peters, Carl, 59, 64, 104, 106
"petitionism", 51
Poland, 87, 159
Polenz, Ruprecht, 151–2, 155, 158–9, 172
Police Zone, 39, 41
Political Committee on Genocide, Apology and Reparations, 158
Politik & Kultur (monthly paper), 111
Ponape, 71
Popular Democratic Movement (PDM), 171
Portugal, 60
Portuguese empire, 30
post-Covid Oktoberfest, 79–80
post-World War II, 12, 25, 29, 98, 116
Potemkin villages, 61
Preußisches Liebesglück (Prussian fortune of love) (oil painting), 92
Priso, Lock (Kum'a Mbappé), 44
Prosperi, 102
"protection treaty", 44, 152
"protection troops" (*Schutztruppe*), 135
Prussia, 92
Prussian Cultural Heritage Foundation, 112, 154
Prussian factories, 43
Prussian militarism, 82
Puttkamer, Jesko von (Governor), 45, 47–8

Qingdao, 67, 74–6

INDEX

"racialisation", 94
raditional Association of Former Schutztruppen and Overseas Forces (Traditionsverband ehemaliger Schutz-und Überseetruppen), 100
Rechavia-Taylor, Howard, 182
Reichstag, 51
Remnants, 88
Renan, Ernest, 188
Report on the Natives of South West Africa and Their Treatment by Germany (the "Blue Book"), 143
Republic, Palace of the, 111
Retzlaff, Christoph, 178
Rhenish Mission Society, 139
Rhenish Missionary Society, 31
Rhineland, 94
Riruako, Kuaima (Chief), 147, 157
Robert Koch Institute, 67
Roma, 4, 191
Roth, Claudia, 7, 9, 185
Roth, Michael, 129, 130
Rothberg, Michael, 99, 196
Rothenbaum Museum—Cultures and Arts of the World (MARKK), 129
Rukoro, Chief Vekuii, 131, 151, 157, 160, 170, 198
Rwanda, 68

Sachsenhausen, 95
Sahel, 178
Salim, Al Bashir bin (Abushiri or Bushiri), 61
Salvation Army, 19
Samoa, 69–72, 78
San (Bushmen), 141, 161, 172
Sansanné-Mango, 53
Sarr, Felwine, 112
Savoy, Bénédicte, 112–13
Schilling, Britta, 136
Schlaga, Matthias, 159
Schleswig-Holstein, 118, 128, 159
Schneider-Waterberg, Hinrich, 127
Schuhplattler, 80
Secretary for Colonial Affairs, 85
Seitz, Theodor, 34

Senator for Culture and Europe, 9
Sepúlveda, Ginés de, 16–17, 20
Serengeti darf nicht sterben (Serengeti Shall Not Die) (documentary movie), 102
Shandong Province, 73, 74
Shandong, 74
Shark Island, 140, 142
Sinti, 191
Slave Coast of West Africa, 31
Social Democratic Foreign Minister, 155
Social Democratic leader, 64
Social Democratic Minister for Economic Cooperation and Development, 146
Social Democratic Party (SPD), 3, 5–6
Social Democrats, 48, 88
  German election, 81–7
"social imperialism", 33, 83
Society for German Colonisation, 32, 59
Soden, Julius von, 47
Sokeh on Ponape (Pohnpei), 71
Solf, Wilhelm, 72
Solidarity Committee of the GDR, 98–9
Songea, 11
Sorbonne, 188
South Africa, 1, 31, 37, 41–2, 90, 109, 141
  colonialism, perspective on, 142–4
South Schleswig Voters' Association, 128
South Sea idyll, 71
South Sea naval squadron, 71
South Sea, 68–72, 73
South West Africa, 2, 6, 34, 35, 37–42, 44, 58, 60–3, 66–7, 75, 78, 80, 85, 97, 104, 136, 142, 144, 150, 182, 186, 195
  colonial Germany, Africans in, 91–6
  colonialism, scholars on, 87–91
  German election, 81–7
  Germany's denial, 144–8

INDEX

negotiating genocide, 154–61
South Westers, 145
southern Kilimanjaro region, 64–5
Southwest Africa, 123–4
Soviet Union, 1
Soyinka, Wole, 183
Spain, 69
Spanish–American War, 69
"Spanish East Indies", 69
Special Rapporteurs, 175–6
Spiecker, Johannes, 139
Stahn, Carsten, 2, 167–8
Stalin regime, 155
Stanley, M., 19
State for International Cultural Policy, Minister of, 150
Steglitz-Zehlendorf, 198
Steinmeier, Frank-Walter, 9–11, 114–15, 130, 133–4, 155
Steinmetz, George, 115
Steyeler Shandong Mission, 73
Stolperstein ("stumbling block"), 95
Strauss, Franz Josef, 80–1, 103
Ströbele, Hans-Christian, 107, 128–9
Stuttgart, 54, 152, 164
Stuttgarter Zeitung (German newspaper), 110
Styria, 62
Sub-Saharan Africa, 178
Swahili, 61
Swakopmund, 140
SWAPO, 147, 160, 164–5, 180
Swartbooi, Bernadus, 171, 175
Sznaider, Natan, 197

Táiwò, Olúfémi, 2
Taku, 76
Tanganyika, 68
Tanzania, 10, 80
Technical University of Berlin, 112
Theurer, Karina, 175, 177, 178–9
Thierry, Lieutenant Gaston, 53–4
Through Darkest Africa (Stanley's travelogue), 19
Thurman, Kira, 96
Time (magazine), 113

Timm, Uwe, 104, 145
Tirpitz, Alfred von, 73, 74
Togo, 32, 35, 52–8, 70, 78–9, 80, 93, 140
Tolstoy, 110
Touré, Aminata, 118
Traditionsverband, 100–1, 105
"trans-imperial", 23
Treptower Park, 119
Tripartite Agreement (1899), 70
Trotha, Lothar von, 63, 75, 123–4, 138–41
Trustees, Board of, 154
Tsingtao Beer, 79
Turkey, 155
Tuskegee, 57
Tuskegee Expedition, 57

Ukraine, 155
Ulm, 131, 132
UN Permanent Forum of People of African Descent, 11
Unified Germany, 146
Union for African Studies in Germany (VAD), 101
United Kingdom (UK), 7, 10, 186
United Nations (UN), 21, 156, 163
United Nations Economic and Social Council (ECOSOC), 142
United Nations General Assembly, 21–2, 158, 177
United Nations High Commissioner for Human Rights, 121
United Nations Human Rights Council, 119–20, 156, 175–6
United States (US), 69, 70, 186, 193
    Black Power movement, 116
    federal court, 157
"unity in diversity", 180
University of Freiburg, 150
USA Inc., 157

VAD conference, 105
Valladolid, 16
VE Day, 134
Vedder, Heinrich, 42

INDEX

Venaani, McHenry, 171, 178
Venezuela, 30
Versailles, Treaty of, 68, 87
Victoria Falls, 63
Victory in Europe (VE), 133
Vogelsang, Heinrich, 38
Volk ohne Raum (People without Space) (Grimm), 90
Völkermord Verjährt Nicht (There Is No Statute of Limitations on Genocide), 151

Wachaga village, 64
Wahehe kingdom, 63–4
Wallace, Marion, 137, 143–4
Warsaw, 159
Washington, Booker T., 57
Waterberg, 129, 138, 147
We Need New Names (Bulawayo), 192–3
"Weimar colonialism", 88
Weimar Republic, 35, 78, 87–9, 91, 94, 121–2
Welle, Deutsche, 158
Welser, Bartholomäus, 30
West Africa, 35, 43, 56
West African territories, 78
West German Africa colonial legacy, analyses of, 100–6
West German Bundestag, 146
West German civil society, 145
West German foreign policy, 100
West German parliament, 166
West Germany, 29, 98–102, 116, 135, 144–5, 188
Whitaker Report, 142
"White Book", 143
Wieczorek-Zeul, Heidemarie, 129, 146–7, 151

Wiedemann, Charlotte, 193
Wildenthal, Lora, 99–100
Wilhelm II, Emperor of Germany, 59–60, 64, 75
Wilhelmine imperialism, 81
Wilhem, von Humboldt, 111
Windhoek, 80, 150, 151–2, 153, 178
Wissmann statue, 100–1
Wissmann, Hermann, 61
  death, 62
Witbooi community, 153
Witbooi, Hendrik, 39, 139–40, 152–3
Woermann, Adolph, 32, 34, 43, 44, 58–9
Working Group (United Nations Human Rights Council), 119–21
Working Group of Experts on People of African Descent, 155–6
World War I, 29, 42, 49–52, 58, 67–8, 71, 76, 87, 94
World War II, 4, 90, 92, 111, 144, 156, 167
World's Fair, 90–1

X (formerly Twitter), 178

Yap, 71
Yazidi, 155
Yellow Sea, 73
Yerushalmi, Yosef Hayim, 184
Yihequan, 74
Youth Remembers, 4
Yugoslavia, 1

Zampa, Martin Paul (Samba), 52
Zanzibar, 59, 61–2, 110
Zanzibar, Sultan of, 61
zurückGESCHAUT | looking back, 119